Sir William Holdsworth

O.M., K.C., F.B.A., D.C.L.

ESSAYS IN
LAW AND HISTORY

BY

SIR WILLIAM S. HOLDSWORTH

FORMERLY VINERIAN PROFESSOR OF ENGLISH LAW
IN THE UNIVERSITY OF OXFORD, AND
FELLOW OF ALL SOULS COLLEGE, OXFORD

EDITED BY
A. L. GOODHART
AND
H. G. HANBURY

THE LAWBOOK EXCHANGE, LTD.
Clark, New Jersey

ISBN 978-1-886363-13-7 (hardcover)
ISBN 978-1-61619-400-0 (paperback)

Lawbook Exchange edition 1995, 2015

The quality of this reprint is equivalent to the quality of the original work.

THE LAWBOOK EXCHANGE, LTD.
33 Terminal Avenue
Clark, New Jersey 07066-1321

*Please see our website for a selection of our other publications
and fine facsimile reprints of classic works of legal history:*
www.lawbookexchange.com

Library of Congress Cataloging-in-Publication Data

Holdsworth, William Searle, Sir, 1871-1994.
  Essays in law and history / by Sir William S. Holdsworth ; edited by A.L.
Goodhart and H.G. Hanbury.
      p. cm.
  Originally published: Oxford : Clarendon Press, 1946.
  Includes bibliographical references and index.
  ISBN 1-886363-13-7   (cloth : alk. paper)
  1. Law—Great Britain—History. I. Goodhart, Arthur L. (Arthur Lehman),
1891- II.
Hanbury, Harold Greville, 1898-III. Title.

KD626.H65 2000
349.42—dc21   99-047234

Printed in the United States of America on acid-free paper

ESSAYS IN
LAW AND HISTORY

BY

SIR WILLIAM S. HOLDSWORTH

FORMERLY VINERIAN PROFESSOR OF ENGLISH LAW
IN THE UNIVERSITY OF OXFORD, AND
FELLOW OF ALL SOULS COLLEGE, OXFORD

EDITED BY

A. L. GOODHART

AND

H. G. HANBURY

OXFORD
AT THE CLARENDON PRESS
1946

OXFORD UNIVERSITY PRESS
AMEN HOUSE, E.C. 4
London Edinburgh Glasgow New York
Toronto Melbourne Cape Town Bombay
Calcutta Madras
GEOFFREY CUMBERLEGE
PUBLISHER TO THE UNIVERSITY

PRINTED IN GREAT BRITAIN

PREFACE

WHEN we think of Holdsworth we naturally associate his name with his world-famous *History of English Law*, but it is a mistake to consider this great work as his only contribution to legal literature. He also wrote such interesting and important books as *Sources and Literature of English Law* (1925), *Historical Introduction to the Land Law* (1927), *The Historians of Anglo-American Law* (1927), *Charles Dickens as Legal Historian* (1928), *Some Lessons from our Legal History* (1928), and *Some Makers of English Law* (1938). In addition to these he published a great number of articles, book reviews, and notes which he has left bound together in eight large volumes. Some of these articles have since their original publication been incorporated in his *History of English Law* while some are now more or less out of date, but many of them show Holdsworth at his best, and deserve a more permanent and accessible form than can be found in the pages of a Law Review. In choosing for this memorial volume those essays which are most valuable, our chief difficulty has been to decide which we must exclude so as not to exceed a single volume. In particular we regret that we have had to leave out his article on 'The Indian States and India'[1] which he wrote after he had been to India as a member of the Indian States Committee 1928, his Rhodes lecture delivered at University College, London, in 1918 on 'The Relation between Commercial Legislation and National Defence' and his article on 'Power of the Crown to Requisition British Ships'.[2]

We are publishing the essays in chronological order because, as they cover such a wide variety of subjects, no other arrangement would be suitable. We have not found it either necessary or desirable to make any alterations of substance in the articles, which are as fresh to-day as they were when they were first published. A few words of explanation concerning our choice of the various articles may not be out of place here because a brief summary may be of use to the reader in determining which of them are of particular interest to him.

[1] (1930) 46 *Law Quarterly Review* 407.   [2] (1919) 35 *L.Q.R.* 12.

The first essay, entitled 'Martial Law Historically Considered', was published in the *Law Quarterly Review* in 1902. In the course of the next forty years Holdsworth contributed to its pages nearly fifty full-length articles together with a great number of notes and book reviews. Only Sir Frederick Pollock exceeded these figures. Holdsworth's first essay was distinguished, as was all his later work, by his ability to present complicated historical data in an orderly and lucid manner, and it furnished an admirable illustration of his thesis, which he explained again and again, that much of modern law cannot be clearly understood if the origins from which it came are not studied. Thus in the case of martial law we must go back to the law administered by the Court of the Constable and the Marshal in the fourteenth century because the modern distinction between military law, which is concerned with jurisdiction over the army at home and abroad, and martial law, which is concerned with jurisdiction over all citizens in time of rebellion, dates from the seventeenth century. To-day military law depends chiefly upon statute and is, in the words of Cockburn C.J. (*Reg.* v. *Nelson and Brand*[1]), 'a precise, ascertained, and well-defined law'. On the other hand, it is doubtful whether martial law as a distinct code of rules does exist, and whether the proclamation of martial law adds in any way to the powers inherent in the government of using force to suppress disorder. Finally Holdsworth discusses jurisdiction over alien enemies which is sometimes called martial law because it is enforced by soldiers, but which, as he points out, differs *in toto* from martial law as a branch of municipal law. The conclusion he reaches is that 'the only reason why powers so dissimilar are called by the same name of martial law is the purely historical reason that they all formed branches of the jurisdiction of the Constable and Marshal's Court'.

The second essay is concerned with 'The Place of English Legal History in the Education of English Lawyers'. Holdsworth begins by pointing out that there are excellent histories of Roman, French, and German law: only English law has no complete history. (This was written in 1910 before Holdsworth had by his own Herculean labours largely filled this gap.) This is all the more curious because

[1] Special Report 86.

a knowledge of the history of English law is essential to the English historian as well as to the lawyer. The answer is to be found in the peculiar history of the education of the English lawyer which was efficient from the fourteenth to the middle of the seventeenth century, and then entered into a long dark age which came to an end less than a hundred years ago. The pages in which Holdsworth describes the course of English legal education are among the most interesting that he ever wrote, and are filled with odd bits of information. How many students at the Inns of Court realize when they consume their fixed number of dinners each term that these are a survival from the time when the residence of members was as compulsory as it is to-day at Oxford and Cambridge? The essay ends on an optimistic note because by 1910 the renaissance of English legal education had begun both in the academic and in the professional schools, but if Holdsworth were writing to-day he could be even more cheerful, for there is general recognition that every lawyer ought to be given an opportunity of acquiring that 'scientific knowledge of the law' which Holdsworth considered an essential part of his legal education.

The period of time which elapsed between the original appearances of Essays 3 and 4 was twelve years. The occasions of their appearances were widely different. Essay 3 was published as an article in the *Columbia Law Review* in 1912; Essay 4 was delivered in 1924 as the Creighton History Lecture at University College, London. Yet the two essays are complementary to one another, and the reader will find in Essay 4 repetition and amplification of some of the content of Essay 3. In the lessons taught by Holdsworth, repetition never spelled satiety. In a sense, both essays are stages in what might not inaptly be styled the Holdsworth–McIlwain controversy. Professor McIlwain's great work *The High Court of Parliament and its Supremacy* appeared in 1910. Holdsworth's article of 1912 was, in its essence, a commentary on that work. In 1917 McIlwain reiterated, and in some ways extended, his main thesis in the *Magna Carta Commemoration Essays*. Holdsworth in his Creighton Lecture of 1924 restated his own position, reinforced by his own unremitting research during the previous decade.

Briefly, McIlwain's thesis is that Parliament remained until modern times essentially a Court rather than a legislative body. Holdsworth retorts that while Hallam judged the sixteenth century too much from the point of view of the later seventeenth and eighteenth centuries, McIlwain tends to the opposite extreme in telling the story too exclusively from the medieval standpoint. There is danger in too much 'medievalism'; the evolution of the English Constitution can better be understood through a comparison with contemporaneous continental developments than by laying continual stress on Anglo-Saxon influences, which are apt grievously to mislead. In Essay 3 he gives us a careful examination of the Cortes of Castile and Aragon, and the Estates-General of France, and shows the two vital reasons why these assemblies failed to become a permanent check on the King and a permanent part of the constitution. Their constitution was defective, and they incurred the hostility of the legal profession. From the English development these two drawbacks were conspicuously absent. The method of legislation by Bill, which emerged in the fifteenth century, 'emphasized the fact that Parliament was a partner with the King in the work of legislation'. Even more important is the fact that at no time in English history do we see any antagonism between the common lawyers and Parliament. On the contrary, there was always a great connexion between them, and the best legal talent was always ready to assist in the development of the powers of Parliament. The result of this alliance was that in England the interpretation of the doctrine of the supremacy of the law came to be, not, as on the Continent, the omnipotence of a fundamental law which no power in the State could change, and only the lawyers could interpret, but the ascendancy of a law which Parliament could change and modify. In other words, in the sixteenth century supremacy of the law came to mean the supremacy of Parliament.

'Evolution, not revolution.' This was the very apt description by Sir Leslie Scott (now Lord Justice Scott) of the Property Legislation of 1925 which is discussed in Essay 5. But Holdsworth shows that Sir Leslie Scott might have made a much stronger case for the firmness of the historical foundation upon which that legislation rests. He

claimed that it had been built up upon the labours of 'more
than half a century of law reformers'. Holdsworth points
out that the period over which the reform has been spread
is really ten times as long as this. Voluminous as were his
writings, he could be, when occasion demanded, a master of
compression, and in this essay he gives us a miniature history
of real property legislation since the time of Edward I.
With a few deft touches he brings out the cohesion and
continuity of the history of English land law, and bestows
generous praise on the work of Dr. Cheshire (who was
destined to succeed him as Vinerian Professor) for the very
reason that it emphasizes the vital importance of the historical
approach to the study of real property law. It is worth
remarking that he reminds us of the agreement by the
members of Sir Leslie Scott's Committee of 1919 that no
attempt should be made to introduce compulsory registration until the Acts had been in operation for ten years.
Holdsworth's hope that at the end of that period a definite
affirmative decision would be taken has hitherto been disappointed. Twenty years have now passed, but the reform,
the urgency of which Holdsworth in several places stressed,
seems to have passed into oblivion.

There is nothing strikingly original in Essay 6, on 'The
Formation and Breach of Contract', but it ought to be read
by every student embarking on the law because nowhere
else has this difficult subject been analysed with such clarity
and precision. The comparison between *causa* and consideration is an old one, but we doubt whether anyone has used it
as effectively as has Holdsworth in these pages, because he
has, in a few masterly paragraphs, traced the history of both
concepts. It is interesting to note that Holdsworth, who
has sometimes been criticized for his enthusiastic conservatism, reached the revolutionary conclusion (at p. 137) that
'consideration should be treated, not as the sole test of the
validity of a simple contract, but only as evidence of its
conclusion'. This view was adopted by the Law Revision
Committee in its Report on the doctrine of consideration
issued in 1937 (Cmd. 5449), but no steps have been or are
likely to be taken to implement its recommendations.

Essay 7, on 'Case Law', contains a brief but beautifully
clear history of the development of precedents in English

law. Holdsworth reaches the conclusion (at p. 159) that
'both the general rule that decided cases are authoritative,
and the reservations with which that rule is accompanied,
are due historically to the very gradual way in which our
modern theory as to the authority of decided cases was
developed'. No one will quarrel with the conclusion that
decided cases must be authoritative, but it is doubtful
whether the reservations, which Holdsworth regarded as
equally important, are as effective to-day as they were during
the eighteenth and nineteenth centuries. It is, to say the
least, open to question whether in those centuries a court
would have felt itself compelled to follow one of its own
decisions if it recognized that it was clearly wrong, but to-
day both the House of Lords and the Court of Appeal are
absolutely bound unless a statutory provision has been disregarded or there is a conflict of precedents. It is odd that
in this essay Holdsworth made no reference to the practice
in the Judicial Committee of the Privy Council, because a
less rigid system seems to have worked well in the highest
court of the Empire.

Essay 8 is Holdsworth's contribution to the series of
articles on the progress of different branches of law which
were written to celebrate the fiftieth anniversary of the *Law
Quarterly Review*. His subject was Equity, and here he was
in especially happy vein. He first underlines the danger of
the tendency, very perceptible in the years immediately
succeeding on the Judicature Act, 1873, to exaggerate its
effects. He reminds his readers of a truth that he was never
tired of bringing home to his pupils, that the only great
pioneer of the law who disliked the dual system of law and
equity, and attempted to approximate their substantive rules,
was Lord Mansfield, and that he did not have his way.
Equity is still equity, and law is still law, though the relations
of the two systems with regard to certain topics took some
time to adjust. Holdsworth refers to *Nocton* v. *Ashburton*.[1]
He always had a great admiration for Viscount Haldane's
speech in this case, which, in his opinion, yielded the key to
the whole equitable conception of fraud. After passing in
review the contributions to the development of equity of
judges and text-book writers, he ends by a strong challenge to

[1] [1914] A.C. 1932.

Maitland's viewpoint, that equity should not now be taught separately from law. He argues that there is a strong 'jurisdictional and procedural bond' which links together all subjects in equity, and that the essential characteristics of the system cannot properly be appreciated if it is taught 'in snippets'.

Essay 9, which deals with the influence of Roman law on English Equity, is a paper which Holdsworth must greatly have enjoyed preparing. It was a report for the International Congress of Comparative Law held at The Hague in 1937, and was actually delivered at a meeting of the Holdsworth Club of the University of Birmingham in November 1936. His old pupil and close friend, Professor Smalley-Baker, was in the Chair. The affairs of the Law Faculty of Birmingham were always very near his heart, and he was at his best when he visited those who had honoured him by calling their Club by his name. Holdsworth, in his modesty, never pretended to be an authority on Roman law, but in this paper he shows himself more than proficient in it. His conclusion is that we must not be misled into mistaking analogies for derivations; English equity is really as insular as English common law, and developed along lines distinct from those of Roman law.

Essay 10 is an article inspired by the decision in *Re Keen.*[1] Holdsworth's unerring historical sense would often lead him to trace to its source an accepted doctrine or distinction, and show that source to be impure. Realizing the importance of secret trusts, and their popularity with testators, he felt uneasiness at the thought of the distinction, established by dicta of judges, who apparently accepted it with complacency, between (*a*) cases in which a person charged with a secret trust is ostensibly designated as beneficial successor, and (*b*) cases in which he is expressly named as trustee, on the face of the will. As the law now stands parol evidence is admissible to prove the *existence* of the trusts in case (*a*) provided that they were communicated to the legatee charged at any time before the death of the testator, but it is not admissible to prove their *identity* in case (*b*) unless the communication was prior to or contemporaneous with the will. Holdsworth here used arguments, which subsequent writers have described as unanswerable, to show that the distinction is quite unsound. His conclusion is, that according to the

[1] [1937] Ch. 236.

logical basis on which the whole theory of secret trusts rests, the rules governing the two cases should be identical, and that the trusts should in both be capable of being established by parol evidence—provided only that the communication took place before the death of the testator.

In 1936 the Syndics of the Cambridge University Press reissued some of Maitland's best work in three volumes, the first of which contained some of the essays already re-published in his *Collected Papers*, the second being his 'Equity', and the third his 'Forms of Action at Common Law'. In Essay 11 Holdsworth gives a commentary on the whole reissue. In discussing Maitland's introduction to the 'Memoranda de Parliamento 1305', he reminds us that in the history of Parliament Maitland was a pioneer, and that the immense value of his work has been amply vindicated by later writers in this field. He cites as the focal point of Maitland's thesis his insistence that 'a session of the king's council is the core and essence of every *parliamentum*'. The other essays in this volume dealt with the theories of corporate personality, and Holdsworth, though his mind was less attuned than was that of Maitland to problems of abstract jurisprudence, yet shows in his analysis a complete understanding of them. He reaches the conclusion that 'the common law, while admitting the reality of corporate, and to some extent of group personality, has always adhered to the Concession Theory'.

Of particular interest are his comments on Maitland's *Equity*. Few subjects more interested Holdsworth than the juristic nature of equitable rights and interests, and few cases were more often cited by him to his pupils than *Lister* v. *Stubbs*,[1] which brings out visibly the vital distinction between the relation of debtor and creditor and that of *cestui que trust* and trustee. The creditor seeks repayment, the *cestui que trust* restitution. It was largely on the foundation of this decision that Holdsworth built up his edifice of thought which resulted in the conclusion that equitable rights are, in all essentials, *iura in rem*. The essay ends with a tribute to Maitland as jurist and historian which is worthy alike of him who is praised and of him who bestows the praise.

'Literature in Law Books' (Essay 12) is not so much an

[1] (1890) 45 Ch. D. 1.

article as an anthology, for here Holdsworth has collected 'a few passages from the books and judgments of the great lawyers of the past'. He begins with Glanvil and ends with Sir Frederick Pollock, so his field is indeed a wide one. It is odd that there are no quotations from Selden's *Table Talk* or from Jeremy Bentham's more vituperative utterances, but it was obviously impossible to include everyone in less than forty pages. Perhaps this collection will tempt others to make similar legal anthologies; there must be hundreds of passages which deserve quotation, because, as Holdsworth emphasizes in his concluding paragraph, 'law is the basis upon which all government rests' and 'law touches all the most important aspects of national life'. Moreover, 'our great lawyers have always been amongst the ablest men of their age', and therefore 'it would be surprising if on a great occasion their exposition of the law did not attain the dignity of literature'.

In view of the recent wealth of polemical literature on the subject of 'Unjustifiable Enrichment', Essay 13 is of especial importance. Not all Holdsworth's veneration for the learning of Lord Mansfield, not all his respect and affection for his old friends, Lord Wright and Professor Winfield, could impel him to recede from his position that the whole idea of quasi-contract is founded on implied contract, and should not now be detached from that pedestal. In this article, which is in the nature of a reply to Lord Wright's paper on *Sinclair* v. *Brougham*,[1] he strenuously urges that it does not follow from the fact that the implied contract need not now be specially pleaded, that the idea of the implied contract should be eradicated from the substantive law. This is one of the most powerful pieces of polemical writing which ever issued from Holdsworth's prolific pen. Those who do not agree with it— and they may be many—will yet assuredly find that it provides them with food for profound and prolonged thought.

Holdsworth always took an eager interest in the work of younger jurists. Two illustrations of this interest are provided by his exhaustive review of Mr. Fifoot's biography of Lord Mansfield,[2] and his 'Terminology and Title in Ejectment—a Reply', which forms the subject-matter of Essay 14. The reply was made to a very able article, bearing

[1] [1914] A.C. 398. Lord Wright's article is in 6 *Camb. L.J.* 305.
[2] (1937) 53 *L.Q.R.* 221.

this title, by Mr. H. D. Hargreaves.[1] The thesis of that
learned real property lawyer is that, despite the introduction
into the land law of the phrase 'estate owner', the conception
of tenure, and not that of ownership, is still the basis of that
law. This article of Holdsworth's is perhaps the most
interesting of the whole collection, for it provides a corrective to those who would write him down a persistent
preserver of medieval learning and theories. For him, in
fact, legal history was never static, but always productive of
new ideas. Hargreaves rightly called his opinions on the
action of ejectment revolutionary. They are restated here
with crisp brevity. Holdsworth does not pray in aid the
legislation of 1925. He takes his stand on the difference
between the trend of the old learning and that of the new;
the former centred round the real actions, the latter round
the action of ejectment, and through the maturity of this
action the conception of ownership developed.

Essay 15, on 'The Relation of English Law to International Law', is concerned with the single question whether
international law is part of the law of England. Holdsworth
reaches the conclusion (at p. 267) that 'international law is
not so much a part, as a source, of English law. In each case
in which the question arises the court must consider whether
the particular rule of international law has been received
into, and so become a source of, English law.' He is thus in
agreement with the view expressed by the majority of the
judges in *Regina* v. *Keyn*,[2] a view which was followed in *West
Rand Central Gold Mining Co.* v. *Rex*.[3] International lawyers
will be particularly interested in the reasons which Holdsworth gives for reaching his conclusion.

Holdsworth's reputation as a great legal historian tended
to obscure the fact that he was also a first-class practical
lawyer. Early in his career he had thoughts of practising at
the Bar, and if he had done so he would undoubtedly have
been eminently successful. Essay 16, 'A Chapter of Accidents
in the Law of Libel', is an illustration of his powers of analysis.
He reaches the conclusion that 'the very confused opinions
given by the House of Lords in the case of *Hulton* v. *Jones*'[4]
leave it open to the House to reconsider its views on the matter.

[1] 56 *L.Q.R.* 376.   [2] (1876) 2 Ex. D. 63.   [3] [1905] 2 K.B. 391.
[4] [1910] A.C. 20.

He argues that the law should be reformed by the establishment of the rule that an intention to defame the plaintiff is an essential condition for success in an action for libel, the condition concerning intention being satisfied if the statement is made recklessly. It is to be hoped that this article will be studied by the Committee, under the chairmanship of Lord Porter, which is now considering possible amendments in the law of defamation, because there is much to be said for Holdsworth's view, as the recent cases have shown.

The final essay which we have included in this volume is the short one on 'Law Reporting in the Nineteenth and Twentieth Centuries'. After tracing the strange history of law reporting, Holdsworth reaches the conclusion that 'in a system of law which depends largely upon judgments in reported cases, the State ought to do something to safeguard the accuracy of the reports of all cases. . . .' Such a reform, as he points out, would be less radical than many of the changes that have been made in the past.

This brief summary has, we hope, made clear the extraordinary interest and value of the essays which we have collected in this volume. They show the many facets of the man whose name, next to that of Blackstone, is the greatest in the distinguished list of Oxford legal scholars. The title we have chosen for the volume was not idly picked. Both as historian and as lawyer was Holdsworth great, and none better than he understood that the function of the one was the indispensable complement of the function of the other. He was the teacher of one of us, the colleague and dear friend of us both. He is no more with us, but we still have his work. Even to re-read it in order to prepare it for the present collection has been to us a vivid though poignant joy, and we give the collection to the world in the certainty that it will provide not only a reminder of his teaching but a source of new instruction to the jurists of the future, whose proudest aim must be to emulate one whose name is for ever inscribed on the roll of those who have, in the words of Sir Frederick Pollock, contributed to the heritage of the law of England.

A. L. GOODHART
H. G. HANBURY

OXFORD
September 1946

CONTENTS

MARTIAL LAW HISTORICALLY
CONSIDERED[1]

IN the Middle Ages martial law meant the law administered by the Court of the Constable and the Marshal. To
that court we must look for the origin of the military and the
martial law of the present day. Both these laws are the result
a development which dates from an early period in our
constitutional history. Questions as to their meaning and
extent have been at different periods political questions of
the day. A body of law so ancient, and developed in such an
atmosphere, is not easy either to state or to understand.

In 1389[2] we have a statutory definition and limitation of
the jurisdiction of the Constable and Marshal's Court. Its
vagueness is characteristic. 'To the Constable', runs the
statute, 'it pertaineth to have cognizance of contracts touching deeds of arms and of war out of the realm, and also of
things that touch war within the realm, which cannot be
determined nor discussed by the common law, with other
ways and customs to the same matters pertaining, which other
Constables heretofore have duly and reasonably used in their
time.' It is clear that the court exercised a certain jurisdiction
over heraldry, over words spoken to the disparagement of
men of honour, and over contracts relating to war made out
of the realm.[3] But for the purposes of our inquiry the two
most important branches of its jurisdiction were (1) jurisdiction over appeals of death or murder committed beyond
the sea,[4] and (2) 'the offences and miscarriages of soldiers
contrary to the laws and rules of the army'.[5] Both these

---

[1] Reprinted from (1902) 18 *Law Quarterly Review*, 117.
[2] 13 Rich. II, St. 1, c. 2.
[3] Rushworth, pt. 2, vol. ii, 1054, 1055; *Roy v. Parker* (1668), Sid. 352;
Oldis v. Donmille (1695), Shower, 58; 2 Knapp, 149 note. One of the cases
cited by Rushworth is curious. A citizen of London went to a 'gentleman well
descended', and applied for payment of a debt. The gentleman not only
refused, but gave him hard words. ' "Then," said the citizen, "surely you
are no gentleman that would not pay your debts, with some other reflecting
language"; and the citizen underwent the censure of the court.'
[4] 1 Hen. IV, c. 14.
[5] Hale, *History of the Common Law*, 42.

B

branches of the court's jurisdiction were recognized in the Middle Ages by the legislature[1] and by the judges.[2]

The office of Constable ceased to be permanently filled in Henry VIII's reign.[3] This was not at once thought to affect the jurisdiction of the Constable and Marshal's Court. But in the seventeenth century the judges of the Common Law Courts showed a disposition to question the legality of any rival court. The victory of the Parliament in 1640 was followed by the suppression of the Council's jurisdiction in England. The Court of the Marshal shared in the end the same fate. It was voted a grievance in 1640.[4] In a case in Anne's reign it was decided that in the absence of the Constable the court was not properly constituted, that if the Marshal alone had ever exercised jurisdiction it was a mere encroachment like the exercise of jurisdiction by the Court of Requests or the Council of York, and that it was not a court of record.[5] In fact the jurisdiction of the Marshal's Court had become confined to pedigrees, escutcheons, pennons, and coat-armour. The last case known to have been tried in it was in 1737.[6] So completely had it disappeared that even Lord Mansfield seems to have been ignorant of its ancient jurisdiction. In *Lindo* v. *Rodney*[7] he said, 'As to plunder or booty in a mere continental land-war . . . it never has been important enough to give rise to any question about it. . . . There is no instance in history or law, ancient or modern, of any question before any legal judicature ever having existed about it in this kingdom.' It is almost certain that in the Middle Ages this was one of the branches of the court's jurisdiction.[8]

---

[1] 8 Rich. II, c. 5; 13 Rich. II, St. 1, c. 2; 1 Hen. IV, c. 14.

[2] Hearne, *Curious Discourses* (ed. 1720), 259, 260, citing Y.B. 37 Hen. VI, Pasch. pl. 8, 'Whereby it appeareth that all the four justices agreed that the Constable and Marshal had a law by themselves, whereof the common law doth take notice, as well as it doth of the ecclesiastical law, being a law of itself from the common'. Hale, *Common Law* (6th ed.), 41 n.d. Fineux C.J., being asked by Henry VIII what was the Constable's jurisdiction, declined to answer, as it was a matter for the law of arms and not for the common law.

[3] Hale, *Common Law*, 41.   [4] Rushworth, pt. 2, vol. ii, 1056.

[5] *Chambers* v. *Jennings* (1701), 7 Mod. 125.

[6] *Sir H. Blount's Case* (1737), 1 Atk. 295, 296; 3 Bl. *Comm.* (1st ed.), 103–6.

[7] (1782), 2 Dougl. at p. 614, note to *Le Caux* v. *Eden.* (1781), 2 Dougl. 572.

[8] Knapp, 149–52 and note; Hale's manuscript treatise on the prerogative

It is, as we have said, to the once extensive jurisdiction of this court that the military and martial law of the present day owe their origin. To use the words of Coke, it was 'the fountain of marshal law'.[1] For the present purpose the jurisdiction can be divided into two main branches which comprehend both of the two more important branches mentioned by Hale.

I. Jurisdiction over the soldiers of the Crown.

II. Jurisdiction over alien enemies.

I. JURISDICTION OVER THE SOLDIERS OF THE CROWN

The army for which the Constable and Marshal's Court was designed was a feudal army. It was called into existence as occasion required. It was not, as in modern times, an army of professional soldiers backed up by an adequate police. We can hardly, therefore, expect to find the modern distinction between a jurisdiction over an army and a jurisdiction over the ordinary citizen in time of rebellion. Ordinary citizens were the soldiers of the Crown, and many of the wars we should now call rebellions. Changes in political manners and military organization will, as we shall see, account for much of the obscurity in which the subject of martial law has been enveloped in modern times. In considering the development of this branch of the jurisdiction of the court we must anticipate later distinctions, and, for the sake of clearness, divide it into two heads—

1. Jurisdiction over the army at home and abroad—the military law of the present day.

2. Jurisdiction over all citizens in time of rebellion—the martial law of the present day.

there cited states: 'In matters civil, for which there is no remedy by the common law, the military jurisdiction continues as well after the war as during the time of it; for that part of the jurisdiction of the Constable and Marshal stands still. This is the proper jurisdiction of the Constable and Marshal, which, though it be called *curia militaris* in respect of the subject matter, yet the jurisdiction is a formal settled jurisdiction, and may be exercised as well in time of peace as war. This is that which is limited by the statute 13 Rich. II, c. 2, i.e. contracts touching deeds of arms, and war without the realm, and things that touch war within the realm, which cannot be determined by the common law, as touching prisoners, prize, &c.' See also a manuscript treatise of Lord Hale (there cited) 'upon certain petitions of late exhibited in the Court of Chivalry'.   [1] 4 *Instit.* c. 17.

*1. Jurisdiction over the army at home and abroad—the
military law of the present day*

'Always,' says Hale,[1] 'preparatory to an actual war, the kings of the realm, by advice of the Constable and Marshal, were used to compose a book of rules and orders for the due order and discipline of their officers and soldiers, together with certain penalties on the offenders; and this was called martial law. We have extant, in the Black Book of the Admiralty and elsewhere, several examples of such military laws; and especially that of the ninth of Richard II, composed by the king, with the advice of the Duke of Lancaster and others.'

It is clear from this passage that this jurisdiction was defined by codes of rules promulgated by the Crown at different periods.[2] These codes are substantially embodied in the articles of war of the seventeenth, eighteenth, and nineteenth centuries, and in the Army Act of the nineteenth century. Mr. Clode says[3] that 'all the essential conditions in relation to the administration of justice can be traced in earlier codes, and that military law as a system, established and understood in the service, has been gradually developed and improved'. After the disappearance of the Court of the Constable and Marshal the jurisdiction was exercised by committees of officers. Hawkins,[4] with some hesitation, considers that the jurisdiction could be lawfully exercised in this manner. Its name also was changed. It becomes known not as martial but as military law. Cockburn C.J. criticized this change of terminology in *Reg.* v. *Nelson and Brand*;[5] but it is now well settled that the jurisdiction of the Crown over the army is called military law.

At common law this jurisdiction could be exercised over the soldier abroad.[6] Over the soldier within the kingdom it could only be exercised in time of war.[7] All doubt on this point was set at rest by the Petition of Right. The Petition of

[1] *Common Law*, 42.

[2] For an account of these rules see Cockburn C.J.'s charge to the Grand Jury in *Reg.* v. *Nelson and Brand* (Special Report), 89–91, and *Black Book of the Admiralty* (R.S.), i. 282–99, 453–72.

[3] *Military and Martial Law*, 3.

[4] *Pleas of the Crown* (2nd ed.), ii. 14, and *Reg.* v. *Nelson and Brand*, 95, 96.

[5] Special Report, 100.

[6] 1 Hen. IV, c. 14. Cp. also Report by Sir James Marriott, King's Advocate, cited Forsyth, *Leading Cases*, 218.

[7] Hale, 1 P.C. 344 seqq., 499, 500.

Right was in form a re-enactment of old law. After stating the old law which was to be re-enacted, and the manner in which it had been infringed, it prays that there may be no such infringements in future.[1] The clauses contained in it with reference to martial law enact nothing new. They assume that martial law was perfectly legal in time of war—a fact which the parliamentary lawyers did not dispute.[2] And in later times the Petition of Right has generally been taken to deal simply with the recent extensions which martial law had received, and to declare them illegal, leaving martial law only applicable to armies in time of war.[3] The question what was a time of war was also clearly settled. 'The time of peace is when the Courts of Westminster are open.' 'If the Chancery and Courts of Westminster be shut up . . . it is time of war, but if the Courts be open it is otherwise; yet if war be in any part of the kingdom, that the sheriff cannot execute the

---

[1] It recites (§ 6) that 'of late great companies of soldiers and mariners have been dispersed into divers counties of the realm, and the inhabitants against their wills have been compelled to receive them into their houses'; (§ 7) that by 25 Ed. III and Magna Carta 'no man shall be forejudged of life or limb against the form of the Great Charter and the law of the land', yet that divers commissioners have been appointed 'with power and authority to proceed *within the land*, according to the justice of martial law, against such soldiers or mariners, or other dissolute persons joining with them, as should commit any murder, robbery, felony, mutiny, or other outrage or misdemeanour whatsoever, *and by such summary course and order as is agreeable to martial law, and as is used in armies in time of war*', to try and execute such offenders according to martial law; (§ 9) that offenders have escaped punishment 'upon pretence that the said offenders were punishable only by martial law'. It therefore prays (§ 10) 'that your Majesty would be pleased to remove the said soldiers and mariners', and 'that the *aforesaid* commissions for proceeding by martial law may be revoked . . . and that hereafter no commissions *of like nature* may issue forth'.

[2] Coke, 1 *Instit.* 249; below, p. 7, note 3 and p. 8, note 1.

[3] Hale, *Common Law*, 42; *Analysis of the Law*, 11; 1 P.C. 500; 1 Bl. *Comm.* 400; *Reg.* v. *Nelson and Brand*, 66; Stephen, Opinion on *Governor Eyre's Case* (Forsyth, *Leading Cases*, 553–5), and *History of Criminal Law*, i. 207, 208. Blackburn J. in *Reg.* v. *Eyre* (Special Report, 73) says, 'I think it would be an exceedingly wrong presumption to say that the Petition of Right, by not condemning martial law in time of war, sanctioned it; still it did not in terms condemn it'. In *Reg.* v. *Nelson and Brand*, 66, Cockburn says that there are two views as to the effect of the Petition of Right: (1) that it was limited to the recent commissions; (2) that it forbade martial law except in the case of armies in time of war. It would be perhaps true to say that both views are correct; for the second is the consequence of the first. See below, p. 13.

king's writ, there is *tempus belli*.[1] With these opinions of Coke and Rolle agrees the opinion of Hale, who cites a case of Edward III's reign.[2]

The definition was perhaps better suited to a feudal age than to the seventeenth century. This will appear from the difficulty which Charles I experienced in putting into force any kind of military law in 1640.[3]

With the Great Rebellion we reach the period of standing armies. The Parliament in 1642 found it necessary to issue a code of rules for the government of their troops.[4] Various codes of a similar nature were framed by Charles II and James II for the troops which Parliament permitted them to retain.[5] The code of 1666 was modelled on that of 1642. Others were drawn up in 1672 and 1686. But the Crown was careful to state in 1672 that it was only intended to enforce its provisions abroad; and in 1685, after the suppression of Monmouth's rebellion, Kirke was directed to send soldiers guilty of more serious crimes to the ordinary courts for trial, as the articles of war were in force only during the actual rebellion.[6] In fact, the legality of applying any of these rules to the soldier in this country in time of peace was as doubtful as the necessity for some such rules was clear.

The Revolution begins a new epoch. Parliament legalized a standing army as a necessary evil. It controlled the powers of the Crown over it at home and in time of peace. It left subsisting the powers of the Crown over it abroad and in time of war.[7] From 1688 to 1879 military law rests partly

---

[1] Rushworth, pt. 2, vol. ii, App. 79, 81.

[2] Hale, 1 P.C. 344; *Common Law*, 42, 43.

[3] Rushworth, pt. 2, vol. ii, 1199. Lord Conway, in a letter to the Archbishop of Canterbury, says: 'My lord of Northumberland did write to me, that having had occasion to look into the power he hath to give commissions, the lawyers and judges are all of opinion that martial law cannot be executed here in England, but when an enemy is really near to an army of the king's, and that it is necessary that both my lord of Northumberland and myself do take a pardon for the man that was executed here for the mutiny; if this be so, it is all one as to break the troops, for, so soon as it shall be known, there will be no obedience.'

[4] Clode, *Military and Martial Law*, 10–12.

[5] Ibid. 12–19.   [6] Clode, *Military Forces of the Crown*, i. 478.

[7] *Barwis* v. *Keppel* (1766), 2 Wils. 314, 318; Clode, *Military and Martial Law*, 74. The Bill of Rights (1 Will. & Mary, Sess. 2, c. 2) states that a standing army *within the kingdom in time of peace* is illegal. It is true that the

upon the authority of the annual Mutiny Acts, partly on the prerogative of the Crown expressed in the articles of war.[1] Into the history of the various modifications of the Mutiny Acts it is not intended to enter here.[2] It will be sufficient to say that they enlarged the powers of the Crown in so far as they gave the Crown power to make articles of war in time of peace and for the soldier within the kingdom; they restricted the powers of the Crown in so far that the Crown could not alter any rule laid down in the Mutiny Act itself.[3] But in cases where the Mutiny Act gave a discretion, or in cases where it was silent and the Crown had such a discretion at common law, the Crown could govern the army by its prerogative.

In 1879 the articles of war and many of the provisions of the former Mutiny Acts were embodied in a statute known as the Army Discipline and Regulation Act.[4] This code of rules for the government of the soldier comes into force for one year by virtue of the annual Mutiny Act.

Military law, therefore, now depends chiefly upon statute. In so far as the Army Act deals with subjects formerly dealt with merely by the articles of war, the prerogative of the Crown is restricted. The Act, however, expressly states that the Crown has power to make articles of war.[5] There is, however, a proviso that no punishment affecting life or limb, or penal servitude, shall be inflicted except for crimes made so punishable by the Act; and that no crime punishable by the Act shall be made punishable in a manner which does not accord with the provisions of the Act. This proviso is not limited, as the corresponding section of the Mutiny Act was limited, to persons within the United Kingdom.

preamble to the first Mutiny Act (1 Will. & Mary, c. 5) states generally that no man may be subjected to any kind of punishment by martial law. But the Act of Anne's reign (1 Anne, St. 2, c. 16) states that no man may be subjected *in time of peace* to any kind of punishment *within the realm* by martial law. The importance of preambles to Acts of Parliament upon a controverted political question may easily be exaggerated. See below, p. 14.

[1] 1 Anne, St. 2, c. 16, § 39; 1 Geo. I, c. 9; 22 Geo. II, c. 5, § 57; Clode, *Military and Martial Law*, 29, 30.

[2] The first Mutiny Act contained 10 sections; the last passed in this form in 1878, 110 sections.

[3] Clode, *Military Forces of the Crown*, i. 502, 517.

[4] 42 & 43 Vict. c. 33, re-enacted with amendments 44 & 45 Vict. c. 58.

[5] 44 & 45 Vict. c. 58, § 69.

This military law is a special code of rules administered by · courts martial, to which the persons defined by the Army Act are subjected.[1] To use the words of Cockburn C.J. 'military law as applicable to the soldier is a precise, ascertained, and well-defined law'.[2]

2. *Jurisdiction over all citizens in time of rebellion—the martial law of the present day*

The jurisdiction of the Crown over the army has thus gradually expanded into the system of military law. On the other hand, the jurisdiction of the Crown over all subjects in time of rebellion has gradually decayed, and has finally altered its shape.

We have seen that in the Middle Ages the Constable and the Marshal's Court had jurisdiction when it was 'a time of war'. We have seen that at a time when every citizen might be called upon to serve in defence of his country jurisdiction over soldiers might be easily confounded with a jurisdiction over all citizens. This confusion was increased by the policy pursued by the Tudors and the earlier Stuarts. They did not consider themselves bound by the legal definition of 'a time of war'. They considered that they might submit ordinary citizens to the jurisdiction of the Marshal or his deputies whenever in their opinion such a measure was necessary to the preservation of order. They may be said therefore to have extended his jurisdiction in two ways: (1) they extended to persons not members of an army powers which existed only over soldiers duly enrolled in the army; (2) they made a time of war mean a time of apprehended disturbance. ·

These extensions were gradually made, and it was difficult to prove that they were extensions.[3] The precise limits of the Constable and Marshal's Court had never been accurately

---

[1] 44 & 45 Vict. c. 58, §§ 175–84.

[2] *Reg.* v. *Nelson and Brand*, 86.

[3] But it is clear that in Elizabeth's reign their legality was doubtful. Camden relates in his *Annales*, s.a. 1573 (cited Prothero, *Documents, &c.* 176), that a fanatic made an attack on Sir J. Hawkins, mistaking him for Hatton: 'Regina ad hoc facinus supra quam solebat ita excanduit, ut in hominem ex jure militari sive castrensi protinus animadverti jusserit; donec a prudentibus fuisset edocta, jus illud non nisi in castris aut temporibus turbulentis adhibendum; domi autem et in pace ex processus judiciaris formula agendum.'

defined. The change from the feudal monarchy of the Middle Ages to the territorial state of the present day left the extent of all kinds of political authority very obscure. The Tudors made use of this obscurity to assume the powers which they considered necessary for the maintenance of the peace. The Stuarts assumed similar powers, but not so much with the bona fide desire to keep the peace as in pursuance of their design to make themselves absolute kings. They pursued this design in the face of a rising parliamentary opposition, and they advertised it by a series of leading cases in constitutional law.

The arguments in these cases of the early Stuart period show how obscure the law really was. If we go back to the twelfth and thirteenth centuries we see none of that separation between the various bodies and persons entrusted with the powers of government to which we are accustomed. Henry II's *curia regis* was the legislature, the executive, and the judicature in one. In the seventeenth century these departments have become fairly distinct. But we see a similar confusion between legal principles, which in modern law we regard as perfectly separate. For instance, in *Bate's Case*[1] and in the *Case of Ship-money*[2] we seem to be taken over the whole field of constitutional law. In *Bate's Case* the judgment considered the power of the Crown over trade, treaties, foreign affairs, and indirect taxation. That case showed the Crown that it could turn its power over foreign trade to fiscal uses. In the *Case of Ship-money* the judgment considered the power of the Crown to provide for the defence of the country, and the measures which it could take when the safety of the country was in danger. In this case therefore the whole question of the extent of the power of the Crown to make use of martial law was exhaustively discussed. The power to make use of martial law was the premiss from which the conclusion was drawn that the tax could be imposed. The Crown was seeking to turn to fiscal uses its powers to act in defence of the country, as in *Bate's Case* it had turned to similar uses its power over foreign trade. It is true that the Petition of Right had negatived the supposed right to use martial law within the kingdom except in times of actual war.

[1] (1606), 2 S.T. 371.
[2] (1637), 3 S.T. 826.

The Petition of Right was evaded by the ruling that it merely confirmed old liberties and enacted nothing new.[1]

In the judgments given in this case we can see clearly the two different views held at that time as to the meaning of the term martial law. From these two different views we may trace historically a divergence of opinion upon this subject which has lasted until the nineteenth century.

The opinion of the majority of the judges was in favour of allowing to the Crown a power to proclaim martial law whenever the country was in danger; and of the existence of that danger they held that the Crown was the sole judge. It followed that in any case of apprehended danger the Crown could act as it pleased. The recent extensions of martial law were therefore upheld to their fullest extent. We may take as an illustration of these views a passage from the judgment of Finch C.J.:[2]

'In time of imminent danger, *tempore belli*, anything, and by any man, may be done, murder cannot be punished; yet, says my brother Crooke, the king cannot charge his subjects in any case without Parliament; no, not when the kingdom is actually invaded by the enemy. But truly I think, as he was the first, so he will be the last of that opinion. . . . There hath been and may be as great danger when the enemy is not discerned as when in arms and on the land. In the time of war when the course of law is stopped, when judges have no power or place, when the courts of justice can send out no process, in this case the king may charge his subjects, you grant. Mark what you grant; when there is such a confusion as no law, then the king may do it. *Dato uno absurdo, infinita sequuntur.* Then there may be a time of war in one part of the kingdom, and the courts of justice may sit. Now whether a danger be to all the kingdom or to a part, they are alike perilous, and all ought to be charged. . . . Expectancy of danger, I hold, is sufficient ground for the king to charge his subjects; for if we stay till the danger comes, it will be then too late. And his averment of the danger is not traversable, it must be binding when he perceives and says there is a danger; as in 1588 the enemy had been upon us, if it had not been foreseen and provided for before it came.'

The opposite view is best represented in the argument of Mr. Holborne, one of Hampden's counsel. He maintained

[1] (1637), 3 S.T. 826, 1109, Berkeley J., dealing with the Petition of Right, quotes Charles I's speech to the two houses, 'that it must needs be conceived that he had granted no new, but only confirmed the ancient liberties'. Finch C.J. at p. 1237 says, 'There was no new thing granted only the ancient liberties confirmed'.   [2] (1637), 3 S.T. 826, 1234.

that mere expectancy of danger gives no additional powers to the Crown. It is only the actual presence of pressing danger which gives to the Crown and to the subject alike the right to do what is necessary to ward off the danger.

'Put the case an enemy was landed, to show what the powers are by our laws in that case for defence; when there is a particular appearance of instant and apparent danger, in that case particular property must yield much to necessity. These cases our books warrant, as building of bulwarks on another man's ground, and burning corn. In 1588 there was an actual danger, and then it was just to take corn or grass or anything to raise supplies. But where do any of our books say that upon fear of danger, though in the king's case, a man can without leave make a bulwark in another man's land? I do not read. As your lordships may observe in this case of apparent danger the power of the king; observe withal the power of the subject, and out of what principle this doth grow; whether out of a form of law or out of necessity. In these cases of instant danger and actual invasion, it is not only in the power of the king, but a subject may do as much in divers cases. For if there be an actual war, the subject may, without any direction, do any act upon any man's land, and invade any property towards defence: it is the law of necessity that doth it. Nay in that case the subject may prejudice the king himself in point of property. . . . *Levis timor* will not serve . . . but such a fear as ariseth from an actual and apparent danger.'[1]

It was clear from the Petition of Right that the actual decision in the *Case of Ship-money* was wrong. It was clear that the Crown could not make use of martial law in a case of merely apprehended danger when the ordinary courts were sitting.[2] But, granted the existence of an instant and pressing danger, was there not some power in the Crown to make use of some form of martial law? Was this martial law merely an illustration, as Holborne had contended, of the right of rulers and subjects to use in an emergency the force necessary to protect life and property?

The question was difficult to answer. Martial law was a term known to the law books. But it was clear that the Constable and Marshal's Court, which originally adminis-

[1] (1637), 3 S.T. 826, 975; cf. pp. 1012, 1013. And Crooke J. at p. 1162, 'Royal power, I account, is to be used in cases of necessity and imminent danger, when ordinary courses will not avail . . . as in cases of rebellion, sudden invasion, and some other cases, where martial law may be used, and may not stay for legal proceedings'.

[2] *Wolfe Tone's Case* (1798), 27 S.T. 613.

tered it, had passed away, and that the most important branches of the jurisdiction of that court were now administered by courts martial acting mainly under statutory authority. It was clear that the law so administered was a law which could be applied only to a certain defined class of persons. It might however be argued that if the Crown had once had a prerogative to govern ordinary citizens by martial law in the case of a rebellion which amounted to a war, and if that prerogative had never been taken away, it still existed. Some weight is given to the view that the Crown possessed this prerogative by the preambles and recitals of certain statutes relating to Ireland. 39 Geo. III, c. 11, passed by the Parliament of Ireland for the statutory exercise of martial law, mentions in the preamble 'the wise and salutary exercise of His Majesty's undoubted prerogative in executing martial law'; and the same Act goes on to provide that, 'nothing in the Act contained shall be construed to take away, abridge, or diminish the acknowledged prerogative of His Majesty for the public safety to resort to the exercise of martial law'. 43 Geo. III, c. 117 contains a reservation of this 'undoubted prerogative'; and there is a similar reservation in 3, 4 Will. IV, c. 4, s. 40. Blackstone, following Hale, speaks of it as a thing permitted in time of war in order to preserve discipline in the army.[1] He does not identify it with the code of military law in force by virtue of the Mutiny Acts.[2] It has therefore been contended with some force that a prerogative to exercise martial law in case of rebellion still remains vested in the Crown.[3]

Rebellion, it is said, is a state of war declared by the Crown.[4] It can, of course, only be declared if a state of war, as defined by the older authorities, really exists. This state of war gives to the Crown the power to use the military forces

---

[1] 1 Bl. *Comm.* 400.

[2] Ibid.: 'At such times [in times of foreign war] particular provisions have been usually made for the raising of armies and the due regulation and discipline of the soldiery; which are to be looked upon only as temporary excrescences bred out of the distemper of the state, and not as any part of the permanent and perpetual law of the kingdom.' At p. 402 he treats separately of the Mutiny Act.

[3] Finlason supported this view in several works—*Treatise on Martial Law*; *Review of the Authorities as to the Repression of Riot and Rebellion*; *Commentaries on Martial Law.*   [4] *Treatise*, xii; *Review*, 53, 54.

of the State as it pleases. Its prerogative is not controlled by the Mutiny Act, which deals only with the regular army as defined by the Act.[1] Persons, therefore, acting under such a proclamation of martial law do not need acts of indemnity for their protection unless they have acted wantonly and without good faith.[2] This prerogative is quite different from the power which all citizens have at common law of using the degree of force which is necessary to prevent outrage. That power merely provides the necessary means for quelling a riot. It merely allows an amount of force exactly proportioned to the necessities of the case. It does not allow, as a proclamation of martial law allows, an absolutely free hand in dealing with the enemy.[3] It is contended that the preambles of the Acts cited bear out this view; and it must be admitted that probably those who passed them did mean something of the kind. Hargrave certainly thought that they must bear this construction.[4]

There seem to be two objections to this view. (1) Suppose that the Constable and Marshal's Court would have had jurisdiction to try by martial law any persons actually combatant in case of rebellion, would this necessarily give the Crown power to subject to martial law all citizens combatant or non-combatant? To contend that this was so would seem to be an extension of the term martial law similar to that made by the Tudors, and condemned by the Petition of Right. It can only be said that it is not clear that the jurisdiction of the court would not have extended to this case. But this would be contrary to the opinion of the parliamentary lawyers of the early Stuart period, and to the opinion of Hale.[5] It is perhaps

[1] *Commentaries*, 16, 18, 19, 93; *Review*, 58.

[2] *Treatise*, xii; *Review*, 46-8.

[3] *Treatise*, xxxi; *Commentaries*, 18, 19, 119, 120.

[4] Forsyth, *Leading Cases*, 190: 'With these statutes before me I am forced to resist any contrary impressions I may have as to the real boundary of martial Law.' See the views of Mr. Headlam (Judge Advocate General) and Sir David Dundas, cited *Reg.* v. *Nelson and Brand*, 101-3.

[5] *Common Law*, 42: 'This indulged law was only to extend to members of the army, or to those of the opposite army, and never was so much indulged as intended to be executed or exercised upon others. For others, who had not listed under the army, had no colour or reason to be bound by military constitutions, applicable only to the army, whereof they were not parts. But they were to be ordered and governed according to the laws to which they were subject, though it were a time of war.' (The reference in the Petition

not possible to say certainly whether the court would have had jurisdiction in such a case. (2) If the Constable and Marshal's Court had jurisdiction, and if therefore the right of the Crown to try persons by martial law could be established, we should have the anomaly of a law without a court to administer it. To a body of law in so destitute a condition the description of Cockburn C.J.[1] would seem very applicable. 'Martial law', he says, 'when applied to the civilian is no law at all, but a shadowy, uncertain, precarious something, depending entirely on the conscience, or rather on the despotic and arbitrary will of those who administer it.' He arrived independently at the same conclusion as Holborne and the parliamentary lawyers of the seventeenth century. Martial law as a distinct code of rules does not exist. It is merely the application of the common law principle 'that life may be protected and crime prevented by the immediate application of any amount of force which, under the circumstances, may be necessary'.[2]

This is the view most strongly supported, especially by the more recent authorities. It is the view of Comyn[3] and Lord Loughborough.[4] It is the view which Hargrave would have considered to be law but for the preambles to the Irish statutes cited above.[5] These statutes Cockburn C.J. explains away.[6] And whatever we may think of the explanation it must be allowed that the necessity for comprehensive Acts of indemnity whenever martial law has been put in force is a strong argument in favour of this view. Such Acts do not as a rule cover cases of wanton wrongdoing. This is the only reason for their existence upon the contrary hypothesis.[7] It is the view which has been taken by distinguished law officers

---

of Right to martial law 'as is used in armies in time of war' (above p. 5, n. 3) points in the same direction.)

[1] *Reg. v. Nelson and Brand*, 86.

[2] Ibid. 85.   [3] *Digest, Parliament, H.* 23.

[4] *Grant v. Gould* (1792), 2 H.Bl. 69, 98.

[5] Forsyth, *Leading Cases*, 190.

[6] *Reg. v. Nelson and Brand*, 72–4. He says that a recital is of great value as forming a presumption as to what the law is, but that it is not conclusive; that it was there weakened because it was not needed, as, whether the Crown had the power to use martial law or not the legislature gave it; that a reservation of the power could give no right if it did not already exist.

[7] *Wright v. Fitzgerald* (1799), 27 S.T. 759.

of the Crown.[1] It is the view which seems to be adopted by the government in the circular upon the subject of martial law addressed in 1867 to the governors of our colonies.[2] It is the view which is taken by Stephen in his opinion on *Governor Eyre's Case*,[3] and in his *History of Criminal Law*.[4]

There are many points of agreement between the two theories. Moreover we shall see that in practice their results are not materially different. Both demand as conditions precedent of a proclamation of martial law a state of war, i.e. a condition of affairs in which it is absolutely necessary to use force. The great point of difference consists in the consequences to the persons acting under such a proclamation. On the first theory the person so acting cannot be made civilly or criminally responsible unless he has acted with malice. On this theory it is only in cases of riot as distinguished from cases of rebellion that a person is civilly or criminally responsible unless he accurately apportions the degree of force used to the necessity of the case. On the second theory there is no such distinction to be drawn between cases of riot and cases of rebellion. The same principles apply to both; for rebellion is but riot 'writ large'.

The law, then, acts on the same principles in judging the conduct of those who have acted under a proclamation of martial law, and in judging the conduct of those who have used force to suppress a riot. The proclamation in no way adds to the powers inherent in the government of using force to suppress disorder. 'The proclamation must be regarded as the statement of an existing fact rather than the legal creation of that fact.'[5]

The question then arises, what are the rights and duties of those who are thus obliged to use force to suppress disorder?

When riot approaches rebellion, when it practically amounts to a state of war, as the necessity is greater, so the discretion of those whose duty it is to restore order is more free. A proclamation of martial law during a rebellion, or

[1] Forsyth, *Leading Cases*, 188 (Opinion of Henley and Yorke, 1757); 194 (Opinion of Sir J. S. Copley, 1824); 198, 204 (Opinions of Sir J. Campbell and Sir R. M. Rolfe, 1838 and 1839).
[2] Clode, *Military Forces of the Crown*, ii. 667.
[3] Forsyth, *Leading Cases*, 551.   [4] i. 207–16.
[5] Opinion of Mr. Cushing, Attorney-General of the United States, viii, Opinions of Attorney-Generals at p. 374.

shortly before it has been entirely quelled, practically gives
to those in authority full powers to do all that is necessary to
restore order.[1] Only acts clearly malicious could give rise to
subsequent legal proceedings. This is illustrated by the case
of *Elphinstone* v. *Bedreechund*.[2] Elphinstone was appointed
(1817) sole commissioner of a territory in India conquered
from Bajee Row, the Peishwa. In February 1818 he issued
a proclamation describing the measures to be taken for the
settlement of this territory, and appointed Captain Robertson
provisional collector and magistrate of Poonah, the capital
of Bajee Row's territory. Since that date certain courts had
been sitting at Poonah. The Peishwa surrendered June
1818. The war did not end till the December of that year. In
May Robertson had seized and imprisoned Narroba, the
treasurer of the Peishwa, until he gave up certain money
alleged to be the property of the Peishwa. Bedreechund, the
executor of Narroba, sued Robertson and Elphinstone in the
Supreme Court of Bombay for this money. The Supreme
Court of Bombay decided that, the courts being open, the
war was over at the time when Narroba was thus imprisoned,
that the property belonged to Narroba, and that therefore
Bedreechund could recover it. This decision was reversed by
the Privy Council. Lord Tenterden said,[3] 'We think that the
proper character of the transaction was that of hostile seizure
made, if not *flagrante* yet *nondum cessante bello*, regard being
had both to the time, the place, and the person; and consequently that the municipal Court had no jurisdiction to
adjudge upon the subject'. The case of *Marais* was, in all
essential particulars, identical with the case *Elphinstone* v.
Bedreechund, and was decided in the same way.[4] When the
courts are sitting it is no doubt a time of peace—but, subject
to the qualification established by these two cases, that they

---

[1] The Lord Chancellor, in the case of *Marais* v. *The General Officer commanding the lines of communication and the Attorney-General of the Colony*,
[1902] A.C. 109, said at p. 115, 'Doubtless cases of difficulty arise when the
fact of a state of rebellion or insurrection is not clearly established . . . but
once let the fact of actual war be established, and there is an universal consensus of opinion that the civil courts have no jurisdiction to call in question
the propriety of the action of military authorities'.
[2] (1830), 2 S.T.N.S. 379.
[3] (1830), 2 S.T.N.S. 379, 449.
[4] [1902] A.C. 109.

are sitting in their own right and not merely as licensees of the military power.

Where the case is a case of riot rather than a case of rebellion, as the necessity is less, so the discretion of those concerned in restoring order is more limited. The principles upon which the courts will act are most clearly pointed out in Lord Bowen's report upon the Featherstone riots.[1] On the one hand, the magistrate is responsible if he neglects to take proper precautions for preserving the peace;[2] and the ordinary citizen, whether a soldier or not, is liable if he does not assist to preserve the peace when required to do so.[3] On the other hand, any person who uses more force than the necessity of the case requires can be made criminally or civilly responsible for the consequences of using excessive force. 'He is bound', said Littledale J.,[4] 'to hit the exact line between an excess and doing what is sufficient.' Mere honesty of intention will be of no avail if he has not come up to the standard which the law requires. But honesty of intention is good evidence to show that he has fulfilled his legal duty by doing or abstaining from doing all that can reasonably be expected from a man of honesty and ordinary prudence and activity, under the circumstances in which he was placed.[5] In coming to a decision upon this question it is only the actual circumstances, in which the person was then placed, which can be considered. Events subsequently occurring, which no person of ordinary foresight would expect, cannot be regarded.[6]

'The framers of the Petition of Right', said the Lord Chancellor, 'knew well what they meant when they made a condition of peace the ground of the illegality of unconstitutional procedure.'[7] Substantially the same distinction between a time of peace and a time of war is recognized in modern law. In this, as in other branches of the law, it is the views of the lawyers who framed the Petition of Right and who argued the *Case of Ship-money* which have prevailed.

[1] *Parliamentary Reports*, 1893, 94.
[2] *Rex* v. *Kennett* (1781), 5 C. & P., 282.
[3] The *Case of Arms* (1597), Popham's Rep. 121; *Burdett* v. *Abbott* (1812), 4 Taunt. 401, 449.
[4] Trial of *Charles Pinney* (1832), 3 S.T.N.S. 11, 510; *Reg.* v. *Eyre* (Blackburn J.), Special Report, 55, 56.   [5] 3 S.T.N.S. 511, 512.
[6] Ibid. 514.   [7] [1902] A.C. 115.

The rise of a standing army, the growth of military law, the disappearance of the Court of the Constable and Marshal may perhaps cause some difference in the terms in which we express the modern law. But, 'when ancient rules maintain themselves ... new reasons more fitted to the time have been found for them, and they gradually receive a new content, and at last a new form, from the grounds to which they have been transplanted'.[1]

II. Jurisdiction over Alien Enemies

It is clear that the power of the Crown over alien enemies rests upon principles quite different to those which govern the power of the Crown over the army or over its own citizens. (1) Wrongs committed by or against an alien in a foreign country do not, as a rule, fall within the jurisdiction of the English Courts.[2] (2) Wrongs committed by or against an alien friend in this country are tried by the ordinary courts.[3] (3) Wrongs committed by an alien enemy in this country cannot be treated as ordinary crimes. 'An alien enemy occupies a portion of the British territory, as the territory of his own sovereign; the laws of his own country are supposed to prevail there as far as he is concerned, and he owes exclusive and undivided allegiance to his own sovereign. If he is captured he is to be treated as a prisoner of war; he can in no shape be tried as an offender for any act of hostility in which he may have participated.'[4] It would appear from *Perkin Warbeck's Case* that such offences fell within the jurisdiction of the Constable and Marshal's Court. It was decided that Perkin Warbeck, being taken in war, could not be indicted for treason as the indictment could not conclude *contra ligeantiae suae debitum*; and that therefore he must be tried before the Constable and the Marshal by martial law.[5] Seeing that this court does not now exist, it would raise an interesting question whether such an alien enemy in this country could be tried at all, if the war was over, and the ordinary courts sitting. It is possible that he might escape altogether.[6]

---

[1] Holmes, *The Common Law*, 36.

[2] Stephen, *History of Criminal Law*, ii. 12.

[3] Forsyth, *Leading Cases* (Opinion of Sir J. Dodson, Sir J. Campbell, and Sir R. M. Rolfe, 1838), at pp. 200, 201.

[4] Ibid.   [5] (1500), cited 7 Co. Rep. 6 b.   [6] Forsyth, 201–4.

(4) In the case of alien enemies in a foreign country the Crown has an absolutely free hand.

It is clearly this species of martial law which the Duke of Wellington had in his mind when he gave his well-known description of martial law.

'Martial law', he says, 'is neither more nor less than the will of the general who commands the army. In fact martial law means no law at all; therefore the general who declares martial law, and commands that it should be carried into execution, is bound to lay down distinctly the rules and regulations and limits according to which his will is to be carried out. Now I have in another country carried out martial law; that is to say, I have governed a large proportion of a country by my own will. But then what did I do? I declared that the country should be governed according to its own national law; and I carried into execution this my so declared will.'

Martial law, in this sense, differs *in toto* from that described above. It is altogether outside the range of municipal law. This distinction is perhaps most clearly pointed out by Mr. Cushing in an opinion which he gave when Attorney-General of the United States.[1]

'Martial law must be distinguished according as it is a foreign or international fact, or as it is a domestic or municipal fact. As exercised in any country by the commander of a foreign army, it is an element of the *jus belli*. It is incidental to the state of solemn war, and appertains to the law of nations. The commander of an invading, occupying, or conquering army rules the invaded country with supreme power, limited only by international law and the orders of the sovereign or government he serves or represents. By the law of nations, *occupatio bellica* in a just war transfers the sovereign power of the enemy's country to the conqueror. Such occupation by right of war, so long as it is military only, *flagrante bello*, will be the case put by the Duke of Wellington of all the powers of government resumed in the hands of the commander-in-chief. . . . This does not enlighten us as to martial law in one's own country and as administered by its military commanders. That is a case which the law of nations does not reach.'

In fact, the only reason why powers so dissimilar are called by the same name of martial law is the purely historical reason that they all formed branches of the jurisdiction of the Constable and Marshal's Court.

[1] viii, Opinions of Attorney-Generals at p. 369.

THE PLACE OF ENGLISH LEGAL HISTORY IN THE EDUCATION OF ENGLISH LAWYERS: A PLEA FOR ITS FURTHER RECOGNITION[1]

THE nineteenth century is notable as the century of the renaissance of historical study. New materials and new methods have seconded the new intellectual point of view, which demands to know something of the origin and growth and environment of an institution, a belief, or an idea, before passing judgment upon it. Thus almost all departments of knowledge have been treated historically with more or less completeness. The one great exception, which the historian of our age will note with surprise, is the law of England. There are excellent histories of Roman law, of Roman-Dutch law, of French law, of German law; but no complete history of English law has ever yet been written, and the list of the partial and fragmentary histories which have been attempted at different periods is very scanty.

Hale's history of the common law, written in the latter part of the seventeenth century, and first printed in 1713, is an able sketch, but it is only a sketch, of the history of English law down to the middle of the seventeenth century. The four volumes of Reeves, written at the end of the eighteenth and the beginning of the nineteenth centuries, terminate with the end of Elizabeth's reign. Though the author's style, and the almost exclusively technical point of view which he adopts, make them unreadable for all but the most determined, they are a creditable performance for the period at which they were written; and they are useful even now if used with discrimination. But it is hardly necessary to say that they are far removed from what a history of English law could be and ought to be at this period. Moreover they are spoilt, I might almost say rendered dangerous to the student, by the labours of Mr. Finlason, the editor of the edition published in 1869. The two volumes of Pollock and Maitland show us how such a history might be written. The inestimable services which their work has

[1] A lecture delivered at All Souls College, Oxford, 22 Oct. 1910.

already rendered both to lawyers and historians is but an earnest of the benefit which would have accrued to the study of law and history if it had been completed by the one English lawyer whose historical reputation was European. But though we must be duly thankful for what we have got, both we and many who come after us will regret that it does little more than lay the foundation for the work of some historian of the future. For the rest, we have histories of legal institutions, and histories of certain branches of the law, which touch upon constitutional development; we have in Stephen's history of the criminal law the history of a single branch of English law; we have in Mr. Justice O. W. Holmes's book on the common law a history of certain parts of the common law, and in Thayer's book on Evidence the last word on the history of the jury; we have in the introduction to some of the volumes of the Selden Society, and in other periodicals, valuable essays on various special topics, many of which are usefully collected in the *Essays on Anglo-American Law*; but we have no history of the law as a whole written by a competent lawyer who is also a competent historian.

If we were not familiarized by long use with the absence of any complete history of English law, and with the absence of general legal history from the list of subjects in which the law student must satisfy his examiners, we should regard these two facts as a very curious phenomenon. How curious it is can easily be seen if we glance for a moment at the importance of a knowledge of the history of English law, in the first place to the English historian, and in the second place to the English lawyer.

1. It can hardly be disputed that some knowledge of the history of a nation's law is needed to understand fully that nation's history. In the laws of a nation we get its considered determinations upon all those parts of the national life which it deems advisable to regulate. They are the best evidence of its ideas at any given period upon such matters as the forms and modes of its government, its attitude to religion, its economic ideas, its social structure, its views as to proprietary relations of its members to itself and *inter se*. In any age the historian of all or any of these sides of national life is brought up against the law—it may be in the form of a statute, it may be in the form of books of authority, it may

be in the form of judicial decisions; and, unless he knows something of the general history of the legal system as a whole, he may easily be deceived as to the bearing or importance of a particular rule. 'It is impossible', said the future Lord Cairns to the Commissioners appointed to inquire into the arrangements made by the Inns of Court for promoting the study of the law—'it is impossible for anyone to be proficient in Roman history who does not understand the history of the civil law. If Gibbon had written his history without a large and explanatory discourse on the civil law, it would have been a very imperfect book.'[1] Legal history, in fact, sheds a brilliant light upon all sides of the national life. The light is shed, it is true, from a single, and that a technical standpoint. But it is an important standpoint; for if legal rules reflect the general course and the general tendencies of national life, those legal rules, when firmly established, give a permanent concrete shape to these tendencies, and thus, in the long run, have had no small share in the creation of distinct national characteristics.

Let us take one or two obvious illustrations from our own history, which will show us that a 'large explanatory discourse' on the common law would elucidate many dark places in our constitutional history. We must know something of the manner in which ideas drawn from the civil and canon law shaped the political theory of western Europe, if we are to understand the medieval history of this or of any other western European country; while we must know also something of the manner in which the English common law shaped the institutions and ideas of a feudal state, if we are to understand the peculiarities of the constitutional history of medieval England. We must know something of the strength and the weakness of the medieval common law if, in the Tudor period, we are to understand why, in England alone, Parliament did not go down before the increasing power of the Crown; why it was necessary to create many new courts and councils, and why the old machinery of law and government was able to hold its own against them. In the Stuart period we must know enough law to reargue those famous constitutional cases in which the claims of Parliament and Prerogative were fought out, if we are to under-

[1] *Report of the Commission on the Inns of Court* (1885), 138.

stand the manner in which the great constitutional questions of the seventeenth century presented themselves to the men of that age. For the eighteenth century, we may remember the words of Seeley to the effect that the expansion of England in the New World and in Asia is the formula which sums up for England the history of that century. We shall assuredly miss the reason why the English nation alone of European nations colonized successfully, unless we bear in mind the manner in which the common law fostered the virtues of self-help, self-reliance, and self-government, teaching the individual to depend little on the State and much on himself. For the nineteenth century it is hardly necessary to speak; seeing that the late Vinerian professor—the only holder of the chair in whom Blackstone has found his peer—has clearly explained the intimacy of the relations between the law of England and its general history.

2. But if a knowledge of legal history is necessary to the English historian, still more is it necessary to the English lawyer. Even if English law were entirely codified it would still be necessary to know something about its history. In the compilation of the *Digest of English Civil Law* which a few of us here are producing under the energetic editorship of Mr. Jenks, we find that a constant recourse to legal history is necessary; and a similar recourse will clearly be necessary to those students who wish to understand the whole import of some of. those short propositions in which we have endeavoured to state the law. But the whole of English law is not yet codified; and, in its present uncodified state, it is no exaggeration to say that it has been necessary to make a careful study of particular topics in legal history in order to arrive at a decision in some of the most important of our leading cases in all branches of the law.[1] Some cases, indeed, it would be safe to say, would have been differently decided if the judges had possessed a greater knowledge of legal history —the *Queen* v. *Millis*[2] and *Beamish* v. *Beamish*[3] are classical

[1] Constitutional Law: *Thomas* v. *the Queen* (1874), L.R. 10 Q.B. 31. Torts: *The Winkfield* [1902], P. 42; *Allen* v. *Flood* [1898], A.C. 1. Contracts: *Nordenfelt* v. *Maxim Nordenfelt Co.* [1894], A.C. 535; [1893], 1 Ch. 630. Real Property: *Foxwell* v. *Van Grutten* [1897,] A.C. 658; *Angus* v. *Dalton* (1881), 6 App. Cas. 740.

[2] 10 Cl. & Fin. 534.

[3] (1859), 9 H.L.C. 274; and cp. the note on both these cases in P. & M. ii. 370.

illustrations. With regard to certain peerage cases, the evil results of the ignorance of legal history upon the law and the lawyers have been recently denounced by one whose exact knowledge of the best evidence for historical facts is only equalled by his power of denouncing its absence in others. Mr. Round[1] says:

'It was not long ago that a learned judge, in the course of addressing a medical gathering, observed that there was this in common between their profession and his own: they both made sure of their facts before forming their conclusions. Now that is precisely what, in my experience, lawyers dealing with the facts of history resolutely decline to do. . . . The historian tests his foundations before he rears his structure. . . . To one who has been trained in these methods . . . his first experience of the lawyers' ways must come surely as a shock; science is exchanged for superstition. . . . What is of most matter in the law is not to learn what the facts were, but what some bygone judge or writer supposed the facts had been. He will gaze in wonder on great intellects bowing themselves in homage before the blunders of the past, acute minds submitting to the fetish worship of "our books", and helpless in the presence of what I have termed "the long ju-ju of the law".'

To such criticism have the lawyers exposed themselves by their neglect of legal history! I might be content simply to copy Mr. Round's words, seeing that they put my case far more forcibly than I could put it. But in fairness to my brother lawyers I must confess I think that, though there is much truth in what he says, he puts his case a little too high; and, as my case is a strong one, I do not wish to injure it by over-statement. It seems to me that Mr. Round has omitted to give due weight to two essential conditions of the lawyer's art. In the first place, lawyers are concerned primarily with deciding present disputes, and only secondarily in extricating the facts of history. They must decide these disputes as quickly as possible, using the best evidence they can get. In the second place, they must follow the law laid down in past cases. They only have a free hand if there is no previous case precisely in point. We must, as Coke says, 'peruse our ancient Authors, for out of old fields must come the new corn'.[2] If it were not so the law would be wholly uncertain; and for certainty in the law a little bad history is not too high

---

[1] *Peerage and Pedigree,* i. 104, 105.　　　　[2] 4 *Instit.* 109.

a price to pay. If historians were similarly situated—if, e.g., Mr. Round were obliged to start by accepting all the late Professor Freeman's conclusions as well as the conclusions of others of our more ancient chroniclers, and could not urge his new conclusions unless he could show that he was dealing with events which none of his predecessors had dealt with, we imagine that 'the ju-ju' of history would equal that of the law in length, and would probably exceed it in acrimony. At the same time Mr. Round is quite right in insisting that the lawyers should acquire more accurate historical knowledge. If certain erroneous decisions arrived at in the past, for lack of that knowledge, are now stereotyped in the law, the lawyers can at least avoid similar errors in the decision of new cases, by learning what historical evidence is, where it can be sought, and how it should be applied.

Why, then, have historians and lawyers alike acquiesced so long in the prevailing ignorance of the history of English law? The answer is, I think, to be found in the peculiar history of the education of the English lawyer. That history possesses what in this country is a striking peculiarity—it has no continuity. There was efficient legal education in the fourteenth, fifteenth, sixteenth, and the first half of the seventeenth centuries. In the course of the nineteenth century the system of legal education, which we know and practise, sprang up. But the two periods are separated by a dark age in which English law was not taught at all.

As to the system of legal education pursued in the earlier period—the readings, the moots, the exercises, and the attendance upon the courts—I do not intend to add anything to what I have said elsewhere.[1] It was a system which gave an intensely practical and professional education. It was eminently suited to the needs of a youthful system of law, the literature of which was as yet of a manageable size. It was perhaps the only system possible for an age in which there were no printed books. When Coke wrote his *Institutes* there were plenty of printed books; and 'timely and orderly reading' was as much an essential part of the student's education as the practice of moots and attendance upon Readings and at the courts.[2] This is illustrated by the fact that, from about this period, increased attention was paid by the various Inns

[1] *History of English Law*, ii. 426, 427.   [2] *Coke upon Littleton*, 70b.

of Court to their libraries.[1] But even at the latter part of Coke's life the old system was beginning to show signs of decay. In spite of the efforts of the judges,[2] and the orders of the Inns of Court, it seems to have become gradually more difficult to secure the services of Readers; and the quality of the Readings fell off—Coke calls the modern Readings 'obscure and dark'.[3] The whole system collapsed during the period of the Great Rebellion. After the Restoration some attempts were made to revive it. Orders were issued by the judges in 1664,[4] and the Inns of Court made some attempt to carry them out.[5] It would appear that at Lincoln's Inn there was a party among the Benchers in favour of this revival. But it succumbed to its opponents in 1677.[6] In fact, during the whole of the second half of the seventeenth century less and less importance was coming to be attached to the educational side of the Reader's duties, and more and more to their social side. Readings were diminishing both in length[7] and in numbers; but the extravagance of the Readers' feasts increased to such a pitch that in 1678 the King interfered.[8] By the end of the century the whole of the old system of legal education had collapsed. If any Readers were appointed, they were not expected to read.[9] In theory the

[1] *Pension Book*, Gray's Inn, xlix; in 1629 the barristers and students of Lincoln's Inn petitioned that the library might be made more convenient for them, *Black Books*, ii. 290, 291; in 1631 general orders were made for the library, ibid. 299; in the Middle Temple the library dates from 1641, A. R. Ingpen, K.C., *Master Worsley's Book*, 107.

[2] General Orders were issued in 1591, *Black Books of Lincoln's Inn*, ii. 20; in 1593, 4, ibid. 31; in 1596, ibid. 47; in 1604, ibid. 81; in 1614, ibid. 440; in 1627, 8, ibid. 451; and in 1630, ibid. 454.

[3] *Coke upon Littleton*, 280b.

[4] *Black Books of Lincoln's Inn*, iii. 445–9.

[5] *Infra*, p. 29, n. 1.   [6] *Black Books of Lincoln's Inn*, iii, xi–xiv.

[7] Ibid. iii.. 10, 12—the Reading is to last one week only.

[8] For the Readers' Feasts see Dugdale, *Orig. Jurid.* 206; in 1678 the King ordered that no Reader, not being a K.C. or the Recorder of London, should spend more than £300 on his Reading, *Black Books of Lincoln's Inn*, iii. 120.

[9] The last Reader appointed in Lincoln's Inn was appointed in 1677, and the last Reading took place in 1680, *Black Books*, iii, xiv; iv, vi; in the Middle Temple they continued to be appointed, but the last Reader who read was Sir W. Whitelock, in 1684, Ingpen, *Master Worsley's Book*, 125; at New Inn there was a Reading on the Statute of Uses, slight in character, as late as 1691, *Collectanea Juridica*, i. 369; cp. *Pension Book*, Gray's Inn, 445, 446, 457 and n. 4.

student's exercises continued. But their theoretical existence was merely an excuse for levying certain fixed payments for failure to perform them.[1]

'For the Common Law', said Roger North,[2] 'there are Societies which have the outward show or pretence of collegiate institutions; yet in reality nothing of that sort is now to be found in them; and whereas, in more ancient times, there were exercises used in the Hall, they were more for probation than institution; now even these are shrunk into mere forms, and that preserved only for conformity to rules, that gentlemen by tale of appearances in exercises rather than any sort of performances, might be entitled to be called to the Bar.'

What these exercises had become in the nineteenth century Mr. Whateley, Q.C., told the Inns of Court Commissioners in 1855:

'When I was a student', he said,[3] 'I used to be marched up to the barrister's table with a paper in my hand, and I said, "I hold the widow". The barrister made a bow and I went away; and the next man said, "I hold the widow shall not"—and the barrister made a bow and he went off; and that was the remnant of performing the exercises.'

The exercises performed at the Benchers' table seem to have been of a precisely similar character—the widow did duty on both occasions.[4] The residence of members once sternly insisted on, because obviously necessary to the efficiency of the old system of legal education, could, like the performance of exercises, be compounded for;[5] and, in the nineteenth century, it has survived only in the liability to keep a fixed number of terms by consuming a fixed number of dinners.[6]

With the disappearance of the old system of legal education, disappeared the whole apparatus of the public teaching

[1] Ingpen, *Master Worsley's Book*, 136, 'It is now usual when a gentleman hath failed, and been fined for so doing, to account his exercise over, he being no more called to that exercise'; see ibid. 211 n. and 212 for the amounts payable; and cp. *Black Books of Lincoln's Inn*, iii. 85.

[2] Cited Ingpen, Introd. to *Master Worsley's Book*, 45.

[3] *Evidence*, p. 54.   [4] *Black Books of Lincoln's Inn*, iv, v. 2.

[5] Ingpen, *Master Worsley's Book*, 143, 144, 210; *Black Books of Lincoln's Inn*, iii, xix. 287.

[6] The modern conditions of call were in substance fixed, in 1762, by an agreement between the four Inns of Court, *Black Books of Lincoln's Inn*, iii. 374, 375.

of English law; for, from the earliest period in our history, the Universities had abandoned this subject to the Inns of Court.[1] It is clear from the preface to *Rolle's Abridgment*, written by Sir Matthew Hale at the end of the seventeenth century, and from a letter written at the beginning of the eighteenth century by Sir Thomas Reeve, Chief Justice of the Common Pleas, to his nephew,[2] that the student must rely upon his own reading for information upon the general principles of the law; and as Bacon had said,[3] there was no really good institutional book which he could read. He must make shift with such books as *Coke upon Littleton*, the *Doctor and Student*, and the *Abridgments*. The study of these books, attendance upon the courts,[4] and reading in chambers were the only methods of gaining instruction in the law of England from the last part of the seventeenth century to the last part of the nineteenth century.[5]

The causes of this disastrous state of things were mainly two. In the first place, the printed book seemed to provide a short cut to knowledge, and led both the students and their teachers to acquiesce in the abandonment of a laborious system of education. The students were not sorry to be relieved of their exercises. The barristers, especially the more senior barristers, upon whom as Benchers the maintenance of the system depended, were not sorry to be relieved of obligations which interfered with their practice.[6]

[1] Holdsworth, *H.E.L.* ii. 415.

[2] Both these are printed in *Collectanea Juridica*, i. 79, 263; cp. the course suggested by Roger North, *Discourse on the Study of the Law*, 41.

[3] *A Proposal for Amending the Laws of England*, Works (ed. 1824), iv. 372, 'For the Institutions, I know well there be books of introductions, wherewith students begin, of good worth, especially Littleton and Fitzherbert's *Natura Brevium*: but they are no ways of the nature of an institution; the office whereof is to be a key and general preparation to the reading of the course'.

[4] From the earliest times, right down to the nineteenth century, places in court were reserved for the students, and judges would sometimes explain to them the gist of the proceedings, or the points of law which were being discussed; for the period of the Year Books see Y.BB. 1 & 2 Ed. II (S.S.) xv, and n. 2; 2 & 3 Ed. II (S.S.) xv, xvi; 3 & 4 Ed. II (S.S.) xli, xlii; for the eighteenth and nineteenth centuries see Campbell, *Lives of the Chief Justices*, ii. 329 and note.

[5] See generally Ingpen, *Master Worsley's Book*, 43–50.

[6] At Lincoln's Inn, in 1605, the Reader-elect said that he had made some progress in his Reading, but 'protested that he coulde not goe throughe and

The old system needed the willing co-operation of students, barristers, and Benchers. All now desired to see the end of it. In 1661 the Masters of the Bench at Lincoln's Inn stated: 'That expresse informacion hath bin made (which they are unwilling to believe) that there is a consent and combinacion interteined and owned by some at least of the gentlemen of the barr to abett and justify such defaults as have already bin made, and to encourage and countenance the like for the future.'[1] There is nothing like a robust faith in the non-existence of facts which we do not wish to see. But the 'expresse informacion' should not have been so very difficult of belief, seeing that, in 1664, it was necessary to pass a rule threatening any Bencher who declined to read with the loss of his seat on the Bench.[2]

In the second place, the life of the lawyers in their Inns were too self-centred and too isolated. We, whose studies are apt to suffer from the opposite defect—from a continual discussion of far-reaching projects of reform, urged upon us by writers in the Press, and by members of our own body—may envy the academic calm of the eighteenth century. But in truth that century suffered from the defect of too little outside interference, as we perhaps suffer from the defect of too much. Robert Lowe hit the nail on the head when he told the Inns of Court Commissioners that the Inns of Court, as at present constituted, were a University in a state of decay.

'They are', he said, 'in the same position, as I understand it, as the University of Oxford was at the end of the last century, when the University had virtually delegated the power of conferring a degree on the Colleges, the consequence of which was that the Colleges, whether from competition among themselves, or having no sufficient motive, had brought the thing down to the very lowest point.'[3]

As the law became more complex, the difficulties of the law student increased. They were, perhaps, at their worst in the first half of the nineteenth century, for he was left to get what instruction he could from his own reading; and there

finishe the same to Reade this sommer withoute refrayninge and loseinge a greate parte of his practize this presente terme and the nexte allso', *Black Books*, ii. 87.

[1] Ibid. iii. 8; for other orders attempting to restore the old system see ibid. 10, 12, 20, 32, 36, 60, 61.   [2] *Evidence*, p. 135.
[3] Ibid. 40.

was but little he could read.[1] His older advisers contemplated his covering the whole body of the law. He could be
'furnished', as Coke put it, 'with the whole course of the law'.[2]
But this had become plainly impossible with the growth in
the bulk and complexity of the law. He had, indeed, Blackstone's *Commentaries*; but he had little else. He was left to
grope his way unassisted amidst the statutes, the reports, and
large treatises wholly unsuited to his needs. We have a description of the position of the law student of the sixteenth
century, when the old system of legal education was in its
prime, and of his position in the nineteenth century, when it
had fallen into utter decay, from two equally competent
eyewitnesses. In the sixteenth century Sir Thomas Smith
tells us that he has such admiration for the conciseness of
statement, the skill in argument, the logical force, the copious
and polished eloquence of the *Londinenses Jurisconsulti* that
he intends to take a long vacation in London in order to
have the pleasure of hearing them dispute together in their
schools.[3] In the nineteenth century Lord Bowen says:[4]

> 'I well recollect the dreary days with which my own experience of
> the law began in the chambers of a once famous Lincoln's Inn con-
> veyancer; the gloom of a London atmosphere without, the white-
> washed misery of the pupil's room within—both rendered more
> emphatic by what appeared to us to be the hopeless dinginess of the
> occupations of the inhabitants. There stood all our dismal text books
> in rows—the endless Acts of Parliament, the cases and the authorities,
> the piles of forms and of precedents—calculated to extinguish all
> desire of knowledge even in the most thirsty soul. To use the language
> of the sacred text, it seemed a dry and barren land in which no water
> was. And, with all this, no adequate method of study, no sound
> and intelligent principle upon which to collect and to assort our
> information.'

The remote germs of our modern system of legal education
must be sought in the apprehensions of that prince of jobbers,
the Duke of Newcastle, and in the suggestion of a Solicitor-

---

[1] See Dicey, 'Blackstone's Commentaries', *National Review*, Dec. 1909,
671.

[2] *Coke upon Littleton*, 70; cp. authorities cited above, p. 28, n. 2.

[3] Extract from Smith's inaugural oration, cited Maitland, *English Law
and the Renaissance*, 90.

[4] Address to the Birmingham Law Students' Society, 1888, cited Cunningham, *Life of Lord Bowen*, 76, 77.

General to a fellow of All Souls. The Solicitor-General, Sir William Murray (the future Lord Mansfield), had perceived in Blackstone, a prominent fellow of All Souls, the makings of a great teacher; and, in 1752, he had recommended the Duke of Newcastle to appoint him to the Chair of Civil Law in this University, which was then vacant. The Duke, not being sufficiently sure of Blackstone's political support, declined to appoint him. Thereupon Murray advised Blackstone to break new ground by giving lectures on English law at Oxford. The wisdom of this advice was abundantly justified. Blackstone's lectures led to the foundation of the Vinerian chair at this University; and the foundation of that chair was the beginning of a new system of legal education. But of Blackstone, and of Blackstone's work, I need say little, after the lecture which the late Vinerian professor gave last year. Blackstone rightly condemned the system under which the student was expected, 'by a tedious, lonely process, to extract the theory of the law from a mass of undigested learning'. He pointed out that it was a mistake to suppose that a knowledge of practice was all that was useful to a lawyer— 'if practice be the whole he is taught, practice must also be the whole he will ever know'; and he concluded that the previous foundations of legal science should, like those of any other science, be laid in one of our learned universities. His own lectures showed the manner in which the learned universities might encourage the study of English law; and these lectures, when published as the *Commentaries on the Laws of England*, were, to use the words of Bacon, the first book 'of the nature of an institution' that the law of England had yet possessed; for they were the first book on English law, the primary aim of which was 'to be a key and general preparation to the reading of the course'. In the New World his words and his example met with a readier response than in his own country. It must indeed be admitted that the reverence of our American cousins for our common law has exceeded our own; for it has borne practical fruit, not only in the elucidation of many dark places in its history, but also in the construction of an original method of legal education which combines the strong features of the old system and the new.[1] In this

[1] See Thayer, 'The Teaching of English Law at Universities', *Harv. Law Rev.* ix. 169–84; Thayer could say with perfect justice in 1895 (op.

country, for reasons which the late Vinerian professor has clearly pointed out, his voice was the voice of one crying in the wilderness. In 1795 Mr. Nolan, a barrister of Lincoln's Inn, in a letter to the Benchers proposing to establish an annual lectureship upon Law and Equity, justly pointed out that, 'Corporate regulations are imposed upon those who wish to become lawyers, and degrees are conferred entitling them to practice, but no person is appointed to deliver that instruction to students on account of which these restrictions were originally imposed'.[1] The proposal of James Mackintosh to deliver a set of lectures, in Lincoln's Inn Hall, on the Law of Nature and of Nations, was with difficulty granted;[2] and a proposal of Lord Brougham's in 1845 that Lincoln's Inn should establish an annual course of lectures on Jurisprudence and the Civil Law, and that the other Inns should be invited to establish lectures on Common Law, Equity, and Conveyancing, was adjourned.[3] It was not till nearly a century after Blackstone lectured and wrote, that any attempt was seriously made to realize his ideal. It was nearly eighty years before there were even faint glimmerings of the dawn.

In 1833 the Inner Temple created two lectureships; but the attendance was small and they ceased after two years. In 1847 the Inner Temple established a lectureship in Common Law, and the Middle Temple lectureships in Jurisprudence and Civil Law; and, in the same year, Gray's Inn established courses of lectureships, moots, and voluntary examinations. In 1851 the Inns of Court established the Council of Legal Education to give lectures and classes; and a call to the Bar was made conditional either on passing an examination, or on attending a certain number of lectures.[4] The inadequacy of these measures was patent to the Inns of Court Commissioners, who reported, in 1855, that 'as regards intellectual qualifications and the professional knowledge of

cit. 169, 170), 'We, in America, have carried legal education much further than it has gone in England. There the systematic teaching of law in schools is but faintly developed'.

[1] *Black Books*, iv. 66.
[2] Ibid. 76; Campbell, *Lives of the Chancellors*, vi. 288–91.
[3] *Black Books*, iv. 229.
[4] *Report*, p. 13; *Black Books of Lincoln's Inn*, iv, vi, vii; Ingpen, *Master Worsley's Book*, 48–50.

a barrister there was no such security as the community is entitled to require',[1] and that we were behind every other European country in this respect.[2] They recommended, among other things, a compulsory examination;[3] but it was not till 1872 that this recommendation was carried into effect.

Long before this, however, the new system of lectures and examinations was well on the way. The 'Society of Attorneys, Solicitors, Proctors, and others, not being barristers, practising in the courts of Law and Equity of the United Kingdom', now called the Law Society, had been incorporated in 1831; and, in 1833, it had established a system of lectures and a compulsory examination. By the middle of the century the Universities had begun to follow the path which Blackstone had pointed out. At Oxford the examination for the B.C.L. degree was started in 1852, and the Honour School of Law and History in 1853; Law and History were, if we may use the metaphor, judicially separated, but not completely divorced in 1872, when our present Honour School of Jurisprudence came into being. At Cambridge the Law Tripos issued its first class list in 1858. When the Society of Public Teachers of Law was formed in 1908, there were found to be, besides the Inns of Court and the Law Society, no less than eight universities teaching, lecturing upon, examining in, and giving degrees in English law.[4] We may fairly say, therefore, that the new system of legal education has been established; and the reproach that there was no teaching of English law—a reproach which had lasted for nearly two hundred years—has been at length removed.

Now I think that this curious history explains to us why the history of English law has never been written and never been taught in any systematic fashion. In the earlier period, when it was possible and necessary to study the whole literature of the law, the lawyers acquired a knowledge of legal history sufficient for their professional work together with their law. But, as Professor Maitland has pointed out, this system of legal education could not lead to the production of any great work upon the history of English law.[5] 'History

[1] *Report*, p. 14.   [2] Ibid., pp. 10, 11.   [3] Ibid., pp. 17–19.
[4] In the United States there were, in 1895, some seventy-five law schools, Thayer, 'The Teaching of English Law in Universities', *Harv. Law Rev.* ix. 173.   [5] *Why the History of English Law is not Written,* 11.

involves comparison, and the English lawyer, who knew nothing and cared nothing for any system but his own, hardly came in sight of the idea of legal history.' Then, in the later period, the peculiar difficulties attending the study of English law rendered it a sealed book to all but the lawyers; and thus we get that peculiarity, noted by Maine,[1] that, while 'Frenchmen, Swiss, and Germans of a very humble order have a very fair practical knowledge of the law which regulates their everyday life', we consider that 'law belongs as much to the class of exclusively professional subjects as the practice of anatomy'. Those qualified to write history knew no law; while the trained lawyer, even if he was acquainted with other systems than his own, had learnt and studied law, not scientifically, but empirically in chambers, with a view to professional practice. Lawyers trained after this fashion, who could devote but a few occasional hours from more absorbing professional pursuits to the needs of the student, were not persons who would be likely to appreciate the importance of legal history in the education of the lawyer; for they had never taught law, nor had they studied it from the point of view of the teacher.

But, in the Society of Public Teachers of Law, we can see that a new school of lawyers has arisen, who make it the business of their lives to teach and study law scientifically; and it is not too much to hope that their united experience may effect some necessary reforms. At the beginning of this lecture, I have tried to give you some reasons for my claim that a reconsideration of the position of the history of English law in the legal curriculum is, of all the needed reforms, the most pressing; and, in conclusion, I should like to make one or two suggestions as to what that position should be.

In the first place, the history of legal institutions, i.e. the history of the courts and their jurisdiction, should be taught at the very beginning of the student's course. To judge from older tracts like the *Articuli ad novas narrationes* and the *Diversité des Courtes*, this has from very early days been considered a necessary branch of elementary knowledge.[2] It should therefore be a part of the first examination; and it could easily and naturally be combined with constitutional

[1] *Village Communities*, 59, 60.
[2] For these tracts see Holdsworth, *H.E.L.* ii. 442, 443.

law and its history. In this way the student will get some idea
(1) of the form and mechanism of the State, the law of which
he is about to learn, and (2) of the judicial machinery by
which that law has been built up. He will learn the meaning
of some of the most fundamental divisions of that law—
the divisions between common law, and equity, and ecclesiastical law, and Admiralty law. He will understand the
reason why there are various divisions of the Supreme Court,
and the principle upon which the judicial work of the State is
assigned to these various divisions.

In the second place, a general outline of the history of the
law should be made part of the final examination. This must
be made part of the final examination because it is impossible
to deal adequately with the history of a technical subject till
its rudiments have been mastered—a fact of which Coke had
some perception when he advised the student to read first the
more recent and then the earlier cases.[1] This subject should
be treated in two parts. The first part should contain a
general account of the chief epochs in the history of the law in
relation to the general history of England, together with an
account of the literature and sources of the law; and the
second part, the history of those branches of legal doctrine
which form part of the examination. Further, the student
should be required to show his capacity to read the two
languages in which the earlier records of the law are written
—Latin and Law French.

The acquisition of a body of knowledge of this kind
would be both of scientific and of practical value. It would
be of scientific value because it would teach the student the
manner in which the law is shaped and developed by the
changing needs and ideas of different ages, and conversely,
the extent to which the law has helped to shape these needs
and ideas; it would teach him at once the permanence and
adaptability of legal rules; it would teach him that apparently
meaningless technicalities once had a meaning, and perhaps
still possess more meaning than may at first sight appear;[2]

[1] *Coke upon Littleton*, 249b.
[2] 'The dullest topics kindle when touched with the light of historical
research, and the most recondite and technical fall into the order of common
experience and rational thought', Thayer, 'The Teaching of English Law at
Universities', *Harv. Law Rev.* ix. 178, 179.

it would teach him the delicacy and difficulty of making successful legislative changes in an old system of law; and, if it is necessary to make some changes, it would the better equip him for the task. It would be of practical value because the student, when he comes to the practical work of his profession, would know something of the authorities which he is constantly using. It would help him to read old books and old reports intelligently. It would put him on inquiry for better evidence if these old books and old reports seemed to be telling impossible tales, or laying down inexplicable law. It would give him a clue to a right conclusion if, seeking authority, he is obliged to wander further and further away from his modern cases, and is even driven to plunge into the Year Books; for it would teach him what parts of the old law were clearly obsolete, and where he might hope to get some light upon a modern case.

The outlines of such knowledge must be acquired, if at all, in a lawyer's student days. If these outlines are then acquired they can and will be added to in later years; for historical methods and historical evidence will be familiar things, and the history of the law will not be a sealed book written in an unknown tongue. Legal history, if thus generally taught, will come to be recognized by the profession as the basis of a scientific knowledge of the law; and our successors will look back to the days when the lawyer was not expected to possess it, and had no adequate means of acquiring it, with as much wonder as we now look back to the days when there was no teaching of the principles of English law.

CENTRAL COURTS OF LAW AND REPRE-
SENTATIVE ASSEMBLIES IN THE
SIXTEENTH CENTURY[1]

THE sixteenth century saw the end of the legal and political ideas of the Middle Ages, and the beginnings of the legal and political ideas of the modern world. Throughout western Europe the legal and political institutions of the medieval state were adapted to the needs of the modern state; and the manner in which that adaptation was made in each particular country affected the whole subsequent history of that country. The legal and political ideas and institutions of the Middle Ages were founded ultimately upon a belief in the existence of absolute rights guarded by a supreme law. In the sixteenth century they were replaced, in most of the countries of western Europe, by a new set of legal and political ideas and institutions founded upon a belief in the sovereignty of the ruler of the State. And thus, as Stubbs has pointed out,[2] while medieval history is, in the main, a history of rights and wrongs, the history of the sixteenth, seventeenth, and eighteenth centuries is, in the main, a history of forces, powers, and dynasties. In England these new ideas and institutions made their appearance. The power of the Crown, and therefore of the executive government, was so strengthened that England became a territorial state of the modern type, and English law public and private was made equal to the task of keeping the peace and of settling the relations between man and man in this new age of Renaissance and Reformation. But the manner in which this change was effected in England was very different from the manner in which it had been effected abroad. It was effected, not, as abroad, by wholly, or almost wholly, replacing medieval institutions by new institutions, but by so improving the efficiency of existing medieval institutions that these medieval institutions were able to meet the new demands made upon them by the modern state. Parliament was controlled by the executive; but it remained the taxing and legislative body in

[1] Reprinted from the *Columbia Law Review*, Jan. 1912.
[2] *Lectures on Mediæval and Modern History*, 329.

the State. The Justices of the Peace were made the centre of a new system of local government. The ordinary courts of common law retained many of their quasi-political functions. The retention of these medieval institutions meant the retention of some of the legal and political ideas which underlay them; and thus at the end of the sixteenth century the English constitution and English public law differed fundamentally from the constitution and the public law of the principal states of western Europe. In England, and in England alone, there had been a continuity of development. That this continuity was possible was due to the fact that the English constitution and English law of the fourteenth and fifteenth centuries were not purely medieval; for, in the twelfth and thirteenth centuries, England had evolved a centralized government under modified medieval forms, and a common law which retained medieval ideas modified, in like manner, to suit the needs of a centralized government. In this century it was the maintenance of this continuity which, more than any other single cause, enabled a successful resistance to be made in England, and in England alone, to the establishment of an absolute monarchy.

It would be difficult, therefore, to exaggerate the importance of the sixteenth century in English constitutional history; and yet that history has never been adequately written. We are beginning to know something of the real meaning of medieval ideas and institutions. We already know much of those constitutional controversies of the seventeenth century, out of which the English constitution of the eighteenth and nineteenth centuries emerged. But, if we except Mr. Protheroe's introductory sketch to his *Select Documents*, we are obliged to look for the constitutional history of the sixteenth century to writers of the type of Hallam, who judge that history exclusively from the point of view of the later part of the seventeenth and of the eighteenth centuries. And yet it is clear that if we are to form a just judgment as to the rights and wrongs of the constitutional controversies of the seventeenth century, we should know something of the political ideas amidst which the chief actors in those controversies had been brought up. To adopt exclusively the standpoint of our modern settled constitutional law, and to content ourselves with taking the Parliament's view of the connexion between precedents drawn from the parliamentary history of the Middle Ages and the new law established as the result of the controversies of the seventeenth century, is to do more than justice to the cause of the Parliament, and less than justice to the cause of the King. Such an attitude prevents us from giving due weight to the manner in which medieval ideas and institutions had been modified by the new ideas and institutions that had come with the sixteenth century.

One recent writer has attempted to tell us something of the constitutional history of the sixteenth century from another point of view. Professor McIlwain's able essay upon *The High Court of Parliament*[1] is a corrective to writers of the type of Hallam, because it looks at parliamentary history from the point of view, not of the late seventeenth and eighteenth centuries, but of the Middle Ages. His conclusions as summarized by himself in the preface to his·essay are as follows:

'(*a*) England after the Norman Conquest was a feudal state, *i.e.*, its political character is better expressed by the word feudal than by the word national. (*b*) As a consequence, her central assembly was a feudal assembly, with the general characteristics of feudal assemblies. (*c*) One of those characteristics was the absence of law-*making*. The law was declared rather than made. (*d*) The law which existed and was thus declared was a body of custom which in time 'grew to be looked upon as a law fundamental. Rules inconsistent with this fundamental law were void. Such a law was recognized in England down to modern times. (*e*) Another characteristic of the times was the absence of a division of labour between different "departments" of government and the lack of any clear corresponding distinctions in governmental activity, as "legislative", "judicial", or "administrative". (*f*) Parliament, the highest "court" of the Realm, in common with the lower courts, participated in these general functions of government. It both "legislated" and "adjudicated", but until modern times no clear distinction was perceived between these two kinds of activity, and the former being for long relatively the less important, we may say roughly that Parliament was more a court than a legislature, while the ordinary courts had functions now properly called legislative as well as judicial. (*g*) "Acts" of Parliament were thus analogous to judgments in the inferior courts and such acts were naturally not treated by the

---

[1] *The High Court of Parliament and its Supremacy*, an historical essay on the boundaries between legislation and adjudication in England.

judges in these courts as inviolable rules *made* by an external omni-
potent legislative assembly, but rather as judgments of another court,
which might be, and were at times, treated as no modern statute
would ever be treated by the courts to-day.'

Our general criticism upon Professor McIlwain's book,
formed after carefully reading it with great profit to ourselves,
is that it suffers from the opposite defect to Hallam's work
in that the story is told too exclusively from the medieval
point of view. The English constitution and the English
common law of the fourteenth and fifteenth centuries were,
as we have said, not purely medieval. Many of Professor
McIlwain's conclusions would be far more applicable to the
French Estates General and to the French Parlements than
to the English Parliaments and the English courts of law,
because, as we shall see, these French institutions retained
many more purely medieval traits than the parallel English
institutions. If the English Parliament and the English
courts of law had been as medieval in character as he maintains they were, we doubt whether they could have been
adapted, as the Tudor kings adapted them, to the needs of
the modern state.

The great merit of Professor McIlwain's book consists
in the fact that it has brought into prominence a neglected
aspect of many facts in English history from the twelfth to
the seventeenth centuries. But it has the defects of its qualities, in that it gives too much prominence to that which was
formerly too much neglected. But our own conclusions and
the points wherein we differ from Professor McIlwain will
appear at large in the following pages, and we must leave our
readers to judge between us.

In some centuries the legal and constitutional history of
England runs very much upon its own lines. The history of
the fourteenth and fifteenth, and the history of the seventeenth centuries can be told without very much reference to
contemporary continental events. In other centuries we must
bear in mind these contemporary continental events if we are
to understand the real significance of the English facts. The
age of Bracton can hardly be understood without some
reference to the events which made the twelfth and thirteenth
centuries an age of legal Renaissance throughout western
Europe. Still less can we understand the significance of the

legal and constitutional history of England in this century of Renaissance, Reformation, and Reception, without some reference to parallel developments abroad. We shall, therefore, in the first place say something of the history of the central Courts of Law and representative assemblies abroad, in order that we may the better understand the unique position to which the English Parliament and the English courts of common law attained during this century.

The Continental Development

In many of the countries of western Europe representative assemblies were to be found in the thirteenth and fourteenth centuries. The Cortes of Castile and Aragon, and the Estates General of France were not unlike the English Parliaments of these centuries. The Cortes of Castile and Aragon controlled taxation and legislation, and sometimes seem to have exercised supervision over all the business of the State.[1] The powers of the Estates General were somewhat more limited. Ordinarily they seem only to have had the right to control taxation, and the right to give counsel to the King.[2] But, with the one exception of the English Parliament, these representative assemblies failed to stem the tide of absolutism in the sixteenth century, and survived, if they survived at all, merely as the shadows of their former selves. The Castilian Cortes, after the revolt of the *communeros* (1520–1) became completely subservient to the King, who bribed or nominated their members.[3] After 1591 the Cortes of Aragon were similarly muzzled.[4] The Estates General lost their powers earlier. The stress of the Hundred Years' War induced them to vote permanent taxes to keep on foot a paid army (1435 and 1439)

[1] Hallam, *Middle Ages*, ii. 24–33, 55, 56.

[2] Esmein, *Histoire du droit Français*, 506 seqq.; Brissaud, *Histoire du droit Français*, 805, 806. Sometimes they exercised extraordinary powers, e.g. in 1355–7 they controlled the administration, and in 1420 they ratified the Treaty of Troyes; they also claimed certain rights of election to the throne in case of a vacancy, certain rights during the minority of the King, and certain rights of sanctioning alienation of the royal domain, Esmein, op. cit. 503–5; but these claims are shadowy—on such matters they did little more than deliberate; their ordinary rights are those stated in the text.

[3] Ranke, *Turkish and Spanish Monarchies* (Kelly's Tr.), 56–8; in 1534 it was said that a place in the Cortes was worth 14,000 ducats; after 1538 the nobles were never summoned.

[4] Ibid. 64, 65.

and they tried in vain to regain their lost control over taxation.[1] By the second half of the sixteenth century their consent or their refusal to consent to a new tax was a matter of no importance. They never acquired a power to legislate. They could advise, complain, or petition; but that was all.[2] The right to petition did not, as in England, develop into a right to consent, to refuse to consent, or to propose new laws.[3] The King was free to act or not as he pleased upon their petitions.[4] These petitions, it is true, often supplied valuable material for the making of laws; but, as in England in the fourteenth century, it was the King who made the laws.[5] Even though their powers were thus diminished, they were distrusted. Their existence gave countenance to democratic claims, which assorted ill with the position which the monarchy had assumed.[6] After 1614 none were assembled till the eve of the Revolution.

The reasons why these representative assemblies failed to become a permanent check upon the King and a permanent part of the constitution were mainly two. In the first place their constitution and procedure were defective. In the second place they excited the hostility of the lawyers, because the position which the lawyers claimed for the law courts seemed to be threatened by the claims of these assemblies.

(1) The constitution of these assemblies was defective.

[1] Esmein, op. cit. 507–10.
[2] Ibid. 511, 512.
[3] Holdsworth, *History of English Law*, ii. 363–6.
[4] 'Le roi était libre absolument de repousser les demandes ou d'y accéder; c'était une supplique qui lui était addressée', Esmein, op. cit. 512; under Philip II the position of the Cortes in relation to the King was very similar, Ranke, op. cit. 59, 60.
[5] Hence, as in the English Parliament, we get complaints that, 'Le pouvoir royal dénaturait les articles des cahiers'; cp. Holdsworth, op. cit. ii. 365.
[6] Hotman, *Franco-Gallia* (ed. 1573), cc. xv–xviii, argues from the history of the Estates General, as English statesmen argued from the history of the English Parliament, that the French monarchy was not absolute— 'Utcumque sit, perspicuum est, nondum centesimum annum abiisse ex quo Francogalliæ libertas, solemnisque concilii auctoritas vigebat, et vigebat versus regem [Louis XI] . . . tanta imperii magnitudine praeditum, quantam nunquam in ullo rege nostro fuisse constat'; cp. H. Lureau, *Les Doctrinés démocratiques de la seconde moitié du XVIe siècle*, 5–10, for instances of claims to the exercise of various powers made by or for the Estates General in the fifteenth and sixteenth centuries.

The nobility and the *tiers état* sat separately. Either the nobility were not summoned; or, if they were summoned, they failed to attend, as in Castile;[1] or, if they attended, they failed to act with the *tiers état*, because their interests were too divergent. Thus in France the exemption of the nobility from the *taille* caused them to take little interest in the struggle to gain control over taxation.[2] The procedure of these assemblies was even more defective. Their activities were seriously limited by old rules which were survivals of a very primitive stage in the history of law. Thus in Aragon, till 1591, the principle that a decision could be arrived at by a majority vote was unknown. A single dissentient could prevent the levy of a tax or the passing of a law.[3] Both in France and in Castile it would seem that, without express powers from their constituents, the deputies could do nothing except present grievances.[4] These rules represented archaic legal ideas which were being rapidly driven from the legal systems of the principal states of Europe by the victorious advance of Roman law.

(2) The preservation of these archaisms partially explains the hostility of the lawyers. The order of legal ideas with which the lawyers of this age of the Reception were familiar was very different from the order of legal ideas which these assemblies represented. But the cause for this hostility really went deeper than this. In many countries, and notably in

[1] Ranke, op. cit. 56, 57.

[2] Esmein, op. cit. 554; in Spain there was a long standing feud between the towns and the nobles, Ranke, op. cit. 56.

[3] Ranke, op. cit. 65; it was enacted in 1591 that for the future, 'the majority of every estate constitutes the estate; even if a whole estate be wanting this shall have no influence upon the constitution of the Cortes, provided that the same shall have been duly summoned according to law'; and see generally as to the Cortes of the Spanish Kingdom in the later Middle Ages, R. B. Merriman, *Am. Hist. Rev.* xvi. 476–95; for some account of the history of the majority principle see Redlich, *The Procedure of the House of Commons*, ii. 261–4; cp. *infra*, p. 53, n. 2.

[4] Esmein, op. cit. 498, 'Les députés aux États généraux étaient, quant à leurs pouvoirs, soumis au régime qu'on appelle le *mandat impératif*. ... Plus d'une fois les députés répondirent aux demandes royales que celles-ci excédaient leurs pouvoirs, et il fallut les renvoyer devant leurs électeurs pour en recevoir de nouveaux'; for a similar rule in Castile see Ranke, op. cit. 58—Charles V got over it by dictating a comprehensive form of credentials which must be given to all deputies; for similar and greater defects in the German diet see *Camb. Mod. Hist.* i. 290, 291.

France, the claim of the central courts to exercise political functions made them the rivals of these assemblies.[1]   As Mr. Armstrong says:

'The jealousy between judicature and legislature has been a prominent rock of offence in the pathway of French constitutional liberty.'[2]

But in order to understand this cause for the jealousy of the lawyers we must explain the constitutional position which they claimed for some of these central courts.

Our own constitutional history teaches us that courts of law were, in the days before the functions of government had become specialized, very much more than merely judicial tribunals.   In England and elsewhere they were regarded as possessing functions which we may call political, to distinguish them from those purely judicial functions which nowadays are their exclusive functions on the Continent, and their principal functions everywhere.   That the courts continued to exercise these larger functions, even after departments of government had begun to be differentiated, was due to the continuance of that belief in the supremacy of the law which was the dominant characteristic of the political theory of the Middle Ages.[3]   The law was a rule of conduct which all members of the State, rulers and subjects alike, were bound to obey.   The whole conduct of government consisted in the enforcement of the law, and in the maintenance of the rights and duties to which it gave rise.   It was a necessary

---

[1]   Esmein, op. cit. 508, 509, tells us that in 1485 the Parlement of Paris turned a deaf ear to the request of the Duke of Orleans that it would assent to the principle that the taxes should not be increased without the consent of the Estates—'C'est qu'il s'agissait des États généraux, c'est à dire d'un pouvoir politique en partie rivale, dont les parlements contrarièrent incontestablement le développement et auquel ils cherchèrent à se substituer'; cp. Armstrong, *French Wars of Religion*, 15, 24, 25, for the events of 1566.

[2]   Op. cit. 15.

[3]   *Supra*, p. 37; cp. Holdsworth, op. cit. ii. 154, 197–200, 361, 362; Esmein, speaking of the Parlement of Paris (op. cit. 379) says, 'Quoique le parlement rendît ses sentences au nom du roi, source de toute justice, dans les arrêts qu'il prononçait, c'était la cour qu'on faisait parler (*la cour ordonne, condamne*) tandis que, dans les arrêts du conseil du roi, le roi parlait toujours en personne (*par le roi en son conseil*)'. This very neatly expresses the contrast between the ideas which underlay the jurisdiction of the older courts, and the ideas which underlay the jurisdiction of the newer courts of the sixteenth century.

consequence of this theory of government that the court should possess political functions; for they existed not merely to do justice as between private persons, but also to see that the law itself was not arbitrarily infringed or altered by the King or any other person.

The two most striking illustrations of the political powers possessed by these medieval courts are the Justiza of Aragon and the Parlement of Paris. Both possessed large powers which were designed to safeguard the supremacy of the law, and to preserve to the individual the rights which it gave him.

The Justiza held his office for life, and was responsible only to the Cortes. He could prohibit any inferior court from proceeding with a case. He was the final judge on points of law arising in all other courts. By the process of *Juris-firma* he could bring any case pending in the lower courts before himself: by the process of *Manifestation* he could bring before himself any person imprisoned, that he might adjudicate upon the justice of the charge made against him. He administered the coronation oath to the King; and often represented him in the Cortes. These powers were evidently designed to protect the subject against any infringements of the law.[1] They existed till the revolt of Saragossa in 1591. After that date the Justiza and his deputies became practically nominees of the King.[2] The new idea that the King's will was law triumphed over the medieval idea and the medieval institution invented to safeguard it.

The Parlement of Paris is a more famous illustration of the same idea. By the end of the thirteenth century it had become a regular court of justice split up into several divisions—the Grand-chambre, the Chambre des Enquêtes, the Chambre des Requêtes, and the Chambre de la Tournelle.[3] But besides this it regarded itself as the guardian of the fundamental laws of the country;[4] and because it possessed

---

[1] Hallam, *Middle Ages*, ii. 48–55.

[2] Ranke, *Turkish and Spanish Monarchies*, 64, 65; *Camb. Mod. Hist.* iii. 516, 517.

[3] Esmein, op. cit. 362–79 for its origins; ibid. 379–84 for its organization, and the description of the functions of these different divisions.

[4] 'Ils se disaient en particulier les gardiens de *lois* fondamentales ou *principes fondamentaux* de la monarchie. On entendait par là certaines règles de droit public, considérées comme si essentielles que le roi lui-même pleinement investi du pouvoir législatif, ne pouvait y déroger', ibid. 518; this is a

these functions it was praised by Machiavelli as one of the wisest institutions in the country.[1] In the sixteenth and seventeenth centuries the reason for their existence was the subject of many conflicting theories.[2] In truth it cannot be understood unless we remember the medieval ideas as to the nature of law, and as to the relation of the law to the court which administered it.

The methods in which it exercised this power were various. In the fourteenth and fifteenth centuries it was sometimes consulted by the King along with the Council.[3] Then and later constitutional questions were sometimes submitted to it.[3] It could take action against offenders against the State.[3] It could make supplementary rules and regulations as to matters which fell within its jurisdiction.[4] But the most important of all these methods was that of remonstrance, and of refusing to register laws submitted to it by the King.[5] It was this last power which for a long time moderated the absolute character of the French monarchy; and it remained at intervals an obstacle to the Crown right up to the end of the ancient régime.[6]

The manner in which the Parlement was composed would seem at first sight to render it an efficient guardian of the law. In France, as in England,[7] property and office were confused. Its members were a body which were practically irremovable, because they had bought their seats, and because they could hand them on to their nominees.[8] But in reality this was a source of weakness. They were a close oligarchical body.[9]

very medieval idea, cp. Holdsworth, op. cit. ii. 367, 368; certain of these matters, such as the descent of the Crown and the inalienability of the royal domain, were enumerated; but, beyond that, they asserted that the principle that the monarchy was not absolute but limited was a fundamental law— 'seulement ici on tombait dans le vague et les parlements avaient beau jeu'.

[1] *Il Principe*, cap. xix.
[2] For these theories see Brissaud, op. cit. 884.
[3] Esmein, op. cit. 519, 520.
[4] 'Arrêts de règlement', ibid. 528–31.   [5] Ibid. 521–6.
[6] See ibid. 531–43; and Brissaud, op. cit. 885–7, for an account of the chief occasions on which this right was exercised.
[7] Holdsworth, op. cit. i. 11, n. 1.
[8] Esmein, op. cit. 401–12; as he says at p. 411, 'Il assura à la magistrature une pleine indépendance; et, sans lui, les résistances politiques des parlements aux XVIIᵉ et XVIIIᵉ siècles ne se comprendraient pas'.
[9] Ibid. 408.

They were often corrupt.[1] It was only occasionally and by accident that they commanded the confidence or sympathy of the public. Another source of weakness was the fact that the King had never ceased to exercise extensive powers over the court. He could not only control the conduct of or the decision in a case,[2] he could also personally intervene. If the King came down in person and held a *lit de justice*, he could force the Parlement to act as he pleased,[3] while it was always possible to intimidate or punish its members, and sometimes to disregard it entirely.[4] If he did not exercise these powers and allowed a modification made by the Parlement he could take credit for his moderation; and this tended to make the rights of the Parlement look as if they were dependent merely upon his pleasure.[5] Again in later times, when provincial Parlements were multiplied, all of them claimed the same rights of refusing to register a law. Thus a law might be in force in some parts of the country and not in others.[6] Thus it happened that, except in times of political excitement, the Parlement was no permanent check on the royal will, for its remonstrances could be disregarded, and its refusal to register a law overridden. ·

Thus neither the representative assemblies of the Middle Ages nor the powers possessed by the central courts of law were able to stand against the new institutions which made for royal absolutism. The constitution and procedure of the representative assemblies were so defective that they were powerless to act efficiently as organs of government in a modern state. They could hamper the activities of the executive government, and they could hinder the development of the State. But they were powerless to critize intelli-

[1] Ibid. 410–12—they had bought their places and wanted to see their money back, cp. Holdsworth, op. cit. i. 221, 228, 229, for similar abuses in the Chancery.   [2] Esmein, op. cit. 431–9.
[3] Ibid. 527.   [4] Ibid. 528.
[5] Cp. Pasquier, *Lettres*, bk. xix, no. 15, 'Nos Roys, par une bienveuillance naturelle qu'ils portent à leurs subjects, réduisants leur puissance absolue sous la civilité de la Loy, obéissent leur Ordonnance'; Henry IV said to the Parlement of Paris, 'J'ai remis les uns d'entre vous en leurs maisons d'où la Ligue les avait chassés et les autres en l'autorité qu'ils n'avaient plus. Si l'obéissance était due à mes prédécesseurs, il est dû d'autant plus de dévotion à moi qui ay restablis l'Estat', cited H. Lureau, *Les Doctrines démocratiques de la seconde moitié du XVIe siècle*, 18, 19.
[6] Brissaud, op. cit. 881.

gently or to control permanently. The lawyers were naturally on the side of the executive government in its efforts to rule efficiently. They were naturally opposed to ineffective assemblies which often voiced the aspirations of a turbulent feudalism, and attacked the abuses of the law. On the other hand, these assemblies had an advantage, the absence of which was fatal to the aspirations of the lawyers to stem the advancing tide of absolutism. They did in a manner represent the nation. The lawyers, as we have seen, in no sense represented the nation. Though the powers which they claimed might have made their courts efficient barriers against arbitrary government, they were the powers of a caste which was often deservedly[1] unpopular. The destruction of their powers roused no national indignation. The enthusiasm for fundamental constitutional laws, administered by the lawyers in their courts, was naturally confined to the lawyers themselves. Nor can we say that the popular instinct was wholly at fault. Fundamental laws generally represent an old order of legal ideas; and thus administered they are apt, in a changing age, to impede the due development of the State.

'*Divide et Impera.*' The new centralized machinery of government, having divided the forces opposed to it, was able to rule supreme. Having suppressed or muzzled the representative assemblies, and having deprived the courts of their political powers, it could exercise supreme authority; and it was able to make that authority felt in every corner of the State, because it was able to supersede the older local officials by delegates responsible only to itself, and subject not to the ordinary law, but to an administrative law which it itself dispensed. The facts were prepared, and the time was ripe. The first political philosopher who could generalize from them could hardly fail to enunciate a theory of sovereignty.

The English Development

The English Parliaments of the thirteenth and fourteenth centuries are, like the Spanish Cortes or the French Estates

---

[1] H. Lureau, *Les Doctrines démocratiques de la seconde moitié du XVIe siècle*, 19, 'Peu à peu les parlements perdent leur véritable caractère, se mettent en lutte contre la royauté sans s'attirer les faveurs de l'opinion publique, et deviennent insupportables et impopulaires'.

General, assemblies in which the King meets the various Estates of his Realm.[1] Like their foreign contemporaries, they aspire to control taxation and legislation. The English courts of common law and the English lawyers, like their brethren on the Continent, believe that king and subject alike are bound to obey the law, and they claim and exercise the power to punish all persons or bodies of persons, save the King, who disobey it.[2] But the constitutional history of the English Parliament, and the constitutional history of the English courts of common law differ entirely from the analogous continental institutions. By the end of the sixteenth century Parliament was recognized as being the 'highest and most authentical court of England',[3] and, under the leadership of Coke, the common lawyers were claiming that the common law administered in their courts was the supreme law, to which even the prerogative of the Crown was subject.[4] An examination of the causes for this divergence between the English and the continental development will show us clearly the reasons why, at the close of the sixteenth century, the English State had assumed a form which was unique in western Europe,[5] and will enable us the better to appreciate the skill with which the Tudor sovereigns maintained an equilibrium amidst the complicated and unstable balance of forces existing in that state.

In the thirteenth century the King's Council was the 'core and essence' of the Parliament; and the term 'Parliament' means rather a colloquy than a defined body of persons. At this Parliament—this colloquy—important cases were decided, and petitions were received.[6] In the course of the fourteenth century this 'colloquy' develops into a body

[1] Redlich, *Procedure of the House of Commons*, i. 5, 6–9.
[2] Holdsworth, op. cit. ii. 154, 197–200, 361, 362.
[3] Smith, *Republic*, bk. 11, c. 2.
[4] See, e.g., Co. 3 *Instit*. 84, 'The common law hath so admeasured the prerogatives of the king, that they should neither take away nor prejudice the inheritance of any'; cp. Bacon's Argument in *Calvin's Case*, Co. *Works* (ed. Spedding), vii. 646, 'Towards the king the law doth a double office. . . . The first is to entitle the king or design him. . . . The second is . . . to make the ordinary power of the king more definite or regular. . . . And although the king in his person be *solutus legibus*, yet his acts and grants are limited by law, and we argue them every day.'   [5] *Infra*, p. 70.
[6] Maitland, *Parliament Roll of 1305* (R.S.), xlvii; Holdsworth, op. cit. i. 171–3; see post, pp. 49, 208.

possessed of a unique set of powers and privileges. From the King's Council in Parliament there is developed the House of Lords, and from the representative knights and burgesses who are summoned to meet the King's Council in Parliament there is developed the House of Commons. Thus from the meeting of the Estates at 'a' Parliament or colloquy with the King's Council, there has emerged 'the' Parliament; and this Parliament has become an essential organ of the English government. 'The High Court of Parliament' has taken a separate and important place among those courts which conduct the government of the medieval state.[1]

During the fourteenth and fifteenth centuries Parliament acquires a definite body of powers, and a procedure which helps to consolidate its position in the State. Under the Lancastrian kings it has asserted its right to be the taxing and legislative authority; and the change in procedure from legislation by way of petition to legislation by way of Bill emphasized the fact that Parliament was a partner with the King in the work of legislation.[2] Mr. Redlich points out[3] that it was the adoption of this procedure by Bill which 'completed the parliamentary edifice'; for it was not till this had taken place that Parliament

'stood out as a representation of the kingdom by means of two corporate bodies with equal rights; nor is it till then that a sure foundation was laid for the equal, or in money matters, the preponderant position of the House of Commons in legislation and politics.'

The distinct corporate character of the House of Commons was further emphasized by the fact that it acquired the right to conduct its debates apart from the Crown, and by the fact that the Crown had no right to take cognizance of debates proceeding in the House;[4] and the distinct corporate character of the two Houses was emphasized by their possession of numerous privileges, which had been successfully asserted during these centuries, and recognized by the courts in wide and ample terms.[5] It is clear that by the end of the fifteenth century Parliament has acquired a position very different from that held by any ordinary court.

---

[1] Redlich, op. cit. i, c. 2.   [2] Holdsworth, op. cit. ii. 364–6.
[3] Op. cit. i. 19, 20; *infra*, pp. 64–6.   [4] Ibid. iii. 37, 38.
[5] Holdsworth, op. cit. ii. 472.

Thus at the close of the medieval period the differences between the English Parliament and the representative assemblies of the Continent were well marked. There were many reasons for this, some of which have often been noted by historians. The fact that the representatives of the counties and the towns united in one House of Commons added to the weight of the representative House. That this alliance was possible was due in part to the commonness of the common law. In part it was due to the absence of anything like the *noblesse* of the Continent; and this again, in an age when property and office and dignity were closely interwoven, was connected with the strict rule of primogeniture which, from an early period,[1] had been the rule laid down by the common law first for the military tenures and then for all the free tenures. The fact that England was free from invasion during a period which was on the whole a period of commercial growth and prosperity, coupled with the fact that the English kings desired to pursue an aggressive and therefore an expensive foreign policy, rendered possible a process of bargaining which necessarily resulted in acquisition and consolidation of the powers of Parliament. We do not overlook the importance of these facts; but we wish to emphasize especially here another, and a more especially legal set of facts, the importance of which was great in the Middle Ages, and even greater in the sixteenth century.

At no period in English history do we see any antagonism between the common lawyers and the Parliament. On the contrary, the lawyers recognize it not only as a court, but as 'the highest court which the king has',[2] in which relief could be given which could be given nowhere else,[3] in which powers could be exercised which neither the King ·nor any other body in the State could exercise,[4] in which the errors of their own courts could be redressed.[5] From an early period

[1] Ibid. iii. 140.

[2] Y.B. 19 Hen. VI, Pasch. pl. 1, p. 63, 'Le Parlement est la court du Roy, et le plus haut court que il ad'; Holdsworth, op. cit. ii. 362, n. 1; see *infra*, p. 79.

[3] Brooke, Ab. *Parlement*, pl. 33, 'Ou matter est enconter reason, et le partie nad remedy al comon ley il suera pur remedy in parliament'.

[4] 49 Ass. pl. 8, 'Le Roy ne purra ny grant cel per sa chartre sans Parliament, ne faire tenements devisable per sa chartre ou ils ne furent pas devisable devant'.

[5] Holdsworth, op. cit. i. 171, 176.

lawyers have been distinguished members of the House of Commons;[1] and the judges and the law officers were from the earliest period members of the Council, which was at first the 'core and essence' of the Parliament. Even when the judges and law officers ceased to be members of the House of Lords, they continued to be summoned, and are still summoned, to that House by writs of attendance.[2] This is a fact of the greatest importance in the history of the English Parliament because it meant that the best legal talent of the day was ready to assist in the development of its powers. It meant that men who were accustomed to the working of the procedural rules of the royal courts were ready to assist it to devise a rational system of procedure. No doubt the procedural rules of the common law were gravely defective;[3] but they had at least one merit—they discountenanced the very archaic legal ideas which so seriously hampered the representative assemblies of the Continent. They were capable of a certain amount of development and adaptation;[4] and the men who spent their lives in working and developing them were the men who were the best fitted to create a workable set of rules for the guidance of a representative assembly. We must not minimize the importance of this question of procedure; for, just as the procedural rules of the common law were the foundation upon which that law was built, so the acquisition by the English Parliament of a reasonable set of procedural rules is the secret of its capacity to develop into an organ of the government of the State.

We know, it is true, but little of the procedure of the medieval Parliaments. But parliamentary procedure, as we see it in the Elizabethan Parliament, was clearly an old growth; and we do know enough of the procedure of the medieval Parliament to see that many of the Elizabethan

---

[1] Porritt, *The Unreformed House of Commons*, 512, 513; but they were sometimes unpopular; in 1330 there was an ineffectual attempt to exclude them from the county representation; and in 46 Edward III an ordinance or statute was passed excluding them (see as to the position of this document the Record Comm. Ed. of the Statutes i. 394 n.); the attempt to exclude them failed, for, as Mr. Porritt says, 'testimony to the presence of lawyers in the House is abundant as soon as the entries in the Journals begin to be full and detailed'.

[2] Redlich, op. cit. ii. 53; *infra*, p. 63, n. 1.

[3] Holdsworth, op. cit. iii. 469–72.

[4] Ibid. ii. 501, 502.

rules are older than the sixteenth century.[1] A few of these rules will show us what a large debt the English Parliament owed in its earliest years to its close alliance with the law and the lawyers, and more especially to the common law and the common lawyers.

(1) From the earliest period in its history the English Parliament has accepted the principle that the wishes of the majority are decisive.[2] It is probable that the principle itself was derived from the canon law. In this, as in many other instances, ideas drawn from the canon law had a large influence upon the minds of those who were creating a common law in the thirteenth century.[3] It is clear from the Year Books that in the fifteenth century it is accepted as an ordinary and obvious principle.[4] (2) We have seen that the procedure by Bill applied to legislation and taxation had much to do with the consolidation of the power of Parliament.[5] It is well to remember that a procedure by Bill, setting out the relief sought, was the ordinary procedure of those who asked some favour or some relief from the Council or the Chancery;[6] and a suit to Parliament for a private Act, doubtless by Bill, was the proper remedy when no relief could be had either at common law or in the Chancery.[7] (3) The committee system which we see in full working order in the Elizabethan Parliaments probably had its roots in the Middle Ages.[8] The

[1] See, e.g., Y.B. 33 Hen. VI, Pasch. pl. 8, for an account of the procedure used in making a statute.

[2] Redlich, op. cit. ii. 261–4; it may perhaps be noted that there is earlier authority for the principle than the *Articuli Baronum* of 1215—the earliest authority cited by Redlich; in the *Leges Henrici Primi*, v. 6, it is stated that in case of conflict the views of the majority will prevail—'Quodsi in judicio inter partes oriatur dissensio, de quibus certamen emerserit, vincat sententia plurimorum'; it was not till 1367 that it was settled that the verdict of a jury might not be given by a majority. Holdsworth, op. cit. i. 157, n. 2; Thayer, *Evidence*, 87, n. 4.

[3] Holdsworth, op. cit. ii. 160, 161, 213–15.

[4] Y.BB. 19 Hen. VI, Pasch. pl. 1, p. 63; 15 Ed. IV, Mich. pl. 2, p. 2, 'Sir, en le Parliament si le greindre partie des Chivaliers des Countys assentent al feasans d'un acte du Parliament, et le meindre partie ne voillent my agreer a cel act, uncore ce sera bon statute a durer en perpetuity', *per* Littleton.

[5] *Supra*, p. 50; *infra*, pp. 64–6.

[6] Holdsworth, op. cit. ii. 365, n. 9.

[7] Brooke, Ab. *Conscience*, pl. 15—Y.B. 8 Ed. IV, Trin. pl. 1; *supra*, p. 51, n. 3.

[8] Redlich, op. cit. ii. 203.

Receivers and Triers of petitions are in principle committees appointed to deal with what was then the chief business of the Parliament.[1] On several occasions the House of Commons appointed Treasurers to receive the subsidy and committees to draw up statutes or to examine accounts;[2] and the idea of a delegation of specific business was familiar to the lawyers. The Chancellor from an early period delegated cases to the masters; and the common lawyers from the earliest period were bound to delegate the decision of all questions of fact to a jury. (4) Mr. Redlich has pointed out that all parliamentary deliberation is cast into the form of a debate upon some specific motion. 'It is not a series of independent orations but is composed of speeches and replies.'[3] But it was a debate as to the issues to be enrolled composed of speeches and replies, which formed, as the Year Books show us, the chief part of the lawyers' work in court;[4] and it is not at all unlikely that it was their influence which thus created one of the leading characteristics of parliamentary deliberation. And it is quite clear that some of the rules of debate—e.g. the rules as to the citation of documents in the House, are founded on the lawyers' rules as to evidence.[5] (5) When we first get a clear account of parliamentary procedure we are struck by the minute attention paid to matters of form. The absence of the proper form of endorsement on a Bill sent to the Lords,[6] the absence of a single letter in a precept addressed by the sheriff to his bailiffs,[7] the use by the Lords of paper instead of parchment for their amendments[8] were serious matters to be gravely discussed. When we remember the character of the common law procedure of the fifteenth

[1] For a note of their early history see McIlwain, *The High Court of Parliament*, 251–6.

[2] In 1340 a joint committee of Lords and Commons was appointed to draw up statutes; in 1406 it was requested that certain of the Commons should be present at the engrossing of statutes; in 1341 a committee was appointed to investigate the accounts of the last subsidy, Redlich, op. cit. ii. 203.

[3] Redlich, op. cit. iii. 51.

[4] Holdsworth, op. cit. iii. 479.

[5] Redlich, op. cit. iii. 60; ibid. at p. 82 the learned author says that probably the rules of debate and the order of procedure are 'real statements of old established usage'.

[6] D'Ewes, *Journal*, 303.

[7] Ibid. 556.   [8] Ibid. 575–7.

century,[1] we cannot help suspecting the influence of the lawyers. (6) Coke says:[2]

'As every court of justice hath laws and customs for its direction, some the civil and canon, some the common law, others their own peculiar laws and customs, so the High Court of Parliament hath also its own peculiar law called the *lex et consuetudo Parliamenti.*'

This law is, like the common law, to be ascertained from the precedents to be found in the parliamentary records;[3] and, in the House of Commons, the relation of the Speaker to this customary law is strikingly similar to the relation of a judge to the common law and to the rules of his court.[4] Thus the whole idea of Parliamentary Privilege, which developed with the consolidation of the powers of Parliament, springs from the notion that it is a court which like other courts must have its peculiar and appropriate privileges; and to the end many of these privileges—notably the power to imprison for contempt—retain a strong analogy to the privileges of other courts.[5] (7) Like the other courts of law in the Middle Ages, Parliament had its separate rolls, which were conclusive evidence of its proceedings.[6]

[1] Holdsworth, op. cit. iii. 471, n. 1.
[2] 4 *Instit.* 14; cp. Y.B. 7 Hen. VII, Trin. pl. 1, p. 16, 'Chescun court sera pris solonque ce que ad este use — et issint de l'Eschiquier et Banc le Roy, et Chancery, et issint del Court de Parlement'.
[3] Redlich, op. cit. ii. 4, 5.
[4] Ibid. ii. 144, 145, 'This duty of the Speaker's [the duty of interpreting the law and custom of Parliament] ... may best be understood by comparing it with the corresponding attitude of an English judge to the law which he administers. The immense and many meshed net of the common law with its thousands of decided cases wraps him in its folds, but gives him in compensation thousands of chances to use the unwritten law stored up in precedents for extending the law itself by exposition, even for creating new law: so, too, is it with the Speaker. Behind the comparatively meagre body of positive enacted rules stretches the wide expanse of century long parliamentary usage, as recorded in the journals of the House. Here, too, the Speaker has the opportunity of drawing new judge-made law out of the old decisions.'
[5] It was said in 1593 (D'Ewes, *Journal*, 514) that, 'This court for its dignity and highness hath privilege as all other courts have; and as it is above all other courts, so it hath privilege above all other courts; and as it hath privilege and jurisdiction too, so hath it also coercion and compulsion'; as Mr. McIlwain says, *High Court of Parliament*, 232, 233, this doctrine was extended with the extension of the powers of Parliament, so that the relations of privileges to the law long remained obscure, ibid. 237 seqq.
[6] Y.B. 33 Hen. VI, Pasch. pl. 8, p. 18, 'Le court de Parlement est le plus

Because, from the first, Parliament had been regarded as possessing the status of a superior court, its powers were never fettered by those archaic rules which had so seriously hampered the usefulness of the representative assemblies of the Continent.[1] Archaic rules. had been already banished from the superior courts by the lawyers of Bracton's school, before Parliament made its appearance as a settled body.[2] Because it was regarded as the highest court known to the law, the lawyers never took a narrow or a technical view of its powers and privileges. The judges in the fifteenth century declined to give an opinion as to their extent.[3] Thus as its powers expanded it was able to develop on its own lines. It was helped by the technical learning of the lawyers, and was not hindered by the narrow unreasonableness of many of their technical rules. Consequently it acquired ample privileges and a flexible code of procedure which made it an organ of the State as definite as the Council, or as any of the courts of common law, but with a perfectly distinct character of its own.[4] Its acts and proceedings were duly recorded like those of the other courts; and this gave them a permanence and an

haut court le Roy ad, et si bien seroit que chescun maner chose ou Act que est material et fait illonques, la reason seroit estre enrole'.

[1] *Supra*, pp. 42–4.
[2] Holdsworth, op. cit. ii. 164.
[3] Ibid. 368, n. 3, 472.
[4] There is an instructive argument in Y.B. 19 Hen. VI, Pasch. pl. 1, p. 64, which illustrates at once the lawyers' rooted habit of regarding Parliament as a court, and the fact that even the lawyers were beginning to see that it was something very different from an ordinary court; counsel argued that a tax granted by Parliament was a profit of the court of Parliament and 'le Roy peut granter les profits de sa Court de Parlement come il peut de ses auters Courts devant que le chose grant soit in luy', but Newton pointed out that grants of taxes by Parliament were wholly different things; for the profits of other courts, 'sont chose a luy accrues per cause d'un forfait fait a sa Ley . . . mes c'est XV est un grant de voluntate populi sui spontanea, qui preuve que il n'est droit en luy devant le grant par inheritance que il ad en ses Courts'; no doubt there is a tendency to talk of statutes as judgments of the Parliament, see, e.g., Y.B. 7 Hen. VII, Trin. pl. 1, p. 15, 'un Act de Parlement n'est forsque judicum', *per* Fineux; but as early as Henry IV's reign the two things were seen to differ, see, e.g., Y.B. 8 Hen. IV, Mich. pl. 13, p. 13, 'Quant a ceo que vous dits que l'ordinance fuit un jugement en le Parlement il n'est my issint', *per* Gascoigne, Y.B. 4 Hen. VII, Trin. pl. 6. Townshend and Brian agree that there is a difference between the repeal of an Act of attainder by another Act, and the reversal of an erroneous judgment.

authority which enabled the power which it had acquired in the Middle Ages to be used as precedents in a later age.[1]

From this alliance between Parliament and the lawyers there flowed two important consequences.

The first, and, from the point of view of legal history, the most important consequence, was the fact that it helped to give a far more definite meaning, and a far larger practical effect to the theories which English lawyers, like some of their continental brethren, held as to the supremacy of the law over all members of the State, king and subject alike. In England the theory that the law was thus supreme was something very much more than a doctrine of the lawyers. It was a large premiss which was used to justify logically the control over taxation and legislation which Parliament had acquired. England, Fortescue explains, is a *dominium politicum et regale*, a kingdom in which the law is supreme, because the King can neither change the laws nor impose taxes without the consent of Parliament.[2] Thus practically illustrated, that which in other countries remained an abstract legal doctrine, became the chief article in the political faith

---

[1] We agree with Mr. McIlwain, *High Court of Parliament*, 230, n. 1, that Professor Redlich is wrong when he maintains (*Procedure of the House of Commons*, i. 24, 25) that the conception of the House of Commons as a court has had no influence on its procedure and order of business but that that procedure and order of business 'have from the first grown out of the political exigencies of a supreme representative assembly with legislative and administrative functions'; we think that the fact that the lawyers were able to regard it as a court made them ready to assist in its development; and they naturally adopted judicial analogies. On the other hand, we think that Mr. McIlwain presses the analogy with a court too far. The lawyers might talk of it as a court; but as the reference to the Y.BB. in the last note shows, they were quite alive to its essential differences from any other court. Mr. McIlwain considers (op. cit. 110) that Parliament was 'thought of first as a court rather than as a legislature at least as late as the assembling of the Long Parliament'. We shall give some reasons for disagreeing with this view, see *infra*, pp. 63, 64.

[2] *De Laudibus*, c. 18, 'they proceed not from the Prince's pleasure as do the laws of those kingdoms that are ruled only by regal government . . . for so much as they are made not only by the Prince's pleasure, but also by the consent of the whole realm . . . and if it fortune those statutes, being devised with such great solemnity and witte, not to fall out so effectually, as the intent of the makers did wish, they may be quickly reformed, but not without the consent of the commons, and states of the realm, by whose authority they were first devised'; cp. *The Governance of England*, c. 3, where the miserable condition of the French peasant is ascribed to the fact that the King can impose taxes without the consent of his estates.

of the English people.[1] Moreover, this doctrine of the supremacy of the law became a far more practically workable principle by reason of its connexion with Parliament. Abroad, as we have seen, the doctrine seemed to take the form of the supremacy of a fundamental law which no power in the State could change, and only the lawyers could interpret.[2] In England, at the close of the Middle Ages it was coming to mean the supremacy of a law which Parliament could change and modify.[3] No doubt a belief in the existence of a fundamental law which no power in the State could change was a reasonable belief when Church and State stood over against one another as rival powers, each claiming a large and undefined allegiance from the same persons.[4] It was occasionally recognized by the pre-Reformation lawyers;[5] and it was used as

[1] It was said in argument in Y.B. 19 Hen. VI, Pasch. pl. 1, p. 63, 'Le Roy peut disinheriter un home et luy mettre a mort que est encontre la Ley, si le Parlement ne fuist' *per* Newton. [2] *Supra*, p. 48.

[3] Holdsworth, op. cit. ii. 368–70. We still hold this view in spite of Mr. McIlwain's criticisms of it, op. cit. 271–81; his instances are taken from cases which turn on the pre-Reformation view of the relationship between Church and State. These cases we regard as a special, and a very intelligible exception to the ordinary rule. Similarly, we think that he has exaggerated the importance in England of the conception of a fundamental law which even Parliament cannot change (op. cit., chap. ii). It is as well to remember that Magna Carta itself, though in form declaratory, was after all enacted law. When the King and Parliament talked of fundamental laws in the seventeenth century (see McIlwain, op. cit. 75–93) they were thinking of the rights which in their opinion the existing law gave to them. These rights they deemed to be fundamental in the sense that they were the basis of the constitution as they conceived it, not in the sense that King, Lords, and Commons could not change them, see *infra*, p. 68. It is only very exceptionally (e.g. in *King* v. *Hampden* (1637), 3 S.T. 826, 1235, and in *Godden* v. *Hales* (1685), 11 S.T. 1165) that we meet with the idea of a law which Parliament cannot change, and then only in the arguments of the extreme prerogative lawyers. Even they avoid using it if they have any more solid reasons to advance. [4] Holdsworth, op. cit. ii. 366, 367.

[5] See, e.g., Y.B. 21 Hen. VII, Hil. pl. 1, pp. 1–5, cited McIlwain, op. cit. 277, 278; we may note that Vavisour (pp. 3, 4) argued that the King could be made a parson by Act of Parliament—various lords, he said, had parsonages, 'issint n'est impertinent que la Roy sera dit parson; et especial per le Act del Parlement. Car en temps le Roy R. 2 il fuit division pur le Pape en temps de vacation, si come il fuit or tard, et pur ceo que il fuit certifie au Roy et son Conseil, que certein Prestres in Anglia avoient offendus in divers points ils furent per Act de Parlement deprives de lour benefices'; to this Frowicke C.J. replied that if lords had parsonages this was by the consent of the Pope, and that, 'Un acte temporal sans le assent del Supreme

a weapon of political controversy by their successors.[1] But it has never in England possessed much practical importance, because, fortunately for the English constitution, the cause of constitutional liberty has never been obliged to place much dependence upon it. The supremacy of a law which could be changed only by Parliament was, as we shall see,[2] far stronger, a far more manageable, a far more efficient protector of that liberty.

In the second place, the existence of this petitioning, taxing, and legislating body helped to introduce the distinction between a judicial court exercising judicial functions, and a legislative body exercising legislative functions. It was an altogether new species of court which was making its appearance in the English State; and it naturally affected very materially the sphere of the activity of the older judicial courts. It is useful to remember that it was the rise of Parliament which tended to make the judicial functions of the itinerant justices their most important functions,[3] and to confine the sphere of activity of the juries, summoned to assist the work of the central courts, mainly to judicial work.[4]

The use which the Tudor kings made of Parliament during the sixteenth century consolidated the powers which it had won in the Middle Ages. At the end of this century it stands out as the supreme legislative and taxing authority in the nation, possessed of an adequate procedure, and protected by well recognized privileges. No doubt Parliament was strictly controlled by the Crown. No doubt the initiative on all important matters was retained by the Crown—though retained at the close of Elizabeth's reign with increasing difficulty. But the picture which D'Ewes draws for us of the Elizabethan Parliaments makes it quite clear that it was this control that was largely responsible for making Parliament,

teste ne poit faire le Roy parson'; the argument based on the anti-ecclesiastical legislation of Richard II's reign is interesting, as it foreshadows Henry VIII's own argument in the preamble to the Statute of Appeals, Holdsworth, op. cit. i. 360, 361; similarly Brian's statement, Y.B. 10 Hen. VII, Hil. pl. 17, that 'Rex est persona mixta car est persona unita cum sacerdotibus Saint eglise', foreshadows the claim to be supreme head of the Church holding directly under God.   [1] McIlwain, op. cit. 75–93; infra. p. 66.
   [2] Infra, pp. 68, 69.   [3] Holdsworth, op. cit. i. 146.
   [4] Ibid. 115, 116; the administrative functions of the jury in connexion with local government had a much longer life.

and more especially the House of Commons, an efficient organ of government in a modern state. That control did for parliamentary power and privilege and procedure what it did for the development of local government under the Justices of the Peace. In both cases the Tudor kings adapted institutions which had begun to develop at the latter part of the medieval period to the needs of the modern state, by enforcing and increasing their powers, and by diligently supervising the exercise of those powers. Just as the Justices of the Peace were educated by the various forms of control which the Crown and the Council applied to them, so Parliament was educated by the use which the Crown made of it, by its constant supervision, by the presence of Privy Councillors in the House of Commons, and by their constant service on its committees.[1] In fact, the increase in the powers and the efficiency of the Justices of the Peace and the increase in the efficiency of the House of Commons helped forward the development of both these instruments of government. (1) The growth of the powers and the efficiency of the Justices of the Peace directly increased the efficiency of the House of Commons, because many of its members were Justices. They were able as members of Parliament to make suggestions for the amendment of the law which their experience as Justices had suggested. This acquaintance with practical affairs possessed by many of its members gave a business-like and a practical tone to deliberations in Parliament to which the deliberations of the continental assemblies never attained.[2] These deliberations were therefore a real assistance to the Council in gauging the feelings of the nation,[3] and in the task of devising the measures which were needed both to guard the State against its numerous enemies, domestic and

[1] We often find all the Privy Councillors in the House put upon committees, e.g. D'Ewes, *Journal*, 157, 345.

[2] See, e.g., D'Ewes, op. cit. 660, 661, 663, 664—a debate on a Bill which involved the increase of the penal jurisdiction of the Justices of the Peace; ibid. 505-7—a debate on a Bill against aliens; ibid. 168-71—a debate on a Bill against non-resident burgesses; ibid. 86—long arguments on a Bill for the increase of the navy.

[3] Thus the Council were well aware from the communications they had received from the Justices that the agitation against monopolies expressed the real feelings of the country, see Hamilton, *Quarter Sessions from Elizabeth to Anne*, 23-7.

foreign, and to adapt its institutions and its laws to the needs of this new age. (2) Conversely, the growth of the power of the House of Commons increased both the efficiency and the independence of the Justices of the Peace. As members of Parliament they had helped to make some of the laws which they administered, and they were therefore in a position to understand them and apply them intelligently.[1] They could the more easily realize that they were no mere officials of the central government, but independent administrators whose powers had been conferred upon them by the law. For both these reasons they were able to bring to the execution of their various duties those qualities of common sense and individual initiative which are apt to wither under a bureaucratic régime.

The result upon Parliament is best described in the well-known words of Sir Thomas Smith:[2]

'The most high and absolute power of the realme of Englande, consisteth in the Parliament. For as in warre where the king himselfe in person, the nobilitie, the rest of the gentilitie, and the yeomanrie are, is the force and power of Englande: so in peace and consultation where the Prince is to give life, and the last and highest commaundement, the Baronie for the nobilitie and higher, the knightes, esquiers, gentlemen and commons for the lower part of the common wealth, the bishoppes for the clergie bee present to advertise, consult and shew what is good and necessarie for the common wealth, and to consult together, and upon mature deliberation everie bill or lawe being thrise reade and disputed uppon in either house, the other two partes first each a part, and after the Prince himselfe in presence of both the parties doeth consent unto and alloweth. That is the Princes and whole realmes deede: whereupon justlie no man can complaine, but must accommodate himselfe to finde it good and obey it. . . . That which is doone by this consent is called firme, stable, and *sanctum*, and is taken for lawe. The Parliament abrogateth olde lawes, maketh newe, giveth orders for thinges past, and for thinges hereafter to be followed, changeth rightes, and possessions of private men, legittimateth bastards, establisheth formes of religion, altereth weightes and measures, giveth formes of succession to the crowne,

---

[1] Thus the Queen addressing the House on its prorogation in 1593 said, 'You that be judges and justices of the peace, I command and straitly charge you, that you see the law to be duly executed, and that you make them [i.e. the statutes just passed] living laws when we have put life into them', D'Ewes, *Journal*, 467.

[2] *De Republica Anglorum*, bk. ii, c. 1.

defineth of doubtfull rightes, whereof is no lawe alreadie made, appointeth subsidies, tailes, taxes, and impositions, giveth most free pardons and absolutions, restoreth in bloud and name as the highest court, condemneth or absolveth them whom the Prince will put to that triall: And to be short, all that ever the people of Rome might do either in *Centuriatis comitijs* or *tributis*, the same may be doone by the parliament of Englande, which representeth and hath the power of the whole realme both the head and the bodie. For everie Englishman is entended to bee there present, either in person or by procuration and attornies, of what preheminence, state dignitie, or qualitie soever he be, from the Prince (be he King or Queene) to the lowest person of Englande. And the consent of the Parliament is taken to be everie mans consent.'

Smith and all other writers[1] of this century speak of Parliament as a court—'the highest and most authentical court of England'—but still a court. This is a significant, but a very intelligible fact. A large part of the government of the country, central and local, was carried on by courts acting under judicial forms. That all governing bodies partook of the nature of courts was therefore an idea which came naturally to those who treated of public law. Moreover, most of the books which treated of the Parliament were written by men who had been trained in the common law;[2] and all of them were familiar with the ideas of the common law. Thus it is not surprising that all writers (whether common lawyers or not) should talk of Parliament as a court. The lawyers found it so treated of in the Year Books; and all could see that its judicial functions and attributes were, and indeed still

[1] e.g. Lambard, Crompton, and Coke.

[2] The chief exception is Smith, who was a Roman lawyer, and a statesman rather than a lawyer; but his book on the Republic of England was meant to be a popular sketch, and he naturally adopts the received terminology. We cannot however agree with Mr. Alston that Smith devotes a large space to the Prince and Parliament only because he regarded the English constitution as consisting primarily of judicial courts; and that he describes them as he does only because 'no account of the judicial system would be complete without them', Introd. xxvii. Smith meant, as his letter to Haddon shows (Alston, Introd. xiv), to raise the question, 'whether what is held in England as law be the better, or what is held here (in France) and in those regions which are administered in accordance with Roman law'. By 'law' Smith clearly meant public rather than private law. But the position of the English Parliament in its relation to the Prince afforded, as we have seen, one of the greatest of contrasts to foreign states. We think that it was mainly for this reason that he describes it so fully.

are, well marked.[1] In fact, for some time after the term 'court' had come to signify simply a judicial tribunal, lawyers will occasionally speak of an Act of Parliament as a 'judgment of the Parliament';[2] and for a yet longer time lawyers and statesmen and ecclesiastics will speak of 'the High Court of Parliament'. They will thus continue to speak of Parliament as a court, partly because ideas derived from the period when it was one among many medieval courts have had a permanent influence upon its powers, its privileges, and its procedure; partly because, in the sixteenth century, the lawyers were a very important class among its members;[3] and partly because in the seventeenth century— the century in which the powers and privileges and procedure of Parliament gained their permanent shape—the lawyers, to whom the conception of a court came naturally, were the leaders and champions of the parliamentary cause.

But we think that too much stress should not be laid upon the fact that Parliament thus continued to be spoken of as a court. We have seen[4] that even in Henry VI's reign the lawyers were beginning to discover that conceptions borrowed from the law as to the jurisdiction of courts could not easily be applied to those powers of taxation and legislation which were fast coming to be the most important functions of a

---

[1] For the various kinds of jurisdiction exercised by the House of Lords see Holdsworth, op. cit. i. 179–93. It should be noted that till quite the end of Elizabeth's reign the judges served on some committees of the House of Lords, not as attendants upon the committee but as members of it, D'Ewes, *Journal*, 22, 67, 99, 101, 108, 142; in 1585 they are named as attendants only, ibid. 319, and on another occasion as members, ibid 322; in 1589 they are also named as members, ibid. 422, but after 1597 as attendants only, ibid. 527; when dealing with private Bills (the procedure upon which is still quasi-judicial) the House of Commons is often styled a court, e.g. ibid. 587; and also when dealing with certain cases of privilege, ibid. 514, 515.

[2] Thus in *Chudleigh's Case* (1589–95), 1 Co. 113, 132, L. Walmesley J. and Periam C.B. said that the Statute of Uses was a 'judgment given by the whole Parliament'; cp. Brooke, Ab. *Parlement*, pl. 73 (39 Hen. VIII); Bacon's argument in *Calvin's Case*, Co. *Works* (ed. Spedding), vii. 671, speaks of two statutes as 'judgments in Parliament by way of declaration of law'.

[3] In 1545 Wriothesley, writing to Paget and Petre as to a proposal to hold the Parliament at Reading, said that, if it were held there, it would be best to adjourn the law term, as, without the judges, sergeants, and other persons engaged at the courts, 'you shall have a very simple assembly', *Letters and Papers*, xx, pt. ii, no. 302.   [4] *Supra*, p. 56, n. 4.

Parliament. As in the case of local government in this century, so in the case of Parliament, non-judicial functions were being rapidly developed. At the end of the century the growth of these functions had made it obvious that Parliament was comparable quite as much to the Council as to a court.[1] 'This court', said Coke, when addressing the House of Commons as Speaker in 1592–3, 'is not a Court alone.'[2] It had indeed become very different from any other court, for in it were represented the King and the three estates of the realm—'The great corporation or body politic of the kingdom'.[3] It was this fact which gave to it its 'high, absolute, and authentical powers'; and it was these powers which were destined to so expand in the following century that the sovereignty of Parliament has become the central and characteristic feature of English constitutional law. As with the Justices of the Peace in the sphere of local government, so with Parliament in the sphere of central government a medieval institution had been so adapted that it was able to satisfy the requirements of the modern state, and develop with its development.

That Parliament, without ceasing to possess some of the characteristics of a court,[4] could be· so used by the Tudor sovereigns that it became a true legislative assembly, is due largely to the manner in which the lawyers had guided its development in the fourteenth and fifteenth centuries, and especially to the substitution of the practice of legislating by Bill for the practice of legislating by petition.[5] So long as legislation took the form of a petition to the King, those petitions which resulted in legislation did not differ materially from petitions which resulted in a judicial decree;[6] and, as

[1] It was so spoken of by Peter Wentworth, D'Ewes, *Journal*, 411; *infra*, p. 68, n. 2.

[2] D'Ewes, *Journal*, 515, 'Though any court of record hath this jurisdiction to make out processes, yet this court cannot. Why? This may seem strange that every court in Westminster, every court that hath causes of Plea, every lords leet, and every court baron hath his powers that they may make out process; yet this court being the highest of all courts cannot; how can this be? The nature of this House must be considered; for this court is not a court alone; and yet there are some things wherein this court is a court by itself, and other things wherein it is no court of itself'; cp. ibid. 434, where the Speaker describes it as 'The highest court of all other courts and the great council also of this realm'.   [3] Coke, 4 *Instit.* 2.

[4] *Supra*, p. 62 seqq.   [5] *Supra*, p. 50.   [6] *Supra*, p. 53.

we have said, a petition to Parliament for a private Act still
retains the judicial characteristics which marked the early
stages in the history of every variety of parliamentary legislation. But there could be no talk of petition in connexion with
the many important Bills which during this period originated
with the Crown; and, as they required the consent of both
Houses, their passage emphasized the fact that Parliament
was a partner in the work of legislation. Bills, whether
originating from the Crown or not, to which the King and
the two Houses had assented, resulted in an Act of the Parliament; and it gradually became clear that even the Bills of
private persons which asked for something in the nature of
a judicial decree fell, if enacted by the same authority, into
the same category.[1] But since their judicial character was
more strongly marked, it was with more difficulty that their
position as legislative Acts was realized. The methods adopted
to sift the sufficiency of the reasons alleged by these peti-
tioners for private Acts were judicial in their nature.[2] The
passage of the ordinary private Bill partook somewhat of the
character of a civil action; and the passage of an Act of
attainder partook somewhat of the character of a criminal
trial. Until Henry VIII's reign it was not clear that the law
would admit the validity of an Act of attainder passed without
hearing the accused in his defence. But in Henry VIII's
reign it was realized that Acts of the Parliament, whether
public or private, were legislative in character; and the
judges were obliged to admit that these Acts, however morally

[1] Y.B. 4 Hen. VII. Mich. pl. 11, 'En le Parlement le Roy voulait que
un tiel soit attaint, et perdrait ses terres, et les Seigneurs assentirent, et rien
fuit plede des Commons purquoi touts les Justices tenirent clerement, que ce
ne fuit Acte, perquoi il fuit restore'.

[2] Thus it was the practice to hear counsel at the Bar of the House on
such Bills, see D'Ewes, *Journal*, 50, 68, 86, 317; at p. 124 (1566) there is
the following entry: 'This morning the Dean of Westminster was present
at the Bar with his counsel; *viz.*, Mr. Edmund Plowden of the Middle
Temple, and Mr. Ford, a civilian. The Dean himself made an oration in
defence of the Sanctuary, and alleged divers grants by King Lucius and
other Christian Kings, and Mr. Plowden alleged the grant of Sanctuary
there by King Edward five hundred years ago: *viz.*, *Dat.* in *an* 1066 with
great reason in law and chronicle; and Mr. Ford alleged divers stories and
laws for the same; and thereupon the bill was committed to the Master of
the Rolls, and others [not named] to peruse the grants, and to certify the force
of the law now for Sanctuaries.'

unjust, must be obeyed.[1] The legislation which had deposed the Pope and made the Church an integral part of the State had made it clear that the morality of the provisions of a law, or the reasons which induced the legislature to pass it, could not be regarded by the courts. '*Nil ineptius lege cum prologo*,' said Bacon in his argument in *Chudleigh's Case*, '*jubeat non disputet* . . . for the law carries authority in itself.'[2]

But when an Act of Parliament had acquired this authority, the last remnants of the idea that there might be fundamental laws, which could not be changed by any person or body of persons in the State, necessarily disappeared. It was obviously difficult to assign any limits to the power of the Acts of a body which had effected changes so sweeping as those effected by the Reformation Parliament. We do not forget that Coke sometimes writes as if he believed in the supremacy of a law which even Parliament could not change.[3] But it would, we think, be a mistake to lay too much stress on isolated statements of this kind.[4] In the first place Coke was often inconsistent

[1] Co. 4 *Instit.* 37, 38, 'I had it of Sir Thomas Gawdye knight, a grave and reverend judge of the King's Bench, who lived at that time, that King H. 8, commanded him to attend the chief Justices and to know whether a man that was forthcoming might be attainted of High Treason by Parliament, and never called to his answer. The Judges answered that it was a dangerous question, and that the High Court of Parliament ought to give examples to inferior Courts for proceeding according to Justice. But being by the express commandment of the King, and pressed by the said Earl [Cromwell] to give a direct answer: they said that if he be attainted by Parliament, it could not come in question afterwards, whether he was called or not to answer . . . *Facta tenent multa, quæ fieri prohibentur*; the Act of Attainder being passed by Parliament—did bind as they resolved.'

[2] Argument in *Chudleigh's Case*, Co. *Works* (ed. Spedding), vii, at p. 625, he is talking of the preamble to the Statute of Uses; the passage runs as follows: 'And whereas a wise man has said, *nil ineptius lege cum prologo, jubeat non disputet*; this had been true if preambles are annexed for exposition; and this gives aim to the body of the statute; for the preamble sets up the mark, and the body of the law levels at it.'

[3] See especially *Bonham's Case* (1609), 8 Co. Rep. 107, 118—'In many cases the law will control acts of Parliament and sometimes adjudge them to be utterly void', cp. Maitland, *Constitutional History*, 300, 301; similarly in *Calvin's Case* (1609), 7 Co. 1, 13*a* and 25*a* there is some loose talk of impossibility of altering even by Parliament a provision of natural law.

[4] We think that Mr. McIlwain, *The High Court of Parliament*, 286 seqq., exaggerates their importance, and we still hold the views expressed in Holdsworth, op. cit. ii. 369, 370; Bacon clearly did not hold this view,

because he had the mind of an advocate, and therefore often allowed himself to be carried away by the argument which he is urging at the moment. In the second place he was so thoroughly steeped in medieval law that he sometimes reproduces ideas which he himself would have admitted to be archaic.[1] In the third place, he is often writing and thinking of the supremacy of the existing law, and not of the question whether Parliament was competent to change it. When Parliament is not sitting it is the existing law, as interpreted by the judges, which is supreme; and when, as in the seventeenth century, the different component parts of the Parliament cannot act together, the same result ensues. In the Fourth *Institute*, when he is dealing specifically with the powers of Parliament, and in other passages, he admits its supremacy freely and fully.[2]

supra, p. 66, n. 2; in other passages in his argument in *Chudleigh's Case* the same view is repeated—thus at p. 623 he says that the judges' authority over laws is 'to expound them faithfully and apply them properly'; at p. 633, to the argument that the limitations in that case should be allowed because they would be a refuge in time of trouble to great houses, he says, 'If force prevail above lawful regiment, how easy will it be to procure an act of Parliament to pass according to the humour and bent of the state to sweep away all their perpetuities'; it is true that in the 'Discourse on the Commission of Bridewell', *Works*, vii. 509–16, he talks (at p. 513) as if he thought that an Act of Parliament which contravened Magna Carta would be void; but such a view is wholly opposed to the latter part of the discourse, when he expressly allows that departures from the clause of Magna Carta, which he is considering, are valid, because they are made by Parliament.

[1] e.g. he says 4 *Instit.* 14, that the Commons may say that they cannot answer without conference with their constituents; see *supra*, p. 43, n. 4, for the archaic character of this idea.

[2] 4 *Instit.* 36, the power of Parliament is, 'so transcendent and absolute that it cannot be confined either for causes or persons within any bounds'; ibid. 37, talking of an Act of attainder, he clearly distinguishes the expediency of a law from the power to make it; ibid. 42, 43, 'Acts against the power of subsequent Parliaments bind not'; cp. 2 *Instit.* 498, where a record of Edward I's reign is cited to the effect that, 'the award of Parliament was the highest law that could be'; Co. Litt. 115*b*, 'the common law hath no controler in any part of it but the high court of Parliament, and if it be not abrogated or altered by Parliament it remains still'; Bl. *Comm.* i. 160, 161; Dicey, *Law of the Constitution* 9th ed., p. 48. We use the word 'Supremacy' advisedly, as we do not think that Coke had fully grasped the doctrine of sovereignty as taught by Bodin and, after his day, by Hobbes—as to this see Alston's ed. of Smith's *Republic*, xxxiii, and cp. Figgis, *Camb. Mod. Hist.* iii. 748; Gooch, *English Democratic Ideas in the Seventeenth Century*, 37.

In the sixteenth century, therefore (whatever may be true of earlier periods), it is clear that the supremacy of the law, taught by Bracton and the Year Books, has come to mean, not the supremacy of an unchangeable law, but the supremacy of a law which Parliament can change.[1] The supremacy of the law is coming to mean the supremacy of Parliament. That the lawyers never placed any difficulty in the way of this evolution was a fact which had large effects upon the future development both of the constitution and of the common law.

Because they did not insist upon the existence of fundamental laws which could not be changed by the ordinary legislative machinery of the State, they were not thrust into a position of political conflict with the Crown. The supremacy of the existing law, so long as Parliament saw fit to leave it unaltered, was guaranteed by the powers of Parliament;[2] and to Parliament they could safely leave any political conflict needed to maintain this position. There was no need therefore for the courts of common law to be anything but useful servants of the Crown; and, for this reason, there was not the same temptation that there was abroad to supersede them by the newer courts which depended more directly upon the King's will. Though many new courts arose in this country, the King was content to allow the ordinary courts to continue to exercise their old jurisdiction. They thus continued to be the guardians and the interpreters of the common law; and since the rules of the common law contained the greater part of the public law of the State, the courts retained many of those political functions of which in foreign

[1] D'Ewes, *Journal*, 164, 'Mr. Morrison said, it were horrible to say, that the Parliament hath not authority to determine of the crown; for then would ensue, not only the annihilation of the statute 35 H. 8, but that the Statute made in the first year of her Majesty's reign of recognition, should also be laid void'; cp. Yelverton's Speech, ibid. 175, 176.

[2] That Parliament identified itself with the cause of the supremacy of the law is clear from D'Ewes—see, e.g., op. cit. 168—a high prerogative speech by Sir Humphrey Gilbert, 'was disliked, as implying many occasions of mischief'; ibid. 176, Yelverton said, 'The Prince could not of herself make laws, neither might she of the same reason break laws'; ibid. 238—Peter Wentworth's speech citing Bracton as to the subjection of the King to the law; ibid. 411—Peter Wentworth asked, 'whether there be any Council which can make, add to or diminish from the law of the Realm, but only this Council of Parliament'.

countries they were deprived by the growth of a system of administrative law.[1]

These political functions exercised by the courts harmonized with the character which the local government of the country had assumed. The officials and communities to which the local government was entrusted originated, as we have seen, at a period when the medieval view that the law was supreme was unquestioned. Their powers and duties were determined for the most part by statutes, and by old rules of the common law. They could be punished by the common law courts for misfeasances and for non-feasances; and, by means of the prerogative writs, they could be ordered to act or to refrain from acting, or their decisions could be questioned. It is clear that authorities of this kind, thus controlled, will not easily become the mere officials of the central authority, nor easily subjected to a system of administrative law.

Thus in England and in England alone the medieval conception of the supremacy of the law was adapted to the needs of a modern state. That it could be thus adapted is due in part to the retention by the Tudors of the medieval machinery of local government, but chiefly to the maintenance of the old alliance between Parliament and the common law. Foreign writers, like Hotman[2] or Duplessis-Mornay,[3] who protested against the growth of royal absolutism, argued from the powers which the representative assemblies and courts of law

[1] See Bacon's discourse on the Commission of Bridewell, Co. *Works* (ed. Spedding), vii. 509–16—many of the old Y.BB. cases are cited to show that the law is supreme, and that the judges can hold to be void grants contrary to law; and at p. 514 he cites a case of Elizabeth's reign in which this view was acted upon—'There was a commission granted forth in the beginning of the reign of her Majesty that now is . . . for the examination of felons and other lewd prisoners. It so fell out that many men of good calling were impeached by the accusations of felons. Some great men and judges also entered into the validity of the Commission. It was thought that the Commission was against the law, and therefore did the Commissioners give over the Commission, as all men know.'

[2] His book—*The Franco-Gallia*—Mr. Figgis calls (*Camb. Mod. Hist.* iii. 760) 'The earliest of modern constitutional histories'.

[3] The *Vindicia contra Tyrannos*, written either by Duplessis-Mornay or by Lanquet, though some contend for a joint authorship of the two men, see Gooch, op. cit. 13, 14; for a good account of the book see Figgis, *Camb. Mod. Hist.* iii. 760–4.

had possessed in the Middle Ages, or adapted to modern needs the medieval theories designed to uphold the supremacy of law. But on the Continent the powers of those assemblies and the theories of the lawyers had never coalesced. It was only in England that the powers of Parliament had come to be regarded as the main security for the supremacy of the law; for it was only in England that the lawyers, by freely admitting the legislative supremacy of Parliament, had gained the support of Parliament and the nation for the medieval doctrine of the supremacy of the law. It was the continuance of this alliance between Parliament and the lawyers, which in the following century finally secured the triumph of a conception which was destined, in yet later centuries, to have a vast influence upon the political ideas and machinery of the old and new world.

THE INFLUENCE OF THE LEGAL PROFES-
SION ON THE GROWTH OF THE ENGLISH
CONSTITUTION[1]

NE sutor ultra crepidam—some of you historians may feel
inclined to apply this proverb to me, a lawyer, setting
out to give this lecture, founded in memory of one of the
greatest and most inspiring historians of the nineteenth century. But in defence I shall put forward three pleas. My
first plea is that I took my first degree in history, and, while
reading history, I studied carefully the whole of Creighton's
great work upon the History of the Popes. My second plea is
that we are living, not in the pre- but in the post-Maitland
days; and one of Maitland's many great achievements was
to renew that early seventeenth-century partnership between
law and history, which has enabled history to humanize law,
and law to correct history. My third plea is that I have
chosen what I may call a border-line subject, which demands
some legal knowledge. But one plea I do not put forward. I
do not intend to minimize the influence of my profession on
the formation of the English constitution. On the contrary,
I intend to show that its influence was by no means the least
of the influences which has made our constitution, and the
principles upon which it is founded, one of the great achievements of the English race—a model not only to our own
Dominions and the United States, but also to many other
nations.

From the end of the eleventh, and during the twelfth
centuries, when our common law began to take shape,
down to the end of the seventeenth century, the common
law and the common lawyers exercised a decisive influence
upon the formation of the constitution; and, when the law of
the constitution was complete, they exercised a considerable
influence upon its later development. The character of that
influence at different stages in the development of the

[1] The Creighton History Lecture delivered at University College, London,
on 1 December 1924.

constitution can, I think, be classified chronologically as follows: In the Middle Ages the evolution of a native common law, the rise of Parliament, and the alliance between lawyers and Parliament, gave to English institutions a shape which was different from that of the institutions of any other country in Europe. Consequently, in the sixteenth century, medieval institutions were not, as in many continental states, swept aside. They were adapted to meet the needs of the modern state; and this adaptation was carried on partly by the legislature, but also to a very large extent by the lawyers. Thus, at the end of the sixteenth century, the differences between English and continental institutions had been broadened and deepened; and the constitution which resulted was a blend of medieval and modern ideas which was quite unique. In the seventeenth century the clash between these medieval and modern ideas was precipitated by the Stuarts, who, like their contemporaries abroad, founded a theory of absolutism on the achievements of their predecessors. Largely by the help of the lawyers in alliance with the House of Commons, medieval ideas were still further adapted to their new situation. As so adapted they prevailed; and a constitution founded on the supremacy of Parliament and the Rule of Law emerged. With the Revolution of 1688 the direct formative influence of the lawyers diminishes; but in the eighteenth and nineteenth centuries their influence can be seen in the manner in which they worked out the implications of the Rule of Law, and made the English state in the eighteenth century, to use Dicey's words, 'the one great free state where arbitrary government was unknown, and individual freedom of speech and action was protected by the rule of fixed law'.[1] In our own times the influence of the lawyers is less direct. Their work consists, partly in the maintenance of tried and tested constitutional principles against criticisms of visionary, and often imperfectly educated, political theorists; and partly in giving a practical shape to projects of reform, by supplying a ballast of common sense, and a spirit of compromise which is not afraid to be illogical. Let us now take a brief survey of these many different kinds of influence exercised by the lawyers, which have all helped to shape the form and the spirit of the constitution under which we live to-day.

[1] Valedictory Lecture on Blackstone, *National Review*, liv. 659.

The fact that, at the close of the medieval period, English institutions differed from the institutions of other European countries, was, I think, mainly due to the evolution of a native common law, to the rise of Parliament, and to the alliance between the lawyers and Parliament. But the manner in which these causes worked together to produce this result has been obscured by the fact that their true bearing has been, to a large extent, unrecognized. This is due to ,two causes. It is due, in the first place, to the habit of tracing back the origins of English law and English institutions to the institutions and laws of the Anglo-Saxons, and of ignoring the resemblances and the differences between the English development and contemporaneous developments in continental states. This habit, which is due mainly to the political use made of the antiquities of early English constitutional history from the seventeenth century onwards, has obscured the fact that the real problem is, Why did the medieval development of English law and English institutions differ so markedly from that of other states? It is due, in the second place, to a natural reaction from this habit of ignoring the medieval development of continental states, and of regarding early English constitutional history from the point of view of later constitutional conflicts. This reaction has led to a treatment and an interpretation of our medieval constitutional history from a point of view which suffers from the defect of being as much too cosmopolitan, as the former point of view was too insular—with the result that again no answer is given to the problem, Why did the medieval development of English law and English institutions differ so markedly from that of other states? I propose, firstly, to say something of these two defective ways of interpreting our medieval constitutional history; and, secondly, to show that the answer to the problem is to be found in the growth of a native common law in the twelfth and thirteenth centuries, and in the reciprocal influence of the common lawyers and Parliament upon one another during the fourteenth and fifteenth centuries.

(1) It was the fashion amongst the lawyers of the seventeenth century to minimize the effects of the Norman Conquest, and to derive English law and English institutions from an Anglo-Saxon, or from an even more remote past.

The publication of Lambard's *Archaionomia* in 1568 had restored the Anglo-Saxon laws to the students of the common law; and in the seventeenth century they were used as a basis upon which pedigrees of English laws and institutions could be constructed, and from which theories as to existing laws and institutions could be deduced. Coke, somewhat naively, said in the Preface to his Third *Institute*, 'to speak what we think, we would derive from the Conqueror as little as we could'; and this attitude of mind no doubt helped him to swallow whole all the fables told by that curious legal romance, *The Mirror of Justices*. Hale, too, in his *History of Common Law*, devotes a whole chapter to minimizing the effects of the Conquest[1]—'in truth,' he said, 'it was not such a conquest as did or would alter the laws of this kingdom'.[2] In the eighteenth and nineteenth centuries this idea passed from the lawyers to the historians. Montesquieu found the origin of the English constitution in the *Germania*.[3] Freeman went back to the institutions of Uri and Appenzell,[4] denounced 'the slavish subtleties of Norman lawyers',[5] and 'the arbitrary influence of the lawyers',[6] and considered that some of the legislation of his own day marked a return to 'those simpler principles which the untutored wisdom of our forefathers never thought of calling in question'.[6]

In truth, the continuity of English history, the legal form into which the constitutional controversies of the seventeenth century were cast, the manner in which in that century both parties interpreted history to suit their own views, and the enduring influence of seventeenth-century politics, has led to an extensive reading back into medieval constitutional history of the ideas of later centuries. No doubt the lawyers were the first offenders. In their search for precedents, and in their use of precedents which they thought they had found, they ignored anachronisms. But the historians followed suit. Even Stubbs once described the Lancastrian period as a period in which 'constitutional pro-

---

[1] Chap. v.   [2] (6th ed.), at p. 49.
[3] *De L'Esprit des Lois*, bk. xi, c. 6: 'Si l'on veut lire l'admirable ouvrage de Tacite sur les mœurs des Germains, on verra que c'est d'eux que les Anglois ont tiré l'idée de leur gouvernement politique. Ce beau système a été trouvé dans les bois.'   [4] *Growth of the English Constitution.*
[5] At p. 21.   [6] At p. 137.

gress had outrun administrative order';[1] but he took a truer view when, in another place, he said of these same contests that 'it was the substance of power, not the theoretical limitation of executive functions, that was the object of contention'.[2] Neither lawyers nor historians really grasped the true problem, which can be stated as follows: it is true that some of the origins of the laws and institutions of England in the Middle Ages can be traced back to a basis of Teutonic customary law of which we find abundant traces in the Anglo-Saxon laws. But the origins of many of the laws and institutions of other states in western Europe can be traced back to a similar basis. Why then did English law and English institutions come to differ so widely from the laws and institutions of other European states? Obviously this is a problem which cannot be solved without looking at foreign as well as English evidence. But English lawyers and statesmen, who were chiefly interested in studying the facts of earlier periods in our constitutional history in order to use them as precedents and arguments for their legal or political views, never came in sight of the true nature of the problem; and as, here again, the historians followed suit, the story of the development of English institutions was related from a purely insular point of view.

I come now to the historians of a very different school, of whom the chief exponent is Professor McIlwain. The point of view of these historians is the point of view of contemporary Europe, in the twelfth, thirteenth, and fourteenth centuries—the centuries during which the English constitution was being made. Professor McIlwain contends in his very able essay on *The High Court of Parliament* that England was a feudal, not a national, state, and that her central governing body was a feudal assembly; that, as in other feudal states, she was governed by a body of customary law, which came to be regarded as a fundamental law, and that laws contrary to this fundamental law were void: that therefore the main work of the governing body was adjudication and interpretation of the law rather than the making of law, so that Acts of Parliament were analogous to the judgments of a court; that all traces of these ideas were not lost till the time of the Long Parliament. Further, he contends, in a

[1] *C.H.* iii. 288. [2] Ibid. ii. 665.

later essay,[1] that Magna Carta was regarded as a part of this fundamental law. Now it cannot be denied that there is an element of truth in Professor McIlwain's picture of the English constitution in the Middle Ages; and it is valuable in that it emphasizes exactly those features which the writers of the older school neglect. But it seems to me that it has the defects of its qualities. If English institutions had continued to be so entirely and exclusively medieval as he represents them to be; if the English Parliament had continued to be simply the assembly of the estates of the realm summoned to speak their mind to the King, which it was in the thirteenth century; why was it that it had, by the fifteenth century, developed into an organ of government possessed of definite privileges, and definite legislative and financial powers? Why was it able, unlike the Cortes in Spain and the Estates General in France, not only to stand its ground in the sixteenth century, but to emerge with its powers and privileges and prestige considerably increased?

I think that we must look for the answer to this problem, which neither the earlier nor the later treatment of medieval constitutional history supplies, to the peculiarities of our legal history. I come therefore to my second head—the effect of the growth of a native common law, and the reciprocal influence of the common lawyers and Parliament on one another in the fourteenth and fifteenth centuries.

(2) We can trace many resemblances between the legal and political ideas of Englishmen and their contemporaries abroad throughout the Middle Ages. We can see in many of the institutions of both the central and the local government the prevalence of those feudal ideas which connected the tenure of land with governmental powers. We can see the influence of that legal Renaissance of the twelfth and thirteenth centuries, which was making for the advance of civilization by introducing the nascent nations of Europe to a higher order of legal and political ideas. We can see the influence of the theory, inherited from the Roman lawyers and the Christian Fathers, that the world must be ruled by law of some kind—the law of God and human law; and that all were subject to a law which, in the last resort, must be enforced even as against the King. But there was this differ-

[1] *Magna Carta Commemoration Essays*, 122–79.

ence between the development of English institutions and English law, and the development of the law and institution of other states: In England the strong and intelligent government of the Norman and Angevin kings had created centralized institutions and a common law. The men who worked those institutions, and who constructed that law, on the basis of the older customary law, were helped, as many lawyers and statesmen all over Europe were being helped, by ideas drawn from the civil and canon law. But the influence of that law was not overwhelming. It supplied a method of reasoning upon matters legal, and a power to create a technical language and technical forms, which enabled precise yet general rules to be evolved from a mass of vague customs. and particular cases. But so effectually was this work done that, at the end of the thirteenth century, a native system of law, in which the new legal ideas and new institutions had been blended with the old customary rules and old institutions, had been created; and this native system of law found itself able to stand by itself and to develop on its own lines. As Maitland tersely puts it:[1] 'The new learning found a small, well conquered, much governed kingdom, a strong, a legislating kingship. It came to us soon; it taught us much; and then there was a healthy resistance to foreign dogma.' Thus the law and institutions of England were far from being based merely upon feudal ideas. The law was *jus commune* for England, as the canon law was *jus commune* for the Church; and, like the civil and the canon law, it was both a rational and a technical system, which was being technically developed by a learned profession to meet new needs. The important institutions of the central government, such as the Council, the courts of common law, and the itinerant justices were royal institutions; and the important officials of the local government, such as the sheriffs and coroners, and, later, the Justices of the Peace, were also royal officials. No doubt there were feudal courts, and franchise courts, some of which were extensive and powerful; but, by the end of the thirteenth century, royal justice and the royal machinery of government had won a decisive victory over feudal, local, and separatist tendencies.

Thus a very different state of things existed in England

[1] P. & M. (2nd ed.), i. 24.

from that which existed in most continental states. Though the new legal ideas which came with the study of the civil and canon law were making way in many countries, notably in France; though centralized institutions staffed by these lawyers were arising; feudal ideas and feudal institutions were not mastered; and therefore many of the institutions of these countries were still of a feudal archaic type. In those countries, therefore, the law laid down and the legal theories taught by the lawyers, who staffed these new centralized institutions, assorted badly with many ideas and institutions which were still alive and active.

This difference has a very direct bearing upon the difference between the medieval and later history of the English Parliament, and that of some of those continental representative assemblies which, like the French Estates General and the Spanish Cortes, were arising about the same period.

These continental assemblies were sometimes hampered by a defective procedure. In Aragon, till 1591, a single dissentient could prevent the levy of a tax or the passing of a law;[1] and in France and Castile, it would seem that, without express powers from their constituents, the deputies could do nothing but present grievances.[2] Sometimes the different estates of which these assemblies were composed failed to act together, because their interests were divergent.[3] In countries where the nobility were exempt from taxation, they naturally took little interest in struggles to gain control over taxation;[4] and the nobility were apt also to voice the aspirations of a turbulent feudalism which did not make for good government. It is not surprising that the lawyers were often hostile to these assemblies. They regarded them, rightly, as ineffective. Moreover, they claimed to exercise political powers which made them their rivals.[5] These political

---

[1] Ranke, *Turkish and Spanish Monarchies*, 65; see *supra*, p. 43.

[2] Esmein, *Histoire du droit français* (11th ed.), 559; Ranke, op. cit. 58; see *supra*, p. 43.

[3] Ranke, op. cit. 56, 57.   [4] Esmein, op. cit. 620.

[5] Ibid. 570–1, tells us how in 1484 the Parlement of Paris turned a deaf ear to the request of the Duke of Orleans that it would assent to the principle that taxes should not be increased without the assent of the Estates—'C'est qu'il agissait des États généraux, c'est à dire d'un pouvoir politique en partie rivale, dont les parlements contrarièrent incontestablement le développement et auquel ils cherchèrent à se substituer.'

powers were the direct consequence of the medieval idea
that the law was a rule of conduct, which subjects and rulers
alike were bound to obey. The lawyers claimed a power to
see that the law was not infringed by the King or any other
person. But this easily slides into the theory that the State
is governed by certain fundamental laws which the lawyers
must enforce. This was the position which the Parlement
of Paris claimed for itself. It claimed, as the guardian of the
fundamental laws, to be able to refuse to register the laws
submitted to it by the King.[1] The result was that the representative assemblies never developed, and remained ineffective; while the opposition of the lawyers could be overridden[2]
—enthusiasm for fundamental laws interpreted by the lawyers
is naturally confined to the lawyers. As Mr. Armstrong has
said,[3] 'the jealousy between judicature and legislature has
been a prominent rock of offence in the pathway of French constitutional liberty'; and the same thing is true in other countries.

Now there was never any of this jealousy in England,
largely because, as we have seen, the law and the institutions
of England were more homogeneous than they were in continental states. From the first the common lawyers recognized Parliament as the highest court which the King has,[4]
as the court in which the errors of their own courts could be
redressed.[5] From an early period the judges were summoned
to attend the House of Lords—they were members of the
Council which was at first 'the core and essence' of the Parliament;[6] and from an early period lawyers took a leading part
in the House of Commons.[7] This is a fact of the greatest
importance in the history of Parliament; for it meant that the
best legal talent of the day was willing to assist in its development. And the lawyers were the men best fitted to devise a
set of procedural rules, which would get rid of those archaic
ideas which hampered the usefulness of the representative
assemblies of the Continent. It is the fact that Parliament,
in the fourteenth and fifteenth centuries, was beginning to

[1] Ibid. 585–93.   [2] Ibid. 591–3.
[3] *French Wars of Religion*, 15.
[4] Y.B. 19 Hen. VI, Pasch. pl. 1, p. 63; see *ante*, p. 51.
[5] Holdsworth, *Hist. Eng. Law* (3rd ed.), i. 360–1.
[6] Maitland, *Parliament Roll of* 1305 (R.S.), lxvii; see *ante*, p. 49; *post*, p. 208.
[7] Porritt, *The Unreformed House of Commons*, 512–13.

acquire such a set of procedural rules, which is the secret of its capacity to develop into an organ of government with definite powers and privileges and records of its own; and it is obvious that their acquisition was largely due to the lawyers.

From this development four consequences followed. In the first place, though the lawyers still talked of Parliament as a court, though it had and still has some of the characteristics of a court, it is clear that, even before the close of the medieval period, the lawyers had begun to see that it was no ordinary court; for it was the body which had exclusive powers of legislation and taxation.[1] By the middle of the sixteenth century it is abundantly clear that it was, as Sir Thomas Smith's description shows,[2] and as the Speaker said in 1589,[3] 'the highest court of all other courts and the great council also of this realm'. In fact Bacon, in his letter of advice to Villiers, said that it was more properly a council than a court.[4] In the second place, long before the end of the Middle Ages, its law-making capacity was recognized. I think that Mr. Plucknett, in his very able book on *Statutes and their Interpretation in the Fourteenth Century*, has proved from the Year Books that it was recognized in that century that statutes could and did make new law.[5] In a Year Book of 1310–11, for instance, it is said that, 'as one canon defeats many *leges*, so the statute defeats many things that were at common law';[6] and this is only one out of many instances.[7] In the third place, this recognition of the law-making capacity of Parliament tended to get rid of the notion of fundamental laws. It is of course true that no medieval lawyer would have ·admitted a theoretically unlimited power to legislate in a merely human legislature. A medieval lawyer would have said that its laws must not contravene those moral rules which the law of nature teaches all mankind; and he would also have denied that Parliament could freely legislate as to matters falling within the ecclesiastical sphere. But, subject to these two modifications, I do not think that, even in the Middle

---

[1] See Y.BB. 8 Hen. IV, Mich. pl. 13, p. 13, *per* Gascoigne; 4 Hen. VII, Trin. pl. 6 *per* Townshend and Brian; 19 Hen. VI, Pasch. pl. 1, p. 64, *per* Newton.   [2] *De Republica Anglorum*, bk. ii, c. 1; see *supra*, pp. 61, 62.

[3] D'Ewes, *Journals*, 434; and cp. ibid. 515 for a similar statement by Coke in 1592–3.   [4] Spedding, *Letters and Life*, vi. 38.

[5] At pp. 26–31.   [6] Y.B. 3–4 Ed. II (S.S.), 162.

[7] Plucknett, op. cit. 30, 69–70.

Ages, he would have asserted that the law—common law or statute law—had so fundamental a character that it could not be altered. In fact there had been too much law-making of one sort or another from the very beginning of the common law. Henry II's Assizes, and Magna Carta itself, were enacted law; and, as we all know, Edward I's reign was one of the greatest periods of legislative activity in our legal history. I do not forget that Coke indulges, in *Bonham's Case*,[1] in loose talk about the power of the law to adjudge Acts of Parliament void. But as against this, let us recall Sir Thomas Smith's emphatic words on the unlimited character of the supremacy of Parliament;[2] and let us also remember that Coke himself said that the power of Parliament is 'so transcendent that it cannot be confined either for causes or persons within any bounds'.[3] In the fourth place, it followed that the lawyers in England came to attach to the phrase 'rule of law' a meaning very different from that which was attached to it by continental lawyers. Abroad it took the form of the supremacy of a law which no power in the State could change, and only the lawyers could interpret. In England it was coming to mean, at the close of the medieval period, the supremacy of a law which Parliament could change; and this, in the succeeding centuries, was a far more manageable, a far more efficient protector of constitutional government, than an unalterable fundamental law.

I think, therefore, that it was largely due to the lawyers: firstly, that the English Parliament, alone amongst the medieval representative assemblies, became a definite and essential part of the government of the State; secondly, that the medieval ideal of the rule of law was so connected with the legislative powers of Parliament that it became a far more practically useful ideal than a reliance on a fundamental law; and, thirdly and consequently, that, because in England alone the lawyers and the estates of the realm united to secure constitutional government, or, as Fortescue puts it, a *dominium politicum et regale*, in England alone, at the end of the Middle Ages, the outlines of such a polity were beginning to emerge. That these results were due to peculiarities in our legal

---

[1] (1609) 8 Co. Rep. at p. 118; see *supra*, pp. 66, 67.
[2] *De Republica Anglorum*, bk. ii, c. 1; *supra*, p. 61.
[3] 4 *Instit.* 36; and for another similar statement see ibid. at p. 43.

G

history is, I think, made the more probable by the analogy afforded by the history of the jury. In the thirteenth century, just as France had her Estates General, so she had a jury system, not unlike that which then existed in England.[1] But her jury system, like her Estates General, never developed as the English jury and the English Parliament developed. And the reason was that, while in France the lawyers under the influence of Roman law adopted a new procedure which had no use for the jury, in England the cessation of the influence of Roman law at the end of the thirteenth century, and the native development of the law, led the lawyers so to develop the jury that it became a unique and an essential part of the procedure of the common law, and in the nineteenth century an institution as widely imitated as the English Parliament itself.

It is not perhaps inappropriate in this lecture, founded in memory of Bishop Creighton, to recall the fact that his views upon the development of the English Church were not unlike the views which I have just expressed as to the development of the English constitution. Dr. Prothero says,[2] 'His view of the position of the English church was that it was neither the mediaeval church nor a church of the continental type, nor yet a mere compromise between two extremes of religious opinion; but that it was a church holding a unique position'. Just so, the medieval development of the English constitution was unique in the manner in which the alliance between the common lawyers and Parliament had developed the Parliament into a true legislature, and, consequently, had given a new and practical meaning to the supremacy of law.

I must now pass to the influence of the lawyers on the development of the constitution in the sixteenth century.

In the sixteenth century the medieval constitution was adapted to the needs of a modern state. But this adaptation did not, as in many continental countries, take the form of a substitution of medieval institutions for a new bureaucratic régime based on the absolute power of the prince, and of a supersession of the medieval law by a new reception of Roman law. On the contrary, the medieval institutions, both of central and of local government, were retained and streng-

---

[1] Holdsworth, *H.E.L.* i. 314–15.   [2] *D.N.B.* (Supplement).

thened; and the medieval common law still held its place. But the machinery of central government was strengthened by the growth of new courts and councils; and, consequently, it was necessary to adapt the legal doctrine as to the prerogative, and its place in the State, to the new political conditions. Modern and medieval ideas were thus blended in a manner which was quite unique; so that, at the end of the sixteenth century, the divergence between the English constitution and the constitutions of continental states, which was already marked at the end of the medieval period, became fundamental.

In this complex process of adaptation the lawyers played a leading part. We can see their influence, firstly, in the new courts and councils by means of which the machinery of the central government was strengthened; secondly, in the manner in which they helped to adapt the machinery of local government, and the procedure of Parliament, to the needs of a modern state; and, thirdly, in the new conception of the prerogative, in which they gave expression to the new position which the King had taken in the State.

(1) The Council was the predominant partner in the Tudor constitution; and it was naturally on its judicial side— in the Star Chamber and the provincial councils—that the influence of the lawyers can be traced. The Chancellor and the Chief Justices, and sometimes some of the puisne judges, were members of the Star Chamber; and it would seem that on the provincial councils the lawyers were the most valuable members. Lee, the President of the Council of Wales, writing in 1540[1] to tell Cromwell of the death of Sir William Sulyard, Chief Justice of Chester, and Mr. Justice Porte, said that he must have 'learned men in their room, as none other is of any help'; and the same thing was also true of the Council of the North.[2] It is clear from what Hudson tells us of Lord Ellesmere's work in the Star Chamber, that he had a large share in making it the regular judicial court, which is pictured for us by Hawarde in his reports; and no doubt the lawyers on the provincial councils had a similar influence. The constitutional importance of this phenomenon is the fact that it was due to this influence of the lawyers that, during the sixteenth century, the Council, the Star Chamber, and

---

[1] L. & P. xv, no. 398. [2] Ibid. xviii (ii), no. 34.

the provincial councils, were fast becoming tribunals, which were administering something very much like administrative law. They heard complaints against servants of the Crown· from the highest to the lowest; and, conversely, the servants of the Crown were protected by them if they found themselves in legal difficulties.[1] If necessary, they overrode the jurisdiction of the ordinary courts—in 1592 there is a case in which the Council directed a jailer to disobey a writ of *habeas corpus*, and to make a return that the commitment was by the Queen's special command.[2] The Council also claimed to exercise the jurisdiction of a *tribunal des conflits*, and to decide disputes as to the jurisdiction of courts.[3] The logical result of these developments is to put the Crown and its servants outside the sphere of the common law, and to subject them to special courts and a special law. It leads to the notion that the Crown is not bound by the ordinary law; and there are clear signs that, though the Council professed to desire to uphold the law in ordinary cases, it would, if necessary, make the ordinary law yield to what it considered to be state necessity.

'This', said Hawarde,[4] 'is the intent of the Privy Councillors in our day and time, to attribute to their councils and orders the vigour force and power of a firm law, and of higher virtue and force, jurisdiction and pre-eminence, than any positive law, whether it be the common law or the statute law. And thus in a short time the Privy Councillors of this realme would be the most honourable noble and commanding lords in all the world.'

We must take some account of these tendencies, and of the part which the lawyers had in developing them, if we would understand the constitutional theory of the royalist lawyers, which emerged in the first half of the seventeenth century.

If we looked only at these legal developments, we might suppose that the English State, like many continental states, was travelling along the road which led to centralized government, based upon royal absolutism, and supported by administrative law. But we shall now see that we get quite a different impression if we look at the manner in which the medieval machinery of local government, and the procedure of Parlia-

---

[1] Holdsworth, *H.E.L.* iv. 85–6, and references there cited.
[2] Dasent, xxiii. 330.   [3] Lambard, *Archeion*, 217.
[4] *Les Reportes del Cases in Camera Stellata*, 78–9.

ment, were being adapted by the lawyers to the new needs of a modern state.

(2) The machinery of local government centred round the Justices of the Peace. They were servants of the Crown, it is true; but they were not merely delegates of the central government. On the contrary, they were unpaid medieval officials, who still did much of their work in sessions, the procedure of which was the medieval procedure of present-ment, indictment, and trial. It is true that, at the end of the sixteenth century, we see signs of the beginnings of a new organization of the justices for administrative work—but only the beginning. As yet much centred round this medieval procedure; and this meant that all the technical rules of com-mon law process and pleading must be observed. These were matters on which the judges claimed to have the last word; and so, side by side with the control of the Council, the control of the common law was retained. And the nature of that control was constantly reminding the justices that they were not mere delegates of the Crown, but independent officials, entitled to act freely, so long as they obeyed the law. It kept alive medieval ideas both as to their own position and as to the rule and the supremacy of the law.

The influence of the lawyers on parliamentary procedure is even more marked; and it is clear from D'Ewes *Journals* that some of the rules of that procedure can be traced to legal influences. Thus, the minute attention paid to matters of form is very reminiscent of a salient characteristic of com-mon law procedure.[1] The idea that parliamentary privilege originates in, and is dependent upon the *lex et consuetudo Parliamenti*, springs from the notion that Parliament is a court, which, like other courts, must have its peculiar law;[2] and some of its privileges, notably the power to imprison for contempt, have a strong analogy to the privileges of other courts.[3] Redlich has pointed out[4] that parliamentary delibera-tion 'is not a series of independent orations, but is composed of speeches and replies'. This is reminiscent of the debate in court as to the issues to be enrolled which formed, as the Year Books show, the chief part of the lawyers' work in

[1] D'Ewes, *Journals*, 303, 556, 575–7.   [2] 4 *Instit.* 14.
[3] D'Ewes, *Journals*, 514.
[4] *Procedure of the House of Commons*, iii. 51.

court; and some of the rules of debate, e.g. the rules as to the citation of documents in the House, are founded on the lawyers' rules of evidence.[1]   I do not for a minute contend that the elaboration of a workable system of procedure is the whole cause of the development of Parliament in the Tudor period. That development was largely due to the use which the Crown and Council made of Parliament, and to the manner in which they controlled it. As in the case of local government, and as in the case of the jury, that control had much to do with the increased efficiency of all these institutions. But I think we may fairly claim that, if the lawyers had not helped Parliament to evolve an adequate procedure, the Tudors could not have made the use of it which they did. The effect upon the position of Parliament is seen in the well-known passage of Sir Thomas Smith's book on the Republic of England, in which he describes it as the body which exercises a supremacy over all other persons and bodies in the State.[2]

It is clear that this growth of Parliament, and the recognition of its supreme legislative powers, will tend to strengthen the medieval idea of the supremacy of the law—common law or statute law. It will tend also to coalesce, firstly, with the idea that the Justices of the Peace, many of whom were members of the House of Commons, were no mere delegates of the Crown, but independent officials, subject only to the laws which, as members of Parliament, they had helped to make; and, secondly, with the ideas of the common lawyers that the State is governed by law—an idea which found its most eloquent expression in the pages of Hooker's *Ecclesiastical Polity*. The result was to consolidate that alliance between the common lawyers and Parliament, to which the medieval development of the English Parliament had owed so much; and to produce that coalescence between the powers of Parliament and the theories of the lawyers, the absence of which was a principal cause for the downfall of the representative assemblies of the Continent.

Thus, in the Tudor constitution, the work of the lawyers in the Council and Star Chamber, and the work of the lawyers in Parliament and in the common law courts, were giving rise to rival constitutional theories as to the position

---

[1] Redlich, op. cit. iii. 60.   [2] Bk. ii, c. 1; see *supra*, p. 61.

of the King and his prerogative in the State. Let us look at the manner in which the lawyers dealt with this difficult problem.

(3) In countries, like France, where the King was fast making good his position to represent the State, Bodin's new theory of sovereignty, and its application to the King, supplied an explanation of political facts, which was both true in substance and scientific in form. No such simple explanation would suit the English facts. Even Henry VIII admitted that 'we at no time stand so highly in our Estate Royal as in the time of Parliament';[1] and the fiscal and legislative powers of Parliament were admitted by all writers of the Tudor period. Similarly it was admitted on all hands that the State should be governed by law. 'Law', said Bacon in his argument in *Calvin's Case*, 'is the great organ by which the sovereign power doth move'; and 'although the king in his person be *solutus legibus*, yet his acts and grants are limited by law, and we argue them every day'.[2] The problem set to the lawyers was thus difficult. They must give legal expression to the position of a King who was the head and representative of the State, but whose powers within it were limited. They solved the problem in the following way: in the first place, they elaborated the distinction, of which we can see the germs in the latter part of the medieval period, between the natural and politic capacity of the King;[3] and this elaboration suggested the idea that the King was a corporation sole. This idea, as Maitland has shown,[4] remained sterile and alien. But the fact that it did so is largely due to the issue of the constitutional controversies of the seventeenth century. The parliamentary party relied on medieval precedents, and their victory revived many medieval ideas. If the victory had remained with the King, and he had ever become identified with the State, I think that something might have been made of the idea that the King was a corporation sole. In the second place, they elaborated the theory that certain prerogatives were inseparably annexed to

[1] *Ferrers's Case, Parlt. Hist.* i. 555.
[2] *Works* (ed. Spedding), vii. 646.
[3] *Case of the Duchy of Lancaster* (1562), Plowden, at pp. 212, 213; and see Bacon, *Works* (ed. Spedding), vii. 667–8.
[4] *Collected Papers*, iii. 251–3.

the person of the King—such prerogatives as the power to pardon would be granted to no other person;[1] and that others were absolute, that is the King had an absolute discretion unfettered by any conditions prescribed by law, as to the mode of their user—for instance the power to make peace or war.[2] The King thus acquired a politic capacity as head of the State; and to that capacity certain prerogatives were inseparably annexed. He himself was not subject to the law; and the exercise of his absolute prerogatives could not be called in question by a law court. But, subject to these qualifications, the extent of the prerogative and the mode of its user were subject to legal limitations which the courts must interpret.[3]

It was an ingenious theory, and it accurately represented the constitutional position in the sixteenth century. But it did nothing to solve the divergence between the two different theories of the State, to which the working of the complex machinery of the Tudor government was giving rise. Elizabeth was an adept in the art of shelving fundamental constitutional questions. But sooner or later a clash between these two different theories of the State was inevitable. It was immediately precipitated by the ignorance of the real nature of English institutions, and the total want of tact, shown by her successors.

The constitutional controversies of the seventeenth century are the high-water mark of the influence of the lawyers upon the formation of the English constitution. James I's claim that the prerogative was in effect the sovereign power in the State brought to a clear issue that divergence between the two very different theories of the State, which had been gradually shaping themselves in the Tudor period. It was this issue which underlay all the constitutional controversies of this century. Both parties appealed to the law and the lawyers to adjudicate upon the general question of the position of the prerogative; and upon the numerous cases in which the extent of particular prerogatives were in issue. It was therefore only natural that the lawyers who favoured the

---

[1] *The Case of Penal Statutes* (1605), 7 Co. Rep. 36.
[2] Smith's *Republic*, Alston's Introd. xxxi–xxxii.
[3] See Hooker, *Ecclesiastical Polity*, bk. viii, § 2. 17.

Crown, and the lawyers who favoured the Parliament, should evolve rival theories on the question of the position of the prerogative in the State.

During James I's reign the lawyers who favoured the Crown evolved a theory as to the position of the prerogative, which gave to James the position which he claimed, and yet could not be said to be clearly contrary to the principles of English law. The corner-stone of this theory was the new twist which was given to the distinction between the absolute and the ordinary prerogative. Instead of saying that the King had certain absolute prerogatives which could not be questioned by Parliament or the courts, and certain ordinary prerogatives which could be so questioned, it was laid down that the King had an overriding absolute prerogative to deal with matters of state; and that no matter in which he chose to exercise this absolute prerogative could be questioned by Parliament or in the courts.[1] Technically this theory had considerable merits. It went a long way towards reconciling the medieval precedents, which supported the view that the prerogative was subject to the control of Parliament and the law, with the practice of the Council and Star Chamber, which ignored these limitations. It enabled a distinction to be drawn between cases in which any exercise of the prerogative was subject to the control of Parliament and the law, and cases in which it was not. It could be represented as the natural development of that line of sixteenth-century cases which gave the King a politic capacity, and certain absolute powers when acting in that capacity. It stopped short, indeed, of attributing sovereign power to the King—it was admitted that he could neither legislate nor tax. But it made the King so much the predominant partner in the State that it was possible by a few further developments to make him in effect sovereign.

The progress of the quarrel between King and Parliament soon showed that it was necessary to make these developments. And they were cleverly made. The Crown lawyers were much too clever to show their hands by large assertions that the prerogative was the sovereign power in the

---

[1] *Bate's Case* (1606), 2 S.T. 371, 389 *per* Fleming C.B.; Spedding, *Letters and Life of Bacon*, iii. 371; James I's Speech in the Star Chamber, *Works*, 557.

State. But they saw that the King had many prerogatives which, with a little extension, could be made to produce this result. His power to issue proclamations could be used to give him a legislative power.[1] His power to imprison persons dangerous to the State could be so used that he could in effect imprison any one who disobeyed his commands.[2] His powers to control trade,[3] and to act freely in defence of the realm,[4] could be so used that they would give him an extra-parliamentary revenue. In fact, it was the development of the consequences of his power to act freely in defence of the realm in the *Case of Ship-money*, which put the coping-stone on the royalist theory. It was laid down, in effect, that, in a time of necessity, as to the existence of which the King was sole judge, he could tax, or, indeed, do as he pleased;[5] and by an extended application of the idea that certain prerogatives were inseparable, it was said that he could not be divested of this sovereign power even by Act of Parliament.[6]

Meanwhile the parliamentary lawyers were developing a rival theory. It was most clearly stated by James Whitelocke (who became a judge of the King's Bench in 1624) in the debate on Impositions in 1610.[7] It too was founded upon a twofold division in the power of the Crown—but a twofold division of a very different kind. 'In the king is a two fold power; the one in Parliament, as he is assisted with the consent of the whole state; the other out of Parliament, as he is sole and singular, guided merely by his own will.' Since the first power was greater than the second, it was clearly the sovereign power in the State. In other words, the sovereign power in the State is the King in Parliament. This theory of parliamentary sovereignty was accepted by the constitutional opposition. In effect it was the complement of Coke's theory of the supremacy of the common law, and it gave expression, in the language of the seventeenth century, to the continuance of that old-standing alliance between the

---

[1] Petition of the House of Commons in 1610, Prothero, *Documents*, 305–6.
[2] *Darnel's Case* (1627), 3 S.T. 1. The real cause for the imprisonment was a refusal to pay a forced loan to the King.
[3] *Bate's Case* (1606), 2 S.T. 371.
[4] *The Case of Ship-money* (1637), 3 S.T. 826.
[5] Ibid. at pp. 1098–9 *per* Berkeley J.
[6] Ibid. at p. 1235 *per* Finch C.J.
[7] (1606) 2 S.T. 371, 482; Parliamentary Debates in 1610 (C.S.), 103–9.

common lawyers and Parliament, to which the victory of constitutional government is largely due. The main defect of the theory is obvious. A royalist writer could fairly say that, in effect, it left the State with no sovereign at all, since it did not provide for the case of a disagreement between King and Parliament; and that his theory was plainly superior because it did provide for such a disagreement. In point of fact both theories were academic and unpractical, until the question whether Parliament or the King as the stronger force in the State had been solved.

After the Restoration it was clear that Parliament had at least as strong a position as the King. The question at issue was no longer whether the prerogative was the sovereign power in the State, but which of these two independent powers—prerogative or Parliament—should be the pre-dominant partner in the State. Charles II and James II, in order to make good their position, took advantage of the semi-religious halo with which the kingly office was invested in the opinion of very many of their subjects; of the defects in the representative system; of the large powers which they had over the composition of the Bench; of their powers over the army; and of their dispensing and suspending powers. The Revolution finally disposed of the theory of divine right; and the Bill of Rights and the Act of Settlement, though they did nothing to correct the defects in the representative system, curtailed the prerogatives which had been the chief weapons of the two last Stuart kings.

Thus the theory of parliamentary sovereignty, pro-pounded by James Whitelocke in 1610, and the supremacy of the common law which Coke had spent his judicial and parliamentary career in advocating, became the accepted theory of the constitution. The sovereign power in the constitution is King, Lords, and Commons. If these three part-ners cannot agree the law is supreme. But, politically, it was an impossible theory. Between three such partners no endur-ing harmony could be expected. If they fell out, one or other must prove the stronger, and cause his will to prevail. That one, whatever the law might say, must be politically the sovereign. Soon after the close of the seventeenth century, the modifications made in the Act of Settlement showed that statesmen were beginning to realize this obvious fact. These modifications have rendered possible the evolution of the machinery of Cabinet government, which has settled the controversies of the seventeenth century by placing the powers of the prerogative at the disposal of the majority of the House of Commons. It has led to the growth of all those conventions of the constitution which regulate the working . of the Cabinet; and it has thus added a new superstructure to that edifice of constitutional law which the Bill of Rights and the Act of Settlement seemed to have completed.

These eighteenth-century developments were the work of the statesmen rather than the lawyers. They were like the parallel developments in local government, which were silently evolving from the medieval judicial machinery by means of which the Justices of the Peace carried on their work, a new machinery for the conduct of the county business.[1] Both these developments were the work of a homogeneous governing class, responsible only to itself. That class easily applied to the conduct of government, both central and local, some of those understandings, rigid and yet within certain limits flexible, permanent and yet eminently adaptable, which their codes of honour or fashion ordained for their personal conduct. It was in other directions that the influence of the legal profession has made itself felt in the eighteenth and nineteenth centuries. .

The maintenance of the supremacy of the common law, which many seventeenth-century statesmen erroneously thought would reconcile all the differences between King and Parliament, has afforded the best of all securities for the protection of the liberties of the subject; and the independent position which the Act of Settlement secured to the Bench, has enabled it to evolve many important principles of constitutional law, more especially in that part of the law which regulates the relations between the State and its subjects.

As against the Crown, the principle that ministers of the Crown are responsible to the law for illegal acts, whether in fact authorized or not by the Crown, was elaborated and applied, not only, as in the Middle Ages, to the humbler servants of the Crown, but even to the highest. Hale[2] and the

---

[1] Webb, *Local Government*, 'The Parish and the County', chap. v.
[2] *Pleas of the Crown*, i. 43–4.

later cases[1] justify it on the ground that, as the King cannot do wrong, he cannot authorize wrong; and that, therefore, whether he in fact authorized the wrong or not, the law must conclusively presume that he has not done so, so that the minister is liable as for an unauthorized illegal act. This principle, and the legal remedy of *habeas corpus*, as improved by the legislature, are two of the best securities ever invented for securing both the liberty of the subject and his other rights against illegal acts committed by the ministers of the Crown. Their efficacy is illustrated in the eighteenth century by such cases as the *General Warrant Cases*,[2] and in our own days by such cases as *Johnstone* v. *Pedlar*,[3] and *ex parte O'Brien*.[4] As against illegitimate extensions of the privilege of Parliament, which threatened the liberty of the subject no less seriously than the illegitimate extensions of the Crown's prerogative, the courts have equally set their faces. The modern law begins with the decisions of Chief Justice Holt in *Ashby* v. *White*[5] and *Paty's Case*;[6] and it is elaborated in many later cases, notably *Burdett* v. *Abbot*,[7] *Stockdale* v. *Hansard*,[8] *The Sheriff of Middlesex's Case*,[9] and *Bradlaugh* v. *Gosset*.[10] These cases established the rule that, though the courts cannot interfere with the exercise of an undoubted privilege, if the privilege is not undoubted, so that the question at issue is its existence, the courts must decide this question as a matter of law; for privilege of Parliament is part of the law.

On the other hand, the rule, which is as old as Bracton,[11] that the Crown could not be sued, had always been mitigated by the power to petition him to do right to a suppliant.[12] The extent of this mitigation was enlarged by the decision of the House of Lords in the *Bankers' Case*,[13] that the remedy of a petition of right was available for breaches of contract; and

[1] See the judgment of Cockburn C.J. in *Feather* v. *The Queen* (1865), 6 B. and S., at pp. 295–6.
[2] *Wilkes* v. *Wood* (1763), 19 S.T. 1153; *Leach* v. *Money* (1765), 19 S.T. 1001.
[3] [1921] 2 A.C. 262.
[4] [1923] 2 K.B. 361; A.C. 603.
[5] (1704) 2 Ld. Raym. 938.
[6] (1705) 2 Ld. Raym. 1105.
[7] (1811) 14 East. 1.
[8] (1839) 9 Ad. and E. 1.
[9] (1840) 11 Ad. and E. 273.
[10] (1884) 12 Q.B.D. 271.
[11] P. & M. i. 500–1; Bracton's *Note Book*, Case 1108.
[12] L.Q.R. xxxviii. 144–56.
[13] (1690–1700) 14 S.T. 1.

that remedy was still further improved by the Petitions of Right Act of 1860.[1]

It was because these various remedies were open to the subject, and it was because they were enforced in the courts of common law, that the English constitution in the eighteenth century compared so favourably with the constitutions of continental states. Abroad the rights of the subject were dependent, not upon the ordinary law and the ordinary courts, but upon administrative law and administrative courts, which applied little law and much administrative discretion; and it was this contrast which so impressed foreigners like Voltaire.[2] In our own days we cannot make a comparison quite so flattering to ourselves. The multifarious activities of the modern state have thrown into striking relief some of the deficiencies of the remedy by way of petition of right—in particular the defect that, because it does not lie for a tort, the courts have, not altogether logically, decided that the Crown cannot, by its machinery, be made liable for the torts of its employees.[3] Legislation, which has vested many powers in boards and local governing authorities, and has deprived the citizen of appeal to the law courts, has made possible much of that oppression which was characteristic of administrative law under the *ancien régime* —a fact which has been abundantly shown in a very able article by my learned friend Mr. C. K. Allen of University College, Oxford, in the *Quarterly Review* of October 1923. As Lord Justice Scrutton said in 1923, in the case of the *Marshall Shipping Co. v. The Board of Trade*,[4]

'I personally feel that the whole subject of proceedings against Government departments is in a very unsatisfactory state . . . and I hope that the committee which is now considering the question of proceedings against the Crown will be able to give the subject more effective remedies against Government departments than he has at present.'

At the same time, while these developments have been taking place in this country, French administrative law, under the influence of the maxim that it is the duty of the State to behave like an honest man, often gives better remedies to the subject than is given by our law.[5]

[1] 23–4 Vict. c. 34. [2] See *Essays in Legal History* (1913), 214.
[3] As to this see *L.Q.R.* xxxviii. 294–6. [4] [1923] 2 K.B. 343, 352.
[5] *Quart. Rev.* vol. 240, 252; cp. Dicey, *Law of the Constitution*, 9th ed.,

What then is the remedy? Is it to introduce the continental system into this country? I do not think that this is desirable, and for this reason: we all know that the custom of the trade has often blinded men to the real character of acts and practices sanctioned by the custom; and that loyalty to colleagues engaged in the same trade, and interested in the maintenance of the custom, has seemed an all-sufficient excuse for very dubious courses of conduct. As Mr. Justice Brett said in 1875,[1] 'When considerable numbers of men of business carry on one side of a particular business, they are apt to set up a custom which acts very much in favour of their side of the business'. It is the same with government departments. The custom and technique developed by the department, the wish to support the policy of the department, even rivalry with other departments, give a sanction to acts which, tested by the moral standards of common life, are wholly indefensible. Sir Frederick Pollock has said that the true test of the soundness of technical language is its capacity to be translated into sensible English.[2] So the soundness of the actions of government departments is their capacity to stand the tests of the ordinary standards of right and wrong applied by judges and juries in the courts. To introduce anything like a system of administrative law is to sacrifice the opportunity of applying this test. Many recent cases, of which the *De Keyser Case*,[3] the *Kelantan Case*,[4] and the *Postmaster General* v. *Liverpool Corporation*,[5] are conspicuous examples, show its value. The true remedy, rather, is to improve and enlarge the remedy by way of petition of right;

368–9, 382–3, 398–401; Harrison Moore, 'Liability for Acts of Public Servants', *L.Q.R.* xxiii. 13.

[1] *Robinson* v. *Mollett* (1874), L.R., 7 H.L. 802, 818.
[2] *Essays in Jurisprudence and Ethics*, 259.
[3] [1920] A.C. 508.   [4] [1923] A.C. 395.
[5] [1923] A.C. 587; in this case Lord Carson said at pp. 601–2, 'the respondents were relieved by the findings of the county court judge from all negligence on their part. On the other hand, the Postmaster General, or rather his predecessors under whom he claimed, were found guilty of improper construction which amounted to negligence, whereby the telephone pipe was exposed to danger which caused the loss in question. I think, My Lords, to attempt to apply S. 8 of the Telegraph Act of 1878 to such a state of facts as that, requires a boldness and a hardihood of construing the Act in support of what was wrong, which has seldom, in my opinion, been surpassed in a Court of Justice.'

to give the courts power to make government departments pay the whole expense of litigation in which they have been unsuccessful; and in cases where, in the opinion of the courts, the litigation has been pursued with a reckless disregard of justice, to order the offending officials personally to pay the whole or some part of the expense incurred. We should thus revert to that old and well tried servant of the law—the sanction of personal responsibility to the law. Its disuse, since the practice of impeachment fell into abeyance, has meant legal irresponsibility in all branches of the public service, from cabinet ministers downwards, and all the evils which legal irresponsibility entails.

Bishop Gardiner relates[1] that Thomas Cromwell once asked him, in the presence of Henry VIII, whether the maxim *quod principi placuit* applied to the King of England—an awkward question in such a presence; and he said that he had answered as follows:

'I had read of kings that had their wills always received for a law, but I told him the form of his reign, to make the law his will was more sure and quiet, and by this form of government ye be established, and it is agreeable with the nature of your people. If ye begin a new manner of policy, how it will frame no man can tell, and how this frameth ye can tell, and I would never advise your Grace to leave a certain for an uncertain.'

This advice is as good to-day as it was in the sixteenth century. The law may need improvement. If so let us improve it; but it would indeed be 'leaving a certain for an uncertain' if we were to abandon the principle of its supremacy. In the fifteenth century, the incapacity of the government to assert its supremacy led to the rise of the over-mighty subject and civil war. In our own day, the deliberate abandonment of its supremacy over trade disputes has led to the growth of those modern analogues of the over-mighty subject—Unions and Trusts, and to disputes which almost attain the dimensions of civil war. In fact, the maintenance of the supremacy of the law over all persons and causes is the first condition precedent for a stable government, and, indeed, for any sort of civilized life. In these modern days, the greatest service which the lawyers can do the State is to impress upon a half-educated electorate the risks of under-

[1] 1 S.T. 588.

mining the foundations of the structure which their predecessors have done so much to build up. To this latest phase
of legal influence I must now turn.

Blackstone tells us[1] that it was a saying of Lord Burghley's
that England could never be ruined but by a Parliament.
The saying may have seemed a clever paradox when it was
first uttered; but to us it is a truism, tinged with a note of
prophecy. In our days many think that to attach much
weight to the learning of the law is a little old fashioned, or
even, in the political jargon of the day, reactionary; and no
doubt this habit of mind is encouraged by the manner in
which an active legislature, responsive to all manner of projects which a glib tongue can make plausible to men without
knowledge, is ready to make experiments at the expense of
the small and largely unrepresented minority who foot the
bill—taxation without adequate representation is now the
order of the day. In the seventeenth century Sir Thomas
Browne once said,[2] 'States are not governed by ergotisms.
Many have ruled well, who could not perhaps define a commonwealth. . . . When natural logic prevails not, artificial too
often faileth.' In these days it is a common fallacy to suppose
that capacity to define a commonwealth, and ingenuity
enough to use artificial logic, are proofs positive of capacity
to rule—the truth being that they merely raise a slight presumption of a capacity to construct some imaginary Utopia.
But it is a fallacy not confined to our own days; and it has
often been exposed—among others by one of our greatest
lawyers and legal historians, Sir Matthew Hale. Hobbes
was one of the first of the philosophers to undertake a serious
criticism of English law, and to plume himself on his capacity
to set the world right by the application of principles which
he had discovered. But as Hale said, in his Reflections on
Hobbes's Dialogue of the Common Law,[3] 'it is a reason for
me to prefer a law by which a kingdom has been happily
governed for four or five hundred years, than to adventure
the happiness and peace of a kingdom upon some new
theory of my own'.[4] And Burke agreed with him. 'It is

---

[1] *Comm.* i. 161.
[2] *Christian Morals*, Works of Sir Thomas Browne (Bohn's ed.), iii. 111.
[3] Printed in Holdsworth, *H.E.L.* vol. v, App. III.   [4] At p. 504.

with infinite caution', he said, 'that any man ought to venture upon pulling down an edifice which has answered in any tolerable degree for ages the common purposes of society.'[1] Lawyers can still give no small help to the development of the constitution, if they can impress upon Parliament and upon the electorate that some knowledge of law, some knowledge of affairs, and some knowledge of history are worth more than a fine imagination.

It is not difficult to make a case against any given institution or any given rule of law; but it is difficult for the half-educated to see through the fallacies of these made cases. A democracy is a hot-bed which freely breeds cranks, faddists, and worse. During the Commonwealth period they abounded almost as freely as they abound to-day. Hale[2] analysed their various species with his usual felicity; and the fact that his analysis is as true to-day as when he wrote, would seem to show that 'progress' so called has made but little headway in eliminating certain human weaknesses. Some would-be re-formers, he points out, wish for novelty—'a certain restless-ness and nauseousness in what they have, and a giddy humour after somewhat which is new . . . possibly upon some over expectations of the benefit of such change, though they have no full or perfect notion of what is to be introduced in the place of what they nauseate'. Others wish for change on account of some piece of injustice which they think the law has inflicted on them. Others 'are possessed with a conceit of a possibility of framing such laws and constitutions as might be faultless . . . and hence if there once occur any incon-venience in a law, presently away with it, and a new frame or model must be introduced and excogitated, and then all will be well'. Others think the laws foolish because they do not understand them; 'and upon this account they will become Solons . . . and frame a law that they themselves may know and approve because they make it, and, as the Israelites in the wilderness, they would have Gods that they may see'. Others are taken with 'some pretty new expedient', which they have adopted, without any consideration of the resulting inconveniences. Others suggest changes merely in order that

[1] *Reflections on the French Revolution*, 90.
[2] *Considerations touching the Amendment of Lawes*, Harv. Law Tracts, 256–63.

their names may be 'enrolled in the number of legislators'. Lawyers can do good service by their criticism of legislative proposals which emanate from these or the like delusions. They can do equally good service in giving a workable form to the substance and wording of legislation which is necessary. In the great periods of legislative reform in the past—in the reign of Edward I, in the Tudor period, in the great codifying Acts of the nineteenth century—the lawyers have always taken an important part. In these ways they can, even in these last days, continue to maintain that alliance between themselves and Parliament, to which the growth and development of constitutional government was in the past largely due.

The legal mould, and the legal forms and concepts, which, in the past, were the media of political discussion, helped to make the growth of the English constitution peaceable and continuous. And even when the lawyers ceased to exercise so direct an influence upon its development as they had exercised in earlier days, the results of their teaching were not wholly lost. To that teaching is due a tradition of respect for law, of national service, and of independence subject to law; and, as the result of that tradition, an instinct for self-government which distinguishes the educated classes of the Anglo-Saxon race. It is possible to copy and transplant to other lands the form of the English constitution—just as it is possible to copy and transplant the academic learning which enables examinations to be passed. It is not possible to copy and transplant that instinct for self-government which gives life and spirit to the bare form—just as it is not possible to copy and transplant the many other qualities, besides academic learning, which fit men to bear rule. The instinct for self-government cannot be transplanted, because, like all instincts, it is the slow product of centuries of that training which our common law has shown itself able to give in fuller measure than any other legal system. It is the possession of that instinct which has enabled us to evolve and to work our constitution, and to colonize and settle distant lands; which has entitled us, because it has fitted us, to govern less gifted peoples.

THE REFORM OF THE LAND LAW
AN HISTORICAL RETROSPECT[1]

BACON, in his *Reading on the Statute of Uses*, used a phrase about the effect of that statute upon the land law of his day, which is not inapplicable to the effect which will be produced by the new Property Acts. He said that the Statute of Uses was 'a law whereupon the inheritances of this realm are tossed at this day as upon a sea'.[2] Bacon's phrase may serve to remind us that the English land law has had, and has survived, other crises before 1 January 1926. Indeed, the legislative ferment of the Tudor period, which produced the Statute of Uses, the Statute of Enrolments, and the Statute of Wills, had a revolutionary effect upon the land law at least as great as the new legislation which has just come into force. This may at first sight seem to be a somewhat incredible statement. It may be thought that it is refuted merely by a comparison between the bulk of the Tudor legislation and the bulk of the new Acts. But such a comparison is wholly misleading for two reasons. In the first place, the new Acts do what has never been done before; they codify and consolidate large parts of the existing common law and statute law relating to property in land. We have had some experience of Acts which codify parts of the common law and consolidate with it the relevant parts of the statute law; the Bills of Exchange Act and the Sale of Goods Act are obvious illustrations. We have also had some experience of Acts which consolidate a principal statute and a number of amending statutes; the Companies (Consolidation) Act, 1908, is an obvious illustration. The new Property Acts are remarkable mainly because they both codify and consolidate on a scale never before attempted. They codify the oldest branch of the common law; and they consolidate, not only the numerous statutes of the nineteenth and twentieth centuries, but also statutes which come from all periods in the history of English law. The large bulk of the new Acts is due very much more

[1] A Lecture delivered at the University of Birmingham on 3 March 1926. Reprinted from (1926) 42 *Law Quarterly Review*, 158.
[2] *Works* (ed. Spedding), vii. 395.

to this fact than to the new matter which they contain. In the second place, I very much doubt whether the new law contained in these Acts is really very much more revolutionary than the new ideas introduced into the common law as the result of the Statute of Uses and the Statute of Wills. If we consider the new developments in the principles of the land law, and in the theory and practice of conveyancing, introduced by these Tudor statutes, and compare them with the new principles as to, for instance, tenure, estates in the land, mortgages, settlements, devolution of real property on intestacy, introduced by the new Acts, we can see that the effects of the Tudor statutes were at least as far-reaching; and I should be inclined to go even further and maintain that, in some respects, the effects of the Tudor statutes were more revolutionary, and therefore more difficult for the legal profession to assimilate. Some of the lawyers of the Tudor period were no doubt familiar with the law as to uses developed by the Chancery. But it was a very difficult feat to introduce into, and to assimilate with, the technical and narrow doctrines of the medieval land law, the elastic and comparatively vague principles which governed these uses; and the more so because they were in very many respects wholly contrary to fundamental principles of that law. On the other hand, the legislation of the nineteenth century has prepared the legal profession for very many of the changes introduced by the new Property Acts. Many of the changes effected by them are, in substance, developments of changes made by that nineteenth-century legislation. The position, for instance, of a tenant for life under the Settled Land Acts has made us familiar with the idea of a person who has complete powers to deal with the legal estate *qua* the outside world, but who must account for the exercise of his powers to many others who have interests in the property; and the Land Transfer Act of 1897 has made us familiar with a representative who is real as well as personal. If anything like the new Acts had been passed—let us say, in 1835—their apparition would have been fairly comparable to the effect upon the legal profession of the passing of the Statute of Uses in 1535. In both cases the legal profession would have been called upon to assimilate many wholly new ideas without any adequate preparation.

All this is, I think, very clearly brought out by Mr. Cheshire's excellent book on *The Modern Law of Real Property*. He has performed with great skill the difficult feat of describing the foundation of old common law and statutory rules as modified by the nineteenth- and twentieth-century statutes, and the codification, consolidation, and partial reconstruction of this amalgam of common law and statutory rules which is effected by the new Acts. There is much new law in these Acts. Old landmarks, such as the Statute of Uses, have disappeared. The old calculus of estates is ruthlessly diminished. The old form of mortgage has gone. But, as we shall see, there is very little new law which has not been foreshadowed, either by actual legislation or by the recommendations of Royal Commissions, which have, from time to time during the nineteenth century, reported upon different topics connected with the land law. It is the great merit of Mr. Cheshire's book that it brings out this continuity between the new law and the old, and so teaches students that the true method of approach to an understanding of the new law is the historical method. Indeed, students are fortunate in having a text-book so skilfully constructed on these lines. I think that the successive editions of this book are destined to instruct many generations of students in the mysteries of the new law of property, even as the work of Joshua and Cyprian Williams has instructed many generations of students in the mysteries of the old law.

In truth, the new Acts are the product of the political and economic conditions of the day, even as other reforms of the land law in past ages were the product of political and economic conditions. It is sometimes supposed that, till the legislation of the nineteenth century, the land law had never, to any great extent, attracted the attention of the legislature. But I hope to show that this is a mistake. It is true that the changes made in the land law by the legislation of the nineteenth century have been more extensive and detailed than at any other period in the history of English law. But this is no peculiarity of the land law. The legislature in that century made changes equally great in many other of the older branches both of law and equity. The changes made in the law of equity and of common law procedure and pleading, and in the criminal law, have been quite as extensive; and the whole judicial system was recast by the Judicature Acts. The truth is that the land law, like other branches of English law, has from time to time been reformed by the legislature; and these reforms have been the starting point, as doubtless these new Property Acts will be the starting point, of new bodies of technical doctrine. No doubt, at the present day, the legislature is a great deal more active than in earlier periods of our legal history. But if it can be persuaded to content itself with the modest task of making the small and necessary amendments which legislation on the scale of these new Property Acts always necessitates, and will abstain for a reasonable time from launching any large new projects for the reform of this branch of the law, the lawyers will create, on the basis of the new Acts, a body of property law as well suited to the needs of our day as the body of law created on the basis of the Statutes of Uses and Wills was suited to the needs of the sixteenth, seventeenth, and eighteenth centuries.

That a statutory reform of the land law is no unprecedented phenomenon in its history is the natural consequence of its importance. It has, in fact, been reformed by the legislature at all those important periods in our legal history, in which changes in political and economic conditions necessitated statutory changes in the law. Taking a very broad survey of the course of English legal history, we can discern six of those periods— the reign of Edward I, the Tudor period, the Restoration period, the period immediately after the Reform Act of 1832, the last half of the nineteenth century, and the post-war movement for reform which has led to the passing of the new Property Acts. I propose very briefly to explain why important statutory changes were needed at those periods, and the manner in which the statutory changes, effected during the first five of those periods, have gone to the making of the law which is contained in the new Acts.

I

The reign of Edward I was an epoch of constructive legislation in all branches of the law, and the statutory changes made in the land law during that reign are still apparent in the new Acts. The occasion for these changes was the need to settle certain outstanding problems in the land law in

accordance with the needs and wishes of the two most powerful parties in the State—the King and the great landholders
—and in accordance with the new position which the free
tenures, and especially tenure by knight service, was coming
to take in the land law of a more settled society.

One of these problems was the question of free alienation.
The King's Courts, although they allowed that the King
could restrain his tenants-in-chief from alienating their land
without his consent, were in favour of the utmost freedom
of alienation. They favoured it partly because it tended to
break up the solidarity of the feudal group, and partly because they regarded the land law as property law pure and
simple; and, under the influence of Roman law, they considered that property connoted freedom of alienation, even
though the thing owned was land. Another problem closely
connected with the first problem was the question of the right
to the incidents of tenure—a question which influenced in
many indirect ways the development of the land law right
down to the abolition of these incidents in the seventeenth
century. It was these incidents which had come, in the case
of tenure by knight service, to be the most valuable of all the
fruits of tenure. 'If', says Maitland,[1] 'tenure by knight service had been abolished in 1300, the Kings of the subsequent
ages would have been deprived of the large revenue that they
drew from wardships, marriages, and so forth; really they
would have lost little else.' The Statute of *Quia Emptores*
(1290)[2] settled the question of the right of the tenant in
fee-simple to alienate freely, but it settled it in such a way that
the tenant's lord secured the incidents of tenure. For the
future every alienation in fee-simple took effect by way, not
of subinfeudation, but of substitution, so that the alienee
held, not of his alienor, but of his alienor's lord. The long
result of this statute has been, not only to secure freedom of
alienation, but also to eliminate mesne tenure, so that one
great obstacle to regarding the land law as property law pure
and simple has been gradually removed. Similarly, it was
the wish to preserve these valuable incidents of tenure which
inspired the statute *De Viris Religiosis*[3]—the earliest statute
of mortmain. A corporation was never under age, never

[1] P. & M. i. 256.   [2] 18 Edw. I, c. 1.
[3] 7 Edw. I.

married, never died, never committed treason or felony. It was, therefore, immune from all those incidents in the life of natural man which were profitable to the feudal lord.

But the landowners, though they were ready to assent to the principle of freedom of alienation, did not wish to be deprived of the power of making family settlements, which would be secure, not only against voluntary alienation by their heirs, but also against the involuntary alienation which followed upon a conviction for treason or felony. They had attempted to make these settlements by the machinery of gifts *in maritagium* and in fee-simple conditional. But the courts, in their desire to secure freedom of alienation, had made settlements effected in this way very insecure. To remedy this the statute *De Donis Conditionalibus* was passed in 1285.[1] It created the estate tail, which was to descend *secundum formam in carta expressam*; and it was decided, early in the fourteenth century, that the estate must continue to descend from heir to heir so long as there was an heir entitled by the terms of the original gift.[2]

. These law reforms of Edward I's reign became the centres of important bodies of doctrine, and the principles which they laid down are still part of the modern law. It is true that the statute *De Donis* is repealed, and that legal estates tail are now impossible; but the effects of the statute still live in the equitable estate tail, and have even been extended by the permission to create these estates in personalty. It is true that the mortmain legislation no longer rests upon the reason which originally inspired it. It depends now on that desire to secure freedom of alienation which was, to a large extent, secured by the statute *Quia Emptores*. But when all deductions have been made it is, I think, true to say that some of the oldest and most permanent parts of the land law owe their origin to the reforms in it which were made by the legislation of Edward I's reign.

II

The land law in the Middle Ages, because it was one of the oldest and the most technical parts of the common law, showed in a marked degree some of the most conspicuous

[1] 13 Edw. I, st. 1, c. 1.
[2] Holdsworth, *H.E.L.* (3rd ed.), iii. 114–16.

failings of the medieval common law. It is true, as Littleton's *Tenures* proved, that it had become a very logical body of principles and rules. But it suffered from the two vices of technicality and rigidity. Its development, through the working of the real actions, had imposed upon it the fetters of the most technical system of procedure which English law has ever seen, and its rigidity is proved by the fact that it so cramped the activities of the landowners, that they had been obliged to appeal to another jurisdiction to get the freedom of disposition, which changing economic and social conditions rendered necessary. By means of uses, as developed by the Court of Chancery, landowners got all the liberty of disposition which they desired. The use imparted an element of flexibility to the land law, which was strikingly absent from the rules of the medieval common law; and the practice of settling land to uses gave to landowners two very highly prized benefits—it enabled them to make a will of their lands, and it enabled them to evade the burdensome incidents of tenure.

It was the latter consequence which inspired Henry VIII's legislation as to uses. The Statute of Uses (1535) was the final result of a struggle, which had lasted for six years, to restore to the King his feudal revenue.[1] It proceeded on the plan of annexing the legal estate to the interest of *cestui que use*, so that landowners got the same free powers of disposition over the legal estate as they had formerly had over the use. For the future shifting and springing uses operated, like remainders, to create legal estates; by making use of the machinery of the statute landowners at length acquired a secret method of conveyance; and by means of powers of appointment they acquired large powers, not only of settling, but of varying the settlements of their property, to meet the needs occasioned by family vicissitudes or the requirements of estate management. From this point of view, Bacon's comment upon the effect of the statute is very apposite. 'The title of the statute is,' he said, '*Statutum de usibus in possessionem transferendis*. Wherein, Walmsly Justice noted well 40 Reginae that if a man look to the working of the statute, he would think it should be turned the other way, *de possessionibus ad usus transferendis*, for that is the course that the

[1] As to this, see Holdsworth, *H.E.L.* iv. 450–61.

statute holdeth to bring possession to the use.'[1] It is true that the statute deprived landowners of the power to make a will. But the outcry against this consequence of the statute was so great that Henry VIII was obliged to restore it in part by the Statute of Wills, which was passed five years later (1540);[2] and the power to devise was given in such wide terms that it enabled landowners to deal with their property by a new species of future interest—the executory devise.

The desire of the King to restore his feudal revenue from the incidents of tenure induced him to press forward these measures of legislative reform which resulted in the Statute of Uses. It was for this reason that, for about a century, the Chancellor refused to disturb the union between the legal and equitable estate effected by the statute, by making a practice of enforcing as a trust a use upon a use.[3] But when in 1660 the incidents of tenure were abolished, this consideration ceased to apply. The Chancellor began to enforce the use upon a use as a trust, and so the existing methods of limiting future estates in the land were duplicated. It was open to landowners to create legal estates by way of remainders, shifting or springing uses, or executory devises, or to create equitable estates by vesting the legal estate in trustees on the appropriate trusts. One of the indirect results of this greatly increased freedom of disposition was to give landowners the power to create 'perpetuities'—the power, in other words, to use their new freedom of disposition in such a way as to destroy that freedom of alienation which the judges had always favoured. The answer of the judges was to confirm the legality of the expedients devised for circumventing the statute De Donis, to pronounce illegal all attempts to create an unbarrable entail, and finally to evolve the rule against perpetuities. Thus, if we look at the effects, direct and indirect, of the Statutes of Uses and Wills, we can see that a very large part of the modern law of real property depended upon these reforming statutes, just as a large part of the medieval law of real property depended upon Edward I's statutes.

[1] Reading, *Works* (ed. Spedding), vii. 417.
[2] 32 Hen. VIII, c. 1, amended by 34 & 35 Hen. VIII, c. 5; see Holdsworth, *H.E.L.* iv. 464–7.
[3] Holdsworth, *H.E.L.* iv. 472–3; v. 307–9; vi. 641–2.

III

A very extensive set of changes in the land law was projected under the Commonwealth.[1] Most of them have been carried into effect in the nineteenth century. But, as most of them were shelved at the Restoration, it is only necessary at this point to allude to two of them—the abolition of the military tenures, and the proposals to establish a register of conveyances.

The abolition of the military tenures was the only one of the projected law reforms of the Commonwealth which was actually carried into effect during the Commonwealth period,[2] and it was confirmed by the Act passed for the same purpose in 1660.[3] The effect of that Act on the modern law was twofold. In the first place, it got rid of a mass of obsolete law. As Hale said in his introduction to Rolle's *Abridgment*:

'Tenures by knight service and their appendix, wardship, value and forfeiture of marriage of the ward, escuage, relief, *aide pur file marier et faire fitz chevalier, primer seisin, livery, offices post mortem, traverses, interpleader,* and monstrans of right in relation thereunto; the several writs of right, of ward, ravishment of ward, *valore maritagii, duplici valore maritagii,* and some other appendixes of this nature, made several great titles in the law, and took up much of the business of the old and latter law books; all, or the greater part whereof, is now pared off, and become unuseful, by the later Act for Alteration of Tenures.'

In the second place, by eliminating many of the consequences of tenure, it took a long step in the direction of assimilating the law of real and personal property—a tendency which had already been helped forward by the virtual supersession of the real actions by the action of ejectment. It is true that a long road remained to be travelled before the assimilation effected by the new Property Acts could be attained; but I think we may say that the reform effected by the Act of 1660 was a condition precedent to any sort of progress along that road.

The proposal made in the Commonwealth period to establish a register of conveyances never matured in the seventeenth century, and similar proposals were only very partially realized in the eighteenth century. But they were persistent

[1] See Holdsworth, *H.E.L.* vi. 416–17.
[2] *Acts and Ordinances,* i. 833; ii. 1043, 1057.
[3] 12 Car. II, c. 24.

from the seventeenth century onwards; and it is necessary at this point to say something of them, because we shall see that the proposal to establish a register was taken up by the Commissioners on the Law of Real Property in 1830, and that the prominence which they gave to it had a large influence in shaping the many suggestions for the reform of the land law, which were made during the nineteenth century.[1]

In the seventeenth century the proposal to establish a register of conveyances was not wholly new. A comprehensive scheme for the registration of conveyances had formed part of Henry VIII's proposals for the reform of the land law.[2] But though his proposal to deal with the problem of the use had taken legislative form in the Statute of Uses, his proposal to establish a register of conveyances never took shape. All that was passed was the Statute of Enrolments,[3] which was, as Bacon said,[4] simply in the nature of a proviso to the Statute of Uses. A scheme for the registration of conveyances was, as I have said, one of the proposals put forward at the time of the Commonwealth; but, unlike other proposals for the reform of the law, it was not lost sight of at the Restoration. Hale, so North tells us,[5] 'had turned that matter in his thoughts, and composed a treatise not so much against the thing (for he wishes it could be) as against the manner of establishing it; of which he is not satisfied, but fears more holes may be made than mended by it'. It is probable that a tract advocating the enrolling and registering of all conveyances of land, which is printed in the Somers *Tracts*,[6] contains Hale's proposals. Francis North favoured a more extensive proposal— a register of titles;[7] and in the eighteenth century Blackstone lamented the secrecy of conveyance which conveyances to uses had rendered possible, and considered that the project of a general register for deeds, wills, and other acts affecting real property, was worthy of consideration.[8]

. A very good account of the attempts made in the sixteenth, seventeenth, and eighteenth centuries to establish some sort of a general register is given by Mr. Tyrrel, in a communication which he made to the Real Property Commission of

[1] *Infra*, pp. 115 et seq.　　[2] Holdsworth, *H.E.L.* iv. 457-9.
[3] 27 Hen. VIII, c. 16.　　[4] Reading, *Works* (ed. Spedding), vii. 432.
[5] *Lives*, i. 142.　　[6] Vol. xi, 81-90.
[7] *Lives of the Norths*, i. 141-2.　　[8] *Comm.* ii. 342-3.

1829.[1] After noticing the proposals in the time of the Commonwealth for the establishment of a general register, he says:

'Bills for the same purpose were brought in . . . during the reign of Charles II in 1663, 1664, 1670, and 1677; in the reign of James II in 1685; in the reign of William III in 1693, 1694, 1697, 1698, and 1699; in the reign of George II in 1734 and 1758; and the last of such bills was introduced by Mr. Serjeant Onslow in 1816, but it was not read a second time. With the exception of the Act for regulating the Bedford Level, the first local Act (for the West Riding of Yorkshire) was passed in 1703, and it was followed in 1706 by the Act for the East Riding, and in 1707 by the Act for Middlesex. The reasons for passing these Acts, which are stated in the preambles, are equally applicable to the whole kingdom. . . . At the same time that the bills were passed for establishing local registers in Yorkshire and Middlesex, similar bills were brought in for the counties of Berkshire and Huntingdonshire. Bills of the same nature were also proposed for Derbyshire in 1732, twice for Surrey in 1709 and 1728, and twice for Northumberland, of which the last was in 1784. However, the only other bill which has passed was that for the North Riding of Yorkshire in 8 Geo. II. It appears that most of these bills were introduced in the House of Commons upon petitions by the Magistrates and the Grand Jury of the county stating "that lands were secretly conveyed by ill-disposed persons, and that several who had purchased lands or lent money thereon, had been undone by prior or secret conveyances or incumbrances".'

Thus, although local registers were established for Yorkshire and Middlesex, all attempts to establish a general register failed. The cause was partly, as Roger North rightly says, the hostility of the legal profession, and partly and consequently the fact that, for the most part, these Bills represented rather crude attempts to legislate upon a very complicated subject.[2] But no doubt the main cause of their failure was the great complication which the Statutes of Uses and Wills, and the doctrines of equity, had introduced into the land law. We shall see that, in the nineteenth century, the outcome of the many discussions by real property lawyers, and the repeated consideration by Royal Commissions of projects of registration, resulted in legislative reforms which, by diminishing these complications, and introducing into the

[1] *First Report,* Appendix, at p. 525.
[2] *Lives of the Norths,* i. 141–2.

law new ideas, helped to render possible the scheme of the new Property Acts.[1]

But though no general register of conveyances or titles was established, legislation of the eighteenth and nineteenth centuries did establish registers of various charges upon land. An Act of 1777[2] established a register for annuities and rentcharges for life or lives, and the Judgments Acts of 1838[3] and 1839[4] established registers of judgments and *lites pendentes* affecting lands. In 1887 provision was made for the registration of deeds of arrangement.[5] As has been pointed out, a register of this kind is quite distinct from a general register of titles or conveyances.[6] It is, in fact, rendered essential by the absence of a general system of registration of title. 'This springs from the fact that, in addition to such charges and encumbrances as may be revealed by an examination of the deeds, there are a whole series of liabilities, not imposed by any deeds, and therefore unmentioned in the deeds, permitted by law, of which a purchaser may be held to have notice, constructive or otherwise, and which therefore become binding on him.'[7] We shall see that the registration of these charges upon land has acquired a greatly increased importance in the new scheme of law inaugurated by the new Property Acts.[8]

IV

'The Blackstonian era', says Dicey,[9] 'was a period of national strength and of most reasonable national satisfaction'; and he adds that 'in the ordinary course of things the law of England would have been amended before the end of the eighteenth, or soon after the beginning of the nineteenth century'.[10] But the French Revolution delayed changes which the rapidly changing social and economic condition of the country rendered absolutely necessary. It was this delay which made necessary the sweeping changes in English law which followed the passing of the Reform Act of 1832.

[1] *Infra*, p. 115 et seq.   [2] 17 Geo. III, c. 26.
[3] 1 & 2 Vict. c. 110.   [4] 2 & 3 Vict. c. 11.
[5] 50 & 51 Vict. c. 17.
[6] J. S. Stewart Wallace, 'The Land Charges Act in Jurisprudence', *L.Q.R.* xli. 179–80.   [7] Ibid. 178.   [8] *Infra*, p. 125.
[9] *Law and Opinion in England* (1st ed.), 79, n. 1.
[10] Ibid. 123.

The Commissioners on the Law of Real Property issued their first report in 1829, their second report in 1830, their third report in 1832, and their fourth report in 1833. The legislation which followed upon those reports, during the first half of the nineteenth century, destroyed many anomalies, and, in the fields of conveyancing and procedure, substituted a simple mechanism for the complex expedients imposed upon the law by its historical development.

'Old abuses fell like leaves in autumn. Fines were not saved by their antiquity, nor recoveries by their absurdity, nor real actions by their costliness. . . . Our sense of historical continuity was not keen enough to save "the casual ejector", or the "common vouchee". A decent oblivion was provided for John Doe and Richard Roe. The law of inheritance itself did not altogether escape the touch of the innovator.'[1]

But, in spite of all the labour and research which are embodied in these four reports and their appendices, the legislation which they produced only resulted in a preliminary clearing of the ground. It did nothing directly in the direction of assimilating the law of real and personal property. The reason for this is to be found in the circumstances of the time, which prevented a just appreciation of the causes which kept these two bodies of law so far apart.

When the Real Property Commission was appointed, and when the Commissioners made their reports, the influence of the great landowners, both in Parliament and in local government, was very great. To a very large extent England had been governed by the great landowners during the eighteenth century; and their political achievement, measured by a comparison between the position and prosperity of the country at the beginning and the end of that century, was one which no merely democratic community is ever likely to be able to show. And even in the narrower field of the land law there is a great deal more to be said for their achievements than is commonly supposed. I have elsewhere pointed out that, till the end of the eighteenth century, the land law met the needs of different classes of landowners.

'No doubt some of its rules were clumsy, some were uncertain, and some were inequitable. But on the whole they were just and flexible rules. The sixteenth century was not marked in England, as it was

[1] Maitland, *Collected Papers*, i. 198–9.

marked in Germany, by a peasant revolt; and the settlement in England of the position of the copyholder removed a set of grievances which, in France, were among the causes of the first French Revolution. Moreover, the rules of the land law impeded neither the economic developments of the sixteenth and seventeenth centuries, nor the progress of the industrial revolution of the latter part of the eighteenth and the beginning of the nineteenth centuries.'[1]

It is true that, at the beginning of the nineteenth century, England was becoming a manufacturing country. But the social and political influence of the landed gentry continued to be felt. Joshua Williams, in 1862, could state as a notorious fact that 'every man who accumulates a fortune immediately lays it out in the purchase of land, with a view to found a family and to perpetuate his name'.[2] Bagehot, writing in 1866, could say that in the House of Commons 'the landed gentry far surpass any other class', and that 'men who study the structure of Parliament, not in abstract books, but in the concrete London world, wonder, not that the landed interest is very powerful, but that it is not despotic'.[3]

It is not surprising, therefore, that the Real Property Commissioners, when they issued their first report in 1829, were influenced by these political and social conditions. They recommended, as we have seen, reforms in many branches of the law, but they gave unstinted praise to its substantive principles. They said:[4]

'We have the satisfaction to report that the Law of Real Property seems to us to require very few essential alterations; and that those which we shall feel it our duty to suggest are chiefly modal. When the object of transactions respecting land is accomplished, and the estates and interests in it which are recognized are actually created and secured, the Law of England, except in a few comparatively unimportant particulars, appears to become almost as near to perfection as can be expected in any human institution. The owner of the soil is, we think, vested with exactly the dominion and power of disposition over it required for the public good, and landed property in England is admirably made to answer all the purposes to which it is applicable. Settlements bestow upon the present possessor of an estate the benefits

[1] Holdsworth, *H.E.L.* vii. 399–400.
[2] *Juridical Society's Papers*, ii. 599.
[3] *English Constitution*, 163, 164.
[4] *First Report*, pp. 6–7.

of ownership, and secure the property to his posterity. The existing rule respecting perpetuities has happily hit the medium between the strict entails which prevail in the northern part of the Island . . . and the total prohibition of substitutions, and the excessive restriction of the power of devising, established in some countries on the Continent of Europe. In England families are preserved, and purchasers always find a supply of land in the market. A testamentary power is given, which stimulates industry and encourages accumulation; and while capricious limitations are restrained, property is allowed to be moulded according to the circumstances and wants of every family. Where no disposition is made by will, the whole landed estate descends to the son or other heir male. This, which is called the Law of Primogeniture, appears far better adapted to the constitution and habits of this kingdom than the opposite Law of Equal Partibility, which, in a few generations, would break down the aristocracy of the country, and, by the endless subdivision of the soil, must ultimately be unfavourable to agriculture, and injurious to the best interests of the State.'

We have seen that the legislation recommended by the Commissioners swept away many archaisms, such as real actions and fines and recoveries.[1] It also made some reforms in the law of inheritance, the law as to prescription, and the law as to the limitation of actions. But the subject which the Commissioners thought most needed reform was the law as to the transfer of real property. In their second report they emphasized the insecurity of titles and the expense of the then existing system of conveyancing, and they made a careful analysis of the causes of these evils. The cure which they advocated was the establishment of a general register of conveyances. No doubt the fact that this project had been discussed at intervals during the seventeenth and eighteenth centuries helped the Commissioners to arrive at the conclusion that this was the best solution of the problem. What they did not see, and what a body of men impressed with the fundamental excellence of the land law could not be expected to see, was the impossibility of combating these evils simply by a mechanical device of this kind. It was impossible to make titles secure, and to get cheap conveyancing, so long as the law permitted a large series of estates, present and future, legal and equitable; so long as it continued to have two sets of rules for succession on intestacy, and two sets of representation on death; so long as conveyances were needlessly lengthy;

---

[1] *Supra*, p. 112.

so long as the system of strict settlement admitted of the creation of all sorts of charges upon land; so long as estates in common were admitted; and so long as the system of mortgaging land remained unreformed.

This erroneous view taken by the Commissioners—first, that little change was needed in the substantive rules of the land law; and secondly, that most of its defects could be cured by establishing a register of titles or conveyances—has had a large effect on the subsequent history of the movement for the reform of the land law. It has led reformers to concentrate on schemes of registration rather than on direct changes in the substantive rules of the land law; and, consequently, it has blinded them to the fact that changes in those substantive rules are a condition precedent to the establishment of a successful system of registration. It was only gradually that this fact became evident during the last half of the nineteenth century. That it then became evident was due partly to the unsuccessful attempts which were made to establish a general register either of titles or conveyances, and partly to changes in economic and political conditions which caused a great change in men's ideas as to the fundamental excellence of the land law. Both these two sets of causes produced reforms in the land law during the last half of the nineteenth century which were the conditions precedent for the final reform made by the new Property Acts.

V

In the latter half of the nineteenth century economic and political ideas were changing. The advantages resulting from the existing system of settlements, and from the law of primogeniture, which were extolled by the Commissioners of 1829, were receding into the background, and the disadvantages resulting from the existing system of conveyancing were coming into the foreground. The Commissioners on the Registration of Title reported in 1857 that 'There is a general insecurity of title and apprehension of risk, even when, to all external appearance, there is an absence of any ground for suspicion'.[1] 'What are the evils of which the public complain?' said Joshua Williams in

[1] *Parliamentary Papers*, 1857, Sess. 2, vol. xxi, 258–9.

1862.[1] 'Chiefly I apprehend these—delay, expense, and uncertainty as to the amount of delay and expense. In-security, when a purchase has once been made, is not an evil that appears to be generally felt; but, with regard to mort-gages, complaints are sometimes heard of the insecurity of a second mortgage, and the difficulty of mortgaging a second time.' In these circumstances, it was only natural that atten-tion should be turned to the remedy which the Commis-sioners had put forward in 1830—the remedy of a general register either of titles or of conveyances. The difference between these two rival schemes of registration was clearly explained by the Commissioners, who reported in 1878–9. They said:[2]

'That registration of titles is in the abstract to be preferred to registration of assurances may at once be conceded, for the former aims at presenting the intending purchaser or mortgagee with the net result of former dealings with the property, while the latter places the dealings themselves before him, and leaves him to investigate them for himself. In one case he finds, so to speak, the sum worked out for him; in the other he has the figures given him, and has to work out the sum for himself.'

A Bill for the registration of legal titles only, and not equit-able interests, was preferred by a Committee, which reported in 1853, to a Bill for the registration of conveyances;[3] and in 1857 the Commissioners appointed to consider the registration of title took the same view, and produced a scheme to give effect to it;[4] and it should be noted that the consideration of this scheme produced suggestions, many of which were endorsed by later Commissions and by dis-tinguished real property lawyers, and some of which have been substantially enacted by the new Property Acts. Thus it was suggested that no form of interest, except the fee, charges on the fee, and leases, should be put on the register,[5] and that trusts should be kept off the register.[6] But Lord

[1] *Juridical Society's Papers*, ii. 589.
[2] *Parliamentary Papers*, 1878–9, vol. xi, *ix*.
[3] Ibid. 1852–3, vol. xxxvi, 399.
[4] Ibid. 1857, Sess. 2, vol. xxi, 245.   [5] Ibid. 277.
[6] Ibid. 281–2; see also the sketch of a Bill, approved by the Commissioners, App. at p. 394 seq. which, *inter alia*, reformed the system of mortgage, and reformed certain technicalities in the creation and limitation of estates.

Westbury's Act of 1862,[1] and Lord Cairns's Act of 1875,[2] which provided for the registration of title, were both failures. As Charles Sweet pointed out: 'Lord Westbury's experiment taught us that a system of registration of title, to be successful, must not be too rigid. Lord Cairns's experiment taught us that a voluntary system is foredoomed to failure.'[3] It is in the Report of a Committee of the House of Commons appointed, in view of this failure, to consider the steps which should be taken to simplify the title to land, to facilitate its transfer, and to prevent frauds on purchasers and mortgagees, that we can find some suggestions which bore immediate fruit in amending Acts, and others which the new Property Acts have at length adopted. We can find also other suggestions which the new Property Acts have adopted in two papers contributed to the Juridical Society in 1862 by Wolstenholme[4] and by Joshua Williams.[5]

The Commissioners were agreed that, as a first step to simplify titles, it was necessary to repeal the Statute of Uses —'that stronghold of conveyancing pedantry';[6] and this was also the opinion of Joshua Williams.[7] They pointed out that the great obstacle to the establishment of a system of registration of titles was the complication of estates and interests which were legally possible.

'If', they said, 'an Act of Parliament could be passed . . . either prohibiting the owner of property from tying it up or charging it except in a particular manner, or giving to the possessory proprietor the right of dealing with it as if it were his own; in other words, if the law either recognized nothing but estates in fee-simple, or gave to the holder of land the same power of disposition which the holder of stock now enjoys, the registration of title would be as easy as the title would be simple.'[8]

Wolstenholme, in 1862, made a proposal, directed towards the same objects, which the new Property Acts have in effect adopted.[9] He proposed that legal estates should be limited to estates in fee-simple and terms of years absolute, and that mines, easements, and rentcharges should only be

[1] 25 & 26 Vict. c. 53.   [2] 38 & 39 Vict. c. 87.
[3] L.Q.R. xxviii. 6.
[4] Juridical Society's Papers, ii. 533–52.   [5] Ibid. 589–628.
[6] Parliamentary Papers, 1878–9, vol. xi, ix.
[7] Juridical Society's Papers, ii. 622–3.
[8] Parliamentary Papers, 1878–9, vol. xi, vi.   [9] Infra, p. 124.

grantable for these two estates.[1] All other estates should be equitable. The tenant for life under a strict settlement should have the legal fee, but should not be able to dispose of it without the consent of the trustees.[2] In case of a sale the beneficial interests should attach to the purchase price, and should cease to attach to the land.[3]

The Commissioners also recommended that a real representative should be appointed for freehold interests in land,. in whom estates of inheritance should vest in the first instance;[4] and to this suggestion Wolstenholme[5] and Joshua Williams[6] agreed. Joshua Williams suggested the abolition of the pernicious system by which conveyancers were paid by the length of the conveyance, and the substitution of *ad valorem* scale of payments;[7] and this opinion was endorsed by the Commissioners, who also recommended that short statutory forms should be substituted for the lengthy common form clauses to be found in all conveyances.[8] Both Joshua Williams[9] and the Commissioners[10] agreed that the existing form of mortgages should be abolished. A charge on land should be substituted which should give the mortgagee the same remedies as were given by the existing form of mortgage. Joshua Williams emphasized the inconvenience of tenancies in common, and suggested that, if tenants in common exceeded a certain number, any person holding a share to a certain amount should be able to compel a sale.[11]

The wisdom of these suggestions was enforced by changes in economic and political conditions. That economic conditions were a main cause of the legislation initiated by the

---

[1] *Juridical Society's Papers*, ii. 544; see also *Parliamentary Papers*, 1878–9, vol. xi, 248.

[2] *Juridical Society's Papers*, ii. 547, 548.   [3] Ibid. 548.

[4] *Parliamentary Papers*, 1878–9, vol. xi, *viii*.

[5] *Juridical Society's Papers*, ii. 547, 548; *Parliamentary Papers*, 1878–9, vol. xi, 248.   [6] *Juridical Society's Papers*, ii. 615.

[7] *Juridical Society's Papers*, ii. 594–601; he said, at p. 598: 'I have before now met with some who seemed to think that their sole duty to their principals consisted, first in expanding every idea into the largest possible number of words, and secondly, in making as many deeds as possible out of every transaction.'

[8] *Parliamentary Papers*, 1878–9, vol. xi, *vii–viii, xiv*.

[9] *Juridical Society's Papers*, ii. 619–20.

[10] *Parliamentary Papers*, 1878–9, vol. xi, *xiii, xiv*.

[11] *Juridical Society's Papers*, ii. 624–5.

Settled Land Act, 1882, was clearly explained by Lord Macnaghten in *Bruce* v. *Marquess of Ailesbury*.[1] He said:[2]

'A period of agricultural depression, which showed no sign of abatement, had given rise to a popular outcry against settlements. The problem was how to relieve settled land from the mischief which strict settlements undoubtedly did in some cases produce, without doing away altogether with the power of bringing land into settlement. That was something very different from the task to which Parliament addressed itself in passing the Settled Estates Acts. In those Acts the Legislature did not look beyond the interests of the persons entitled under the settlement. In the Settled Land Act the paramount object of the Legislature was the well-being of settled land.'

Maitland, in his paper on the 'Law of Real Property', which was written in 1879, passed by in silence the argument of the Commissioners on the Law of Real Property in 1829 for the maintenance of primogeniture—the argument that it was a mainstay of the aristocracy—and showed that it was unfair to children, and that the law of inheritance, of which it was a part, introduced endless complications into the law.

'The advocates of primogeniture are fond of laying stress on the fact that few landowners die intestate. Is it not a little one?—This is their favourite plea. No, we reply, the abuse is not a little one. It is for the sake of the heir-at-law that we disorder the whole of our jurisprudence. In order to postpone women to men, in order to make a will which no one wants made, we render our law unknowable by any save experts. If after all our efforts we fail in attaining our worthless objects, if daughters and younger sons are not disinherited, this is but an additional argument for reform. We undergo all the evils of having two systems of property law, and have nothing to show for it. You cannot prove that a law is good by showing that all sensible men contrive to evade it.'[3]

The result of the discussions of schemes for the registration of title, and of these economic and political reasons for reform, was not the establishment of any general and compulsory system of registration of title, or changes in any of the fundamental principles of the law of real property. The Act of 1875,[4] which provided for the registration of title, was, as we have seen, a purely voluntary Act, and it was not

---

[1] [1892] A.C. 356.
[2] Ibid. at pp. 364–5.
[3] *Collected Papers*, i. 193–4.
[4] 38 & 39 Vict. c. 87.

till 1897 that Lord Halsbury provided machinery for applying it compulsorily to a county or a part of a county.[1] The
chief result of all these movements for reform was the passing of much legislation to effect those reforms in the law
which had been shown to be obviously necessary. In 1857
the Commissioners on Registration of Title had expressed
the opinion that 'the establishment of a register should only
be part of a general plan for amending the law of real
property',[2] and Joshua Williams agreed with this view. In
1862 he said: 'The remark that a general measure of registration should follow rather than precede beneficial alterations in the law itself, is one in which I entirely agree. If the
alterations be beneficial the sooner they are introduced the
better.'[3] This, in fact, was the course pursued. The Parti-
tion Act, the Vendor and Purchaser Act, the Conveyancing
Acts, the Settled Land Acts, and the Land Transfer Act,
1897, introduced many of those partial reforms which had
been advocated during the latter part of the nineteenth century. But they were all partial and, to a large extent, unconnected reforms. They all helped on the simplification of
conveyancing, but, with the exception of Part I of the Land
Transfer Act, 1897, they did little to effect any assimilation
between the law of real and the law of personal property.
The main essential features of the law of real property still
held their ground. Dicey called attention to this fact in 1905
in his paper on 'The Paradox of the Land Law'.[4] He said:

'To the student of legal history the development of the English land
law from 1830 to 1900 presents this paradox: incessant modifications
or reforms of the law, which extend over seventy years, and have
certainly not come to an end, have left unchanged, in a sense almost
untouched, the fundamentals of the law with regard to land. . . . The
paradox of the modern English land law may thus be summed up: the
constitution of England has, whilst preserving monarchical forms,
become a democracy, but the land law of England remains the land
law appropriate to an aristocratic State.'[5]

This state of things was attributed by Dicey to the state of
public opinion on the subject of the reform of the land law.

[1] 60 & 61 Vict. c. 65.
[2] *Parliamentary Papers*, 1857, Sess. 2, vol. xxi, 299.
[3] *Juridical Society's Papers*, ii. 607.
[4] *L.Q.R.* xxi. 221.   [5] Ibid. 221, 222.

The landowners desired no fundamental changes, and those who wished for reform were divided; and so, though piece-meal reforms which cured obvious evils were effected, no large and thoroughgoing reform was undertaken. But I think that it was due in part to the fact that the need for fundamental changes in the substantive principles of the law, had been obscured by the manner in which those who desired such changes had concentrated their energies, not on schemes for the reform of the substantive law, but on schemes for the registration of titles or conveyances; and the pursuance of this policy was, I think, not unconnected with the views held by the Real Property Commissioners of 1829.

VI

After the war many causes made it impossible to leave the land law in the condition in which it was in 1914. The para-dox, to use Dicey's phrase, had become too glaring; and public opinion was prepared for larger measures of reform. One cause, Sir Leslie Scott tells us,[1] was his experience as chairman of the Lands Requisition Committee, which showed up 'the expenses and delays of land transfer in England as compared with newer countries'. Another cause which made some reform necessary was the break-up of large estates. This process was assisted by the dissipation of the nation's capital, which is the necessary result of the burden of heavy death duties; for they prevent saving, by taking and spending (often on very questionable objects) money which would otherwise be profitably invested, and they encourage extra-vagance by penalizing thrift. These causes rendered it necessary to facilitate and cheapen the transfer of land, and it was inevitable that many other rules of the land law— notably the law of primogeniture—should come under review. Sir Leslie Scott's Committee, which reported on land transfer in 1919, at length took the step of denying directly the view which had been taken by the Commis-sioners on the Law of Real Property in 1829. Instead of praising the law of real property and putting most of the

[1] For the facts contained in this and the ensuing paragraphs I have relied mainly on Sir Leslie Scott's little book, *The New Law of Property Explained*; it contains his speech on the second reading of the Law of Property Bill, 1922, with an introduction, and it also contains notes by B. B. Benas.

blame for its admitted inconvenience on the system of conveyancing,[1] it gave effect to a view which had for some time
been gaining ground, and said that 'the main defects in the
existing system of Conveyancing do not lie in the Conveyancing Acts or in the practice of Conveyancing, but in the
general law of Real Property'.[2] This view was not only
technically correct; it was also in accordance with the trend
of public opinion. It was clear that institutions which,
according to the Commissioners of 1829, were the buttresses
of aristocracy, were likely to fare even worse in our post-war
than they had fared in our pre-war society.

It was clear in 1919 that no extension of the system of
registration of title was possible—opinions were then, and
still are, too much divided; and so it was decided to follow
deliberately the course which, almost accidentally, had given
rise to very many of the reforms of the nineteenth century.
We have seen that the various Commissions which had
reported on schemes of registration of title, and the various
statutes which had been passed in consequence of their
recommendations, had not succeeded in introducing any
general compulsory system of registration of title, but that
they had been the means of suggesting many useful reforms
in the law.[3] It was now resolved to follow up this method of
approach—to begin by reforming the substantive law of real
property and by simplifying conveyancing. Necessarily the
existing Land Transfer Acts, dealing with registration of
title, were amended and altered so as to bring them into line
with the new law. But it was agreed that there should be no
attempt to introduce any further measure of compulsory
registration of title till the Acts had been in operation for ten
years. At the end of this period the working of the Acts may

---

[1] *Supra*, pp. 112–14.

[2] *Reports*, &c., 1919 (Cmd. 424), vol. xxix, p. 9; this was the view of
Charles Sweet in 1912, see *L.Q.R.* xxviii. 10–11, 25; and of the Land Transfer Commissioners (1909–11), ibid. 21, 25, n. 1—though it was beyond the
scope of their commission to report on the advisability of amendments to the
Law of Real Property. Sir Arthur Underhill in his pamphlet entitled *The
Line of Least Resistance* (Butterworth, 1919), p. 38, has pointed out that this
was also the view of the Committee of 1878 on Land Titles and Transfer—
'To legislate for the registration of titles without, as a preliminary step,
simplifying the titles to be registered, is to begin at the wrong end'.

[3] *Supra*, pp. 115–20.

result in a definite decision of the long controverted question as to the expediency of a general compulsory system of registration of title.

The history of the manner in which the new Acts have assumed their present shape is shortly as follows: The story begins with a Bill of 1895, drafted by Wolstenholme and Sir Benjamin Cherry, which dealt with the subject-matter of Part I of the Act of 1922, i.e. the assimilation of the law of real and of personal property. This was followed by Draft Bills dealing with Settled Land, Conveyancing, Trustees, and Personal Representatives. In 1908 a Royal Commission was appointed to consider the working of the Land Transfer Acts, which was presided over by Lord St. Aldwyn. This was followed by Lord Haldane's Bill, introduced just before the war, the main object of which was to assimilate the law of real and personal property. The Committee set up in 1919 to advise as to the action to be taken to facilitate and cheapen the transfer of land, endorsed the views of the Royal Commission of 1908; and, with that object, requested Sir Benjamin Cherry to recast and put into one Bill the series of Draft Bills dealing with various parts of the land law. This Bill was introduced in the House of Lords by Lord Birkenhead in 1920. After many amendments in a Joint Committee of both Houses, and consultations with the Law Society and many other bodies, the Bill finally passed both Houses in 1922—a result which was, as Sir Leslie Scott has pointed out, due in great measure to the skill, knowledge, and tact of Lord Birkenhead. Subsequently the Act of 1922 (except those parts of it which relate to enfranchisement of copyholds, extinguishment of manorial incidents, and the conversion of perpetually renewable leases into long terms) was repealed, and its contents were split up into the series of Property Acts which have come into force this year. The whole series is, therefore, as follows: The parts of the Law of Property Act, 1922, which were not repealed, as amended by the Law of Property (Amendment) Act, 1924, and the Law of Property (Amendment) Act, 1924; the Law of Property Act, 1925; the Land Charges Act, 1925; the Settled Land Act, 1925; the Trustee Act, 1925; the Administration of Estates Act, 1925; the Land Registration Act, 1925; the Universities and College Estates Act, 1925.

The contents of these Acts to a large extent assemble, consolidate, and carry to their logical conclusion the reforms already made in the law by the legislation of the nineteenth century; and, where they introduce new law, in order to carry those reforms to their logical conclusion, they often reproduce suggestions which had already been made with this object in view. The simplification of tenure effected by getting rid of copyhold was thought desirable, but not possible, by the Real Property Commissioners in 1832;[1] but it is the logical result of the diminution of copyhold, which has followed from the facilities given for its enfranchisement by the legislation of the nineteenth century. Obviously the abolition of such customs as borough English and gavelkind was also the logical consequence both of the simplification of tenure and of the new scheme of intestate succession introduced by the Acts. We have seen that the reduction in the number of estates to estates in fee-simple and for a term of years absolute had been suggested by Wolstenholme as early as 1862,[2] and that the repeal of the Statute of Uses had been suggested by Joshua Williams in the same year, and by the Commissioners who reported in 1878–9.[3] That a new system of intestate succession for all kinds of property was needed had been emphasized by Maitland in 1879.[4] It was, in fact, necessary, both in order to assimilate the law of real and personal property and in order to pave the way to a simplified law as to the administration of assets. From the latter point of view, it carries to its logical conclusion the change made by Part I of the Land Transfer Act, 1897. The change in the manner of effecting a mortgage had been suggested by Joshua Williams in 1862, and by the Commissioners who reported in 1878–9.[5] The abolition of tenancies

---

[1] 'Having explained the reasons why it appears to us so expedient that copyhold tenure should be changed into common socage, we are obliged to confess that, after deep deliberation, we have not been able to discover any means of speedily attaining so desirable an object. . . . We have found the difficulties great in proportion as the need for change is urgent', *Third Report*, 17.   [2] *Supra*, p. 117.   [3] Ibid.

[4] *Collected Papers*, i. 171 seq.; *supra*, p. 119.

[5] Above, p. 118. Mr. Lightwood, *Law Journal*, xl. *N.S.* 46–7, has shown that in earlier days a mortgage by the demise of a term was the most usual way of effecting a mortgage; he points out that this is so stated by Davidson (2nd ed.), vol. ii, pt. ii, 852 note, and that it was the form required by section 27

in common had been suggested by Joshua Williams as early as 1862.[1] The great change made in the direction of cheapening and facilitating the transfer of land consists in the careful provisions for keeping equities off the title. To effect this object the Acts contain many new provisions, but these provisions had been, to some extent, foreshadowed by the machinery of the Settled Land Acts and the Land Charges Acts. This clearly appears from the memorandum of 1921 on the Law of Property Bill:[2]

'Whilst preserving the present law that a purchaser for value of a legal estate in land can in good faith, without notice, obtain a good title, it reduces the number of cases in which a purchaser will be affected by notice to a minimum. This reduction is effected—(a) by introducing a trust for sale in certain cases; (b) by adopting and extending the principle of the Settled Land Acts, by which the conveyance by a person having the power of disposition overrides all the equities subsisting under the settlement—the equities attaching to the proceeds of the sale; (c) by requiring certain rights affecting the land to be registered in one of the registers kept under the Lands Charges (Registration and Searches) Acts, and making such rights liable to be overridden on a conveyance of the legal estate to a purchaser, unless the rights are registered, notwithstanding that the purchaser may have notice of them.'

This review of the statutes which have reformed the land law at different periods shows that, throughout the long history of this branch of the law, and right down to the recent legislation, three main tendencies have been apparent. In the first place, contrary to the usually received opinion, the legislature has had a larger share in shaping the land law than it has had in shaping any other branch of private law. At all periods in the history of the land law, statutes have been the parents of a great many of its fundamental principles, and the starting points of new epochs in its development. In the second place, the tendency, which Maitland discerned in the law of the thirteenth century, to make what

of the University and College Estates Act, 1858. This is also borne out by the fact that in the second edition of Bridgman's *Conveyances* (1690) there are several precedents of mortgages by demise, and only one of a mortgage in fee. For the reasons why this form was superseded see Davidson, loc. cit. and Mr. Lightwood's article.　　　　　　　　　　[1] *Supra*, p, 118.

　　[2] *Reports*, &c. 1921 (Cmd. 1287), vol. xxix, at p. 4.

was formerly the law for the great men the law for all, is also discernible all through its history. It was the desire of the owners of great estates to make permanent settlements of their property which caused directly the development and elaboration of some of the most salient characteristics of the land law of the eighteenth century, and indirectly the development of that rule against perpetuities which set a definite limit to the fulfilment of this desire. Most of the large powers which the law, as thus developed and elaborated at the instance of the owners of great estates, conferred on these landowners, belong now to all the landowners; for the new Acts allow nearly all the results, which could formerly be accomplished by the creation of legal estates, to be accomplished by the creation of equitable interests. In the third place, from the sixteenth century onwards, the law of real property and the law of personal property have exercised a reciprocal influence upon one another. This is very evident if we compare the law relating to chattels real with the law relating to freehold interests. The law relating to chattels real borrowed from the law relating to freehold interests some of its rules as to tenures and estates, and some of its rules relating to covenants which run with the land. On the other hand, the law relating to freehold has borrowed more from the law relating to chattels real. It has borrowed the power of devise, the form of action by which freeholds came to be protected, and the machinery by which they devolved upon the heir or devisee. Moreover, the rule against perpetuities, devised in the first instance to govern settlements of land, was extended to all kinds of property as soon as the necessity for so extending it appeared. The new Acts merely push this tendency to its logical conclusion. On the one hand, the rules regulating conveyances of land are designed to make (so far as this is possible) these conveyances as simple and cheap as the conveyances of personalty—the simplicity of a conveyance of stock and shares has been taken as an example to be followed; and one of the rules formerly only applicable to personalty—the rule in *Dearle* v. *Hall*—has been applied to land. On the other hand, the capacity to create an entailed interest has been extended to owners of personalty. For all kinds of property a new uniform system of succession on intestacy has been devised, which is much more akin to the old rules as to personalty than to the old rules as to realty.

Sir Leslie Scott, speaking of the new Acts, has said: 'This vast monument of human energy has been built by the hands of many builders. More than half a century of law reformers have contributed to it.' This is a considerable under-statement. If there is any truth in the history which I have endeavoured to relate in this paper, it would be more true to say that some five centuries of law reformers have contributed to it. Revolutionary as the new Acts may at first sight appear, they are historically the product of a long series of reforming statutes; and their provisions are a striking illustration of the continuity of the history of the legislative reform of the land law. They are, as Sir Leslie Scott has said, 'not revolution but evolution'. Like the other great reforms in the past, they will, no doubt, become the foundation upon which the judges will build up a new fabric of property law, related to the old in somewhat the same way as the modern law of real property, constructed on the basis of the Statutes of Uses and Wills, was related to the medieval land law.

THE FORMATION AND BREACH OF CONTRACT[1]

SOME of the rules of English law on the subject of the formation and the breach of contract differ widely from the law of countries on the continent of Europe, and of countries in other parts of the world which have been influenced by the law of continental Europe. The parts of English law relating to the formation of contract which present this contrast are, first, the classification of contracts into the two divisions of contracts under seal or specialty contracts, and contracts (verbal or written) which are not under seal or simple contracts; and, secondly, the rule that no simple contract is valid unless accompanied by a consideration. The parts of English law relating to the breach of contract which present this contrast are the rules which relate to the conditions under which the equitable remedies of specific performance and injunction can be obtained. It is the purpose of this paper to deal with the reasons why the rules of English law on these two matters have come to differ from other systems of law.

The Formation of Contract

Both in England and on the Continent we must begin the continuous history of the law of contract from the legal renaissance of the twelfth and thirteenth centuries. Justinian's *Corpus Juris* then began to be studied again in the original texts, and Gratian's *Decretum* began the *Corpus Juris Canonici*. Thus western Europe was introduced to the Roman law of contract; and, partly under the influence of modern needs, but chiefly under the influence of the canon lawyers, who insisted that it was a moral duty to keep faith, a law of contracts, which was based upon and yet was different from the law laid down in the *Corpus Juris*, began to be formed. English law felt these influences. This is evident from Glanvil's book which comes from the end of the twelfth century, and, more especially, from Bracton's book which comes from the middle of the thirteenth century. Since

[1] Reprinted from the *Tulane Law Review*, vol. ii, Feb. 1933.

English law in the time of Bracton had no developed law of contract, the part of Bracton's book which deals with contracts is based upon the Roman law which he had derived mainly from Azo. In fact Bracton uses the works of the civilians and canonists in very much the same way as the French lawyers who wrote summaries of the French customary law in the *pays de coutumes* in the thirteenth, fourteenth, and fifteenth centuries. He uses them to supply a theory of contract, and to fill up other gaps in the common law.[1] If the King's courts had continued to be staffed by men like Bracton, who were learned in *utroque jure*, the theory of contract taught by the civilians and canonists might have become the theory of English law, and English rules as to the formation of contract would have been the same as those of the Continent. But, at the end of the thirteenth century, judges of the school of Bracton gave place to judges of another kind. The Bench began to be recruited from practitioners in the King's courts—from men who knew little else than their own native system of law. That meant that the law of contract, like other branches of English law, began to be developed on native lines, and therefore began to diverge widely from those systems of law upon which the influence of civilian and canonist doctrine was continuous. As Maitland has said, the new learning of the civilians and the canonists, 'found a small, well conquered, much governed kingdom, a strong, a legislating kingship. It came to us soon; it taught us much; and then there was healthy resistance to foreign dogma.'[2]

It was this cessation of the direct influence of the civil and canon law on English law at a comparatively early date, and the continuance of that influence on systems of continental law, which are the causes of the divergence of the English rules as to the formation of contract from the continental rules. Let us glance briefly first at the continental development,[3] and then at the English development.

---

[1] Holdsworth, *H.E.L.* (3rd ed. 1922), ii. 270; Esmein, *Histoire du droit Français* (15ᵉ éd. 1925), 791–2, 796–840.

[2] Pollock and Maitland, *H.E.L.* (2nd ed. 1899), i. 24.

[3] Lorenzen, 'Causa and Consideration in Contracts', *Yale L. Journ.* xxviii. 621 (1919); Walton, 'Cause and Consideration in Contracts', *L.Q.R.* xli. 306 (1925); Holdsworth, op. cit. viii. 42–8.

The civilians, following the Roman texts, insisted that a pact was not a contract unless it was accompanied by a *causa*. *Ex nudo pacto non oritur actio*. But it was difficult to see in what the *causa* consisted in the case of the consensual contracts and the *pacta vestita*. Substantially in these cases nude pacts were actionable. The canonists, insisting that faith must be kept, either dispensed with a *causa*, or so generalized and attenuated the requirement of *causa* that it tended to become almost invisible. In Italy and Germany and Scotland the *causa* disappeared, and it was recognized that nude pacts would give rise to an action. In France and in Roman-Dutch law the need for a *causa* was still insisted on; but it was a generalized and an attenuated *causa*. Sir Frederick Pollock, speaking of the *causa* of French law, says: 'The existence of a natural, *i.e.*, moral obligation, or even of a real or supposed duty in point of honour only, may be quite enough. Nay, the deliberate intention of conferring a gratuitous benefit, when such intention exists, is a sufficient foundation for a binding unilateral promise';[1] and a decision of the Judicial Committee of the Privy Council shows that the same propositions are true in Roman-Dutch law.[2] It is not, therefore, surprising to find that considerable difficulty has been experienced in making a satisfactory definition of this attenuated *cause* or *causa*. Consequently there is a strong tendency to follow the law of those countries which have rejected the necessity for any kind of *causa*. This tendency is observable both amongst French and Roman-Dutch lawyers. Professor Lee, for instance, calls the requirement of *causa* 'a juristic figment', and says that it means little more than that 'an agreement to be legally enforceable must be entered upon with a serious and deliberate mind'.[3]

Azo, speaking of the consensual contracts, had said that, in their case, the vestment which clothed the nude pact was *elegans et tenuis*.[4] This *elegans et tenuis* vestment was in fact, like the new clothes of the emperor in Hans Andersen's fairy tale, no clothes at all; but it has taken a long time to

[1] Pollock, *Contracts* (5th ed. 1889), 692.
[2] *Jayawickreme* v. *Amarasuriya*, [1918] A.C. 869, 875.
[3] Lee, *Introduction to Roman-Dutch Law* (2nd ed. 1926), 198 (cf. ibid., 4th ed., 441).
[4] Walton, 'Cause and Consideration in Contracts', *L.Q.R.* xli, 306, 313 (1925).

find out the fact—so great has been the influence of the civil law. That the fact has now been discovered by many writers on French and Roman-Dutch law is clear. Professor Lee, speaking of Roman-Dutch law, says, 'any pact whatever is enforceable, provided only that it is freely entered upon by competent persons for an object which is physically possible and legally permissible';[1] and the same description, it would seem, might be given either of the actual state of the law, or of the state to which it is approximating, in all civilized countries which are not governed by the English common law.

The English development of the law of contract was very different. Owing to the cessation of the influence of the civil and canon law at the end of the thirteenth century, English lawyers were obliged to construct for themselves their own law of contract. They constructed it, as they constructed other branches of English law, on the foundation of the royal writs, that is, on the foundation of the remedies provided by the royal courts for the redress of injuries. The substantive law grew up gradually round these royal writs; and the main outlines of that law still retain many marks of its origin. These writs gave birth to distinct forms of action; and, as Maitland has said,[2] though 'we have buried these forms of action they still rule us from their graves'. Since the English law of contract was constructed in this way it is not surprising to find that some of its principal rules as to the formation of contract bear abundant marks of, and can only be explained by, their procedural origin.

At the end of the thirteenth century the two writs which were available for the enforcement of certain kinds of contract were the writ of convenant and the writ of debt. The writ of covenant was a general remedy which covered almost the entire field of agreement, but it was only available if the agreement was in writing and under seal. Hence agreements in writing and under seal (specialty contracts) fall into a distinct class; and in course of time come to differ in several respects from contracts not under seal (simple contracts)— e.g., the length of time which bars the right of action upon them differs, and for a long time the specialty debts of a

---

[1] Lee, op. cit., 4th ed., 225.
[2] Maitland, *The Forms of Action at Common Law* (reissued 1936: see *infra*, p. 216), 2.

deceased person were paid, before his debts upon simple contracts. The writ of debt was not a purely contractual remedy, but it could be used to enforce a contract if one of the parties thereto had performed his part, and could show that, in consequence, the other owed him a fixed sum of money. Hence it came to be said that an agreement was enforceable by writ of debt if the plaintiff could prove that he had given a *quid pro quo* to the defendant, and so conferred a benefit upon him. The benefit which was thus conferred by the plaintiff on the defendant has had some influence in the formation of that doctrine of consideration which is the most distinctive feature in the English law as to the formation of contract. But, as we shall now see, the origins and the most essential features of that doctrine originated in another form of action which, in course of time, superseded the action of debt.

Old procedural rules made the action of debt an inconvenient action, but its greatest defect was its incapacity to enforce executory contracts. A general remedy for the breach of simple contracts was found in the rise and gradual extension of a new action—the action of assumpsit. This action was originally an offshoot of the actions of trespass and deceit, and, when it first made its appearance, it was a delictual action. It lay when a man had agreed (assumpsit) to do something, and had done it badly, with the result that the plaintiff was injured. Later it was extended to cases when a man had agreed to do something, and had failed to do it, with the result that the plaintiff was injured, provided that the plaintiff, as the result of and relying upon the making of the agreement, had altered his position to his detriment. Finally it was extended to cases when a man had promised to do something in return for a counter-promise by the other party—in other words it was extended to remedy the breach of purely executory contracts. The action of assumpsit thus became the principal remedy for breach of contract, and the only available remedy for most simple contracts. It is to it that we must look for the origin of the doctrine of consideration; for that doctrine is, for the most part, simply the compendious word which describes the different conditions under which the action of assumpsit lay.

The classical definition of consideration runs as follows:

'A valuable consideration in the sense of the law, may consist either in some right, interest, profit, or benefit accruing to the one party, or some forbearance, detriment, loss, or responsibility, given, suffered, or undertaken by the other.'[1]

The idea that consideration may consist in a benefit accruing to one party is derived from the *quid pro quo* which a plaintiff must prove that he had given in order to succeed in an action of debt. The idea that consideration may consist in some detriment suffered by the other party is derived from the conditions under which the action of assumpsit lay. To succeed in that action a plaintiff must prove either that he incurred a detriment on the faith of the promise made to him by the other party, or that he made a counter-promise in return for the other party's promise.

In the same way other rules as to what is, and what is not, a valid consideration are logical inferences from the conditions in which the action of assumpsit lay. Thus, a past act done by A for the benefit of B, which is wholly unconnected with a subsequent promise made by B to A, is not a valid consideration for that promise.[2] Suppose, for instance, A rescues B from drowning, and then B writes to A expressing his gratitude and promising to pay A £100, the rescue is not a valid consideration for the promise. It is merely a motive for the promise, and motive is not the same thing as consideration.[3] On the other hand, suppose A does a service for B, which at the time both parties recognize must be paid for, a subsequent promise to pay is treated 'either as an admission which evidences, or as a positive bargain which fixes, the amount of that reasonable remuneration on the faith of which the service was originally rendered'.[4] The service here is an executed consideration for the promise. It follows that a merely moral obligation is not a valid consideration for a promise, for such an obligation is regarded either as a past act unconnected with the subsequent promise, or merely as a motive for the promise.[5] In fact, as Lord Denman said in the case of *Eastwood* v. *Kenyon*,[6] the doctrine that a moral obligation was a sufficient consideration 'would

[1] *Currie* v. *Missa* (1875), L.R. 10 Ex. 153, 162.
[2] *Roscorla* v. *Thomas* (1842), 3 Q.B. 234.
[3] *Thomas* v. *Thomas* (1842), 2 Q.B. 851.
[4] *Stewart* v. *Casey*, [1892] 1 Ch. 104, 115–16.
[5] *Eastwood* v. *Kenyon* (1840), 11 Ad. & E. 438.   [6] Ibid. at p 450.

annihilate the necessity for any consideration at all, inasmuch as the mere fact of giving a promise creates a moral obligation to perform it'. Again, although the detriment to the plaintiff need not have resulted in any benefit to the defendant, the form of the action made it necessary that the detriment incurred on the faith of the promise should have been incurred by the plaintiff to whom the promise was made. In other words, consideration must move or come from the promisee.[1] So, too, if A is bound by his contract with B to pay him a certain sum, the payment of a less sum cannot be a valid consideration for a promise by B to give A a discharge for his debt;[2] and on the same principle the performance by A of his contractual duty to B is probably no consideration for a promise by C to A; for A has only done what he is legally liable to do, just as when he pays part of his debt to B.[3] In neither case is there any detriment to A, the promisee, which can afford a consideration for a further promise. Thus, just as the doctrine of consideration is derived mainly from the conditions in which a contract was enforced by the action of assumpsit, so the main rules which make up that doctrine are logical deductions from those conditions.

The fact that an exposition of the English theory of the formation of contract must take account, first of the division into specialty and simple contracts, and, secondly, in the case of simple contracts, of the doctrine of consideration, is a striking testimony to the manner in which the English law of contract has been built up around, and has been conditioned by the development of, the common law actions by means of which contracts were enforced. We shall now see that this fact explains and illustrates the essential continuity of common law doctrine; and that it is also one of the most striking illustrations of the strength of the common law tradition, as compared with other elements which have gone to make up the fabric of modern English law.

In the history of English law there were two periods when

---

[1] *Tweddle* v. *Atkinson* (1861), 1 B. & S. 393, 121 Eng. Rep. R. 762.

[2] *Foakes* v. *Beer* (1884), L.R. 9 A.C. 605.

[3] Pollock, *Contracts* (11th ed.), 150. Probably a promise by A to C to perform his (A's) contractual duty to B is good consideration for a promise by C to A, since a promise is a valid consideration for a promise, see ibid. 200, 201; Holdsworth, op. cit. viii. 40, 41.

this common law theory of contract might have been replaced by a very different theory of contract—a theory which would have brought English law into much closer touch with continental law. The first of these periods was the fifteenth century. The inadequacy of the remedies given by the common law for breach of simple contract was the occasion of many applications to the equity of the Chancellor, who, as we shall see, was prepared to supplement, and, if necessary, correct the inadequacy or harshness of common law rules, on grounds of fairness and justice.[1] The records of the Chancery show that the Chancellor, in cases of contract, was prepared to accept those rules of the civilians and canonists which enforced all agreements which were accompanied by a *causa* or *cause* of the very generalized type which has been described above.[2] If the common lawyers had not so developed their action of assumpsit that it became an adequate remedy for the enforcement of contracts, the English theory of contract might have been developed by the Court of Chancery on these lines. But the development of that action by the common lawyers caused the Chancery to abandon a general jurisdiction over the law of contract, and to retain it only when the common law remedy of damages was insufficient.[3] The effects of this retention in the case of one particular class of contracts will be dealt with in a subsequent part of this paper.[4] Here we need only note that the abandonment by the Court of Chancery of a general jurisdiction over the law of contract left the theory of the formation of contract to the common law. The second of these periods was in the latter part of the eighteenth and the beginning of the nineteenth centuries. Lord Mansfield, who was the Chief Justice of the King's Bench from 1756 to 1788, was one of the greatest commercial lawyers England has ever produced, and the greatest legal mind of the eighteenth century. He tried to establish two revolutionary propositions in the law of contract. In the first place, he held that consideration was not essential to the validity of a simple contract, but was only evidence of its conclusion; so that if

[1] Holdsworth, op. cit. ii. 344–7.
[2] Ibid. v. 294, 295.
[3] Ibid. 321, 322.
[4] *Infra*, p. 139.

a contract was reduced to writing no consideration was necessary.[1] In the second place, he held that a moral obligation
was a valid consideration.[2] The first of these propositions
was soon overruled;[3] but the second obtained for some time
a considerable measure of acceptance.[4]

Lord Mansfield, being a Scot, had something of the mentality of the Scottish lawyer. Lord Macmillan, in what was
perhaps the most interesting of the papers read at the International Congress of Comparative Law, held at The Hague
in 1933, has explained that the mind of Scottish lawyers,
because it had been trained in Roman law, was orderly,
systematic, and logical. 'The Scottish nation', he says, 'has
always been credited with a special aptitude for philosophy
and a special devotion to logical principles. Consequently the
systematic and orderly scheme of the Roman law appealed
with an irresistible attraction to the Scottish national genius.'
Moreover, these intellectual characteristics were accentuated
by the severely logical character of the Calvinistic theology
of their Presbyterian churches. On the other hand, the English lawyer had built up his system by the inductive and empirical case system. Logic he had—the system of special
pleading was often dominated excessively by pure logic. But
his logic was always subordinated to the rules which had been
gradually and to a large extent empirically developed from
the cases. And the theology taught by the English Church
was, as compared with the logical Calvinistic creed, a somewhat eclectic compromise. Hence, as Lord Macmillan says,
the contrast between the English and the Scottish lawyer is a
contrast 'between the two main schools of legal thought, the
logical and the empirical'. It was therefore only natural that
Lord Mansfield should seek to rationalize and reduce to
some sort of principle many of those rules of English law
which could be explained historically, but could hardly be
justified logically. Therefore he tried to do for the rules relating to the formation of contract what he tried to do for the
rules of seisin and the rules as to the relationship of law and
equity. But in all these cases he failed to make any impres-

[1] *Pillans* v. *Van Mierop* (1765), 3 Burr. 1663.
[2] *Hawkes* v. *Saunders* (1782), 1 Cowper 289.
[3] *Rann* v. *Hughes* (1778), 7 T.R. 350.
[4] Holdsworth, op. cit. viii. 30-3.

sion on the settled rules of English law. If he had succeeded he would have made the rules of English law more rational; but he would have made a large break in the continuous development of those rules. In particular, if his views as to the nature of consideration, or as to the efficacy of a moral obligation, had been received as orthodox doctrine, a considerable approach would have been made to the continental theory of contract.[1]

In the nineteenth century both of these propositions were rejected. The procedural origin of the doctrine of consideration was recalled, and the modern law was, as we have seen,[2] settled on this basis. No doubt the resulting theory of contract has its strong points. As Sir Frederick Pollock has said, 'roughly stated it seems plain and sensible, the courts will hold people to their bargains, but will not enforce gratuitous promises unless they are made in solemn form'.[3] But of recent years many lawyers have come to the conclusion that this theory of contract is somewhat of an anachronism, and that its disadvantages outweigh its advantages.[4] Since the substantive law has long ago broken loose from the leading strings of the forms of action, it is an anachronism that the law as to the formation of contract should still perpetuate, in the distinction between specialty and simple contracts, the limitations of the writ of convenant; and that the law as to simple contracts should still be dominated by a doctrine which has been historically developed with great logical precision from the procedural requirements of the form of action by which those contracts were enforced. There is, I think, much to be said for Lord Mansfield's view that consideration should be treated, not as the sole test of the validity of a simple contract, but only as evidence of its conclusion. If the legislature were to adopt that view, and if, at the same time, it got rid of the distinction between simple and specialty contracts, English law would make a much closer approach to continental law. For the result would be that any lawful agreement into which the parties to it entered with the intention of affecting their legal relations, would, if

[1] Ibid. 34; Pollock, *Contracts* (11th ed.), 145.
[2] *Supra*, pp. 133, 134.
[3] Pollock, *Genius of the Common Law* (1912), 91.
[4] Holdsworth, op. cit. viii. 46, 47.

it could be proved by adequate evidence, be enforceable.[1] But, as the law of continental states shows, it would then be necessary to make some provision as to the necessary evidence to be adduced to prove, first the formation of an agreement, and, secondly, the fact that the parties intended, when they agreed, to affect their legal relations. To meet these difficulties I have suggested in the *History of English Law* that it might be advisable to enact that all lawful agreements, intended by the parties to affect their legal relations, should be enforceable as contracts either if consideration was proved, or if they were put into writing and signed by the parties thereto.[2]

Breach of Contract

Perhaps the most distinctive feature in the English legal system is the manner in which the rules of the common law and the rules of equity have been kept separate. The distinction between law and equity is not peculiar to the English legal system. That distinction is as old as Aristotle; and it was known in substance to the classical Roman lawyers and to the medieval canonists and civilians.[3] It is based, as Lord Ellesmere said in the *Earl of Oxford's Case*[4] on the fact that 'men's actions are so divers and infinite, that it is impossible to make any general law which may aptly meet with every particular act, and not fail in some circumstances'. It is in fact a universal distinction. What is peculiar to England is the sharpness of the separation between the rules of law and equity. That phenomenon is due to the fact that the rules of law and the rules of equity were administered by distinct tribunals using a distinct procedure; and that in consequence two separate systems of rules grew up, which occasionally conflicted with, but were more often supplementary to, one another. The historical reason for this peculiarity of English law is the fact that, in the fourteenth century, the rules administered by the common law courts

---

[1] Holdsworth, op. cit. viii. 47, 48.

[2] Ibid. 48; cf. Sixth Interim Report of the Law Revision Committee (1937), 18.

[3] Pollock, *Essays in Legal History* (1913), 286; Vinogradoff, 'Reason and Conscience in Sixteenth Century Jurisprudence', *L.Q.R.* xxiv. 374, 375 (1908); cf. Vinogradoff, *Historical Jurisprudence* (1914), ii. 63, 64.

[4] (1615), 1 Ch. Rep. 1, 6.

had become so rigid and so technical that they failed to find any place for equity, and, consequently, failed to provide adequate remedies for litigants.[1] Litigants who needed equity applied to the King, who referred them to his Chancellor—the keeper of his conscience. Thus the Chancellor and his department, the Chancery, came to be the court which administered equity. That court was not fettered by the rigid procedural rules of the common law courts, and it deliberately set out to remedy, on equitable grounds, the defects of the common law. Thus in England, law and equity came to be administered by distinct courts, and not, as at Rome, by the same court. It is for this reason that Justinian was able to effect what the English Judicature Acts could not effect. He fused law and equity: they, for the most part, only fused the courts and the procedure of the courts which administered law and equity. This dualism has left its mark upon many branches of English law. In the law of contract it is most marked in its effect on the law as to the remedies available for breach of contract.

We have seen that there was a time when the common law conception of contract was so narrow that it seemed likely that the development of the law of contract would be taken over by equity. But we have seen that the common law courts, menaced by this competition, so extended the action of assumpsit that the common law acquired an adequate conception of contract.[2] The Court of Chancery therefore withdrew from the greater part of the field of contract, and accepted the conception of contract worked out by the common law courts; for equity did not interfere with the law when the law was adequate. But in one respect the common law was still defective—for the breach of a contract it gave only damages. If, therefore, something more than damages was wanted, it was still necessary to have recourse to equity. Thus the rules as to the kinds of specific relief which are available for breach of contract, and the conditions under which this relief can be obtained, are the product of equity.

The rules of equity were at first nebulous. The Chancellor tried to come to the ideally just decision after examining all the facts of each case. Hence Selden's gibe that the

[1] Holdsworth, op. cit. ii. 344–7.
[2] *Supra*, p. 135.

Chancellor's equity was a wholly uncertain thing; for, he said, the consciences of individual Chancellors are as various as the size of their feet. But, by degrees, the principles upon which the Chancellor administered equity were reduced to system. This process was complete at the end of the eighteenth century. Lord Eldon said in 1818 that nothing would give him greater pain than the thought that he had done anything to justify the reproach that the equity of the Court of Chancery varies like the Chancellor's foot; and that the doctrines of equity 'ought to be as well settled and made as uniform, *almost*, as those of the common law'.[1] Note the word 'almost'. There is still an element of discretion about some of the rules of equity, and the remedies given by equity are always discretionary. If a contract is broken, the injured party has a legal right to recover the damages due to him in accordance with the rules of law which fix the measure of damages. But, if he is asking for an equitable remedy, the court can withhold it if, in the circumstances, it thinks it ought not to be given.

This contrast between legal and equitable remedies for breach of contract is illustrated by the case of *Re Scott and Alvarez's Contract*.[2] A purchaser bought property and paid a deposit under a condition of sale which barred him from making inquiries into the title. In fact the vendor had no title at all. It was held that the condition of sale precluded him from bringing an action at law to recover the deposit; but that, in the circumstances, the court would refuse specific performance of the contract.[3] Therefore, because the dif-

---

[1] *Gee* v. *Pritchard* (1818), 2 Swans. 402, 414.

[2] [1895] 2 Ch. 603; the actual decision in this case is no longer law, since, by the Law of Property Act (1925), § 49 (2), the court, if it refuses specific performance, may order the repayment of the deposit; but the statement of principle in that case illustrates the distinction between the rigid conditions which govern the award of legal remedies, and the discretionary character of equitable remedies.

[3] After holding that the purchaser could not recover his deposit by an action at law, Lindley L.J. said: 'When we come to the remedy of specific performance we get into an entirely different region of law. The extraordinary remedy of specific performance is always more or less open to discretion; and I am not aware of any case in which, unless the condition has been extremely clear, a court of equity has ever forced a purchaser to take a title which is shown to be bad, and which will expose the purchaser to an immediate law suit against which he will have no defence . . . The vendor

ferent forms of specific relief are the creation of equity, there is an element of discretion in awarding them which is not present in the common law remedy of damages.

The two forms of specific relief about which I propose to say a few words are the remedy of specific performance for the breach of executory contracts, and the remedy of injunction.

Specific Performance

By far the most common class of cases in which the remedy of specific performance is sought are contracts for the sale of interests in land. This is due to two causes. In the first place, damages are not a sufficient remedy for the breach of a contract to buy an estate in land. It is not possible, as in the case of a contract to buy ordinary chattels, to go into the market and buy with the money awarded as damages, a precisely similar estate. In the second place, on a contract for the sale of specific chattels the property in the chattels passes without delivery: on a contract for the sale of land the property does not pass. It does not pass until a conveyance in pursuance of the contract has been made. As Fry says in his book on *Specific Performance*:

'In a jurisprudence where contract and transfer are effected by the same instrument, a jurisdiction in specific performance could hardly arise: but when contract is separated from conveyance by all the formalities and delay of an examination into title, and the preparation of a formal deed, it would be a necessity to anything like a civilized system of law.'[1]

Because, in the first place, the grant of the remedy of specific performance was an equitable remedy, and therefore discretionary, equity has laid down certain rules as to the conditions under which it will grant the remedy, which differ from the common law rules as to the conditions under which damages can be obtained. Because, in the second place, this remedy is generally applied for in contracts for the sale of interests in land, and because the English land law is very complex, equity has developed many detailed rules as to the

must not come and invoke the extraordinary jurisdiction of a court of equity to do what would be a manifest injustice.' *Re Scott and Alvarez's Contract,* [1895] 2 Ch. 603, 612–14.
    [1] Fry, *Specific Performance,* 6th ed. (1920), § 37.

incidents of these contracts, which have no parallel in the common law rules as to contracts which are not specifically enforceable. Let us look briefly at these equitable rules from these two points of view.

(1) Equity has always refused to grant the remedy unless it is certain that it would be fair to both parties to grant it. This has led equity sometimes to refuse to grant it although there is a perfectly valid contract. For instance, equity will never specifically enforce a contract at the suit of a party who has given no consideration, although it is under seal:[1] and it will never grant this remedy unless both the parties to the contract have a right of action upon it. Thus an infant can at law bring an action upon a contract to buy land, but no action can be brought against him. In such a case there is said to be 'a want of mutuality'; and this 'want of mutuality' is a defence to an action for specific performance.[2] Conversely, equity, in at least one case, grants specific performance, although the contract is not enforceable at law. Equity has always acted on the principle that the parties to a contract must not make the provisions of a statute, which enacts that a contract or other transaction shall be drawn up with certain formalities, an instrument of fraud or sharp practice. The Statute of Frauds provides that contracts for the sale of interests in land shall not be enforceable by action unless they are in writing and signed by the party to be charged. But suppose that there is a verbal contract between A and B that A shall buy B's house, and suppose that B allows A to take possession of the house, and spend money on it on the faith of the contract, equity regards it as unfair that B should then repudiate the contract, and, when sued, rely on the defence of the Statute of Frauds. On this ground equity specifically enforces this verbal contract, though no action at law can be brought upon it. This is known as the equitable doctrine of part performance.[3]

(2) The incidents of a contract for the sale of an interest in land are necessarily very different from the incidents of a contract for the sale of chattels. The title to the property must be examined, and the law lays down rules as to the length and kind of title which must be shown. These rules

[1] Fry, *Specific Performance* (6th ed.), § 116.   [2] Ibid., § 460.
[3] Ibid., §§ 561, 578, 585, 586.

as to title may be varied by conditions of sale; and there is much law as to the construction of clauses in these conditions of sale. Questions as to the acreage and description of the property, which is the subject of the contract, have given rise to many questions. When the court is asked to grant specific performance it may have to consider problems arising out of these questions, and ask itself whether it is fair, in the circumstances, to grant the remedy; and, if it decides to grant it, it may consider it fair that the contract should be enforced, not as it stands, but with some variations, some abatement of the price, or some compensation for a slight defect in acreage.

In these ways, then, through the working of the remedy of specific performance, equity has created the largest part of the law relating to contracts for the sale of interests in land. Because these contracts have been developed by equity, the law which regulates their incidents differs from the law which regulates the incidents of contracts for the sale of chattels. The question whether or not this separation between law and equity, and the consequent diversity of legal and equitable rules, is convenient, and beneficial to the English legal system as a whole, will be dealt with later. Here it will be sufficient to say that even if the law as to the remedies for the breach of contracts to sell land and chattels had been developed in the same jurisdiction, and not in the separate jurisdictions of law and equity, the differences in the physical characteristics of land and chattels, and of still greater differences in the law as to property in land and property in chattels, would have caused the law relating to the sale of interests in land to differ considerably from the law relating to the sale of chattels. I pass now to the remedy of an injunction.

Injunctions

An injunction is an order issued by the Chancery Division of the High Court ordering a person to forbear from a course of conduct or to do a specific act. The most common class of injunctions are prohibitory—they order a forbearance. But the court can issue a mandatory injunction—an injunction ordering an act to be done. The power of the court to issue injunctions has had large effects on many different branches of English law. In the sphere of public law and of company law injunctions have helped to develop the doctrine of *ultra vires*. In the sphere of the law of tort they have helped to make the law more effective by restraining threatened and continuing torts—notably nuisances and the infringement of easements. In the sphere of property law they have created the law as to equitable waste, and the law as to those negative covenants which run with the land in equity; and they have developed the law as to the infringements of such rights as trade names, trade marks, and copyright. In the sphere of the law of contract, they have, as we shall now see, added a valuable remedy for certain breaches of contract.

The use of injunctions to enforce the obligations of parties to contracts has given rise to a complex body of law which is closely related to the analogous topic of specific performance. It would be impossible, even in outline, to describe this body of law. All I can do is to state one or two illustrations of the sort of cases in which an injunction can be used to remedy a breach of contract.

First, if a contract to sell land is specifically enforceable, an injunction will be granted in aid of specific performance. Thus, if an action for specific performance is pending, and it is clear that there is a contract to sell, the court will grant an injunction to restrain the vendor from dealing with the property pending the action.[1] Secondly, if there is an express negative stipulation in a contract, a party to the contract is prima facie entitled to an injunction to restrain the breach of it; but, in the case of a positive stipulation, the court must consider, *inter alia*, the physical possibility of enforcing it in this way, whether damages would be an adequate compensation, and whether, in the circumstances, an injunction would do justice to the parties.[2] Thirdly, the court will not grant an injunction to enforce a positive covenant, if the contract is not specifically enforceable, e.g., a contract for personal services.[3] Fourthly, if the case is one in which an injunction ought to be granted, it will be issued to stop, not only a com-

---

[1] *Preston* v. *Luck* (1884), 27 Ch. D. 497.

[2] *Doherty* v. *Allman* (1878), 3 A.C. 709, 719–21, *per* Cairns L.C.

[3] *Whitwood Chemical Co.* v. *Hardman*, [1891] 2 Ch. 416, 427, *per* Lindley L.J.

pleted breach of contract, but also an apprehended breach.[1]
These illustrations make it clear that the equitable remedy
of an injunction is a flexible and very valuable addition to
the common law remedy of an action for damages.

I have admitted when dealing with the formation of contract, that the doctrine of consideration, because it is simply
the translation into terms of substantive law of the procedural necessities of the action by which single contracts
were enforced, is, at the present day, an anachronism.[2] Is
it also true to say that this distinction between legal and
equitable remedies for breach of contract, because it is based
on the originally separate jurisdiction of the courts of common law and the Courts of Chancery, is equally an anachronism? I think that the answer is in the negative. It is true
that a legislator, preparing a code of laws on logical principles, would never divide the field of law, as English law
is divided, into the two supplementary parts of law and
equity. But I think that it may be maintained that the
system under which different remedies are granted under
different conditions in case of the breach of different kinds
of contract is defensible in principle; and I think that it can
also be maintained that, in practice, the relations of law and
equity are so adjusted that no inconvenience is caused to
suitors. It might, indeed, appear at first sight that the co-
existence of two separate systems of law and equity would be
productive of great inconvenience. At the end of the eighteenth century Lord Mansfield tried to bring about a certain
measure of fusion. He failed to effect this; and the two systems continued to be separate supplementary systems, which
worked in harmony with one another.[3] The Judicature Acts
effected a fusion between the courts of law and equity, made
provision for a uniform code of procedure, and gave to the
judges of the High Court the power to administer both law
and equity. But they did not fuse the substantive rules of
common law and equity. Matters which formerly fell within
the jurisdiction of the common law courts are decided by
legal rules, and matters which formerly fell within the

[1] *Tipping* v. *Eckersley* (1855), 2 K. & J. 264, 270.
[2] *Supra*, p. 137.
[3] Holdsworth, 'Blackstone's Treatment of Equity', *Harv. L. Rev.* xliii. 1,
8–10, 16–21 (1929).

jurisdiction of the court of Chancery by equitable rules. They provided, indeed, that in case of a conflict the rules of equity were to prevail. But the fact that very few cases of conflict have emerged, proves that the working arrangement between the two sets of rules had been skilfully effected, and had been successful in practice.[1]

In fact there is a long tradition of co-operation between the two sets of rules, and the results produced are not unsatisfactory. It must always be remembered that, in considering the merits and defects of a legal system, considerably more stress must be laid upon the convenience to suitors, to practitioners, and to judges, of adhering to a system to which they are accustomed, than upon the claims of pure logic. However logical a code may be, if it is not understood by those who apply it and by those whom it governs, it will not produce results as good as a less logical system which has worked well for a long time, and which is understood. In time the action of the legislature, and the working of a uniform Supreme Court of Judicature with a uniform code of procedure, may produce a fusion between law and equity; and in time, the fact that the different remedies provided by the law for breach of contract were originally legal or originally equitable may be a matter of merely antiquarian interest. But, even if this happens, the substantial conditions upon which the different remedies can be obtained must continue to differ very much as they differ to-day. If that is true, I think that it can be maintained that the divergence between the legal remedies for breach of contract dispensed by the King's Bench Division of the High Court, and the equitable remedies dispensed by the Chancery Division, is not productive of practical inconvenience.

[1] Maitland, *Equity* (reissued 1936), 16–17, 149–59.

CASE LAW[1]

O F recent years there has been a good deal of discussion, from the jurisprudential point of view, of the merits and demerits of the Anglo-American system of case law. Outstanding contributions to this discussion are Professor Winfield's chapter on Case Law in his *Chief Sources of English Legal History*;[2] Professor C. K. Allen's two chapters on the nature and history, and on the authority and operation, of precedent in his *Law in the Making*;[3] and more especially Professor Goodhart's inaugural lecture on 'Precedent in English and Continental Law', which is published in the *Law Quarterly Review* of this year.[4] In this paper I propose to say something of the final establishment of the modern theory as to the authority of decided cases, of the reservations and conditions subject to which that theory has been accepted, and of some of the criticisms which have been passed upon it.

The modern theory as to the authority of decided cases was reached substantially by the end of the eighteenth century.[5] If we look at it superficially, it appears to be a simple theory. A decided case makes law for future cases, and will bind all inferior courts and generally courts of co-ordinate jurisdiction. But the more closely the theory is examined the less simple does it appear. Let us look at two statements of that theory. (i) One of the ablest books on this subject, entitled *The Science of Legal Judgment*, was published by

[1] Reprinted from (1934) 50 *L.Q.R.* 180.   [2] Chapter vii.
[3] Chapters iii and iv.   [4] 50 *L.Q.R.* 40–65.
[5] Dr. C. K. Allen, *Law in the Making* (3rd ed.), 150–1, says that the modern theory 'is certainly a product of the nineteenth century'; I do not agree to this statement; I think that the modern theory was reached a good deal earlier. It seems to me that Professor Allen has not sufficiently observed the distinction between the general theory and the reservations with which that theory has been and is accepted; with these reservations I deal below (pp. 152–8); it is true that the character and force of these reservations have differed from age to age, and that some judges have at all periods attached more weight to some of them than other judges; but these facts do not affect the truth of the view that, subject to those reservations, they accepted the modern theory. [In the 3rd ed., p. 222, Dr. Allen writes, 'The substance (of the modern doctrine of precedents) ... had reached a high state of development by the end of the eighteenth century, but needed the continually improving mechanism of the succeeding age to give it final and definitive form.' Eds.]

James Ram in 1834. Ram states the theory in this way:[1]
'a case decided is called a precedent; and is an authority,
which, under many circumstances, binds a court to make the
same decision in a future similar case'. (ii) Sir Frederick
Pollock thus states the modern rule:[2] 'the decisions of an
ordinary superior court are binding on all courts of inferior
rank within the same jurisdiction, and though not absolutely
binding on courts of co-ordinate authority nor on that court
itself, will be followed in the absence of strong reasons to the
contrary. The decisions of a Court of Appeal are binding on
all courts of co-ordinate rank with the court below, and
generally, according to English practice, on the Appellate
Court itself.' These are guarded statements. The first says
that 'under many circumstances' a decision is authoritative.
The second tells us that in the case of a co-ordinate court,
appellate or otherwise, a decision will be followed 'in the
absence of strong reasons to the contrary', or that it is
'generally' binding. It is clear that, if we would understand
the modern theory as to the authority of decided cases, we
must try to discover the meaning, not only of the rule that
a decided case is an authority for deciding a similar case,
but also of the qualifications of that rule which make it
necessary to use such terms as 'under many circumstances',
or 'in the absence of strong reasons to the contrary', or
'generally'. We can only discover the meaning of the rule
and its qualifications if we examine the way in which the
modern theory was developed during the sixteenth, seventeenth, and eighteenth centuries.

In the Year Books of the later years of the Middle Ages
cases were cited and distinguished somewhat in the manner
in which they were cited and distinguished in later law.[3]
They were regarded as precedents of some authority. If
they had not been regarded as being of some authority it
would be difficult to see what value the Year Books would

[1] At p. 112.
[2] *A First Book of Jurisprudence* (6th ed.), 321–2.
[3] Holdsworth, *H.E.L.* ii. 541–2; see T. Ellis Lewis's papers on 'The
History of Judicial Precedent', *L.Q.R.* xlvi. 215–24, 326–60; xlvii. 411–27;
cf. Professor C. K. Allen, *Law in the Making* (3rd ed.), 178–91. I think that
Professor Winfield minimizes too much the part played by precedent during
the period of the Year Books in his *Sources of English Legal History*, 148–57.

have been to the legal profession.[1] But the modern theory as to the authority of decided cases could not begin to be developed, till the changes made at the end of the fifteenth and the beginning of the sixteenth centuries in the system of pleading concentrated the reporter's attention, not upon the oral debate in court as to what the pleading should be and what issue should be reached, but upon the decision of the court upon an issue reached by the written pleadings of the parties before the case had come into court.[2] It was the change in the style of law reporting, which followed upon this transition from the system of oral to the system of written pleadings, which made the growth of the modern theory as to the authority of decided cases possible;[3] and therefore, in the latter half of the sixteenth and at the beginning of the seventeenth centuries, the general rule that decided cases were authoritative was recognized in the Courts of Common Law,[3] in the Court of Chancery,[4] and in the Court of Star Chamber.[5] In fact from the sixteenth to the nineteenth century a chain of authority can be cited for this general rule.

In the early seventeenth century Bacon said: 'decided cases are the anchors of the laws, as laws are of the state.'[6] 'Our Booke Cases,' said Coke,[7] 'are the best proofes what the law is. . . . Booke Cases are principally to be cited for deciding of cases in question, and not any private opinion, teste me ipso'; and the multitude of citations of cases in his reports and other writings show that he believed in this statement.[8] This view is also taken by Hobart and Jenkins

[1] Thus Prisot C.J. said (Y.B. 33 Hen. VI, Mich. pl. 17, p. 41): 'Et Sir si ce serra or adjuge nul plee, come vous tenes, vraiment ce serra mal ensample aus juvenes apprentices que sont studients en Termes; car ils ne unques voillont doner credence a lour livres, si tiel jugment que ad este aussi moults fois ajuge en lour livres sera or ajuge le contrary.'

[2] Holdsworth, *H.E.L.* iii. 654–5; v. 371–3.

[3] Ibid. v. 372–3.   [4] Ibid. 275–6.

[5] Ibid. 162–4; Coke, 4 *Instit.* 64, records a case where 'the presidents of this court were to be searched; for except presidents could make a difference between this court and others, the defendant could not be sentenced'.

[6] 'Iudicia enim anchorae legum sunt, ut leges reipublicae', *De Augmentis*, bk. viii, Aph. 73.

[7] Co. *Litt.* 254a; cp. also f. 81b.

[8] Gray, *Nature and Sources of Law*, § 459, says, 'the contrast between all or any of the earlier reporters and Lord Coke is enormous, for with Lord Coke the citation of cases reached a height which it has never equalled since'.

in their reports.[1] It is true that, in the latter half of the seventeenth century, Vaughan C.J., after distinguishing mere *obiter dicta* from opinions necessary to the decision, and therefore truly judicial,[2] says that another court is not bound to follow a judicial opinion if it thinks that the judgment given was not according to law.[3] But Hale,[4] writing at the same period, though he admits that the courts cannot

'make a law properly so called; for that only the King and Parliament can do; yet they have a great weight and authority in expounding, declaring, and publishing what the law of this kingdom is, especially when such decisions hold a consonancy and congruity with resolutions and decisions of former times, and though such decisions are less than a law, yet they are a greater evidence thereof than the opinion of any private persons, AS SUCH, whatsoever. First, because the persons who pronounce those decisions, are men chosen by the king for that employment, as being of greater learning, knowledge, and experience in the laws, than others. Secondly, because they are upon their oaths, to judge according to the laws of the kingdom. Thirdly, because they have the best help to inform these judgments. Fourthly, because they do, *sedere pro tribunali*, and their judgments are strengthened and upheld by the laws of this kingdom, till they are by the same law reversed or avoided.'

In the eighteenth century it was realized that the distinction which Hale drew between a law properly so-called, and a decision which for the reasons he gives is a very strong evidence of law, was a little thin. In 1754 Lord Hardwicke .

[1] See the cases cited by Professor C. K. Allen, *Law in the Making* (3rd ed.), 194–5; I doubt whether the distinction there drawn between precedents in matters of pleading and procedure, and in other cases, is really important— decisions on these matters often involved a decision as to the substantive law.

[2] 'An extra judicial opinion given in, or out of Court, is no more than the prolatum or saying of him who gives it. . . . An opinion given in Court, if not necessary to the judgment given of record, but that it might have been as well given if no such, or a contrary, opinion had been broach'd, is no judicial opinion; but a mere gratis dictum. But an opinion, though erroneous, concluding to judgment, is a judicial opinion, because delivered under the sanction of the judge's oath': *Bole* v. *Horton* (1673), Vaughan, 360, 382.

[3] 'If a Court give judgment judicially, another Court is not bound to give like judgment, unless it think that judgment first given was according to law. For any Court may err. . . . Therefore, if a judge conceives a judgment, given in another Court, to be erroneous, he being sworn to judge according to law, that is, on his own conscience, ought not to give the like judgment, for that were to wrong every man having a like cause, because another was wrong'd before': Vaughan C.J. 360, 383.   [4] *Hist. of the Common Law* (6th ed.), 90.

said:[1] 'I think authorities established are so many laws; and
receding from them unsettles property; and uncertainty is
the unavoidable consequence.' This was in substance the
view of Blackstone.[2] It is true that he admits that a decision
which is contrary to reason or divine law cannot stand.[3] That
is only to be expected since he even denied the validity of
a statute which was contrary to divine law.[4] But he states
the general rule to be that the judges must 'abide by former
precedents when the same points come again in litigation'—
otherwise there could be no certainty in the law;[5] and he
minimizes the force of his admission that a decision contrary
to reason or divine law cannot stand, by saying that 'even in
such cases the subsequent judges do not pretend to make
a new law, but to vindicate the old one from misrepresentation'.[6] Precedents must, he says, be followed unless 'flatly
absurd and unjust'; and that is so even if they appear unjust
to us, if they lay down settled law and are not repugnant to
natural justice;[7] for 'they are the evidence of what is common
law'.[8] The binding force of precedents is stated even more
strongly by Douglas in the preface to his reports.[9] In 1803

[1] *Ellis* v. *Smith* (1754), 1 Ves. 11, 17.
[2] *Comm.* i. 69–71.
[3] Ibid. 69–70; this was also stated by Hobbes, *Leviathan*, f. 143, cited
C. K. Allen, *Law in the Making* (3rd ed.), 200, and was really a commonplace
in an age which believed in the overriding force of the divine law or the law
of nature; see Holdsworth, *H.E.L.* vi. 290–1, 293–4.
[4] Bl. *Comm.* i. 41.
[5] 'As well to keep the scale of justice even and steady, and not liable to
waver with every new judge's opinion; as also because the law in that case
being solemnly determined, what before was uncertain, and perhaps indif-
ferent, is now become a permanent rule, which it is not in the breast of any
subsequent judge to alter or vary from, according to his private sentiments:
he being sworn to determine, not according to his own private judgment, but
according to the known laws and customs of the land': ibid. 69.
[6] Ibid. 70.   [7] Ibid. 70–1.
[8] 'Upon the whole we may take it as a general rule, that the decisions of
courts of justice are the evidence of what is common law: in the same manner
as in the civil law, what the emperor had once determined was to serve for a
guide for the future': ibid. 71.
[9] 'It has been found expedient to entrust to the wisdom and experience of
judges, the power of deducing, from the more general propositions of law,
such necessary corollaries, as shall appear, though not expressed in words, to
be within their intended meaning. Deductions thus formed and established
in the adjudication of particular causes, become in a manner part of the text

Lord Eldon followed cases of which he did not wholly approve because 'it is better the law should be certain than that every judge should speculate on improvements in it'.[1] In 1832 Lord Tenterden C.J. said: 'the decisions of our predecessors, the judges of former times, ought to be followed and adopted, unless we can see very clearly that they are erroneous, for otherwise there will be no certainty in the administration of the law.'[2]

The general rule is clear. Decided cases which lay down a rule of law are authoritative and must be followed. But in very many of the statements of this general rule there are reservations of different kinds. Let us look at these reservations which have been made by the judges at different periods, and at their practical results; for, unless we realize their importance, we can neither understand the nature of the authority which decided cases have in our modern law, nor estimate the truth of the criticisms which have been passed upon this mode of developing a legal system.

The fundamental principle upon which all these reservations ultimately rest is the principle stated by Coke, Hale, and Blackstone, that these cases do not make law, but are only the best evidence of what the law is. They are not, as Hale said, 'law properly so called',[3] but only very strong evidence of the law. They are evidence, as Coke said, of the existence of those usages which go to make up the common law; and, conversely, the fact that no case can be produced to prove the existence of an alleged usage is evidence that there is no such usage.[4] It is clear that the adoption of this point of view gives the courts power to mould as they please the conditions in which they will accept a decided case or a series of decided cases as authoritative. If the cases are only

of the law. Succeeding judges receive them as such, and, in general consider themselves as bound to adhere to them no less strictly than to the express dictates of the legislature': Preface, iii–iv.

[1] *Sheddon v. Goodrich* (1803), 8 Ves. 481, 497.

[2] *Selby v. Bardons* (1832), 3 B. & Ad. 2, 17.   [3] *Supra*, p. 150.

[4] 'Hereby is appeareth how safe it is to be guided by judicial presidents, the rule being good, *Periculosum existimo quod bonorum virorum non comprobatur exemplo*. And as usage is a good interpreter of Lawes, so non-usage when there is no example is a great intendment, that the Law will not bear it': Co. *Litt.* 81*b*; Coke there points out that no 'Act of Parliament by non-user can be antiquated or lose his force'.

evidence of what the law is the courts must decide what weight is to be attached to this evidence in different sets of circumstances. The manner in which they have decided this question has left them many means of escape from the necessity of literal obedience to the general rule that decided cases must always be followed. They have allowed many exceptions to and modifications of this rule, if in their opinion a literal obedience to it would produce either technical departures from established principles, or substantial inconveniences which would be contrary to public policy.

First, Coke is never tired of insisting that the fact that a rule would lead to inconvenient results—inconvenient either technically or substantially—is a good argument to prove that the rule is not law.[1] The principles of the common law must be maintained 'even though a private man suffer losse';[2] and so firmly did he believe this thesis that he even said that these principles could not be overridden by an Act of Parliament.[3] Obviously, according to this view, only those cases could be regarded as authoritative which were in accordance with those principles. Coke, as usual, stated this principle in an exaggerated form. It was quite clear that no one really believed, not even Coke himself, that the principles of the common law could control an Act of Parliament;[4] and it was clear that, if the authority of decided cases could be disregarded whenever the judge thought that substantial inconvenience would be caused by following them, very little authority could be attached to them—a conclusion which was contrary both to Coke's theory and to his practice. Vaughan C.J. pointed out that 'when the law is known and clear, though it be unequitable and inconvenient, the judges must determine as the law is, without regarding the unequitableness or inconveniency';[5] and that 'if incon-

---

[1] 'Here note three things. First, that whatsoever is against the rule of Law is inconvenient. Secondly, that an argument *ab inconvenienti* is strong—to prove it is against Law. . . . Thirdly, that new inventions . . . are full of inconvenience': Co. *Litt.* 379*a*; cp. ibid. 66*a*, 152*b*, 178*a*, 258*b*, 279*a*.

[2] Co. *Litt.* 152*b*; 'it is better, saith the law, to suffer a mischiefe (that is peculiar to one) than an inconvenience that may prejudice many', ibid. 97*b*.

[3] *Bonham's Case* (1609), 8 Co. Rep. 107, 118; Holdsworth, *H.E.L.* ii. 442; iv. 186–7.

[4] Holdsworth, *H.E.L.* ii. 442; iv. 187; v. 475.

[5] *Dixon* v. *Harrison* (1670), Vaughan, 36, 37.

veniences necessarily follow out of the law only the Parliament can cure them'.[1] It followed from this view that the authority of decided cases must be respected, even though the judge thought they led to inequitable and inconvenient results. It is true that Vaughan C.J. gives the judges a larger latitude than they possess to-day, or probably than they possessed then, of refusing to follow a judgment which they considered to be erroneous.[2] But it is important to remember that the judges have always assumed the power to disregard cases which are plainly absurd and contrary to principle. Blackstone admits that they have this power,[3] Parke B. makes a similar admission;[4] and the power has been used in modern times.[5] It is largely a question of the extent of this power. Lord Mansfield made a large use of it when he attempted to reform the doctrine of consideration[6] and the law of quasi-contract,[7] to make a fusion between law and equity,[8] and to rationalize the doctrine of seisin.[9] But the failure of his attempts to effect these large objects showed that it was a power which could only be exercised within a much narrower compass; for it was the weight of the decided cases which secured that failure, by proving that the principles which

---

[1] 'Judges must judge according as the law is, not as it ought to be. But then the premises must be clear out of the established law, and the conclusion well deduc'd before great inconveniences be admitted for law. But if the inconveniences necessarily follow out of the law, only the Parliament can cure them': *Craw* v. *Ramsey* (1670), Vaughan, 274, 285.

[2] *Supra*, p. 150.   [3] *Supra*, p. 151.

[4] 'Our common law system consists in the applying to new combinations of circumstances those rules of law which we derive from legal principles and judicial precedents; and for the sake of obtaining uniformity, consistency, and certainty, we must apply those rules, where they are not plainly unreasonable and inconvenient, to all cases which arise; and we are not at liberty to reject them, and to abandon all analogy to them, in those to which they have not yet been judicially applied, because we think that the rules are not as convenient and reasonable as we ourselves could have devised': *Mirehouse* v. *Rennell* (1833), 1 Cl. & Fin. 527, 546.

[5] *Drummond* v. *Drummond* (1866), L.R. 2 Eq. 335, 339, where previous cases decided in ignorance of a statute were disregarded; *Collins* v. *Lewis* (1869), L.R. 8 Eq. 708, where Stuart V.-C. declined to follow what was clearly a mistaken decision; and see *Farquharson* v. *Floyer* (1876), 3 Ch. D. 109, where *Collins* v. *Lewis* was followed.

[6] Holdsworth, *H.E.L.* viii. 26–34.

[7] *Harv. Law Rev.* xliii. 21–3.   [8] Ibid. 8–10.

[9] Holdsworth, *H.E.L.* vii. 43–4.

he wished to apply were not law.[1] The modern cases show, as Parke B. pointed out,[2] that it can only be used if a rule laid down by a case is 'plainly unreasonable and inconvenient'— that is, if it is obviously contrary to a statute or to well-established principle.[3] Similarly, if a case arises which is covered by no authority, a recourse must be had to principles. In such a case Lord Mansfield would have attached little weight to precedents which might suggest an analogy;[4] but Parke B. attached much greater weight to them;[5] and his is now the accepted view.

Secondly, in the eighteenth century when the reports were made by private reporters, the reports of decided cases possessed very different degrees of authority. It was always possible for a judge who was trying a case to decry the authority of a report which laid down a rule with which he disagreed. Lord Mansfield, when he was pressed by a case which laid down a rule which he did not like, was rather too apt to take this line.[6] It is no doubt a line which became less possible to take as the reports improved in quality, and as reporting became more standardized and more stereotyped. But within limits this censorship of reports is both legitimate and necessary.[7] For, after all, what is authoritative is not

[1] Ibid. 44; viii. 34–5.
[2] *Supra*, p. 154, n. 4.
[3] Lord Hanworth, in his life of Pollock C.B. 198, prints a letter from the Chief Baron in which he says: 'the common law of England is really nothing more than "summa ratio"—*the highest good sense*—even Parke, Lord Wensleydale (the greatest legal pedant that I believe ever existed), did not always follow even the House of Lords; he did not *overrule*—(oh no! μὴ γένοιτο) but he did not *act upon* cases which were *nonsense* (as many are).'
[4] 'The law would be a strange science if it rested solely upon cases; and if after so large an increase of commerce, arts, and circumstances accruing, we must go to the time of Rich. I to find a case and see what is law. Precedent indeed may serve to fix principles, which for certainty's sake are not suffered to be shaken, whatever might be the weight of the principle, independent of precedent. But precedent, though it be evidence of law, is not law itself; much less the whole of the law': *Jones* v. *Randall* (1774), Lofft. 385; for a less pointed version of this dictum see Cowp. 39.
[5] *Supra*, p. 154, n. 4.
[6] Wallace, *The Reporters*, 504–5.
[7] Thus in the case of *Chillingworth* v. *Esche*, [1924] 1 Ch. at pp. 112–13, Warrington L.J. said: 'there are one or two points raised by Mr. Micklem with which I think I ought to deal. He relies on *Moeser* v. *Wisker* ((1871), L.R. 6 C.P. 120). In my opinion that is a case which never ought to have

the report, but, so far as it goes,[1] the record. The reports, as
Blackstone said, only 'serve as indexes to, and also to explain,
the records; which always in matters of consequence and
nicety the judges direct to be searched'.[2] For this reason a
report can, as Sir Frederick Pollock has said, 'always be
contradicted by a more accurate report or even by the clear
recollection of the Court or counsel, though this does not
often happen'.[3]

Thirdly, though ·the English legal system was a very
centralized system, though, for the most part, only the decisions of the central courts of law and equity were reported,[4]
yet, before the Judicature Act, there were a considerable
number of these courts. There were three courts of common
law, there were the courts held by the judges of assize, there
was the Court of Exchequer Chamber, the Court of Chancery, and the House of Lords. The cases decided by these
courts were sometimes conflicting, and the weight to be
attached to their decisions was different. The result was
that it was often by no means clear that a previous decision

been reported. It was an *ex parte* application. The judges seized on a single
fact, and decided on that fact. The purchaser in that case had no opportunity
of stating his view.'

[1] As Douglas points out in the preface to his reports, p. v, though the
record is indisputable so far as it goes, it does not go far; and 'since the most
material parts of the case cannot be gathered from the record', recourse must
be had to the reports, so that it is upon their fidelity and accuracy that 'the
evidence of a very great part of the law of England entirely depends'; it was
because the record omitted some of the most essential parts of the case that
the writ of error, which lay only for errors on the record, became comparatively useless: Holdsworth, *H.E.L.* i. 215–16, 223–4.

[2] *Comm.* i. 71; and see ibid. 69.

[3] *Essays in the Law*, 233; cp. Ram, *The Science of Legal Judgment*, 7.

[4] The practice of reporting the decisions of the itinerant justices began
late and was soon discontinued; the reports of their decisions begin with
Peake (1790–4), and end with Foster & Finlason (1858–65); cp. Pollock,
A First Book of Jurisprudence, 322–3. When the new county courts were
established in 1846 English lawyers showed their instinctive sense of one of
the main conditions for the success of a system of case law by abstaining from
reporting their decisions; for, as Bacon pointed out, *De Augmentis*, bk. viii,
c. 3, Aph. 78, 'nihil tam interest certitudinis legum . . . quam ut scripta
authentica intra fines moderatos coerceantur, et facessat multitudo enormis
authorum et doctorum in jure; unde laceratur sententia legum, judex fit
attonitus, processus immortales, atque advocatus ipse, cum tot libros perlegere
et vincere non possit, compendia sectatur'.

given by one of three courts might not be reversed, if the same or a different court at a later date thought that some other line of authority ought to be followed. The position in 1834 was thus summed up by Ram:[1] '(1) Modern cases in Bank stand in opposition to each other. . . . (2) Modern cases at Nisi Prius stand in opposition to each other. . . . (3) One decision in Bank does not always bind the courts to make the same decision in Bank on similar circumstances in another case: one such decision is often overruled by another. (4) One decision at Nisi Prius does not bind the courts to make the same decision at Nisi Prius on similar circumstances in another case: often one such decision overrules another. (5) Consequently, one decision at Nisi Prius does not so settle the point decided, as to exclude all hope of a different result on a second Nisi Prius trial of the like question.' (6) The same is true of two or more cases decided at Nisi Prius. (7) 'One case decided in Bank does not so settle the point decided, as to exclude all hope of a different result on a second case in Bank on the like question.' (8) The same is true of two or more cases decided in Bank. In fact the three independent courts of common law, like the Proculians and Sabinians in Roman law, sometimes followed different rules on certain matters.[2] The Judicature Act, by abolishing these separate courts and substituting a High Court split up into Divisions, and a Court of Appeal, has got rid of the principal cause of those divergencies. But it is still not quite certain how far judges of the High Court are obliged to follow each other's decisions;[3] and quite recently conflicting decisions have been given by the Court of Criminal Appeal[4] and the Court of Appeal.[5]

[1] *The Science of Legal Judgment*, 6-7.
[2] Thus in the sixteenth century, and till the decision in *Slade's Case* in 1602 (4 Co. Rep. 92b) the Courts of Common Pleas and Queen's Bench took different views on the question whether assumpsit could be brought for a debt without an express subsequent promise: Holdsworth, *H.E.L.* iii. 443-4; in the nineteenth century there was a difference of opinion between the Courts of Exchequer and Queen's Bench as to the kind of misrepresentation which would support an action for deceit.
[3] *Supra*, p. 148.   [4] *R. v. Denyer*, [1926] 2 K.B. 258.
[5] *Hardie and Lane* v. *Chilton*, [1928] 2 K.B. 306; though the correctness of *R. v. Denyer* was denied in this case, Hewart C.J. on 23 April stated that, for the purpose of the administration of the criminal law, *R. v. Denyer* would

Fourthly, Bacon pointed out that 'it is a sound precept not to take the law from the rules, but to make the rule from the existing law. For the proof is not to be sought from the words of the rule, as if it were the text of law. The rule, like the magnetic needle, points at the law, but does not settle it.'[1] This truth was emphasized by Lord Hardwicke when he said that 'neither law nor equity consists merely of casual precedents, but of general rules and principles by the reason of which, the several cases coming before the courts of justice, are to be governed';[2] and by Parker C.B. when he said that 'the law of England is not confined to particular precedents and cases but consists in the reason of them, *ratio legis est anima legis* and *ubi eadem est ratio idem est jus* are known maxims'.[3] Lord Mansfield agreed with them;[4] and this principle has been reasserted by Sir Frederick Pollock, who says:[5]

'Judicial authority belongs not to the exact words used in this or that judgment, nor even to all the reasons given, but only to the principles recognised and applied as necessary grounds of the decision. Therefore it has never been possible for the courts to impose dogmatic formulas on the Common Law, and the efforts of text writers to bind it in fetters of verbal definition have been constantly and for the most part happily frustrated by the reconsideration and restatement of guiding principles in the judgments of the highest tribunals.'

It is with these reservations that English law accepts the

be followed till reversed 'by the only competent tribunal', the House of Lords: *L.Q.R.* xliv. 436. [The point at issue has been resolved by the House of Lords in *Thorne* v. *Motor Trade Association* [1937] A. C. 797. Eds.]

[1] 'Recte jubetur, ut non ex regulis jus sumatur; sed ex jure quod est, regula fiat. Neque enim ex verbis regulae petenda est probatio, ac si esset textus legis. Regula enim legem (ut acus nautica polos) indicat, non statuit': *De Augmentis,* bk. viii, c. 3, Aph. 85—the translation is Spedding's.

[2] *Gorton* v. *Hancock,* Har. MSS. 353, f. 122, cited P. C. Yorke, *Life of Hardwicke,* ii. 492; in *Ellis* v. *Smith* (1754), 1 Ves. 2, 17, he is reported to have denied a dictum of Bacon cited at the Bar and said that 'many uniform decisions ought to have weight that the law may be known'; if Bacon's dictum was the dictum cited above this statement is not directly contradictory to it, and the dictum in *Gorton* v. *Hancock* agrees with its spirit.

[3] *Omichund* v. *Barker* (1748), 2 Eq. Cases Ab. 401.

[4] 'The law does not consist of particular cases, but of general principles, which are illustrated and explained by those cases': *R.* v. *Bembridge* (1783), 3 Dougl. 327, 332.

[5] *Continental Law in the Nineteenth Century* (Continental Legal History Series), xliv.

authority of decided cases. Both the general rule that decided cases are authoritative, and the reservations with which that rule is accompanied, are due historically to the very gradual way in which our modern theory as to the authority of decided cases was developed. As the result of that evolution English lawyers have invented a wholly original method of developing law. It is a method of developing law which preserves the continuity of legal doctrine, and is, at the same time, eminently adaptable to the needs of a changing society.[1] As I have pointed out in my *History of English Law*, Coke's Reports restated the medieval common law, and adapted it to the needs of the seventeenth century;[2] and, in the nineteenth century, a succession of eminent judges adapted to the needs of that century of change the law of the seventeenth and eighteenth centuries. Such a method of developing law `could only have been invented by a learned self-governing profession, responsible only to itself. It was the leaders of this profession who made or employed the men who made the Year Books. It was they who, in a later age, made the reports. It was they who applied to these reports an intelligent criticism which has established a professional tradition as to which of these reports are good, which bad, which indifferent. It was they who worked out in theory and applied in practice the general rule that decided cases are authoritative, the reservations to that general rule, and more especially the principle that the authority of a decision is attached, not to the words used, nor to all the reasons given, but to the principle or principles necessary for the decision of the case. But even such a profession could not have evolved this method of developing law if the courts had not been staffed by an independent bench of judges, sufficiently well paid to secure that they were, as a general rule, more able than the Bar. It is true that barristers have sometimes exercised some kind of censorship over the cases

---

[1] Burke said: 'nothing better could be devised by human wisdom than agreed judgments publicly delivered, for preserving unbroken the great traditionary body of the law, and for marking . . . every variation in the application and the construction of particular parts': Report (30 April 1794) of a Committee of the House of Commons on the proceedings in the trial of Warren Hastings, *Works* (Bohn's Ed.), vi. 453.

[2] Vol. v, 489.

which they have reported.[1] But it is the criticism of the
Bench, and the use made by the Bench of prior decisions,
upon which the success of a system of case law in the long
run depends. A system of appointing judges which does not
secure both the presence of the ablest lawyers on the Bench,
and security of tenure, will never be able to operate successfully our English system of case law.

No doubt this system of case law has its defects; and Bentham and Austin, who looked at the legal phenomena of their
day merely analytically, and therefore superficially, exercised
their ingenuity in stressing its imperfections. Bentham's
contemptuous description of it is well known:

'It is the judges that make the common law. Do you know how
they make it? Just as a man makes laws for his dog. When your dog
does anything you want to break him of, you wait till he does it and
then beat him. This is the way you make laws for your dog, and this
is the way the judges make laws for you and me.'[2]

Austin emphasized the difficulty of extracting the *ratio deci-
dendi*, the fact that case law is made in haste, its *ex post facto*
character, its bulk, the uncertainty as to the validity of
many of its rules, its fragmentary character, its tendency to
make the statute law unsystematic.[3] It is impossible to deny
the truth of some of these criticisms. But I think that an undue emphasis is laid upon them by the manner in which the
analytical jurists treat case law, not as one of the means and
one of the means only, by which English law has been
developed, but as an isolated phenomenon. If we look at the
various sources of English law we see that, though case law
is a principal source, it is not the only source, and that the
existence of other sources of that law, such as books of
authority and statutes, has gone some way to diminish some
of the defects emphasized by this school of jurists.

---

[1] For instance, Campbell; Atlay, *The Victorian Chancellors*, ii. 138,
says: 'Campbell was no mere stenographer; he exercised an absolute discretion
as to what decisions he reported and what he suppressed, and sternly rejected
any which appeared to him inconsistent with former rulings or recognised
principles. He jocularly took credit for helping to establish the Chief Justice's
reputation as a lawyer, and he used to boast that he had, in one of his drawers,
material for an additional volume in the shape of "bad Ellenborough law".'

[2] *Truth v. Ashhurst (Works*, v. 235).

[3] Austin, *Jurisprudence* (3rd ed.), ii. 671–82.

In more recent times an insufficient attention to the many reservations with which the theory of the binding force of decided cases is received, has led some comparative lawyers to depreciate unduly this method of developing a legal system as compared with the continental method,[1] which attaches binding force, not to the decision of individual cases, but, to use a French term, to a 'jurisprudence', that is, to 'a series or group of cases creating a practice'.[2] Let us examine some of their criticisms.

It is said that the English method of developing a legal system makes for greater rigidity than the continental method—the custom declared to be law by a decided case is for ever fixed and cannot, as under the continental practice, be varied as the custom varies.[3] The answer to this criticism is that the English method has the merit of making the custom and therefore the law certain. If inconvenience arises in the future the legislature can easily see the exact point requiring remedy, and can therefore easily make a law to fit the new circumstances. It is said, again, that the English method is too conservative, and that we want a better reason for a rule of law than the fact that it was approved by our ancestors.[4] But the history both of Roman and of English law shows us that an element of conservatism is needed for the construction of 'a durable system of jurisprudence';[5] and the reservations with which the English system of case law is received[6] enable the judges, within fairly wide limits, to apply to old precedents a process of selection and rejection which brings the law into conformity with modern conditions. Mr. Justice Holmes has truly said that, 'it is revolting to have no better reason for a rule of law than that so it was laid down in the time of Henry IV. It is still more revolting if the grounds upon which it was laid down have vanished long since, and the rule simply persists from blind

[1] See Professor Goodhart's paper on 'Precedent in English and Continental Law', 50 *L.Q.R.* 40.

[2] Ibid., p. 42.

[3] 'In so far as the English method does succeed in incorporating custom into law, it is obvious that it must be the custom which existed at the time of the precedent case, while under the Continental procedure the practice of the Courts may change as the popular custom changes': ibid., p. 46.

[4] Ibid. pp. 47–9.

[5] Maine, *Ancient Law*, 75–6.   [6] Above, pp. 152–8.

imitation of the past.'[1] But, in fact, this process of selection
and rejection has been applied to the law laid down in the
Year Books;[2] and generally the rules there laid down, which
are still part of modern law, have survived because they suit
modern needs. It is not, I think, true to say that the English
method of developing law by means of decided cases makes
the law unpractical, because it is based, not on a series of
experiments, but on single authoritative cases, which preclude further experiments.[3] The reservations with which the
English method is accompanied[4] provide opportunities for
further experiments.[5] It is true to say that this method keeps
the law in touch with life, and prevents much unprofitable
speculation upon academic problems which serves only to
·illustrate the ingenuity of the speculator. I think, in fact,
that it is true to say that it hits the golden mean between too
much flexibility and too much rigidity, for it gives to the
legal system the rigidity which it must have if it is to possess
a definite body of principles, and the flexibility which it must
have if it is to adapt itself to the needs of a changing society.
If it gives less flexibility than the continental system, it also
gives more certainty; and it is generally less rigid than the
enacted law. If we compare the medieval common law with
the law of the sixteenth and seventeenth centuries, and the
law of the sixteenth and seventeenth centuries with the law
of the nineteenth and twentieth centuries, this flexibility is

[1] *Collected Legal Papers*, 187.
[2] Especially by Coke, Holdsworth, *H.E.L.* v. 490, and the process has
continued from his day to our own.
[3] Professor Goodhart says, 50 *L.Q.R.*, p. 50: 'A system of law to be
truly practical must be one based on a series of experiments, tested by trial
and error; this, however, is not the method of English law, for owing to the
doctrine of precedent, the first experiment must also be the last. In contrast
to this, the Continental practice in fact is based upon experience, for *la
jurisprudence* only becomes fixed if the result of the cases shows that a rule,
heretofore tentatively applied, is a desirable one. There is, therefore, room
for a certain amount of judicial experimentation which is impossible under
the common law.'
[4] Above, pp. 152–8.
[5] Professor Williston, *Some Modern Tendencies in the Law*, 125, cited
50 *L.Q.R.*, p. 54 says: 'Uniform decisions of three hundred years on a particular question may, and sometimes have been overthrown in a day, and the
single decision at the end of the series may establish a rule of law at variance
with all that has gone before.'

apparent; and it is not difficult to see that this result is the consequence both of the English system of case law and of the reservations with which that system is applied in practice. It is true that the application of that system makes the law bulky and technical, and it is true that it imposes upon the lawyers a high degree of technical skill.[1] But is that too high a price to pay for the benefits of a legal system, which combines the virtues of certainty and flexibility in such a way that it has been found capable of continuous adaptation to the needs of successive ages, of a legal system which has enabled the lawyers to construct a body of scientific doctrine which is matched only by that constructed by the classical jurists of Rome? I agree with Professor Allen when he says[2] that the weaknesses of our system of case law 'do not outweigh its substantial merits'; and that 'the amount of irrationality introduced into the law by certain inevitable difficulties of application is inconsiderable beside the solid and rational jurisprudence which the Common Law, built up on example and analogy, has erected to so high a position in European civilization'.

The study of comparative law is a very valuable study which is necessary to students both of legal history and of modern law. But it has its pitfalls. One of these pitfalls is the risk that it may lead us to depreciate unduly our own law and our own legal institutions. If the student of foreign law and foreign legal institutions has a close and practical acquaintance with the working of his own law and legal institutions, which make him painfully aware of their defects, and merely an academic knowledge of foreign law and foreign legal institutions, he will be apt to stress the weak points of his own, and magnify the strong points of the foreign, law and legal institutions of which his knowledge is more distant and theoretical. If his knowledge of his own law and institutions is equally distant and theoretical he will necessarily judge both by reference only to their appearance on paper, and will praise or condemn on merely theoretical grounds, which will often leave out of sight the real strength and weakness of both. In the sixteenth century Starkey thought that the best cure for the defects of English

[1] 50 L.Q.R. pp. 47–8.
[2] Law in the Making (3rd ed.), 304.

law would be a reception of the Roman civil law; but it is
clear that his knowledge of the civil law was of the bookish,
academic kind, which overlooked the fact that in practice the
laws of those countries which had received the Roman civil
law suffered from defects quite as great as those from which
English law suffered.[1] It seems to me that to-day some of the
critics of our system of case law, and some of the critics of our
English judicial system and of our jury system, have made
a mistake similar to that made by Starkey in the sixteenth
century.[2] They pass over the strong points of their own law
and institutions almost in silence, and they stress the weak
points. They condemn too strongly the apparent anomalies
of their own system, and they praise too strongly the
apparent logic and neatness of continental systems. To make
a perfectly fair comparison it is necessary to have a thorough
and first-hand knowledge of the practical working of both
the systems which are compared. But it is as rare to possess
a thorough first-hand knowledge of the practical working
of two legal systems as it is to be perfectly bilingual. Consequently, those who make these comparisons, without this
intimate knowledge, are often unconscious of the fact that
the imitation of foreign examples, which they advocate, may
result in changing the inconveniences which they know of for
the greater inconveniences from which the virtues of our own
laws and institutions have saved us.

[1] Holdsworth, *H.E.L.* iv. 259–60.
[2] This it seems to me is the weak side of Mr. Ensor's instructive little book
on *Courts and Judges in France, Germany and England*; thus at p. 8 he under-
values the advantage of an Appeal Court which is nation-wide and not
regional; and at p. 9 he refuses to admit that there is any advantage in a jury
trial in civil cases; similarly, in his anxiety for the ease of the litigant, he
refuses to take due account of the advantage to the law which is afforded by
the appellate jurisdiction of the House of Lords; the fact that the English
judge is not constantly looking for promotion is not, as he seems to think,
the only or the most important reason why the quality of justice he dispenses
is so good; there is more to be said in favour of the circuit system than he
admits; and his denunciation of the unpaid magistracy rests mainly on a few
and comparatively rare hard cases.

EQUITY[1]

THE Judicature Acts came into force on 1 November 1875.[2] The group of statutes generally known as the Property Acts came into force on 1 January 1926. Thus 1 January 1885, the birthday of this *Review*, and 1 January 1935, its jubilee, both occur some nine years after the enactment of legislation which has had a profound effect upon equity; so that both the beginning and end of this period of fifty years have this one common feature—the possibility of reaching some tentative conclusion as to the effect of these important legislative changes. On 1 January 1885 some conclusions as to the effect of the working of the Judicature Acts were beginning to emerge just as on 1 January 1935 there are beginning to emerge some conclusions as to the effect of the working of the Property Acts. But, apart from this chronological accident, these two great legislative changes have hardly any common feature.

The changes made by the Judicature Acts were more far-reaching and more complex than the changes made by the Property Acts; and they were very different in their character. The Judicature Acts recast the whole judicial system, provided a new code of procedure for the Supreme Court which it had created, and put the relation of equity to law on a new basis. The Property Acts have made large alterations directly and indirectly in some of the substantive principles and rules of equity, and they have consolidated and restated in statutory form many more of these principles and rules. Broadly speaking, it would be true to say that the Judicature Acts affected mainly adjective law, and the Property Acts mainly substantive law. But, whilst the Judicature Acts made changes of such magnitude that it has taken very many years fully to work out their effects, the experience of the

---

[1] Reprinted from (1935) 51 *Law Quarterly Review*, 142.
[2] The first Judicature Act, 36 & 37 Vict. c. 66, was passed in 1873; it was intended to come into operation on 2 November 1874 (section 2), but that date was postponed by 37 & 38 Vict. c. 83 to 1 November 1875; it came into force on that day as amended by the Act of 1875, 38 & 39 Vict. c. 77.

last nine years shows, I think, that it will take less time fully to work out the effects of the Property Acts. This is due partly to the fact that the changes effected by those Acts are less far-reaching and complex—they affect some only of the substantive rules and principles of law and equity, and partly to the care with which they were drafted.

It follows that, in this survey of Equity during the last fifty years, it is necessary to begin with the Judicature Acts. Those Acts dominate the whole of this period. They have determined the conditions under which equity has been developed by the legislature and the courts, and they determine the manner in which the Property Acts will be applied and interpreted. In the first place, therefore, I shall say something of the way in which the Judicature Acts have affected the development of equity; in the second place, I shall glance very briefly at the work of one or two of the Lord Chancellors and judges and other lawyers who have shaped that development; in the third place, I shall say something of developments in equity which have been made by the legislature; and, lastly, I shall say something of the present position of equity in the English legal system.

The Judicature Acts and their Effects

It was inevitable that there should be, at the start, some misconception as to the effect of the Judicature Acts. In the first place, lawyers were inclined to exaggerate the importance of the section of the Act of 1873 which provided that, in cases of conflict between the rules of law and equity, the rules of equity should prevail.[1] In the second place, there were for a long time some divergent views as to the effect of the Act on the substantive rules of law and equity.

(1) Augustine Birrell, in a lecture on the changes in the procedure and principles of equity, which he gave in 1900,[2] after quoting section 25, sub-section 11 of the Act, said: 'Like truth, equity has finally prevailed by statute. . . . No triumph can be completer than this. The judges of the Queen's Bench Division are by statute required to administer, even though they may fail to understand, the Rules of

[1] 36 & 37 Vict. c. 66, s. 25, sub-s. 11.
[2] *A Century of Law Reform*, 196–7.

Equity.' Birrell's words illustrate the prevailing tendency to exaggerate the effect of this section of the Act. This tendency prevailed till the publication of Maitland's *Lectures on Equity* in 1909. He showed that this section of the Act has had a very small effect because, throughout their history, the relations of law and equity had been relations, not of conflict, but of partnership.[1] In fact, from the first, the theory upon which the Chancellors justified their equitable modifications of, or additions to, the law, postulated a partnership. *The Doctor and Student*, which sums up the medieval development of equity, over and over again emphasizes the fact that the law is the foundation and starting-point of the rules of equity; for these rules are called into existence by the presence of some hardship resulting from the manner in which the law had dealt with a particular case.[2] The writers of the early seventeenth century were no less emphatic. Bacon admitted that 'the common law hath a kind of rule and survey over the chancery, to determine what belongs to the chancery';[3] and Norburie said that 'Law and Conscience are so linked together that they are hardly to be severed, and conscience must always be founded on some law'.[4] In the late seventeenth and eighteenth centuries the Chancellors and the judges so skilfully worked out the terms of the partnership between law and equity, on the basis of a differentiation between the exclusive, the concurrent, and the auxiliary jurisdiction of the court, that the occasions for conflict between law and equity were minimized. How skilfully they had devised and worked this partnership was seen from the fact that, since the Judicature Act, very few cases in which this section has been called into operation have occurred.[5] It is true that it was more often unsuccessfully appealed to in argument; but, as we shall now see, that was due to the divergent views which prevailed as to the effect of the Act on the substantive rules of law and equity.

---

[1] *Lectures on Equity* (reissued 1936), 17–19, 153–6.
[2] Bk. i, cc. 16, 19, 26, cited Holdsworth, *H.E.L.* iv. 280–1.
[3] Reading on the Statute of Uses, *Works* (ed. Spedding), vii. 415.
[4] Hargrave, *Law Tracts*, 444–5.
[5] Maitland, *Lectures on Equity*, 155–6, cites *Job* v. *Job* (1877), 6 Ch. D. 562, and *Lowe* v. *Dixon* (1885), 16 Q.B.D. 455; to which we must add *Berry* v. *Berry*, [1929] 2 K.B. 316.

(2) Before 1885 the courts had come to the conclusion that the Act had not abolished the distinction between legal rights and equitable rights, and between legal remedies and equitable remedies. In the case of *Joseph* v. *Lyons*[1] Cotton L.J., in answer to the contention that the Judicature Acts had swept away the distinction between legal and equitable rights, said:[2]

'it was not intended by the Legislature, and it has not been said, that legal and equitable rights should be treated as identical, but that the Courts should administer both legal and equitable principles. . . . It was not intended that a conveyance void at common law, should, after the passing of these statutes, become valid as a conveyance at common law.'

In the case of *Britain* v. *Rossiter*[3] it was held that the equitable doctrine of part performance could only be applied to those contracts over which equity had had jurisdiction before the Judicature Acts, i.e. to specifically enforceable contracts. Brett L.J. said:[4]

'the doctrine [of part performance] was not extended to any other kind of contract before the Judicature Acts: can we so extend it now? I think that the true construction of the Judicature Acts is that they confer no new rights; they only confirm the rights which previously were to be found existing in the Courts either of Law or Equity; if they did more they would alter the rights of parties, whereas in truth they only change the procedure.'

But upon certain other matters some of the judges did not always speak so clearly. Thus in the case of *Walsh* v. *Lonsdale*[5] Jessel M.R. stated very broadly[6] that

'there are not two estates as there were formerly, one estate at common law by reason of the payment of the rent from year to year, and an estate in equity under the agreement. There is only one court and the equity rules prevail in it. The tenant holds under an agreement for a lease. He holds, therefore, under the same terms in equity as if a lease had been granted, it being a case in which both parties admit that relief is capable of being given by specific performance.'

But, as Farwell J. pointed out in the case of *Manchester*

[1] (1884), 15 Q.B.D. 280.   [2] At p. 286.
[3] (1879), 11 Q.B.D. 123.   [4] At p. 129.
[5] (1882), 21 Ch. D. 9.   [6] At p. 14.

Brewery Co. v. *Coombs*,[1] this statement must be accepted with considerable limitations.

'Although it has been suggested that the decision in *Walsh* v. *Lonsdale* takes away all differences between the legal and equitable estate, it, of course, does nothing of the sort, and the limits of its applicability are really somewhat narrow. It applies only to cases where there is a contract to transfer a legal title, and an act has to be justified or an action maintained by force of the legal title to which such contract relates. It involves two questions: (1) Is there a contract of which specific performance can be obtained? (2) If yes, will the title acquired by such specific performance justify at law the act complained of, or support at law the action in question?'

Thus the doctrine will not apply if the rights of the parties are purely equitable; nor can it affect the rights of third parties.

'Thus a contract by a landowner to sell the fee simple of land in possession to A would not enable A to maintain an action of ejectment or trespass against a third person, because such actions are purely legal actions requiring the legal estate or possession respectively to support them, and the contract relied on is not made with the defendant.'

Similarly, it took some time to adjust the legal and the equitable conceptions of fraud, and the conditions upon which the legal and equitable remedies for fraud would be given. Equity did not clearly differentiate a fraudulent from a non-fraudulent representation. It adopted the view of Roman law that *culpa lata aequiparatur dolo*. This view was taken by Jessel M.R. in the case of *Smith* v. *Chadwick*;[2] and he went on to say that fraud as so defined would give rise to an action of deceit.[3] This view of the law was followed by the Court of Appeal in the case of *Peek* v. *Derry*.[4] But the House of Lords reversed the latter decision, and laid it down that to succeed in a common law action of deceit fraud as defined by the common law must be proved; and that the common law did not hold a statement to be fraudulent if the person making it believed it to be true, even though he had been grossly

---

[1] [1901] 2 Ch. 608, 617–18.   [2] (1882), 20 Ch. D. 27.

[3] 'A man may issue a prospectus, or make any other statement to induce another to enter into a contract, believing that his statement is true, and not intending to deceive; but he may through carelessness have made statements which are not true, and which he ought to have known were not true, and if he does so he is liable in an action for deceit', (1882), 20 Ch. D. 27, 44.

[4] (1887), 37 Ch. D. 541.

careless in making it and believing it.[1] In other words, the common law drew the distinction between a knave and a fool much more precisely than it was drawn by equity or by Roman law. This decision gave rise to the impression that both law and equity recognized as fraud only that species of fraud which must be proved to exist in order to succeed in an action of deceit. That impression was corrected by Lord Haldane's judgment in the case of *Nocton* v. *Lord Ashburton*.[2] He said:[3]

> 'It must now be taken to be settled that nothing short of proof of a fraudulent intention in the strict sense will suffice for an action of deceit. That is so whether a Court of Law or a Court of Equity, in the exercise of concurrent jurisdiction, is dealing with the claim. . . . But when fraud is referred to in the wider sense in which the books are full of the expression, used in Chancery and describing cases which were within its exclusive jurisdiction, it is a mistake to suppose that an actual intention to cheat must always be proved. A man may misconceive the extent of the obligation which a Court of Equity imposes on him. His fault is that he has violated, however innocently because of his ignorance, an obligation which he must have been taken by the Court to have known, and his conduct has in that case always been called fraudulent, even in such a case as a technical fraud on a power.'

This distinction between the legal and the equitable conception of a fraud was justified, Lord Haldane pointed out, by the fact that the law was concerned with enforcing a duty of universal obligation—the duty to be honest; while equity, which acts *in personam*, was concerned also with enforcing duties of particular obligation arising from the circumstances and relations of the parties.[4]

The courts have, for the most part,[5] worked out logically and skilfully the principle that the Judicature Acts have not, in most cases, affected the substance of legal and equitable rules; but that their main operation has been upon the tribunals and the procedure by which legal and equitable rights are enforced. The result has been that those Acts have made no breach in the continuity of the development of

[1] (1889), 14 App. Cas. 337.   [2] [1914] A.C. 932.
[3] At pp. 953–4.   [4] At pp. 954–5.
[5] Two cases in which there may have been some misconception as to the correct adjustment of legal and equitable rights and remedies are *Hurst* v. *Picture Theatres*, [1915] 1 K.B. 1; 31 *L.Q.R.* 217; and *Re Wait*, [1927] 1 Ch. 606; 43 *L.Q.R.* 293.

equitable principles. They have preserved the most salient
feature of English equity—its development as a separate
system; and they have achieved this result because, though
they effected a very radical reform, they were the logical
consequence of the shape taken by a series of statutes which
begin in the second quarter of the nineteenth century. The
reason why these reforms, which culminated in the Judicature Acts, took this shape can only be explained historically.

Lord Hardwicke, in the case of *Wortley* v. *Birkhead*,[1] said
that the doctrine of *tabula in naufragio* could never have been
evolved in a country in which law and equity were administered in the same courts, but was due entirely to the fact that
in England law and equity were administered in separate
courts. As Blackstone pointed out,[2] and as I have shown in
my *History of English Law*,[3] this is the most distinctive
feature of equity in the English legal system. It has made
equity a very separate body of principles and rules, with
technical characteristics of its own, as marked as, but very
different from, the technical characteristics of the common
law. In the seventeenth century this distinctive feature of
the administration of equity in England did not escape the
notice of Bacon; and he expressed a preference for it.[4] In the
eighteenth century, Hardwicke, differing from Kames who
preferred the Scottish system of administering law and
equity in the same court, agreed with Bacon.[5] In fact, the
only great lawyer of the eighteenth century who disliked
the separation between the rules of law and equity, which
was the consequence of the English system, was Lord Mansfield. If he had had his way the future relations of law and
equity would have been very different. The substantive
principles of law and equity would have gradually approxi-
mated to one another; and the Judicature Acts might have
effected a fusion both of substantive and adjective law. But
his views were rejected; and law and equity developed in the
eighteenth and nineteenth centuries, as they had been developing during the latter part of the seventeenth century, in
partnership, but each on its separate technical lines. These

[1] (1754), 2 Ves. Sen. 571, 573-4.
[2] *Comm.* iii. 50.
[3] Vol. i, 446, 449.
[4] *De Augmentis*, bk. viii, c. 3, Aph. 45.
[5] Yorke, *Life of Hardwicke*, ii. 553.

relations of law and equity were not disturbed by the reformers of the second and third quarters of the nineteenth
century. They considered that what stood most in need of
reform was, not the substantive principles of law and equity,
but the inconveniences resulting from the separation of the
courts of law and equity, and from their systems of procedure.
The removal of these evils was the object upon which these
reformers concentrated their energies; and the Judicature
Acts were the logical culmination of the reforms which they
made with this object. They abolished the courts of law and
equity, handed over their jurisdiction to a Supreme Court,
and provided a uniform code of procedure for that court.
They did not fuse law and equity; and so it was necessary
to divide the High Court into a Chancery Division and a
King's Bench Division. Perhaps it was thought that the
judges of those Divisions would be freely interchangeable.
But it was soon found that this would be inconvenient; and
the experiment of sending the judges of the Chancery
Division on circuit was soon abandoned.[1] Thus a continuous
development of the principles of equity in the Chancery
Division has been secured; for that Division has inherited the
traditions of the old Court of Chancery, just as the King's
Bench Division has inherited the traditions of the old courts
of common law. The different genesis of the rules applied
in these Divisions, and the different outlook of lawyers
trained in the equity and common law traditions, ensure the
continued separation of those substantive rules of law and
equity which the Judicature Acts did not attempt to join
together.

It follows, therefore, that during the last fifty years, both
the principles of equity evolved by the Chancellors of the
eighteenth and nineteenth centuries, and the new principles
and rules introduced by the legislature, have been developed
by the Chancellors and judges and other lawyers with no
break in their historical continuity. With this professional

---

[1] In 1875, Atlay tells us (*Victorian Chancellors*, ii. 418 n. 1), 'the Chancery
judges and the members of the Court of Appeal were put on the *rota* for circuit. Let "blushing glory" draw a veil, or, in allusion to a once famous anec-
dote, a waistcoat, over the years that followed. The unwilling intruders went
back to their own places . . . and the hungry sheep in the Court of King's
Bench still look up and are not fed.'

development of the principles of equity, and with the modifications made by the legislature, I shall deal in the two following sections of this paper.

The Professional Development of the Principles of Equity

During the eighteenth and the first few years of the nineteenth centuries, the professional development of the principles of equity was in the hands of the Lord Chancellor and the Master of the Rolls, assisted, in cases which came before the House of Lords, by those peers who were learned in the law. To them the legislature had added first one[1] and then two more Vice-Chancellors,[2] and the Lords Justices in Chancery.[3] As the result of the Judicature Acts and the Appellate Jurisdiction Act,[4] the professional development of the principles of equity was entrusted to the judges of the Chancery Division, the Master of the Rolls, the Lords Justices of the Court of Appeal, and the Lords of Appeal in Ordinary. The Master of the Rolls became the president of one of the Courts of Appeal; and, since his jurisdiction is no longer exclusively equitable, he is no longer appointed exclusively from lawyers whose training has been in the courts of equity. Since neither the Court of Appeal nor the House of Lords are divided, like the High Court, into Divisions, Lords Justices and the Lords of Appeal, whose professional training has been in the common law, have taken some part in this development, in the same way as Lords Justices and Lords of Appeal, whose professional training has been in equity, have taken some part in the development of the common law—to the advantage of both systems. I propose, in the first place, to say something of the contributions of one or two of the Chancellors, Lords of Appeal, and other judges, whose training has been in equity, to the development of equitable principles; in the second place to say something of the contributions of lawyers whose training has been in the common law; and, in the third place, to say something of the contributions of the lawyers who have written books on equity as a whole or on some branch of equitable doctrine.

(1) Roundell Palmer, Earl of Selborne, who took a prin-

[1] 53 Geo. III, c. 24.
[2] 5 Vict. c. 5.
[3] 14 & 15 Vict. c. 83.
[4] 39 & 40 Vict. c. 59.

cipal share in framing and passing the Judicature Acts, was Lord Chancellor when the first number of this *Review* appeared—he resigned when Gladstone's Government fell on 9 June 1885. Of all the Chancellors who have held office during the period 1885–1934 he has, I think, left the deepest mark on our system of equity. He had, it has been well said, 'that intuitive insight into legal principles, and power of grasping and expounding facts, which are certain tests of legal genius';[1] and to these gifts he added an enormous industry. He seldom delayed his judgments for more than a few weeks; and, as Lord Davey has said, in those judgments 'it was his habit to comment on the previous decisions and point out the distinctions between them, and put them into their proper places', with the result that his judgments 'are often a complete commentary on the particular branch of law, and recognized as the *dernier mot* on the subject'.[2] Good illustrations of his powers are to be found in his judgments in *Maddison* v. *Alderson*,[3] *Kendall* v. *Hamilton*,[4] and *Speight* v. *Gaunt*.[5] He was a strong churchman; and Lord Rosebery happily said of him that 'there was something in his austere simplicity of manner which recalled those great lawyers of the Middle Ages who were also churchmen, for to me Selborne always embodied that great conception and great combination'.[6] Of the other Chancellors, trained and practised in the courts of equity, who, during this period, made important contributions to the principles of equity, perhaps the most distinguished was Lord Haldane. His grasp of the principles of equity and his powers of exposition are illustrated by such cases as *Nocton* v. *Lord Ashburton*[7] and *Kreglinger* v. *New Patagonia Meat Co.*;[8] and in the case of *Mason* v. *Provident Clothing Co.*[9] he helped to put the law as to covenants in restraint of trade on its

---

[1] Veeder, 'A Century of Judicature', *Essays in Anglo-American Legal History*, i. 826.
[2] *Memorials Personal and Political*, ii. 442–3.
[3] (1883), 8 App. Cas. 467, 470–82.
[4] (1879), 4 App. Cas. 504, 537–41.
[5] (1883), 9 App. Cas. 1, 4–15.
[6] Cited Veeder, op. cit. 826.
[7] [1914] A.C. 932, 943–58.
[8] [1914] A.C. 25, 33–45.
[9] [1913] A.C. 724, 729–34.

modern footing. Nor should we omit the work of Lord Cave. His judgments were not spectacular, but they were more often right than the judgments of other lawyers who possessed more spectacular gifts; for he had, it was said, in a very high degree the quality of judgment—'that quality which helps people to arrive at a right conclusion, quite distinct from cleverness or even brilliance'.[1]

Amongst the equity lawyers who became Lords of Appeal in Ordinary Lord Davey holds a very high place. He was a master of equity on all its sides. His judgments often sum up all the preceding authorities in clear and precise language, and lay down the law for the future. Some of them are for that reason leading cases. One instance is the case of *Pledge* v. *White*,[2] in which he settled the principles of the doctrine of consolidation; and another is the case of *Hunter* v. *The Attorney-General*,[3] in which the principles applied when property is given on trusts, some of which are charitable and some are not, are lucidly summed up. Lord Parker, too, was a very great equity lawyer. In the case of *Elliston* v. *Reacher*,[4] which he decided as a judge of first instance, he summed up the law as to conditions under which the court will hold that a building scheme exists, and the rules as to the enforceability of covenants in the leases granted in pursuance of the scheme. In such cases as *Hammerton* v. *Dysart*[5] and *Attorney-General of the Commonwealth of Australia* v. *Adelaide Steamship Co*.[6] he showed his mastery of old law and his power to apply it to modern conditions. But the greatest of the equity lawyers who became Lords of Appeal was Lord Macnaghten. His mastery of the principles of equity was as unique as his power of summing up the whole matter in a witty epigram or a happy turn of phrase. In this power he resembles Maitland. Just as Maitland could infuse some humour into his account of the Anglo-Saxon hide, so Lord Macnaghten, in the case of *Van Grutten* v. *Foxwell*,[7] could infuse some humour into his historical account of the adventures of the rule in *Shelley's Case*—so much humour

[1] Mallet, *Life of Cave*, 205.
[2] [1896] A.C. 187, 191–9.
[3] [1899] A.C. 309, 323–4.
[4] [1908] 2 Ch. 374.
[5] [1916] 1 A.C. 57, 78–95.
[6] [1913] A.C. 781.
[7] [1897] A.C. 658, 669–77.

that an eminent real property lawyer, now deceased, refused
to cite the case in his book because he said that he did not
like the disrespectful way in which Lord Macnaghten had
spoken of the rule. He is one of that select band of judges
whose judgments are sometimes literature—a good example
is to be found in his judgment in the case of *Gluckstein* v.
Barnes;[1] and at the same time many of them give the clearest
and best exposition of equitable principles—examples are
such cases as *Tailby* v. *Official Receiver*,[2] *Commissioners of
Income Tax* v. *Pemsel*,[3] *Trego* v. *Hunt*,[4] and *Ward* v. *Dun-
combe*.[5]

Amongst the many other eminent equity lawyers who have
done good work on the Bench in applying, explaining, and
developing equitable principles, it is difficult, and perhaps
invidious, to select particular names. But mention should be
made of Lord Justice Fry, who, besides writing the standard
book on Specific Performance, was, it has been said justly,
'one of the greatest technical masters of equity';[6] and Lord
Cozens-Hardy, who was one of the first judges to give a clear
exposition of the relation of the provisions of the Real
Property Limitation Act to the doctrine of seisin;[7] and who,
in the case of *British South Africa Co.* v. *De Beers Mines*,[8]
gave a lucid exposition of the application of the principle that
equity acts *in personam*.

(2) Amongst the common lawyers who have contributed
to the development of equity a high place must be assigned
to Bowen—'the great judge', said Lord Davey,[9] 'who steered
the ship in the transition from the old system to the new'. The
literary quality of his judgments is equalled only by that of
Macnaghten and Sumner. His capacity for subtle reasoning,
and his power of summing up a situation in a happy phrase,
is equalled only by the thoroughness with which he stated
basic principles, explained them in all their bearings, and
deduced from them logically the answer to the point at issue.

[1] [1900] A.C. 240, 248–55.
[2] (1888), 13 App. Cas. 523, 541–52.
[3] [1891] A.C. 531, 574–92.
[4] [1896] A.C. 7, 22–5.
[5] [1893] A.C. 369, 383–95.
[6] Veeder, op. cit. 816–17.
[7] *Re Atkinson and Horsell's Contract*, [1912] 2 Ch. 9.
[8] [1910] 2 Ch. 502, 513–15.   [9] *L.Q.R.* x. 215.

Many of his judgments, said a colleague, were essays 'which can be handed down to our successors as models of absolute perfection'.[1] At the same time he never lost sight of the need to adjust these principles to modern needs and conditions. His judgments in such cases as *Dashwood* v. *Magniac*,[2] *Allcard* v. *Skinner*,[3] *Re Hodgson*,[4] and many others, show that he has left a considerable mark on the principles of equity. Lord Herschell was primarily a great commercial lawyer, who was remarkable for his grasp of legal principles and the lucidity with which he expounded them. But he, too, made important contributions to equitable principles in such cases as *Commissioners of Income Tax* v. *Pemsel*,[5] *Trego* v. *Hunt*,[6] and *Reddaway* v. *Banham*.[7] Lord Sumner, like Lord Herschell, was primarily a commercial lawyer. He, too, made some important contributions to the exposition of equitable principles—for instance, on the question of the extent of the equitable modification of the legal rules as to the invalidity of an infant's contracts,[8] on the principle upon which equity enforces secret trusts,[9] and on the distinction between legal and equitable assets.[10]

But the lawyer who, starting as a common law judge, added almost more than any other single man to our system of equity, was Nathaniel Lindley—the last of the serjeants, and successively judge of the Court of Common Pleas and of the Common Pleas Division, Lord Justice, Master of the Rolls, and Lord of Appeal in Ordinary. He was a student of Roman law, and his first published work was a translation of Thibaut's *System des Pandektenrechts*. He studied law scientifically and historically, and, as Sir Frederick Pollock has told us,[11] taught his pupils to follow his example. He had a large Chancery practice, and was the author of authoritative

[1] Cited Cunningham, *Life of Bowen,* 157.
[2] [1891] 3 Ch. 306, 358–67.
[3] (1887), 36 Ch. D. 145, 189–93.
[4] (1885), 31 Ch. D. 177, 187–92.
[5] [1891] A.C. 531, 568–74.
[6] [1896] A.C. 7, 10–21.
[7] [1896] A.C. 199, 207–15.
[8] *Leslie* v. *Sheill*, [1914] 3 K.B. 607, 613–19.
[9] *Blackwell* v. *Blackwell*, [1929] A.C. 318, 333–40.
[10] *O'Grady* v. *Wilmot*, [1916] 2 A.C. 231, 269–75.
[11] See the dedicatory letter prefixed to his book on Contracts.

books on Partnership and Companies. It is not surprising, therefore, that he showed a mastery of equity, as indeed of other branches of English law, which was surpassed by none. His judgments have none of the brilliance which characterizes some of the judgments of Bowen, Macnaghten, and Sumner. They are plain statements of principle expressed with the simplicity and clarity which comes from complete mastery. His short judgment in *West* v. *Williams*[1] is a brilliant piece of legal reasoning; and his judgments in such cases as *Chillingworth* v. *Chambers*[2] and *Hardoon* v. *Belilios*,[3] and many others, are recognized as complete and final statements of the principles which are expounded therein. By reason both of his great abilities and industry, and of the length of his tenure of his judicial offices, he has left a very deep mark upon the development of very many branches of English law, and, not least, on the development of equity.

(3) Some of the great treatises on different branches of equity have been written by lawyers who have attained judicial rank. Such treatises as Williams on Executors, Fry on Specific Performance, Lindley on Partnership, and Buckley on Companies, have done much to summarize the results of the case and statute law, and to state those results in a logical and systematic form. The same sort of work has been done by the editors of successive editions of White and Tudor's *Leading Cases in Equity*. But perhaps the greatest improvement in the literature of equity in the last fifty years has been in the text-books for students. When I first began to study equity, the standard text-book was Snell, which was then edited by Archibald Brown. Under his editorship it was not a very satisfactory students' book. In fact it was very different from the good text-book which it has become in the hands of its present editors. Two of the best students' books in my day were Pollock's *Partnership*, and Underhill's *Trusts*— then a students' book. For the rest, I learnt most from the lectures of Sir Alfred Hopkinson who was then Reader in Equity at the Inns of Court. Now there are many more good books to help the student on his way. Two of the most important are Ashburner's book which has just been well

---

[1] [1899] 1 Ch. 132, 142–4.
[2] [1896] 1 Ch. 685, 695–700.
[3] [1901] A.C. 118, 120–8.

edited by Mr. Dennis Browne, and, above all, Maitland's *Lectures on Equity*.

Maitland touched nothing which he did not illuminate, nothing which he did not put in a new and true and attractive form. 'The mark of a master', says Mr. Justice Holmes,[1] 'is that facts which before lay scattered in an inorganic mass, when he shoots through them the magnetic current of his thought, leap into an organic order, and live and bear fruit.' And that is what Maitland's *Lectures on Equity* did for his hearers; for the editors of these lectures have said that after hearing them, 'equity, in our minds a formless mystery, became intelligible and interesting.' I think that no one had before so clearly explained the nature of equity, its place in the English legal system, and its relation to law. No one else had so clearly explained that the relation of equity to law was a relation of partnership and not of conflict, and so enabled lawyers to estimate the effect of the Judicature Acts on that relation. No one had so clearly pointed out that equity was not, like the common law, a self-sufficient system; but rather a collection of appendices to, or glosses upon, various branches of the common law, which were united by no very close substantive bond, but only by a 'jurisdictional and procedural bond'. Moreover, till Maitland wrote his paper upon the trust concept,[2] nobody had any idea of the magnitude of the juristic feat which English lawyers had accomplished when they invented that concept. No one had any idea of the large space which that concept has filled, and still fills, in our public and private law.

This short account of the manner in which equity has been shaped by many judges and other lawyers is brief and inadequate; and, because it is necessary to be brief, it has taken somewhat the shape of a catalogue. But it is necessary to make some attempt to estimate the professional development of the principles of equity during the last fifty years, because it was by means of this professional development that our modern system of equity has been created. By its means the old doctrines evolved by the eighteenth- and early nineteenth-century Chancellors, the new doctrines evolved

---

[1] *Collected Legal Papers*, 37.

[2] 'Trust and Corporation', *Collected Papers*, iii. 321–404; cp. his Introduction to Gierke's *Political Theories of the Middle Age*. See post., p. 210.

by the Chancellors and judges since the Judicature Acts, and the changes made by the legislature, have been blended into a body of doctrine which has absorbed many new ideas, and yet has maintained its connexion with the basic principles ascertained in preceding centuries. Therefore, fully to understand the achievement of the Chancellors and judges, and the considerable changes in and development of equitable doctrine during the last fifty years, we must say a few words of those statutory changes, which have made many additions to and modifications of the form and substance of the equitable doctrines of the eighteenth and a considerable part of the nineteenth centuries.

The Developments made by the Legislature

Until after the middle of the nineteenth century there had been very few legislation changes in the substantive principles of equity. A few small changes had been made in the administration of assets by Locke King's Acts[1] and Hinde Palmer's Act,[2] and in the series of laws which made small changes in the land law. Great changes do not begin till the last twenty years of the nineteenth century. In 1881 came the Conveyancing Act, and in 1882 came the Settled Land Act. These Acts, it is true, concern the law of property rather than the principles of equity. But they have some bearing upon the sphere which equity has come to occupy in the English legal system, because, by that time, jurisdiction over most of the problems to which the land law gave rise had been appropriated by the Chancery Division. The reason why that had come about is, I think, the indirect result of two clauses in the Chancery Procedure Amendment Act of 1852. The old Court of Chancery in the eighteenth and early nineteenth centuries had never exercised so exclusive a jurisdiction. It is true that an eighteenth-century writer,[3] after pointing out that it was then usual 'to convey long terms in trust and make the several limitations of the estates the uses of the trust', said: 'The consequence of this is, that trustees being known only in the Court of Chancery;

---

[1] 17 & 18 Vict. c. 113; 30 & 31 Vict. c. 69; 40 & 41 Vict. c. 34.
[2] 32 & 33 Vict. c. 46.
[3] Edward Wynne, *Observations on Fitzherbert's 'Natura Brevium'*, 47; the tract was written in 1760.

all such suits, to which they must necessarily be parties, become suits in equity'—so that 'little will be left to the Courts of common law, but petty contracts and trifling assaults'. But this was an exaggeration. So long as future legal estates were created by strict settlements and by wills, the common law courts necessarily retained some jurisdiction, because the Court of Chancery could not act in any case of doubt, till the parties or the court had ascertained from a court of common law the true interpretation of the effect of the limitations contained in these settlements and wills. But the Chancery Procedure Act of 1852 prohibited the Court of Chancery from directing cases to be stated for a court of common law, and gave the court power to determine such questions of law; and it further provided that, in cases when it refused equitable relief till the rights of the parties had been determined by an action at law, the court might determine those rights.[1] It followed that for the future it was no longer necessary to apply to a court of common law to ascertain the rights of the parties under settlements and wills, so that the jurisdiction of equity over most of the questions arising out of settlements and wills came to be the exclusive property of equity.

One other great change, which had a very large effect upon an important branch of the equitable jurisdiction, had been made before 1885. That was the change effected in the proprietary status of married women by the Married Women's Property Act, 1882. But that Act did not adopt the straightforward course of assimilating the proprietary position of a married woman to that of a man or an unmarried woman.[2] Instead, it applied, with some modifications, the equitable rules as to the separate property of married women, to all married women. It preserved the effect of settlements, and it made it possible to attach a restraint upon anticipation to this statutory separate estate. Some very difficult problems were thus set to the Chancery Division, which could only be solved by an application of the equitable principles applicable to the separate property of married women, and of some of the legal rules as to their status, to the new situation created by the

[1] 15 & 16 Vict. c. 86, ss. 61, 62.
[2] That course has, however, now been adopted by the Law Reform (Married Women and Tortfeasors) Act, 1935. [Eds.]

clauses of the Act. The judges have shown much skill in the solution of these problems. The fact that the result is not wholly satisfactory is due to the legislature rather than to the judges.

In 1888 and 1893 came two comprehensive Trustee Acts. Those Acts are partly a codification of existing equitable rules and practice, and partly a modification of those rules and that practice. The most notable change was made by section 8 of the Trustee Act of 1888 which gave to trustees, under certain conditions, the benefit of a statute of Limitation. That section is still in force, since, for some reason which is not very obvious, it has not been absorbed into the Trustee Act, 1925.[1] Other statutes which made important modifications in the law of Trusts were the Judicial Trustees Act, 1896, and the Act of 1906 establishing the Public Trustee. A useful clause in the former Act gave the court power to relieve a trustee from the consequences of a breach of trust if it appeared that he had acted honestly, reasonably, and ought fairly to be excused.

In 1890 the Partnership Act, very skilfully drawn by Sir Frederick Pollock, codified the law of Partnership. In 1897 Part I of the Land Transfer Act made a new departure in the law as to administration of assets, by making all property, except the legal estate in copyholds, devolve upon the personal representative. But, from the point of view of the ambit of the equitable jurisdiction, the most important legislation is the series of Company Acts which begin in 1844 and extend to the Companies Act, 1929. These Acts are important from this point of view, because they have given equity a far larger jurisdiction in commercial cases than it would otherwise have had. In the earlier part of the eighteenth century the Court of Chancery had shared with the courts of common law jurisdiction in commercial cases. But its system of procedure made it a very unsatisfactory tribunal, and it added very little to mercantile law. It lost this jurisdiction after Lord Mansfield had so reformed the procedure of the Court of King's Bench that it became a very much more convenient tribunal for the trial of commercial cases, and after he had, by his decisions, laid down the leading principles of our modern mercantile law. Almost the only species of mercantile jurisdiction left to the Court

---

[1] It is now replaced by sect. 19 of the Limitation Act, 1939. [Eds.]

of Chancery was its jurisdiction in bankruptcy. But the manner in which this jurisdiction was exercised was most unsatisfactory, and the court was deprived of it in 1831.[1] The effect of the Company Acts upon equity has been to entrust to it the task of solving the many new problems which the rise of these new commercial entities have created, and to give back to it some of that control over commercial problems which it had lost in the eighteenth century.

Thus, before the Property Acts came into effect on 1 January 1926, many new developments in equity had been made by the legislature. The Property Acts have had, and will have, a profound effect upon the development of equity. In so far as they affect the law of property and conveyancing, they affect a branch of the law which had become almost exclusively the domain of equity; and the carrying out of their object of assimilating as far as possible the law of real and personal property has had large effects upon many equitable doctrines. One obvious illustration is the manner in which they have largely diminished, though in one small respect they have extended,[2] the importance of the doctrine of conversion. Two of these Acts—the Trustee Act and the Administration of Estates Act, together with some of the clauses of the Judicature Act, 1925[3]—have had a very large direct effect upon important bodies of equitable doctrine. The Trustee Act both consolidates many previous Acts on the subject of trustees, and makes some considerable changes in the law. The Administration of Estates Act has effected very skilfully a much-needed reform and restatement of the very complex law of executors and administrators, of the administration of assets, and of intestate succession. Since, for the most part, these Acts deal with matters which fall within the province of the Chancery Division, they have had, and will have, a large effect upon the future development of equity. But very many of their provisions are simply restatements, with or without modification, of existing equitable principles; and it is obviously contemplated that the powers and discretions which they give to the court will be exercised

[1] 1 & 2 Will. IV, c. 56.
[2] *Re Kempthorne*, [1930] 1 Ch. 268.
[3] Certain of the clauses of the Administration of Estates Act were repealed and substantially re-enacted in the Judicature Act.

in accordance with the same principles. They must therefore be interpreted in the light of the older cases in which those principles are stated, and in which the court has been accustomed to look for guidance as to the manner in which it ought to exercise the powers and discretions entrusted to it. They will no doubt create a new era in the development of many branches of equity—just as the Married Women's Property Acts have created a new era in the development of a particular branch of equitable doctrine. But, like the Married Women's Property Acts, they have not created, and they will not create a decisive break in the historical continuity of the evolution of equitable doctrine, or, consequently, in the present position of equity in the English legal system.

The Present Position of Equity

Maitland in his *Lectures on Equity* gave the authority of his great name to the view that, since the Judicature Acts, equity need not be taught or learned as a separate system. He said:[1]

'When some years ago the new scheme for our Tripos was settled, we said that candidates for the second part were to study the English Law of Real and Personal Property and the English Law of Contract and Tort, with the equitable principles applicable to these subjects. It was a question whether we ought not to have mentioned equity as a separate subject. I have no doubt, however, that we did the right thing. To have acknowledged the existence of equity as a system distinct from law would in my opinion have been a belated, a reactionary measure. I think, for example, that you ought to learn the many equitable modifications of the law of contract, not as a part of equity, but as a part, and a very important part, of our modern English law of contract.'

This view is based partly on the undoubted fact, which Maitland explained clearly for the first time, that equity is not a self-sufficient system, but a series of glosses on, or appendices to, various branches of the common law,[2] and partly on the fact that the bond between them was a 'jurisdictional and a procedural bond',[3] which the Judicature Acts had dissolved. He added that 'the day will come when lawyers will cease to inquire whether a given rule be a rule of equity or a rule of

---

[1] *Lectures on Equity*, 21–2.
[2] Ibid. 18–20.
[3] Ibid. 20.

common law: suffice it that it is a well-established rule administered by the High Court of Justice'.[1] It is thought by
some that, now that so many of the rules of equity have, as a
result of the Property Acts, ceased to be rules of common law
or equity, and have become statutory rules, the day en-
visaged by Maitland has come.

I think that neither the fact that equity is not a self-
sufficient system, nor the results of the Judicature Acts and
the Property Acts, support this conclusion.

In the first place, it does not follow from the fact that
equity was not a self-sufficient system, but a series of glosses
on, or appendices to, various branches of the common law,
only bound together by a jurisdictional and procedural bond
which has been dissolved, that it is not necessary to teach it
or learn it as a separate whole. So to reason involves a serious
underestimate of the strength and consequences of that
jurisdictional and procedural bond—an underestimate of the
same kind as that which Blackstone made in his treatment
of equity.[2] The matters which made up the system of equity
may have been disparate; but, because the jurisdictional and
procedural bond ensured a similar technical approach to all
these matters, it gave a unity to many of the principles which
underlie them. The true meaning of these principles, and of
the cases upon which these principles depend, cannot be
grasped unless equity is studied as a separate whole. Both
the principles and the cases may easily be misunderstood
unless some knowledge of the technical environment in
which they were born is present to the mind of the student.
That knowledge will never be acquired if equity is studied
in snippets. It may be that the old jurisdictional and procedural bond has been dissolved. But its effects remain. Like
the forms of action, 'it rules us from its grave', because it
lives in the very distinct technical approach, and the very
distinct intellectual characteristics, which it imposes upon
those who study the principles and rules of equity.

In the second place, I think that this view rests upon an
exaggerated estimate of the effects of the Judicature Acts—a
view which, as we have seen,[3] was held by eminent judges
immediately after the passing of the Acts, but which has

---

[1] Ibid. 20.
[2] As to this see *Harv. Law Rev.* xliii. 14.   [3] Above, pp. 167–70.

now been corrected. Maitland began to lecture on equity in 1888; and if the resolution he mentions as to the Tripos was made 'some years ago', we are brought very near to the time when the Judicature Acts first came into operation, and when these exaggerated views prevailed.

In the third place, I do not think that the conversion of many of the rules of equity into statutory rules by the Property Acts, and by the legislation which preceded them, at all advances the argument for this thesis. On the contrary, I think that they are an argument for the teaching of equity as a separate system. The Law of Property Act has largely increased the number of purely equitable interests, and has consolidated the dominion of equity over large parts of the law of property. It is clear, therefore, that a knowledge of the principles of equity is more than ever necessary to those who are called upon to interpret and apply its provisions. The same knowledge is needed by those who are called upon to interpret and apply those numerous clauses of the other Property Acts which restate or modify existing equitable principles; and that knowledge can, I think, only be acquired by those who have studied equity as a separate and distinct system. I entirely agree with the opinion expressed by an American writer that 'attempts to teach equity here and there as parts of courses on property, contract, and tort can never be satisfactory, if for no other reason than because violence is done by that process to the history of equity in its relation to the common law, and because of the essential and fundamental difference between legal and equitable relief'.[1]

In fact, as I have shown in this paper, both the Judicature Acts and the numerous other Acts which have restated, developed, modified, or added to the principles of equity, have all assumed the existence of this distinct and separate system of equity. They have been interpreted and applied and harmonized (as their framers intended) with the existing principles of equity, by a succession of able Chancellors and judges, who were masters of those principles. The result is that the historical continuity of those principles remains. It follows, therefore, that the study of that historical system

[1] William F. Walsh, 'Review of Powell's Cases on the Law of Trusts and Estates', *New York Law Quart. Rev.* xi. 669.

as a whole is more than ever necessary to the student who wishes to understand the true meaning and scope of the modern statutory rules, which are founded upon, and pre-suppose the existence of, the principles evolved by the old Court of Chancery and its successors—the Chancery Division and the Court of Appeal. That study has flourished during the last fifty years—may it continue to flourish.

THE INFLUENCE OF ROMAN LAW ON ENGLISH EQUITY[1]

THE separation of the English legal system into the two distinct departments of common law and equity is peculiar to England; and the sharpness of this separation is due to the circumstance that the administration of common law and equity was, from the latter part of the fourteenth century down to the coming into force of the first Judicature Act in 1875, entrusted to separate courts which acted upon principles and by means of rules of procedure which were quite different from one another.

Both the fact and its cause have been noted by English lawyers from an early period. The separation of the English legal system into the two departments of law and equity was noted as a peculiarity of the English legal system by Bacon[2] and James I[3] in the early part of the seventeenth century; and in the eighteenth century its origin was rightly attributed both by Hardwicke[4] and Blackstone[5] to the fact that in England alone law and equity were administered in separate courts.

The result has been that the substantive rules of the English system of equity and its rules of procedure are as different from anything which is to be found in continental legal systems as the substantive rules and the rules of procedure of the common law. But though equity and common law are sharply separated in one respect there is a similarity between them. Both the English system of equity and the English common law have been less influenced by Roman law than continental legal systems; but neither have been wholly uninfluenced by it. It is the purpose of this paper to

[1] An address prepared as a report for the International Congress of Comparative Law to be held at The Hague in July 1937, and delivered at a meeting of the Holdsworth Club of the University of Birmingham, held at the University, Edmund Street, on 27 November 1936.
[2] *De Augmentis*, bk. viii, c. iii, Aph. 45, cited Holdsworth, *H.E.L.* v. 486 n. 3.
[3] *Works of James I*, 559, cited Holdsworth, *H.E.L.* iv. 279 n. 4.
[4] *Wortley v. Birkhead* (1754), 2 Ves. Sen. 571, 574.
[5] *Comm.* iii. 49.

examine the nature and extent of that influence on the English system of equity.

It would, I think, be true to say that though the ways in which and the time at which Roman law influenced equity, differed from the ways in which and the time at which it influenced the common law, yet the character of that influence and its results have not been dissimilar. A rapid glance first at the ways in which Roman law influenced the common law, and then at the way in which it influenced equity will make this fact clear.

The period when the influence of Roman law upon the common law was most strongly felt was during the latter half of the twelfth, and the first half of the thirteenth centuries—the age of Glanvil and Bracton. The civil and canon law, as expounded by the school of the glossators, helped the statesmen and lawyers who then staffed the King's court to construct a common law; and they did their work so well that, from the end of the thirteenth century, the common law took its place as an independent system, and developed along its own insular lines. As Maitland has said, this Roman learning 'came to us soon; it taught us much; and then there was a healthy resistance to foreign dogma'.[1] But at later periods in the history of the common law the influence of Roman law on particular topics was felt. Some use was made in later centuries of the Roman doctrines which Bracton had borrowed in order to liberalize the common law—the classic instance is the case of *Coggs* v. *Bernard* in 1704,[2] in which the principles of the law of bailments, as summarized by Bracton from Roman law, were stated by Holt C.J. as part of the law of England; and in the eighteenth century the works of continental lawyers, which were based ultimately on the technical concepts of Roman law, helped Lord Mansfield to found the English system of mercantile law. Many different doctrines of the common law have been influenced by Roman law; but the Roman doctrines thus received have never been continuously developed on Roman lines. They have been naturalized and assimilated into the English legal system, and have thus helped that system to develop to meet new needs on its own

[1] Pollock and Maitland, *H.E.L.* (2nd ed.), i. 24.
[2] (1704), 2 Ld. Raym. 909.

lines.[1] Thus Lord Wright, speaking of commercial law, has said that 'until well into the nineteenth century English judges frequently relied on citations from foreign jurists, such as Pothier, Emerigon, the Civilians, and indeed the Digest, which Blackburn often quoted', but that he cannot recall any instance in the present century in which a judge has had recourse to these foreign sources.[2]

The influence of Roman law on equity has had a history which, in its main outlines and in its effects, is not dissimilar. Since the origin and development of the English system of equity are later in date than the origin or development of the common law, the period when the influence of Roman law was most marked came later; but in both cases that influence was felt in the initial stages of development. Just as the period of the greatest influence of the Roman law on the common law was during its infancy in the late twelfth and early thirteenth centuries, so the period of the greatest influence of the Roman law on equity was during its infancy in the late fourteenth and early fifteenth centuries. Just as the Roman influence on the common law was felt through judges who had studied the civil and canon law, so the Roman influence on equity was felt through Chancellors and their officials who were ecclesiastics and canonists.

The late Professor Vinogradoff pointed out that the Latin version of St. Germain's Dialogue between a Doctor of the Canon Law and a Student of the Common Law shows that the writer, when dealing with the equitable doctrines, which he puts into the mouth of the Doctor, 'started in the same way from scholastic philosophy and Canon law as Bracton started from Roman law in his time. . . . Azo was the interpreter of Civil law for the thirteenth century lawyer, John Gerson was the leading exponent of school doctrines for the sixteenth century jurist.'[3] St. Germain takes his definition of equity, and the reason for its existence side by side with law, from Aristotle through Gerson;[4] and from Gerson also he takes his definition of the conception of Sinderesis (συντή-

[1] Holdsworth, *H.E.L.* iv. 293.

[2] *Some Developments of Commercial Law in the Present Century*. The Presidential Address of Lord Wright to the Holdsworth Club of the University of Birmingham, 1935, p. 2.

[3] *L.Q.R.* xxiv. 374.   [4] Ibid. 374–5.

ρησις), i.e. the power of distinguishing good from evil and of choosing the good.[1] That power, St. Germain points out, enables conscience to operate in individual cases to distinguish right from wrong, and so to redress the hardship which sometimes arises from that generality of the rules of law which Aristotle had said was the occasion for rules of equity. On the question how conscience should be applied in individual cases St. Germain borrows from two fifteenth-century *Summae Confessorum* which were specially concerned with concrete moral problems of this kind.[1]

But as with the common law, so with equity, this canonist and civilian influence was not permanent; and though in later times the obvious analogies, such as those between the Praetor's *jus honorarium* and the Chancellor's equity, and between the *fidei-commissum* and the trust, are referred to, there is no evidence that the later in date of these analogous conceptions was derived from the earlier. No doubt equity took over certain Roman concepts from the ecclesiastical courts when it assumed the jurisdiction over legacies and administration of assets which those courts had once exercised; and in the discussion of cases of this sort many references are made to Roman law.[2] It may also be that when the Court of Chancery followed the rule of the common law, and upheld the validity of a bequest of chattels to B subject to 'the use and occupation of' those chattels by A during his life,[3] it was influenced by the views of the ecclesiastical lawyers, who were familiar with the Roman rule that a testator could bequeath the usufruct of a *res* to A, and the *dominium* in it to B;[4] and it may be that it was influenced by the Roman rule when it asserted the invalidity of such a

[1] Ibid. 378.
[2] See, e.g., *Ward* v. *Turner* (1752), 2 Ves. Sen. 431 (*donatio mortis causa*); *Ashburner* v. *MacGuire* (1786), 2 Bro. C.C. 108 (ademption of a legacy); *Scott* v. *Tyler* (1788), 2 Bro. C.C. 431 (legacy given under a condition restraining marriage). As Kerly says, *History of Equity*, 189, 'the sources from which the passages from the Institutes and Digest which were cited in equity were almost invariably taken—the text-books of ecclesiastical law, Godolphin and Swinburne—indicate clearly the uses to which they were applied.'
[3] Holdsworth, *H.E.L.* vii. 474; *Vachel* v. *Vachel* (1669), 1 Ch. Cas 129; *Hyde* v. *Parratt* (1695), 1 P.Wms. 1; *Tissen* v. *Tissen* (1718), 1 P.Wms. 500.
[4] Holdsworth, *H.E.L.* vii. 474; cf. Bordwell, 'Interests in Chattels', *Missouri Law Rev.* i. 128.

bequest in the case of *res quae usu consumuntur*, and laid down
the rule that in such a case A became the absolute owner.[1]
But these cases do not cover much ground; so that I think
that Kerly is right in his contention that the debt of equity
to Roman law is not large.[2]

In fact, just as the doctrines taken by Bracton from
Roman law, and the later borrowings from Roman law,
were never continuously developed on Roman lines, but
were assimilated into the common law system, so the
doctrines of equity taken from Gerson and the Canonists and
Civilians, and the later borrowings from similar sources, have
been assimilated into the English system of equity, which is
as insular in its contents as the common law. What Lord
Wright has said of the earlier practice of citing the civilians
in commercial cases, and the cessation of that practice in
modern times, is equally true with respect to equity. Maine
says that earlier Chancellors sometimes borrowed from the
Corpus Juris Civilis; and that, during the eighteenth century,
'the mixed systems of jurisprudence and morals constructed
by the publicists of the Low Countries appear to have been
much studied by English lawyers, and from the Chancellorship of Lord Talbot to the commencement of Lord Eldon's
Chancellorship these works had considerable effect on the
rulings of the Court of Chancery'.[3]   But nowadays such
authorities are rarely if ever cited. The growth of purely
English rules recorded in the cases has made a recourse to
foreign authorities unnecessary.

It was in fact inevitable that equity should develop mainly
on native lines. In the first place, the place and function
assigned to equity in relation to law by the canonists and
civilians of the fifteenth century emphasized its dependence
on the law of the State. In the second place, that dependence
was still further emphasized by the course of English legal
history.

(1) The place and function assigned to equity by St.
Germain were accepted by later lawyers; for, right down to
Blackstone's day and later, his book was accepted as authori-
tative. On this matter I shall summarize what I have said in

---

[1] *Randall* v. *Russell* (1817), 3 Mer. 190, 194–5.
[2] *History of Equity*, 101–1, 189.
[3] *Ancient Law*, 44–5.

my *History of English Law*.[1] St. Germain adopts the view held by all medieval lawyers that the world is ruled primarily by the law of God or nature or reason, and only secondarily by the human law of the State. No human law which was contrary to these universal laws was valid. But a human law might conform to these universal laws, and so be valid; and yet when it came to be applied to a particular case it might work manifest wrong. It was particular cases of this kind which called for the intervention of equity. It follows that the human law of the State is the foundation of the rules of equity; for they are called into existence by the presence of some hardship resulting from the manner in which this human law has dealt with particular cases. Thus the law of the State is the starting-point of equity. Two consequences follow: first, though civil and canon law treatises might be useful as illustrating the working of the rules of equity as applied to those systems of law, they were of small importance in England, as compared with treatises upon the common law, upon which in England the rules of equity must be based. Secondly, though in England equity developed into a very distinct system because it was administered in the separate Court of Chancery, it never lost its dependence upon the law. At the end of the sixteenth century Bacon said that 'the common law has a kind of rule and survey over the Chancery to determine what belongs to the Chancery';[2] and at the end of the nineteenth century Maitland pointed out that equity was a 'supplementary law—a sort of appendix added on to our code on a sort of gloss written round our code', which, 'at every point presupposed the existence of common law'.[3] Inevitably, therefore, the conceptions, principles, and rules of the common law played a much greater part in the development of equity than the conceptions, principles, and rules of Roman law.

(2) This dependence on the common law was emphasized by the course of English legal history. One of the results of the Reformation in Henry VIII's reign was the replacement of the ecclesiastical Chancellors by Chancellors who were English lawyers. Cardinal Wolsey was the last

[1] *H.E.L.* iv. 279–83.
[2] 'Reading on the Statute of Uses', *Works* (ed. Spedding), vii. 415.
[3] *Equity*, 18, 19.

of the ecclesiastical Chancellors of the medieval type. He was replaced in 1529 by Sir Thomas More—an eminent common lawyer and the son of a common law judge; and the teaching of canon law in the Universities was suppressed. It is true that down to the middle of the seventeenth century some of the Masters in Chancery and some of the Masters of the Rolls continued to be civilians. It is true that in those few parts of the jurisdiction of the Court of Chancery which had been taken from the ecclesiastical courts, rules of the civil and canon law continued to be followed. But it is clear that when the Chancellors came to be chosen invariably from men who had made their career as English lawyers, and when the Masters in Chancery and the Masters of the Rolls came likewise to be chosen from English lawyers, the influence of the concepts and principles and rules of the common law would become the predominating influence in the development of the system of equity.

This change of personnel did not in any way diminish the separation between equity and law, nor did it affect the theory upon which equitable interferences with or additions to the law were made. The ecclesiastical Chancellors had established equity as a separate system; and St. Germain's book had caused the theory upon which they acted to be the theory which was accepted by their successors. But the change of personnel, coupled with the continued separation between the Court of Chancery and the courts of common law, had this result: it caused the principles and rules of equity, which these lawyers, Chancellors and Masters, were developing in their Court of Chancery, to develop on lines which were quite distinct both from the rules of the common law and from the rules of Roman law.

I propose to take two instances to illustrate this fact: first the system of procedure and pleading, and secondly some features in the development of the law of trusts.

(1) In any system of law which has developed independently on its own lines, its rules as to procedure and pleading are the first to be developed, and are a fair index to the manner in which its substantive rules will be developed. Both the system of procedure and the system of pleading which were developed by the Court of Chancery were quite unique. In both cases ideas borrowed from the Roman canon and

civil law united with very different ideas taken from the common law to produce a system which was remarkable for its delay and expense. The procedure used by the ecclesiastical Chancellors of the Middle Ages was influenced by the summary procedure of the canon law; and the fact that, in the Middle Ages and later, some of the Masters were civilians, ensured some infiltration of ideas drawn from the civil and canon law. Thus the idea that witnesses should be examined privately and by an official of the court, and the idea that their evidence should not be divulged till published, are reminiscent of rules of the civil and canon law. So, too, is the form of the judgment. In the common law courts the court simply decided the specific issue raised by the pleadings: in equity the court considered the whole of the circumstances of the case, and made a decree which could give effect to the rights of the parties in those circumstances.[1] On the other hand, the process used to get the parties before the court resembled the dilatory process of the common law; and sinecure officials and saleable offices, which helped to make procedure slow and expensive, were even more common in the Court of Chancery than in the common law courts.[2] The result of these two sets of influences was that the Court of Chancery developed a system of procedure which resembled neither the Roman system nor the common law system. It was the same with its system of pleading. In the sixteenth and seventeenth centuries we can see in the system of equity pleading ideas taken from Roman law, and ideas taken from the common law. In the plaintiff's bill and the defendant's answer, in the discovery which the defendant was obliged to give, and in the liberty of amendment, we can see ideas taken from Roman law; in the fact that the pleading took place out of court, in the nature of the pleas and demurrers open to the parties, and in the joinder of issue, we can see ideas taken from the common law.[3] The clash of these two separate sets of ideas resulted, in the eighteenth century, in the creation of a system which was quite unique. The ideas taken from the common law were eliminated; and a wholly original system was developed, which centred round the bill

[1] Holdsworth, *H.E.L*, ix. 337–8.   [2] Ibid. 339.
[3] Ibid. 376–9.

and answer. Though it was freed from the subtleties of the common law system of special pleading, it was quite as artificial and technical, and infinitely more dilatory and expensive.[1]

(2) The law of trusts is the most important and the unique contribution of equity to the jurisprudence of the world. The modern trust is derived from the medieval use; and early writers on the use had no hesitation in looking to Roman law for its origin. Gilbert, Sanders, Blackstone, Spence, and Digby all point out the analogy which exists between the position created by the grant of a *usus* or a *usus-fructus* or the bequest of a *fidei-commissum*, and that created by the gift of property to A to the use of B.[2] But, as Bacon realized,[3] the existence of an analogy is one thing; the proof that the later in date of these two analogous things is derived from the earlier is another. It is now generally agreed that Bacon was right in regarding these institutions of Roman law as analogies of a superficial kind. The late Mr. Justice Holmes pointed out that the root idea underlying the use or trust is to be found amongst the Germanic tribes—the idea, that is, that a person to whom property has been conveyed for certain purposes must carry out those purposes.[4] But since in very many cases the common law refused to compel a person to whom property had been thus conveyed to do his duty, it was necessary for equity to intervene; and its intervention has in course of time created a body of law which has no parallel in any other legal system. 'If we were asked', says Maitland,[5] 'what is the greatest and most distinctive achievement performed by Englishmen in the field of jurisprudence I cannot think that we should have any better answer to give than this; namely, the development from century to century of the trust idea.' Since the law of trusts is the largest and most important part of the English system of equity, since its influence upon that system is all-pervading, these words of Maitland make it clear that the doctrines of equity are, like its system of procedure and pleading, and like the doctrines of the common law, essentially native.

[1] Holdsworth, *H.E.L.* ix. 406.
[2] Ibid. iv. 410 and n. 1.
[3] 'Reading on the Statute of Uses', *Works* (ed. Spedding), vii. 407–8.
[4] *L.Q.R.* i. 162; Holdsworth, *H.E.L.* iv. 410–12.
[5] 'The Unincorporate Body', *Collected Papers*, iii. 272.

LAW ON ENGLISH EQUITY

No doubt the conception of equity and its relation to the law was derived from Aristotle through the canon lawyers; and no doubt the system of equity procedure and pleading owed something to the civilians and canonists. But since the underlying theory as to the occasions when equity could modify the law made it in a sense a satellite to the law, and since the common law was, to use the words of Holt C.J., 'the overruling jurisdiction in this realm',[1] it followed that the contents of its rules were determined far more by defects of, and lacunae in, the common law, which made its interference necessary, than by the Roman or any other system of law. Though Roman rules, and, as Maine indicated,[2] the speculations of foreign writers on Roman law and jurisprudence, might be referred to in order to indicate what was the fair and reasonable rule to apply to a given state of facts,[3] the main current of the development of equity was determined by the need to add to, or to render more efficacious, the rules of the common law; and, since that development was made by a separate court, the contents of its rules were elaborated mainly by the practice of the court, and through the agency of that system of case law, which, in the course of the seventeenth century, it followed the common law in adopting.

It is, I think, safe to say that the English system of equity owes practically nothing to classical Roman law; and that the equity of the Praetor, to which Lord Hardwicke and other Chancellors sometimes compared it,[4] is merely an interesting parallel and not a source from which it is derived.

This conclusion is supported by what Professor Buckland has said in his interesting lectures on *Equity in Roman Law*. The conception of equity and its relation to law, which St. Germain took from Aristotle and the canon lawyers, assumes the principle which runs all through English equity —the principle that it acts *in personam*; for if it is the hardship in individual cases resulting from the generality of the

---

[1] *Shermoulin* v. *Sands* (1697), 1 Ld. Raym. 272.
[2] Above, p. 192.   [3] Kerly, *History of Equity*, 189.
[4] Thus Lord Hardwicke in the letter which he wrote to Lord Kames on the administration of equity in England talks of 'the Praetor', and of the work of equity 'under the head *adjuvandi vel supplendi juris civilis*', P.C. Yorke, *Life of Hardwicke*, ii. 554, 555.

rules of law which is the occasion for equity, equity must act *in personam*—it must consider the circumstances of the particular case which justify each litigant in appealing to equity. 'But', says Professor Buckland, 'we shall look in vain in Roman law for any such rule as that which underlies all our equity principles, that "Equity acts *in personam*" ', and 'nowhere is there any sign of a special duty on the Praetor, or any other administrator of the law, to deal with persons who do injustice under cover of legal right, by methods which put pressure on the conscience of the wrongdoer'.[1] It may be, as he says, that 'the legal logic of the classical Roman lawyer is much the same as that of the English lawyer',[2] so that both when set to solve a concrete problem arrive at much the same conclusion. But because the underlying principles upon which the equity of the Roman lawyer and that of the English lawyer are based are fundamentally dissimilar, direct descent of English principles and rules from the classical Roman law can rarely be shown.[3]

---

[1] At page 3.   [2] At page 127.   [3] At page 122.

SECRET TRUSTS[1]

R*E Keen*, [1937] 1 Ch. 236; 106 L.J. Ch. 177 decides two points in the law relating to secret trusts. The first point is this: if a communication by a testator as to the terms of the trust is contained in a sealed envelope, which is not to be opened till after the testator's death, the giving of the envelope to the trustees is a sufficient communication of the trust before death, because, said Lord Wright M.R., 'the trustees had the means of knowledge available whenever it became necessary and proper to open the envelope' (at pp. 242–3). On this point the Court of Appeal followed a hypothetical opinion of Kay J. in *Re Boyes* (1884), 26 Ch. D. at p. 536, and reversed the decision of Farwell J. in this case. The second and more important point is this: if property is left by a testator to X in trust, the trusts declared cannot be carried out unless their terms are communicated to X at or before the date of the will. In this case the property was to be held by the trustees 'upon trust and disposed of by them among such person, persons, or charities as may be notified by me to them during my lifetime'. Since this provision in the will was construed as reserving to the testator the power to make new notifications as to the trusts on which the property was to be held after the date of the will, it was held to be invalid. It follows that the law draws a hard-and-fast line between cases of the type of *McCormick* v. *Grogan* (1869), L.R. 4 H.L. 82 where property is left to a person without any mention of a trust, but a trust is established *aliunde*, and cases where the property is left on trust and evidence is necessary to establish the terms of the trust. In the former class of cases the communication of the trust may be made at any time before the testator's death—in *McCormick* v. *Grogan* it was made after the date of the will: in the latter class of cases it must be made at or before the date of the will. In neither case can the communication be made after the date of the testator's death, because that would enable a testator to make a *post-mortem* disposition of his property by a document which is not executed as

[1] Reprinted from the (1937) 53 *Law Quarterly Review*, 501.

required by the Wills Act. Thus, if the trusts were contained in a sealed envelope, and the trustees had no notice of its existence till after the death, the trusts would not be binding.

The distinction thus established by *Re Keen* is founded on the decision of Parker V.-C. in the case of *Johnson* v. *Ball* (1851), 5 De G. & Sm. 85, 91. He said: 'A testator cannot by his will prospectively create for himself a power to dispose of his property by an instrument not duly executed as a will or a codicil'; he deduced from this rule the consequence that it was impossible to give effect to the communication of a trust made subsequently to the making of the will; and he distinguished the case where no trust appears on the face of the will. The authorities cited by Parker V.-C. for his decision are *Croker* v. *Marquis of Hertford* (1844), 4 Moo. P.C. 339, and *Briggs* v. *Penny* (1849), 3 De G. & Sm. 525. But the first of these cases was not a case of a secret trust. It was a case where a testator tried to reserve to himself a power in his will to make future direct dispositions of his property by unexecuted papers. It is an authority only for the proposition that a testator cannot reserve to himself this power, because, if he were able to reserve such a power and he used it, he would be able to make a *post-mortem* disposition by a document not evidenced as required by the Wills Act. The second of these cases was, so far as it applied to a secret trust, the case of a communication made after the death of the testator. Knight-Bruce V.-C. said (at p. 547):

'I apprehend that a testator, by a will, . . . could not enable himself to make a disposition of any part of his property by any means which, if the will had not been made, he could not effectually have used. . . . The power of a testator to incorporate in his will another existing paper which the will, by specific reference and description, identifies, and the prevention of fraud, by compelling a legatee to perform, after the testator's death, a promise made by him to the testator, upon the faith of which the testator, to the knowledge of the legatee, gave the legacy, are scarcely exceptions or qualifications.'

It is clear that this reasoning is no authority for the distinction drawn in the case of *Johnson* v. *Ball* between the case where no trust appears on the face of the will, and the case where a trust appears. The three later cases in which this distinction between the case of an absolute gift and the case where the property is left on trust is recognized—*Re Fleet-*

wood (1880), 15 Ch. D. 594, *Re Huxtable*, [1902] 2 Ch. 793, and *Blackwell* v. *Blackwell*, [1929] A.C. 318—are all cases in which the communication was made at or before the date of the will. The distinction therefore rests ultimately on the case of *Johnson* v. *Ball*, the decision in which was based on cases which cannot be regarded as authorities for drawing any such distinction.

In fact the reasoning in the case of *Johnson* v. *Ball* rests upon a failure to distinguish between four distinct things: (1) an attempt by a testator to reserve to himself a power to make a direct disposition of his property by an instrument not executed as required by the Wills Act; (2) a disposition by way of secret trust not communicated by a testator to the trustee till after the testator's death; (3) a disposition by way of secret trust communicated by the testator to the trustee at or before the making of his will; (4) a disposition by way of secret trust communicated by the testator to the trustee after he has made his will and before his death.

It is necessary to distinguish carefully between the first two and the second two of these states of fact for the following reason: In the first two cases there is an absolute *post-mortem* gift which cannot take effect unless it is contained in a document executed as required by the Wills Act. In the second two of these cases there is no absolute *post-mortem* gift because both the will and therefore the communication of the gift contained in it are revocable during the testator's life-time. In the case of *Moss* v. *Cooper* (1861), 1 J. & H. 352, 367, Page Wood V.-C. said 'it is altogether immaterial whether the promise [made by the trustees to hold the property on trust] is made before or after the execution of the will, that being a revocable instrument'. But if the fact that a will is a revocable instrument till the death is the true principle upon which the validity or invalidity of a secret trust is based, it is clear that the distinction drawn in *Re Keen*, *Blackwell* v. *Blackwell*, and *Johnson* v. *Ball*, between the case where a trust appears on the face of the will and where it does not, is illogical, because in neither case is there an absolute *post-mortem* gift.

My contention is that the true principle is that indicated by Page Wood V.-C.—the fact that till death a will is re-vocable, and therefore till death conveys nothing. It follows that if before the death of a testator a trust is communicated to persons who on the face of the will take beneficially, or if before the death the terms of a trust are communicated to persons who on the face of the will take in trust, those persons, when the death occurs and the will becomes operative, take their estates with notice of the trust, and ought therefore to be bound by it. No valid or logical distinction can be drawn between these two cases, because in both cases there is a person who takes property with notice of a trust. On the other hand, if in either case the communication is made after the testator's death, the beneficiary under the will has taken an estate without notice of a trust. He gets a good estate both in law and in equity, which cannot be affected by any subsequent notice, partly because he had no notice when he took his estate, and partly because to decide otherwise would allow a person to make a *post-mortem* disposition of his property in a form which does not comply with the Wills Act.

The principle upon which equity recognizes and enforces secret trusts was explained with great clarity by Lord Sumner in *Blackwell* v. *Blackwell*. But in a passage in his judgment (which was not necessary for the decision in that case) he expressly approved of the distinction drawn in the case of *Johnson* v. *Ball*. That passage was the foundation of the judgment of the Court of Appeal in *Re Keen*, and led it to sanction this unfortunate distinction. But the distinction is not easily reconcilable with the principle previously stated by Lord Sumner upon which equity recognizes and enforces secret trusts, and, as the Court of Appeal recognized in *Re Keen*, it works in an arbitrary fashion, with the result that the intentions of testators are disappointed. Let us look at the reasoning in *Blackwell* v. *Blackwell* and the decision in *Re Keen* from these points of view.

Lord Sumner's account of the principle underlying the doctrine of secret trusts is contained in the following passages from his judgment in the case of *Blackwell* v. *Blackwell*. He dealt first with the case where there is an absolute gift and no trust appears on the face of the will. On that point he said ([1929] A.C. 318, 334):

'In itself the doctrine of equity, by which parol evidence is admissible to prove what is called "fraud" in connexion with secret trusts, and effect is given to such trusts when established, would not seem to conflict with any of the Acts under which from time to time the legislature has regulated the right of testamentary disposition. A Court of conscience finds a man in the position of an absolute legal owner of a sum of money, which has been bequeathed to him under a valid will, and it declares that on proof of certain facts relating to the motives and actions of the testator it will not allow the legal owner to exercise his legal right to do what he will with his own. This seems to be a perfectly normal exercise of general equitable jurisdiction. The facts commonly but not necessarily involve some immoral and selfish conduct on the part of the legal owner. The necessary elements on which the question turns are intention, communication, and acquiescence. The testator intends his absolute gift to be employed as he and not as the donee desires; he tells the proposed donee of this intention and, either by express promise or by the tacit promise, which is signified by acquiescence, the proposed donee encourages him to bequeath the money in the faith that his intentions will be carried out.'

It may be noted that this reasoning gives very little countenance to the distinction between cases of the type of *McCormick* v. *Grogan*, where no trust appears on the face of the will, and cases where a trust appears on the face of the will. After all a trustee is just as much 'the absolute legal owner' as a person to whom the legal ownership has been given without any mention of a trust. Lord Sumner then proceeded to consider the case where the trust appears on the face of the will. On that point he said (at p. 335):

'To this two circumstances must be added to bring the present case to the test of the general doctrine: first, that the will states on its face that the legacy is given on trust but does not state what the trusts are, and second, that the legatees are acting with perfect honesty, seek no advantage to themselves, and only desire, if the Court will permit them, to do what in other circumstances the Court would have fastened it on their conscience to perform. Since the current of decisions down to *Re Fleetwood* and *Re Huxtable* has established that the principles of equity apply equally where these circumstances are present as in cases where they are not, the material question is whether and how the Wills Act affects this case. It seems to me that apart from legislation, the application of the principle of equity, which was made in *Fleetwood's* and *Huxtable's* cases, was logical, and was justified by the same considerations as in cases of fraud and absolute gifts.'

The last sentence makes it clear that Lord Sumner drew no distinction between the equitable principle applicable to cases where no trust appears on the face of the will, and the equitable principle applicable to cases where it does appear, provided, as he said later, that the communication is made at or before the making of the will. But if the case where the property is left on trust is justified 'by the same considerations as in cases of fraud and absolute gifts', it is a little difficult to see why in both cases the communication cannot be made by the testator after he has made his will.

Both Lord Buckmaster (at pp. 330–1) and Lord Sumner (at p. 339) accepted the correctness of the distinction drawn in *Johnson* v. *Ball* between the case where no trust appears on the face of the will and the case where it does appear; and it was upon the passage in Lord Sumner's judgment in which he accepted that distinction that the decision in *Re Keen* is based. Lord Sumner said (at p. 339):

'A testator cannot reserve to himself a power of making future unwitnessed dispositions by merely naming a trustee and leaving the purposes of the trust to be supplied afterwards, nor can a legatee give testamentary validity to an unexecuted codicil by accepting an indefinite trust, never communicated to him in the testator's lifetime. . . . To hold otherwise would indeed be to enable the testator to "give the go-by" to the requirements of the Wills Act, because he did not choose to comply with them.'

It is clear from this passage that Lord Sumner puts into the same category a communication to a trustee made by a testator during his life, and a communication made to a legatee after the testator's death. In other words, he confuses the case where there is no absolute *post-mortem* gift because the communication is made in the testator's lifetime, and the case where there is an absolute *post-mortem* gift because the communication is made after the testator's death. But in the earlier passages already cited in which he explains the *rationale* of the doctrine of secret trusts, this confusion does not appear. Indeed, the passage cited from p. 339 is hardly consistent with these earlier passages; for if, as he says in a sentence which follows the passage cited from p. 339, 'it is communication of the purpose to the legatee, coupled with acquiescence or promise on his part, that removes the matter from the provision of the Wills Act and brings it within the law of trusts, as applied in this instance to trustees, who happen also to be legatees', it is difficult to justify the distinction between communications made by a testator at or

before the making of the will and those made by him after
the making of his will.

If, as I think, the whole distinction between the cases
where no trust appears on the face of the will and cases where
it does appear rests upon a confusion of thought in the
reasoning of Parker V.-C. in the case of *Johnson* v. *Ball*,
which arises from a failure to distinguish a gift which is an
absolute *post-mortem* gift from a gift which is not; and if it is
contrary to the principle upon which the doctrine of secret
trusts rests, it is not surprising that the reasonableness of the
distinction is open to question. It is not clear why communication at any time before death should be operative in one
class of case and not in the other; for there is no difference in
principle between admitting evidence to establish the existence of a trust, and admitting evidence to establish the terms
of a trust. In both cases the trustee has accepted the trust in
the testator's lifetime. In neither case is the testator overriding the Wills Act by a *post-mortem* communication. In
neither case therefore is he making a *post-mortem* disposition.
In fact, as Lord Wright M.R. admitted in *Re Keen*, the
distinction may lead, as it led in this case, to a frustration of
the intention of a testator by an accident in drafting; for, as
he said, if the clause had been worded so as to apply to trusts
previously indicated by the testator, then, according to the
decision in *Blackwell* v. *Blackwell*, evidence of the communication made to the trustees would have been admissible.
In fact the judgment of the Court of Appeal on this second
point is barely consistent with its judgment on the first point.
A communication by a testator to a trustee at or before the
execution of the will as to the terms of the trust, which is contained in a sealed envelope which is not to be opened till after
his death, is a valid communication of the terms of the trust.
But the giving of the envelope is in effect simply a notice that
he is to take as trustee, and yet the terms of the trust may be
communicated not only after the execution of the will but
after the death of the testator. If that is the law, it is a little
difficult to see why a gift to a legatee on trust cannot be followed by a communication of the terms of the trust at any
date after the execution of the will and before the death.

The case of *Blackwell* v. *Blackwell* was a decision as to a
trust communicated contemporaneously with the will. What

was said as to trusts communicated after the will and before the death was therefore only *dictum*. If the reasoning of *Johnson* v. *Ball* is founded on a confusion of thought, it is still open to the House of Lords to apply logically Lord Sumner's statement of the principle upon which the doctrine of secret trusts rests, to follow the implications of the reasoning of Page Wood V.-C. in *Moss* v. *Cooper*, and thus to simplify the law by getting rid of a distinction which is unreasonable and works substantial injustice.

MAITLAND REISSUED[1]

THE first of these books[2] contains seven of Maitland's papers—the most essential parts of his introduction to the 'Memoranda de Parliamento 1305', 'The Corporation Sole', 'The Crown as Corporation', 'The Unincorporate Body', 'Trust and Corporation', 'Moral Personality and Legal Personality', 'The Body Politic'. Mr. Lapsley has edited the first of these papers, Professor Hazeltine the fourth and fifth, and Professor Winfield the rest. The papers fall into four groups. The first deals with constitutional history, the second and third with English legal history, the third and fourth with the problem of group and corporate personality, and the last with political science.

Since Maitland wrote the first of these papers, much has been written on the early history of Parliament, and many unpublished Rolls of Parliament and other documents relating to Parliament have been printed. To this large literature Mr. Lapsley's preface is an invaluable guide. From it, I think, emerges the fact that Maitland's paper began a new epoch in the study of the early history of Parliament. In this paper, as in all his other historical work, Maitland tells his story from the original documents and from the point of view of the men who wrote those documents; and here, as elsewhere, he portrays the ideas of these men with amazing clarity. This method of writing the early history of Parliament, when applied by a man of unique historical and literary genius, produced results which were perhaps more revolutionary than those produced by any of his other works. The reason why it produced these revolutionary results is as

[1] Reprinted from the *Yale Law Journal*, 1937.
[2] *Selected Essays*, by F. W. Maitland. Edited by H. D. Hazeltine, G. Lapsley, and P. H. Winfield. Cambridge: at the University Press; New York: The Macmillan Co. 1936. Pp. ix, 264. $3.65. *Equity: A Course of Lectures*, by F. W. Maitland. Edited by A. H. Chaytor and W. J. Whittaker. Revised by John Brunyate. Cambridge: at the University Press; New York: The Macmillan Co. 1936. Pp. xxiv, 343. $4.00. *The Forms of Action at Common Law: A Course of Lectures*, by F. W. Maitland. Edited by A. H. Chaytor and W. J. Whittaker. Cambridge: at the University Press; New York: The Macmillan Co. 1936. Pp. xi, 92. $1.25.

follows: The protagonists in the constitutional conflicts of the seventeenth century had used the events of parliamentary history to prove their political creeds. The victory of Parliament in 1688 was thought to have established not only the legal but also the historical correctness of the views held by those who supported the Parliament. Thus there was established a traditional view of parliamentary history; and that traditional view had, during the eighteenth and nineteenth centuries, coloured the interpretation of the sources, and given rise to a set of doctrines as to the constitution of Edward I's parliaments which suffered from the fatal defect of looking at medieval facts from the point of view of the modern theory of the constitution. Maitland's account of what a parliament of Edward I's reign really was and what it really did presented so great a contrast to the received view on these matters that, as Mr. Lapsley says, it was some time 'before scholars grasped completely the bearings and implications of his essay or realized how strong a solvent of orthodoxy it was destined to be'. It was pioneer work—as were many other of Maitland's works; and though very much has been published on these lines since, it is wonderful how well his work has stood the test of comparison with the results of later researches in this field. This fact will be apparent if we look at some of the conclusions of Messrs. Richardson and Sayles in their Introduction to the *Unedited Rolls of Parliament 1279–1373*.[1]

Maitland insisted that 'a session of the king's council is the core and essence of every *parliamentum*'. This is accepted as obviously true by Messrs. Richardson and Sayles when they say:

'The king had always a council round him, a comparatively small body which was largely ministerial. On special occasions this small body would be afforced according to the needs of the moment, and parliament was a specially solemn occasion. Under Edward I the council summoned to parliament probably varied a great deal in composition; but when really important business had to be despatched every effort would be made to include all magnates of influence in church and state, and certainly every highly placed minister.'

Maitland pointed out that the records of the audience of,

[1] *Rotuli Parliamentorum Anglie Hactenus inediti mcclxxix–mccclxxiii*, Camden Soc., 3rd series, vol. li (1935).

and the answers to, petitions take the largest space in the roll of 1305; and precisely the same point is made by Messrs. Richardson and Sayles. They say also that 'the decisions of the council in parliament were apt to be directions as to the means of obtaining justice or of reaching a settlement rather than final judgments'. Exactly the same thing is said by Maitland, and, indeed, as Maitland points out, by Hale. Similarly Maitland's observation that 'by no sharp line can the petitions of the assembled lords and commons be marked off from the general mass of petitions' is said by Messrs. Richardson and Sayles to be generally true; but they think that some of this class of petitions did not pass through the hands of the receivers and triers, but went straight to the council. These few illustrations show the soundness of Maitland's conclusions. They show that the soundness of those conclusions was due to his capacity for seeing into the minds of those who composed the documents which he was interpreting—a capacity which has never been equalled by any other historian.

The fourth and fifth of these papers on 'Trust and Corporation' and 'Moral Personality and Legal Personality', are two of the most important papers in this collection. They have been very well edited by Professor Hazeltine. He has translated the German phrases, he has added notes which give references to books in which Maitland's theories have been discussed, and at the end he has given us a comprehensive bibliography of the continental and English literature on these subjects. These papers are important because in them Maitland introduced English lawyers to a new body of thought, and explained why it was a new body of thought to Englishmen. Both his account of the continental controversies to which it had given rise, and his explanation why these controversies had had no English counterpart, shed a new light on English institutions and English law.

The accepted continental theory of corporations had unduly restricted liberty of association. It was generally held that the only persons whom the State would recognize were either natural persons or fictitious persons. Fictitious persons were corporations; and it was only the sovereign who could create a fictitious person. The logical consequence of this view was what is known as the 'Concession Theory'—'the corporation is, and must be, the creature of the State. Into its nostrils the State must breathe the breath of a fictitious life, for otherwise it would be no associated body but individualistic dust'.[1] Thus the existence of all groups and communities were subordinated to the will of a sovereign state. Under the influence of this theory the old communities of the Middle Ages were dissolved, and therefore the liberty to associate was strictly limited. It was not till the beginning of the twentieth century that French law relaxed these limitations. In these circumstances those who desired to obtain a greater liberty of association attacked the theory upon which these limitations were based. Associations, it was said, were not fictitious. They were real things, as real as the human beings who composed them. They did not depend for their existence on the authorization of the State. The State therefore should recognize them in the same way and for the same reasons as it recognizes natural men. Thus the question whether group personality was fictitious or real became an important practical question because upon it depended the extent of the liberty of association and the powers of these associations.

Maitland pointed out that this had never been so important a practical question in England, partly because English law had never ceased to recognize some of the medieval communities such as counties and hundreds and Inns of Court, and partly because it had in the Trust a medium whereby many different associations could live and flourish without any authorization by the State. For the first time he pointed out the importance in this connexion of that medieval element in English law, the survival of which had been secured by the victory of the Parliament and the common law in the seventeenth century; and for the first time he pointed out the significance of the Trust Concept in our public and semi-public law. What theories English lawyers had had upon corporate personality were of a superficial kind; for, like other branches of the common law, the law as to corporations had grown up gradually and depended very little upon philosophical theory. Maitland's papers set lawyers thinking, and made them realize the need

[1] Gierke, *Political Theories of the Middle Age* (1900), xxx.

to acquire some clearer ideas as to the theoretical foundations upon which their law rested. I think that the result of that investigation has been to show that in the main the common law view of corporate personality is a sensible theory; but that the somewhat hand-to-mouth manner in which it has grown up has had its dangers, more especially in these latter years when the liberty to associate allowed by the common law, and the ease with which statutes allow corporate form to be assumed, have multiplied both the number and power of these various associations. The following conclusions have, I think, emerged:

In the first place, the question whether corporate personality is real or fictitious, though practically important in continental speculation because it was bound up with the question of liberty of association, is not fundamentally important for lawyers. The law recognizes persons, not from the biological point of view, but as the subjects of rights and duties. That being so, a group of persons, corporate or otherwise, which is the subject of rights and duties, is a person no less and no more than a natural person. No doubt it is a different sort of person because it is artificial, and no doubt its artificial quality gives it a different legal status. But it is just as real a person as a natural person. As Professor H. A. Smith has said,[1]

'a confusion is sometimes created by not distinguishing clearly between the legal and the philosophical, or the legal and the historical aspects of the matter. Thus, for example, if we ask the familiar question "Has the corporation a real group will as distinct from that of its individual members?" the answer will usually be for the philosopher. The lawyer is under no obligation to answer such a question, and the law does not generally provide him with an answer unless litigation has proved or legislation has anticipated its necessity. Now it is almost impossible to imagine any law suit in which the judge must find himself driven to pronounce upon the existence or non-existence of a group-will. The semi-philosophical expressions we find here and there in the Reports are invariably *obiter dicta*, and the true method of handling, or rather refusing to handle, such questions is well illustrated by the Privy Council in *Citizens Life Assurance Company* v. *Brown*[2] where Lord Lindley says: "If it is once granted that corporations are for civil purposes to be regarded as persons, i.e. as principals acting by agents

[1] Smith, *The Law of Associations* (1914), 128-9.
[2] [1904] A.C. 423, 426.

and servants, it is difficult to see why the ordinary doctrines of agency and of master and servant are not to be applied to corporations as well as to ordinary individuals".'

Secondly and consequently, the common law, without indulging in much speculation as to the nature of a corporation's personality, has evolved the common-sense view that a corporation has, so far as is consistent with its artificial nature and with the purpose with which it is created, the capacities and liabilities of a natural man.

Thirdly, the common law has always adhered to the rule that corporate form can be conferred only by the State. Those continental speculators who wished to get a larger liberty of association thought that, when they had disproved the fictitious nature of corporate personality and proved its reality, they had also proved the falsity of the Concession Theory. They thought that from the proof of its reality it followed that no authorization of the State was needed for its recognition as a legal *persona*. But this conclusion really rests upon a confusion of thought which is due to the circumstances in which the continental controversies had arisen. It is perhaps arguable that it is a weak spot in Maitland's brilliant exposition of these continental theories that he does not clearly point out that proof that unincorporate groups have a real life of their own, though it disproves the Fiction Theory, has no logical bearing on the Concession Theory. Therefore the common law, while admitting the reality of corporate and, to some extent, of group personality, has always adhered to the Concession Theory. I think that it may be maintained that it was because the law recognized the reality of the life of a group that it insisted that, for a legal life, it must have the authority of the State. The State is thus able to impose conditions which will prevent these corporate groups from menacing the peace of the State and the liberty of the individual.

But fourthly, the gradual and untheoretic way in which the English law as to groups and associations has grown up was dangerous in an age which demanded this liberty to associate in groups which tended to increase in size and power. The absence of any clear theory as to the basis of the law caused lawyers and legislators to ignore this danger. It caused them to ignore the implications of Burke's aphorism that 'liberty

when men act in bodies is power'. The excessive liberty
given to Trade Unions, and the absence of all power in the
Company Acts to provide any machinery for disincorporating
a company which is guilty of wrong-doing, are illustrations.

For all these reasons I think that it may be maintained
that these papers of Maitland, though dealing largely with
speculations evoked by causes which are not operative in
England, are of great importance to English lawyers and
statesmen. They are important, first because they have elucidated the theories adopted by English law upon the topic
of corporate and unincorporate personality; secondly because
they point to certain defects in that law; and thirdly because
they elucidate the historical importance of certain aspects of
English public law, and in particular the large part which the
Trust Concept has played in different branches of public
and semi-public law. They are of great importance to
students of jurisprudence because they contain clear reasoning upon fundamental principles and problems which helps
students to think for themselves. They are of great importance to students of comparative law because they show in
the clearest way the divergent manner in which, under the
stress of different conditions, similar problems are discussed
and solved.

The two papers on 'The Corporation Sole' and 'The
Crown as Corporation' are studies in two topics of English
legal history which had been very little explored till Maitland
wrote about them. They are interesting histories of the
failure to adapt the new law, which was beginning to grow
up round the corporation, to old bodies of legal doctrine,
which had been elaborated in the days when this new law had
not been heard of. But I think that the failure of the attempt
to apply the conception of a corporation sole to the Crown
was due, not so much, as Maitland would seem to suggest,
to the conception itself, as to the course of English constitutional history. Parliament won its victory over the Crown
with the help of medieval precedents which regarded the
King as a natural man. Those precedents assorted badly
with the doctrines of the Tudor lawyers which made the
King a corporation sole, the head and representative of
the State, and the possessor of many mystical qualities. If
the Stuart kings and the prerogative lawyers had had their

way King and State would have been identified, and the conception of a corporation sole might have been valuable. But the result of the victory of the Parliament was that the Crown, though it remained a corporation sole with many extraordinary qualities, did not become coextensive with the State. The ambiguous position which the Crown thus occupied between the old theories and the new accounts for the failure of the concept of the Crown as a corporation sole. The two papers on 'The Unincorporate Body' and 'The Body Politic' are less important. The first deals mainly with the relation of the Trust Concept to corporation law, and explains why it has 'given us a liberal substitute for a meagre law of corporations'. The second enters a protest against the view that 'we are within measurable distance of a sociology or an inductive political science which shall take no shame when set beside the older sciences'.

In Mr. Brunyate's new edition of Maitland's *Lectures on Equity*[1] the text has very wisely been left unchanged, except for the omission of two passages dealing with topics which have been rendered obsolete by the Property Legislation of 1925. In fact Mr. Brunyate tells us that, because the book deals mainly with the basic principles of equity, 'surprisingly little revision has been found necessary'. But the footnotes, which were not Maitland's work, have been added to and altered. In addition Mr. Brunyate has added six notes which deal with the cases of *Oliver* v. *Hinton*[2] and *Walker* v. *Linom*,[3] Restrictive Covenants, Trusts, the Law of Property since 1925, the Administration of Assets, and Election. Mr. Brunyate has done his editorial work very skilfully, and his notes are just what is wanted—not too long, and at the same time clear and accurate. The book will be more valuable than ever as an introductory book for students, and it will still be valued by all lawyers, because it continues to describe in Maitland's clear and effective style the root principles of equity, the relation of equity to law, and its place in the English legal system.[4]

[1] Maitland, op. cit. *supra*, p. 207, n. 2.
[2] [1899] 2 Ch. 264.   [3] [1907] 2 Ch. 104.
[4] There is only one remark that I should like to make about the text. It is curious that at page 45, where the relation of debtor and creditor is

I regret that Mr. Brunyate has not given us his opinion as to Maitland's thesis that equitable rights are essentially *jura in personam;* for, as he says, Maitland's views on this point 'pervade the book and are of the essence of it'. Mr. Brunyate thinks that the discussion and criticism of Maitland's views on this point are not the function of a reviser. I think that he might easily have given us another note on this topic. In fact, the excellence of the notes which he has given us will cause his readers to regret the omission.

My own opinion on this controverted topic is that it is the one case in which Maitland's views upon equity have been materially modified by subsequent discussion. I think that this modification is justified by two reasons. In the first place, there is weighty authority against Maitland's views; and, in the second place, his insistence on the predominately personal character of equitable rights obscures the true nature of equitable ownership.

First, authority is against Maitland. Lindley L.J. in the case of *Lister* v. *Stubbs,*[1] and Lord Parker in the case of *Sinclair* v. *Brougham,*[2] emphasized the proprietary character of equitable rights. In the former case Lindley L.J. said that the fallacy of the plaintiff's argument was in failing to distinguish between the debtor-creditor and the trustee-*cestui que trust* relation 'in confounding *ownership* with obligation'.[3] In the latter case Lord Parker said of equity that, 'starting from a personal equity, based on the consideration that it would be unconscionable for anyone who could not plead purchase for value without notice to retain an advantage derived from the misapplication of trust money, it ended, as was so often the case, *in creating what were in effect rights of property*, though not recognized as such by the common law'.[4]

Secondly, I think the insistence of the predominately personal character of equitable rights obscures the true nature of equitable ownership. No doubt a *cestui que trust* has rights contrasted with the relation of trustee and *cestui que trust*, neither Maitland nor Mr. Brunyate cites the case of *Lister* v. *Stubbs* (1890), 45 Ch. Div. 1 which turns on this very difference.

[1] (1890) 45 Ch. Div. 1.
[2] [1914] A.C. 398.
[3] *Lister* v. *Stubbs* (1890), 45 Ch. Div. 1, 15. The italics are mine.
[4] *Sinclair* v. *Brougham,* [1914] A.C. 398, 441–2. The italics are mine.

in personam against his trustee; but he has many other rights both against his trustee and against third persons. It is these other rights which give him equitable ownership. What then is this equitable ownership? The answer is that its main characteristic is the fact that it is a right as against all the world except as against a bona fide purchaser for value without notice of the legal estate. This characteristic is due to the relation in which equity has always stood to the law. Equity has always followed the law, and, when the equities are equal, has always allowed the law to prevail. It seems to me impossible to say that ownership of this character has not got predominately proprietary characteristics merely because there is one possible person as against whom it cannot be asserted. Indeed, it is impossible to maintain this thesis without denying the existence of equitable ownership—which seems to me to be absurd. At any rate the doctrine of following trust property shows that, whatever the law might say, equity always regarded these equitable rights as something very different from merely personal obligations; for the essence of that doctrine is this—even if the property has got into the hands of a bona fide purchaser for value, so that the equitable ownership of it has ceased to exist, the former owner is given a proprietary right to or in any property which can be identified as its proceeds, and is thus enabled to take it in preference to creditors whose rights are merely personal.

In the first edition of the *Lectures on Equity* there was included a set of 'Lectures on the Forms of Action'. The latter set of lectures have been detached from the *Lectures on Equity*, and are printed in their original form and without annotation in a separate volume.[1] Of that volume it is only necessary to say that it is still an indispensable introductory volume to the study of English legal history. There has, it is true, been some controversy as to the connexion of Chapter 24 of the Statute of Westminster II[2] with action on the case.[3]

---

[1] Maitland, op. cit. *supra*, p. 207, n. 1.

[2] Statute of Westminster 2nd, 1285, 13 Edw. I, c. 24.

[3] Plucknett, 'Case and the Statute of Westminster II' (1931), 31 *Col. L. Rev.* 778; Landon, 'The Action on the Case and the Statute of Westminster II' (1936), 52 *L.Q.R.* 68; Plucknett, 'Case and Westminster II' (1936), 52 *L.Q.R.* 220.

It is possible that it may be necessary to revise somewhat the traditional view which Maitland states.[1] With that exception these lectures hold the field as the best account for the beginner, and, like all Maitland's work, however elementary, they have much that is of value to the mature student.

Sir Frederick Pollock has said of Maine's writings that 'they are classics in their kind, and accordingly their standard and worth are little or not at all affected by the changes which the learning of posterity may bring to specific propositions contained or assumed in them';[2] and of his genius he has said that it 'was not only touched with art, but eminently artistic; and art is immortal'.[3] This and more than this can be said of Maitland's writings. He was more alive than Maine to the human aspects of the history of law. It is easy, as I have said elsewhere, when dealing with theories, and doctrines, and institutions, to forget that they were made and used and developed and abused by men of like passions with ourselves. Maitland never forgot this. He can extract human traits from a plea roll and a Year Book. And this characteristic of his genius was developed by his sense of humour and his gaiety of manner which conceal the learning and research underlying the brilliant argument which flows so easily. Moreover, to this sense of humour and this gaiety there was added a talent for epigram, which clinches the argument, and sums up in some memorable phrase the conclusion of the whole matter. And I think that it can be maintained also that Maitland was a greater lawyer and legal historian than Maine. He was one of the great lawyers of his age, and one of the greatest historians, legal or otherwise, that this country has ever produced. This may seem to be an extravagant claim. But I am not alone in this opinion. Mr. G. M. Young in his brilliant picture of Victorian England has said:

'I dwell on the name of Maitland partly because, outside his own profession, England has never done justice to that royal intellect, at once as penetrating and comprehensive as any historian has ever possessed: but more because no other English writer has so perfectly apprehended the final and dominant object of historical study: which is, the origin, content, and articulation of that objective mind which

[1] (1931), 47 L.Q.R. 334.
[2] Pollock, Oxford Lectures (1890), 151.   [3] Ibid. at 154.

controls the thinking and doing of an age or race, as our mother tongue controls our speaking; or possessed, in so full a measure, the power of entering into that mind, thinking with its equipment, judging by its canons, and observing with its perceptions.'[1]

To us who are lawyers he is one of those fixed stars who takes his place with such men as Bracton, Littleton, Coke, Hale, and Blackstone. And because he takes this rank students will always wish to study his *ipsissima verba*, to know what his views were, even though it has been proved by later research that they must be modified. It seems to me that in these circumstances what is wanted is not so much selected fragments of his works with annotations, as the works themselves. What is wanted is two or three omnibus volumes printed on thin paper in legible type which contain all he wrote. I should exclude the *History of English Law*, but nothing else. All else, beginning with his introduction to *The Select Pleas of the Crown for the County of Gloucester*, and including his introductions to *Bracton's Note Book* and to the volumes of the Selden Society, which he edited, ought to be printed exactly as he wrote them. No introduction would be needed—merely a list of important dates in his life; and of course the dates of publication would be affixed to each work. I am sure that these volumes would satisfy a want which has long been felt by lawyers and historians. I am sure that they would have a rapid sale, and that the demand for them would continue, even as the demand for the works of the other classics of our legal and historical literature continues. Many of these books were published by the Cambridge University Press, and that Press ought to publish these omnibus volumes. Let us hope that the Syndics of that Press will see that it is to their interest not to refuse thus to recognize the needs of students and the outstanding qualities of Maitland's work—prophet though he is from their own country.

[1] Young, *Victorian England, the Portrait of an Age* (1934), 185–6.

LITERATURE IN LAW BOOKS[1]

THE phrase 'literature in law books' may seem to have in it a considerable element of paradox. And there is some justification for this view; for it is true that though law books often contain straightforward, well-reasoned, and clear expositions of principles and rules, they are not as a rule literature. It is not often that a lawyer, gifted with literary power, is moved by the importance or interest of his theme to make a statement of a principle or rule which rises to the level of literature. But the phrase is not wholly a paradox because there is a certain amount of literature, sometimes great literature, in legal text-books and in the reports. This fact was brought to my attention some years ago in the following way. The Oxford University Press were publishing an anthology of English prose, and it occurred to someone that there might be hidden away in the reports specimens of great prose fit to be included in such an anthology. I was asked whether this was so but was told that I must confine my attention to modern times, since the specimens of the prose of earlier periods had been already printed. I selected some extracts from the judgments of Lords Bowen, Macnaghten, and Sumner; and those extracts were put before the editor, Sir Arthur Quiller-Couch. He was quite enthusiastic about their merits and seemed really surprised to find a new vein of great literature, of the existence of which he, a professor of English literature, had been quite ignorant. Since then I have thought over this question of literature in law books; and it has occurred to me that it might be useful to vindicate the literary capacity of lawyers by putting together a few passages from the books and judgments of the great lawyers of the past. My selection is necessarily only a selection; and others may be able to make a different and a better one. But I think that it is an interesting selection, and that it will prove that the title of this paper is not wholly paradoxical.

[1] A lecture delivered to the Faculty of Law in the University of Birmingham on November 18, 1938, and to University College, Hull, England, on December 5, 1938. Reprinted from *Washington University Law Quarterly*, Feb. 1939.

The earliest law books were not written in English but in Latin or French. But we must take some account of these books because in two of them—in Glanvil and Bracton—there are passages which can be said to be literature.

The passage in Glanvil, and I think the only passage, which can be said to be literature, describes Henry II's institution of the trial by the grand assize on a writ of right as an alternative to trial by battle. Thayer says of it, 'In the midst of the dry details of his treatise we come suddenly upon a passage full of sentiment, which testifies to the powerful contemporaneous impression made by the first introduction of the organized jury into England.'[1] It is contained in chapter 7 of Glanvil's second book and, translated into English, runs as follows:

'That assize is a certain royal favour, given to the people by the mercy of the king, with the advice of his nobles, by means of which such healthy provision is made for the life and condition of men, that each may keep the freehold which rightfully is his, and all can avoid the doubtful issue of battle. And by this means it comes to pass that each can escape the last punishment of unexpected and untimely death, or at least the shame of perpetual infamy arising from the cry of that hateful and shocking word [Craven] which the conquered utters as the result of his disgrace by defeat. This institution is the product of the highest equity. For the establishment of the right which after many and long delays is hardly ever attained by battle, is attained by its means more easily and quickly. The assize does not allow so many essoins as the battle, and so labour and expense are saved to the poor. Moreover by as much as the testimony of several credible witnesses outweighs in actions that of one only, by so much is this institution more equitable than the battle. For while the battle depends upon the testimony of one sworn person this institution requires the oaths of at least twelve lawful men.'

The literary qualities of Bracton's work are well known and well recognized; for both Lord Campbell and Maitland have stressed them. Many passages might be cited in support of their opinions—notably Bracton's introductory pages on *Justitia* and *Jus*. They are inspired no doubt by Ulpian; but, as Maitland says, they are no mere cant or common form, 'for he feels that he is a priest of the law'.[2] I shall cite

---

[1] *A Preliminary Treatise on Evidence at the Common Law* (1898), 41–2.

[2] Pollock and Maitland, *History of English Law* (1st ed. 1895), i. 187, n. 2.

two passages, both of which illustrate Bracton's persuasion that the law is a sacred thing. The first of these passages stands at the beginning of his treatise:

'But since these laws and customs are often abused by fools and unlearned men, who ascend the judgment seat before they have learned the law, by men who are ever in doubt and unable to decide; and since they are often perverted by the majority, who decide cases according to their arbitrary whims and not according to the authority of the laws; for the instruction of the minority at least, I, Henry of Bratton, have braced my mind to study the old judgments of the just. I have perused diligently, not without night watching and labour, their acts, their counsels, and their opinions; and whatever I have found worthy of note I have digested into one book divided into titles and paragraphs. I have compiled it without prejudice to its correction by better opinion, committing it to writing for the verdict of posterity, asking the reader that if he find anything superfluous or weak he will correct and amend it or pass it over, since to remember everything and to be infallible is divine rather than human.'

The second of these passages deals with the most acutely controverted question in Henry III's reign—the position of the King in the State and his relation to the law. Many passages in Bracton's book show that he was intensely interested in this question; and to his treatment of it the parliamentary party frequently appealed in the constitutional controversies of the first half of the seventeenth century. Here is one of the most eloquent of the passages in which he sets out his view of these questions:[1]

'The king ought to be superior to all his subjects in power. He ought not to have an equal and much less a superior, and especially in the administration of justice. . . . Though in his capacity to receive justice he is no greater than the least in his kingdom, and though he is superior to all in power, yet, since the heart of the king ought to be in the hand of God, lest his power should be unbridled, let him apply the bridle of temperance and the reins of moderation, so that unbridled power may not lead him to do injustice. For a king can do nothing on earth save that which he may lawfully do, seeing that he is the servant and vicar of God. Nor is it any answer to say that "what the king wills has the force of law", because at the end of that law, the reason follows "since by the Lex Regia which was passed concerning his power"; that is, not whatever may be suddenly presumed to be the king's will, but what by the council of the magnates, with the authority

[1] Ff. 107a and b.

of the king, and after due deliberation, has been rightly determined, is the law. His power is a power to do right not wrong, and since he is the author of right, he from whom rights arise ought not to give occasion to wrongdoing, and he whose office it is to restrain others from wrong should not himself do wrong. The king therefore ought to use his power to do right as the vicar and servant of God on earth, because that is the power of God alone, but the power to do wrong is the power of the devil and not of God, and of him whose works he does the king will be the servant. Therefore while he administers justice he is the vicar of the eternal king, but a servant of the devil if he turns aside to do injustice. . . Let him therefore temper his power by the law which is the bridle of his power, so that he may live according to law, for human laws are sanctified when they bind their maker, and moreover it is worthy of the majesty of a reigning king that he should proclaim that he is bound by the law. Nothing is so fitting to a ruler as a life obedient to law, and to submit his authority to law is greater than empire; and in truth he ought to give to the law the authority which the law has given to him; for it is the law which makes him king.'

After the age of Bracton we get no great law books till the close of the Middle Ages. At the close of the Middle Ages there are Littleton's great book on *Tenures* and Fortescue's *De Laudibus* and his *Governance of England*. Littleton's book is a classic in that it sums up with great terseness and accuracy the medieval land law. From that point of view it resembles Stephen's classic work on pleading which sums up the common law rules on that subject. But neither of these books is literature. On the other hand, there are passages in Fortescue's books which have a distinct literary quality. I shall cite one short passage from the *Governance of England*, which is the earliest piece of English literature to be found in any law book. Fortescue is advocating the better endowment of the Crown, so that the king may be able to master the lawlessness from which the country was suffering. Here is the passage with the English modernized:[1]

'But this manner of endowment of his crown shall be to the king a great prerogative, in that he has then enriched his crown with such riches and possessions, as never king shall be able to take from it without the assent of his whole realm. Nor may this be to the hurt of the prerogative or power of his successors; for as it is showed before, it is no prerogative or power to be able to lose any good, or to be able to waste or put it away. For all such things come of impotency, as doth

[1] *The Governance of England* (1885), c. 19.

power to be sick or wax old. And truly, if the king do thus, he shall do thereby daily more alms than shall be done by all the foundations that ever were made in England. For every man of the land shall by this foundation every day be the merrier, be surer, be far better in body and all his goods, as every wise man may well conceive. The foundation of abbeys, of hospitals, and such other houses, is nothing in comparison hereof. For this shall be a college, in which shall sing and pray for evermore all the men of England spiritual and temporal. And their song shall be such among other anthems: Blessed be our Lord God, for that he hath sent king Edward IV to reign upon us. He hath done more for us than ever did king of England, or might have done before him. The harms that have fallen in getting of his realm, be now by him turned into our altogether good and profit. We shall now be able to enjoy our own goods, and live under justice, which we have not done of long time, God knoweth. Wherefore of his charity it is that we have all that is in our homes.'

It is not till the latter end of the Tudor period—till the Elizabethan Age—that we find any more literature in law books. Then we find it in the writings of the two great lawyers of that age, Coke and Bacon.

The great bulk of Coke's writings is not literature. But Coke was well read in literature, classical and modern. It is not surprising therefore that he can pen a fine phrase—e.g. 'the gladsome light of jurisprudence', '[the laws of England are] the golden met-wand whereby all men's causes are justly and evenly measured'; and it is not surprising that his enthusiasm for his theme has sometimes produced passages which are literature. I give two illustrations. The first of them deals with a theme on which Coke was always eloquent, viz. the excellence of the common law; the second, with the happy effect of the wise settlement by the Tudors of the position of the copyholder. The first passage runs as follows:[1]

'There is no jewel in the world comparable to learning; no learning so excellent both for prince and subject as knowledge of laws; and no knowledge of any laws (I speak of human) so necessary for all estates and for all causes, concerning goods, land, or life as the common laws of England. If the beauty of other countries be faded and wasted with bloody wars, thank God for the admirable peace wherein this realm hath long flourished under the due administration of these laws: if thou readest of the tyranny of other nations, wherein powerful will and pleasure stands for law and reason, and when, upon conceit of

[1] 2 Co. Rep. (1658), viii–xi.

mislike, men are suddenly poisoned, or otherwise murdered, and never
called to answer; praise God for the justice of thy gracious sovereign
who (to the world's admiration) governeth her people by God's good-
ness, in peace and prosperity by those laws, and punisheth not the
greatest offender, though his offence be *crimen laesae majestatis*,
treason against her sacred person, but by the just and equal proceedings
of law. . . . Cast thine eye upon the sages of the law that have been
before thee, and never shall thou find any that hath excelled in the
knowledge of these laws, but hath sucked from the breasts of that
divine knowledge, honesty, gravity, and integrity. . . . For hitherto
I never saw any man of a loose or lawless life attain to any sound and
perfect knowledge of the said laws: and on the other side, I never saw
any man of excellent judgment in these laws, but was withall (being
taught by such a master) honest, faithful, and virtuous.'

Here is the second passage:[1]

'But now copy holders stand upon a sure ground, now they weigh
not Lord's displeasure, they shake not at every sudden blast of wind,
they eat, drink, and sleep securely; only having an especial care of the
main chance [viz.] to perform carefully what duties and services soever their Tenure doth exact, and Custome doth require: then let
Lord frown, the copy holder cares not, knowing himself safe, and not
within any danger. For if the Lord's anger grow to expulsion, the
Law hath provided several weapons of remedy; for it is at his election
either to sue a *Subpoena* or an action of trespass against the Lord.
Time hath dealt very favourably with Copy-holders in divers respects.'

Bacon, with the possible exceptions of Maitland and
Pollock, is the most literary of all our lawyers. As we might
expect, his literary genius is apparent even in his arguments
on dry points of law; and his other legal works are often
illumined by striking phrases and apposite illustrations.
What better description was ever given of the effect of the
Statute of Uses than that in the opening words of Bacon's
Reading?[2]—'a law, whereupon the inheritances of this
realm are tossed at this day, as upon a sea, in such sort that
it is hard to say which bark will sink, and which will get to
haven'. I have selected two passages from his legal writings.
The first is from his argument in *Calvin's Case*. It deals with
the most pressing of all the constitutional questions of the
day—the relation of the prerogative to the law. It is re-

---

[1] Coke, *Compleate Copy-Holder* (1641), sec. 9.
[2] Bacon, *Works* (Spedding's ed. 1879), vii. 395.

markable not only for its literary power but also for the fact that it shows that the views of a moderate prerogative lawyer like Bacon were then not so very far removed from the views of the parliamentary lawyers. Perhaps if James had allowed Bacon to guide his policy, a *modus vivendi* might have been reached. Here is the passage:[1]

'Law no doubt is the great organ by which the sovereign power doth move, and may be truly compared to the sinews in a natural body, as the sovereignty may be compared to the spirit: for if the sinews be without the spirits, they are dead and without motion; if the spirits move in weak sinews, it causeth trembling: so the laws, without the king's power, are dead: the king's power, except the laws be corroborated, will never move constantly, but be full of staggering and trepidation. But towards the king himself the law doth a double office or operation: the first is to intitle the king, or design him: and in that sense Bracton saith well—*Lex facit quod ipse sit Rex*; that is, it defines his title; as in our law, That the kingdom shall go to the issue female; that it shall not be departable among daughters; that the half-blood shall be respected, and other points differing from the rules of common inheritance. The second is,—that whereof we need not fear to speak in good and happy times, such as these are,—to make the ordinary power of the king more definite or regular. For it was well said by a father, *plenitudo potestatis est plenitudo tempestatis*. And although the king, in his person, be *solutus legibus*, yet his acts and grants are limited by law, and we argue them every day.'

The second passage is taken from his argument in *Chudleigh's Case*. It is the best statement of the reasons why, on grounds of public policy, the common lawyers at the end of the sixteenth and the beginning of the seventeenth centuries were waging so fierce a war against perpetuities. The passage runs as follows:[2]

'But we should consider the perils immanent in the present estate; who see in this time the desperate humours of divers men in devising treason and conspiracies; who being such men that, in the course of their ambition or other furious apprehensions, they make very small or no account of their proper lives; if to the common desire and sweetness of life the natural regard for their posterity be not adjoined, the bridle, I doubt, will be too weak: for when they see that whatever comes of themselves, yet their posterity shall not be overthrown, they will be made more audacious to attempt such matters. Also another

[1] Bacon, *Works* (Spedding's ed. 1879), vii. 646.
[2] Ibid. 633–5.

reason of State may be added . . . and that is the peril which necessarily grows to any State, if the greatness of men's possessions be in discontented races; the which must necessarily follow, if notwithstanding the attainder of the father, the son shall succeed in his time and estate.

'But omitting these considerations of state and civil policy, let us come to consideration of humanity.

'A man is taken prisoner in war. Life and liberty are more precious than lands or goods. For his ransom it is necessary for him to sell. If then he be shackled in such conveyances, he is as much captive to his conveyances as to his enemy, and so must die in misery to make his son and heir after him live in jollity. . . .

'So passing over the consideration of humanity, let us now consider the discipline of families. And touching this I will speak in modesty and under correction. Though I reverence the laws of my country, yet I observe one defect in them; and that is, there is no footstep there of the reverend *patria potestas* which was so commended in ancient times. . . . This only yet remains: if the father has any patrimony and the son be disobedient, he may disinherit him; if he will not deserve his blessing he shall not have his living. But this advice of perpetuities has taken this power from the father likewise; and has tied and made subject (as the proverb is) the parents to their cradle, and so notwithstanding he has the curse of his father, yet he shall have the land of his grandfather.'

The great constitutional controversies of the seventeenth century gave rise to floods of oratory and some memorable statements of the law in the courts and elsewhere; but not, I think, to any absolutely first-rate literature. Eliot's great speech on Buckingham's impeachment and Strafford's in his own defence are political rather than legal documents. Nor do the law books of the second half of the century add much. There are a few striking phrases of Lord Nottingham—'Chancery mends no man's bargain but it sometimes mends his assurance';[1] 'With such a conscience as is only *naturalis et interna* this Court hath nothing to do; the conscience with which I am to proceed is merely *civilis et politica*; and it is infinitely better for the public that a trust security or agreement, which is wholly secret, should miscarry, than that men should lose their estates by the mere fancy and imagination of a chancellor'.[2] Some of the direful consequences which would ensue if wives could pledge their husbands' credit

---

[1] *Maynard* v. *Mosely* (Ch. 1676), 3 Swanst. 653, 655.
[2] *Cook* v. *Fountain* (Ch. 1672), 3 Swanst. 585, 600.

without their authority, were set out in picturesque language by Wyndham J. in the case of *Manby* v. *Scott*: 'The husband will be accounted the common enemy; and the mercer and the gallant will unite with the wife, and they will combine their strength against the husband'; 'Wives will be their own carvers, and, like hawks, will fly abroad and find their own prey'; 'It shall be left to the pleasure of a London jury to dress my wife in such apparel as they think proper'.[1] Wyndham J. must either have been a bachelor judge or have had an extravagant wife.

In the eighteenth century there is a considerable amount of literature in law books. I must therefore make a selection. I must pass over famous passages in Lord Camden's judgment in the case of *Entick* v. *Carrington*[2] and Erskine's orations in defence of the freedom of the press in many cases, notably in his speech in defence of Thomas Paine.[3] I shall give you three passages—one from a judgment of Lord Mansfield, a second from a judgment of Lord Stowell, and a third from Blackstone's *Commentaries*.

The first of these is from Lord Mansfield's famous judgment reversing the outlawry of Wilkes in 1768.[4] He held that the errors alleged by Wilkes's counsel were not sufficient to justify a reversal; but he went on to point out other errors which did justify it. Lest, however, it should be thought that he had yielded to popular clamour, he introduced into his judgment the following statement as to the position of the law and the duty of a judge:

'But here let me pause. It is fit to take some notice of the various terrors hung out; the numerous crowds which have attended and now attend in and about the hall . . . and the tumults which have shamefully insulted all order and government. Audacious addresses in print dictate to us, from those they call the people, the judgment to be given now, and afterwards upon the conviction. Reasons of policy are urged, from danger to the kingdom, by commotions and general confusion. Give me leave to take the opportunity of this great and respectable audience, to let the whole world know, all such attempts are vain. Unless we have been able to find an error, which will bear

---

[1] (K.B. 1662–3), 1 Sid. 109, 122.
[2] (K.B. 1765), 19 How. St. Tr. 1030.
[3] *Rex* v. *Paine* (1792), 22 How. St. Tr. 437.
[4] (K.B. 1770), 19 How. St. Tr. 1075, 1111–14.

us out, to reverse the outlawry, it must be affirmed. The constitution does not allow reasons of State to influence our judgments: God forbid it should! We must not regard political consequences, how formidable so ever they might be: if rebellion was the certain consequence we are bound to say *fiat justitia ruat caelum*.'

Lord Stowell was a master of literary style, and he took infinite pains with his judgments, from which many striking passages could be selected. One of the best known of these passages is his judgment in *The Indian Chief*,[1] in which he explains why an American residing in Calcutta must be deemed to have a British commercial domicil. He said:

'Wherever even a mere factory is founded in the eastern parts of the world, European persons trading under the shelter and protection of those establishments are conceived to take their national character from that association under which they live and carry on their commerce. It is a rule of the law of nations, applying peculiarly to those countries. and is different from what prevails ordinarily in Europe and western parts of the world, in which men take their present national character from the general character of the country in which they are resident; and this distinction arises from the nature and habit of the countries. In the western parts of the world alien merchants mix in the society of the natives; access and intermixture are permitted: and they become incorporated to almost the full extent. But in the East, from the oldest times, an immiscible character has been kept up; foreigners are not admitted into the general body and mass of the society of the nation; they continue strangers and sojourners as all of their fathers were— *Doris amara suam non intermiscuit undam*.'

The literary merits of Blackstone's *Commentaries* were acknowledged even by his enemy Bentham in an often cited passage from his *Fragment on Government*; and Bentham's praise was endorsed by Gibbon, who said that Blackstone's book 'may be considered as a rational system of the English Jurisprudence, digested into a natural method, and cleared of the pedantry, the obscurity, and the superfluities which rendered it the unknown horror of all men of taste'. Many passages could be selected from the *Commentaries* which take rank as literature. I have selected a passage descriptive of the mixed English constitution of the eighteenth century, which has more substantial truth in it than those who read

[1] (Adm. 1801) 3 C. Rob. 12, 28–9.

back nineteenth-century ideas into eighteenth-century institutions have realized. It runs as follows:[1]

'And herein indeed consists the true excellence of the English government, that all the parts of it form a mutual check upon each other. In the legislature the people are a check upon the nobility, and the nobility a check upon the people, by the mutual privilege of rejecting what the other has resolved; while the king is a check upon both, which preserves the executive power from encroachments. And this very executive power is again checked and kept within due bounds by the two houses, through the privilege they have of inquiring into, impeaching, and punishing the conduct (not indeed of the king, which would destroy his constitutional independence, but, which is more beneficial to the public) of his evil and pernicious counsellors. Thus every branch of our civil polity supports and is supported, regulates and is regulated, by the rest: for the two houses naturally drawing in two directions of opposite interest, and the prerogative in another still different from them both, they mutually keep each other from exceeding their proper limits; while the whole is prevented from separation, and artificially connected together by the mixed nature of the Crown, which is a part of the legislative, and the sole executive magistrate. Like three distinct powers in mechanics, they jointly impel the machine of government in a direction different from what either, acting by itself, would have done; but at the same time in a direction partaking of each, and formed out of all; a direction which constitutes the true line of the liberty and happiness of the community.'

During the greater part of the nineteenth century there are many passages of clear statement and much logical reasoning in the judgments of great masters of the law, such as Cockburn C.J., Lord Cairns, Lord Herschell, and Jessel M.R. But, as a rule, they are just not literature. There is, however, a passage in the judgment of James L.J. in the case of *Salvin* v. *North Brancepeth Coal Co.*[2] which easily qualifies. The Lord Justice is emphasizing the rules that substantial present damage must be proved before an action can be brought for nuisance. He says:

'It would have been wrong, as it seems to me, for this Court in the reign of Henry VI to have interfered with the further use of sea coal in London, because it had been ascertained to their satisfaction, that by the reign of Queen Victoria both white and red roses would have ceased to bloom in the Temple Gardens. If some picturesque haven

[1] *Comm.* i. *154–5.   [2] (1874), 9 Ch. 705, 709–10.

opens its arms to invite the commerce of the world, it is not for this Court to forbid the embrace, although the fruit of it should be the sights, and sounds, and smells of a common sea port and shipbuilding town, which would drive the Dryads and their masters from their ancient solitudes.'

At the end of the nineteenth and the beginning of the present century three great judges and two great professors have contributed to the literature of the law. The three great judges are Lords Bowen, Macnaghten, and Sumner. The two great professors are Maitland and Pollock.

Many passages of polished English prose could be selected from Lord Bowen's judgments. His style has been aptly compared to miniature painting. I have selected the following passage from his judgment in *Mogul Steamship Co. v. MacGregor*:[1]

'What then are the limitations which the law imposes on a trader in the conduct of his business as between himself and other traders? There seem to be no burdens or restrictions in law upon a trader which arise merely from the fact that he is a trader, and which are not equally laid on all other subjects of the Crown. His right to trade freely is a right which the law recognizes and encourages, but it is one which places him at no special disadvantage as compared with others. No man, whether trader or not, can however justify damaging another in his commercial business by fraud or misrepresentation. Intimidation, obstruction, and molestation are forbidden; so is the intentional procurement of a violation of individual rights, contractual or other, assuming always that there is no just cause for it. . . . But the defendants have been guilty of none of these acts. They have done nothing more against the plaintiff than pursue to the bitter end a war of competition waged in the interests of their own trade. To the argument that a competition so pursued ceases to have a just cause or excuse when there is ill will or a personal intention to harm, it is sufficient to reply that there was here no personal intention to do any other or greater harm to the plaintiffs than such as was necessarily involved in the desire to attract to the defendants' ships the entire tea freights of the ports, a portion of which would otherwise have fallen to the plaintiffs' share. I can find no authority for the doctrine that such a commercial motive deprives of "just cause or excuse" acts done in the course of trade which would but for such a motive be justifiable. So to hold would be to convert into an illegal motive the instinct of self-advancement and self-protection, which is the very

[1] (1889), 23 Q.B. 598, 614–15.

incentive to all trade. To say that a man is to trade freely, but that he is to stop short at any act which is calculated to harm other tradesmen, and which is designed to attract business to his own shop, would be a strange and impossible counsel of perfection.'

In all the series of the law reports there are no judgments which exhibit such a combination of wit and learning as Lord Macnaghten's. Many of them are great literature. Perhaps the best known is his account in the case of *Foxwell* v. *Van Grutten*[1] of the history of the rule in *Shelley's Case*. Here is part of it:

'Things were not going well with the rule. Its feudal origin was a disgrace. Some judges thought that on these grounds it ought to be "discountenanced". Then it was constantly made a matter of complaint that the rule disappointed the intention, as if that were not its very end and purpose. . . . It was always being disparaged, and, what was perhaps worse, it was always being explained. It led to profound discussions and to some very pretty quarrels. One object of Mr. Fearne's famous work was to refute Lord Mansfield's heresies in *Perrin* v. *Blake* then under appeal to this House. Unfortunately in a later edition the author suggested or proved that Lord Mansfield had not always been true to his own mistaken creed. That, of course, was an imputation not to be borne: it was resented and repelled from the bench; and so Lord Mansfield and Mr. Fearne differed and quarrelled. Lord Thurlow and Mr. Hargrave agreed in everything, and they quarrelled too. They had been friends. "The rule in *Shelley's Case*", so Mr. Hargrave tells us, "had often been discoursed upon" between them. Their friendship stood that strain. But when Mr. Hargrave laid the fruits of his labours before Lord Thurlow, and proposed to introduce a complimentary reference to the Chancellor, who had shown in *Jones* v. *Morgan* that he once enjoyed a vision of the true doctrine in its primitive simplicity, Lord Thurlow felt it was time to draw back. He acknowledged the imperative character of the rule. On that point he was as sound as Mr. Hargrave. . . . So far these great lawyers were at one. But Lord Thurlow thought that Mr. Hargrave was making too much fuss about his work of discovery or restoration, and he was not, I fancy, altogether certain what part was being reserved for the Lord High Chancellor, whether he was to come in as the master or the disciple. At any rate his reply was cold and distant. "For himself," he writes, "he really does not remember the time when he thought the application of the rule in *Shelley's Case* could depend upon anything else but the question whether the word 'heirs' was the designation of some particular person, or included successively all who

[1] [1897] A.C. 668, 669–71.

might pretend to inheritable blood." That was putting the case in a nutshell. But it is one thing to put a case like Shelley's in a nutshell and another thing to keep it there.'

His judgment in the case of *Gluckstein* v. *Barnes*[1] is another of his famous pronouncements. Gluckstein and others had promoted a company, and Gluckstein was one of its directors. The directors had made a secret profit of £20,000. In the liquidation of the company the facts came to light and proceedings were taken. Gluckstein was ordered to pay this money to the company; and from this decision he appealed to the House of Lords who dismissed the appeal. Lord Macnaghten sketched the genesis of the company in the following passage:[2]

'These gentlemen set about forming a company to pay them a handsome sum for taking off their hands a property which they had contracted to buy with that end in view. They bring the company into existence by means of the usual machinery. They appoint themselves sole guardians and protectors of this creature of theirs, half fledged and just struggling into life, bound hand and foot while yet unborn by contracts tending to their private advantage, and so fashioned by its makers that it could only act by their hands and only see through their eyes. They issue a prospectus representing that they had agreed to purchase the property for a sum largely in excess of the amount which they had, in fact, to pay. On the faith of this prospectus they collect subscriptions from a confiding and credulous public. And then comes the last act. Secretly, and therefore dishonestly, they put into their own pockets the difference between the real and the pretended price.'

Gluckstein had argued that he ought not to be ordered to pay the whole of this sum, that some part should be collected from his fellow directors. As to that Lord Macnaghten said:[3]

'My Lords, there may be occasions in which that would be a proper course to take. But I cannot think that this is a case in which any indulgence ought to be shown to Mr. Gluckstein. He may or may not be able to recover a contribution from those who joined with him in defrauding the company. He can bring an action at law if he likes. If he hesitates to take that course or takes it and fails, then his only remedy lies in an appeal to that sense of honour which is popularly supposed to exist among robbers of a humbler type.'

[1] [1900] A.C. 240.   [2] Ibid. at 248.   [3] Ibid. at 255.

Lord Sumner had so great a liking for an epigram and a biting phrase that it sometimes obscured his argument. But he was a master of English prose. His discussion of the basis and limits of religious toleration in the case of *Bowman* v. *The Secular Society* is one of the finest pieces of prose to be found in the law reports. He said:[1]

'The words, as well as the acts, which tend to endanger society differ from time to time in proportion as society is stable or insecure in fact, or is believed by its reasonable members to be open to assault. In the present day meetings or processions are held lawful which a hundred and fifty years ago would have been deemed seditious, and this is not because the law is weaker or has changed, but because, the times having changed, society is stronger than before. In the present day reasonable men do not apprehend the dissolution or the downfall of society because religion is publicly assailed by methods not scandalous. Whether it is possible that in the future irreligious attacks, designed to undermine fundamental institutions of our society, may come to be criminal in themselves, as constituting a public danger, is a matter that does not arise. The fact that opinion grounded on experience has moved one way does not in law preclude the possibility of its moving on fresh experience in the other; nor does it bind succeeding generations, when conditions have again changed. After all, the question whether a given opinion is a danger to society is a question of the times, and is a question of fact. I desire to say nothing which would limit the right of society to protect itself by process of law from the dangers of the moment, whatever that right may be, but only to say that experience having proved dangers once thought real to be now negligible, and dangers once very possibly imminent to have now passed away, there is nothing in the general rules as to blasphemy and irreligion, as known to the law, which prevents us from varying their application to the particular circumstances of our time in accordance with that experience. If these considerations are right and the attitude of the law both civil and criminal towards all religions depends fundamentally on the safety of the State and not on the doctrines or metaphysics of those who profess them, it is not necessary to consider whether or why any given body was relieved by the law at one time or frowned on at another, or to analyse creeds and tenets, Christian or other.'

Let us turn now to the two professors.

An anthology of pieces of fine prose and sparkling epigrams could be compiled from Maitland's books, for

[1] [1917] A.C. 406, 466–7.

everything which he wrote bears the stamp of genius. The two extracts from his works which I have selected illustrate two sides of his genius—his power to enliven a dull subject by a witty presentation of it and his power to extract new and important truths from familiar things.

Just as Lord Macnaghten could put humour into a history of the rule in *Shelley's Case*, so Maitland could put humour into that most dreary of all topics in Anglo-Saxon history—the hide. Here is his description of what historians have called 'beneficial hidation':[1]

'Long ago the prevailing idea may have been that team-land, house-land, pound-land, and fiscal hide, were or ought normally to be all one; and then the discovery that there are wide tracts, in which the worth of an average team-land is much less or somewhat greater than a pound, may have come in as a disturbing or differentiating force, and awakened debates in the council of the nation. We may, if we like such excursions, fancy the conservatives arguing for the good old rule "One team-land, one hide", while a party of financial reformers has raised the cry, "One pound, one hide". Then "pressure was brought to bear in influential quarters", and in favour of their own districts the witan in their moots jobbed and jerrymandered and rolled the friendly log, for all the world as if they had been mere modern politicians.'

No collocation of names is more familiar to lawyers than that of Coke and Littleton. But who before Maitland realized that there was a paradox in that collocation? Here is his statement:[2]

'Perhaps we should hardly believe if we were told for the first time that in the reign of James I a man who was the contemporary of Shakespeare and Bacon, a very able man too and a learned, who left his mark deep in English history, said, not by way of paradox but in sober earnest, said repeatedly and advisedly, that a certain thoroughly medieval book written in decadent colonial French was "the most perfect and absolute work that ever was written in any human science". Yet this was what Sir Edward Coke said of a small treatise written by Sir Thomas Littleton, who, though he did not die until 1481, was assuredly no child of the Renaissance. . . . A lecturer worthy of that theme would—I am sure of it—be able to convince you that there is some human interest, and especially an interest for English-speaking mankind, in a question which Coke's words suggest: How was it, and why was it, that in an age when old creeds of many

[1] *Domesday Book and Beyond* (1897), 448.
[2] *English Law and the Renaissance* (1901), 3–5.

kinds were crumbling, and all knowledge was being transfigured, in an age which had revolted against its predecessor, and was conscious of the revolt, one body of doctrine and a body which concerns us all remained so intact that Coke could formulate this prodigious sentence and challenge the whole world to contradict it?'

The series of obituary notices of Pollock in the *Law Quarterly Review* of January 1937 has done justice to the range and variety of his literary gifts and to his devotion to the study of the law. My first extract shows how his wit and imagination and his profound knowledge of the law, which enabled him to write such books as *Leading Cases Done into English*, was exercised upon the confusion introduced into the land law by the coming of shifting and springing uses and executory interests:[1]

'The arbitrary legislation of the Tudor period plunged us into a turbid ocean, vexed by battles of worse than fabulous monsters, in whose depths the gleam of a *scintilla juris* may throw a darkling light on the gambols of executory limitations, a brood of coiling slippery creatures abhorred of the pure Common Law, or on the death struggle of a legal estate sucked dry in the octopus like arms of a resulting use; while on the surface a shoal of equitable remainders may be seen skimming the waves in flight from that insatiable enemy of their kind, an outstanding term.'

My second extract is perhaps the finest statement ever made of the creed of all true students of the law—the creed expounded throughout English legal history by such men as Bracton, Coke, and Mansfield. After describing Watts's great fresco in Lincoln's Inn Hall in which the great law-givers of the world are portrayed, he says:[2]

'There you shall see in very truth how the spark, fostered in our own land by Glanvil and Bracton, waxed into a clear flame under the care of Brian and Choke, Littleton and Fortescue, was tended by Coke and Hale, and was made a light to shine round the world by Holt and Mansfield, and the Scotts, and others whom living men remember. You shall understand how great an inheritance is the law of England, whereof we and our brethren across the ocean are partakers, and you shall deem treaties and covenants a feeble bond in comparison of it; and you shall know with certain assurance that, however arduous has been your pilgrimage, the achievement is a full answer. So

[1] *The Expansion of the Common Law* (1904), 13.
[2] *Oxford Lectures and Discourses* (1890), 111.

venerable, so majestic, is this living temple of justice, that immemorial yet freshly growing fabric of the Common Law, that the least of us is happy who hereafter may point to so much as one stone thereof, and say, The work of my hands is there.'

With this great piece of prose my anthology ends. I hope that these extracts from legal text-books and reports will prove that there is some justification for the title of this paper, 'Literature in Law Books'. In fact, I think that it would, for several reasons, be surprising if no such literature was to be found in them. In the first place, law is the basis upon which all government rests, and without it no civilized life would be possible. It is the foundation upon which all the social sciences are built. As the writer of the Year Book of 1432 said,[1] 'The law is the highest inheritance which the king has; for by the law he and all his subjects are ruled, and if there was no law there would be no king and no inheritance'. Naturally lawyers realize this fact more fully than laymen; and its realization has, from the time of Bracton to our own times, inspired some of the most striking of the passages which I have here quoted. In the second place, law touches all the most important aspects of national life. Great constitutional questions, vital economic questions, and many social questions raise issues which arouse much party feeling and party strife. Lawyers set to decide such questions feel their importance; and, for that reason, their exposition of the legal principles which should be applied to solve the particular legal disputes which they occasion are coloured by their sense of the great issues involved, and animated by their desire to command assent to their views. For that reason they sometimes assume a supremely literary form. In the third place, the continuity of English legal history will often make it necessary to trace the manner in which a principle or a rule or an institution has been moulded under the pressure of political, social, or economic needs and theories. In the hands of an historically minded lawyer gifted with literary power such an exposition may easily lead him to write passages which rank as literature. In the fourth place, the curious results which a too technical development of the law sometimes produces may induce a great lawyer with a sense of humour to expound the history of a doctrine and its

[1] (1441) Y.B. 19 Hen. VI, Pasch. pl. 36.

present position in a passage which is, to the initiated, a gem of literary exposition. Lastly we must not forget that our great lawyers have always been amongst the ablest men of their age, and that some of them have studied many other things besides law. It would be surprising if on a great occasion their exposition of the law did not attain the dignity of literature. For all these reasons I think that it may be maintained that there is literature in law books which, though relatively to the great mass of law books small in quantity, yet is of such a quality that it adds appreciably to the distinction of the large body of great English prose.

UNJUSTIFIABLE ENRICHMENT[1]

WHEN can a person who has been unjustifiably enriched at the expense of another be compelled to make restitution? That is a problem which all legal systems must endeavour to solve. They have generally solved it by means of a set of principles and rules which are placed under the rubric 'quasi-contract'. The word 'quasi' has in this connexion a negative meaning. It denotes the absence of that consent without which there can be no contract. On the other hand, the word 'contract' appended to the word 'quasi' denotes that the obligation which the law imposes has some resemblance to a contractual obligation. That resemblance consists, as Professor Winfield has pointed out,[2] in the fact that, like contract, and unlike tort, the relation created by a quasi-contract is to a particular person.

The conditions under which English law will impose a quasi-contractual obligation to restore an unjustifiable enrichment depend, as in other branches of English law, partly upon the rules of the common law and partly upon the rules of equity; and those rules fall into two distinct branches—rules which give a proprietary remedy, and rules which give a personal remedy. It is, as we shall see, the rules which give a personal remedy which have given rise to a controversy, which is by no means settled, as to the principle upon which that remedy should be based. I shall deal first with the proprietary remedy; secondly, with the personal remedy; and thirdly, with the controversy as to the principle upon which the personal remedy is based.

The Proprietary Remedy

An owner who has been deprived of his property can, as a general rule, recover it from anyone in possession of it. That is true both of land and chattels. But since it is in respect of chattels that the quasi-contractual concept of unjustifiable enrichment has most frequently come before the courts, I shall confine myself to that aspect of the question.

[1] Reprinted from (1939) 55 *Law Quarterly Review*, 37.
[2] *The Province of the Law of Tort*, 188.

An owner who has been deprived of his chattel can recover that chattel or its value by means of an action of detinue or trover; and he can recover it, not only if it still exists in its original form, but also if it has been converted into another form, provided that it is clearly identifiable as his chattel in its changed form. In the case of *Taylor* v. *Plumer*[1] money was entrusted to a broker by his principal for the purpose of purchasing Exchequer bills for his principal. The broker bought instead American stock and bullion with which he intended to abscond to America. He was caught, and surrendered the stock and bullion to his principal. The question to be decided in the case was whether the principal was entitled to the stock and bullion, or the trustee in bankruptcy of the broker. It was held that the principal was entitled to it. Lord Ellenborough C.J. said:[2]

'It makes no difference in reason or in law into what other forms, different from the original, the change may have been made, . . . for the product of or the substitute for the original thing still follows the nature of the thing itself, as long as it can be ascertained to be such, and the right only ceases when the means of ascertainment fail, which is the case when the subject is turned into money, and mixed and compounded in a general mass of the same description. The difficulty which arises in such a case is a difficulty of fact and not of law, and the dictum that money has no ear-mark must be understood in the same way, i.e. as predicted only of an undivided and undistinguishable mass of current money. But money in a bag, or otherwise kept apart from other money, guineas, or other coin marked . . . are so far ear-marked as to fall within the rule on this subject, which applies to every other description of personal property whilst it remains (as the property in question did) in the hands of the factor, or his general legal representatives.'

It is clear, therefore, that if the original chattel or the product into which it had been converted could not be identified, the common law could give no proprietary remedy. It is at this point that equity supplemented the common law by means of its doctrine of following trust property. Although a broker, or other person holding property in a fiduciary capacity, had converted the chattels into an undistinguishable mass of money, and had placed that money to his credit at his bank, equity gave a proprietary remedy. It allowed the

[1] (1815), 3 M. & S. 562.   [2] At p. 575.

money, which represented the converted chattel, to be followed. The main principles which regulated the conditions
under which property could be thus followed were laid down
in 1879 in the case of *Re Hallett's Estate*.[1] As Atkin L.J.
said in the case of *Banque Belge* v. *Hambrouck*,[2] 'If in 1815
(the date of *Taylor* v. *Plumer*) the common law halted outside
the banker's door, by 1879 equity had had the courage to lift
the latch, walk in, and examine the banker's books'. The
reasons why equity was able thus to supplement the rules
of the common law were partly the fact that the machinery
of the Court of Chancery enabled it to trace the money into
which a chattel had been converted, and partly the fact that
it regarded the right of the *cestui que trust* as not only a personal equity as against the trustee or person in a fiduciary
position, but also as equitable ownership. If, therefore, it
could fix on any property in the hands of the trustee which
represented the original trust fund, it subjected that property to the trust, and regarded the *cestui que trust* as its
equitable owner.

The case of *Sinclair* v. *Brougham*[3] showed that the proprietary remedy, as thus extended by equity, was in some
circumstances able to give a remedy in a case of unjustifiable
enrichment which the personal remedy was unable to give.
In that case a building society started and developed an
ultra vires banking business. When the society was wound up
questions of priority arose between the outside creditors, the
unadvanced shareholders, and the depositors in the bank.
When the outside creditors had been paid in full, not
enough was left to pay the whole of the claims of the two
other classes of creditors. How should the assets be divided
in these circumstances? The depositors could not recover
anything by the personal remedy of an action for money had
and received because, as we shall see, that remedy depends
on the question whether the law could imply a contract to
repay them. Since 'the implied promise on which the action
for money had and received is based would be precisely that
promise which the company or association could not lawfully
make',[4] no such action lay. Nor could the money be identi-

---

[1] (1879), 13 Ch. D. 696.   [2] [1921] 1 K.B. 321, 335.
[3] [1914] A.C. 398.
[4] [1914] A.C. 398, 440, *per* Lord Parker.

fied, so that the depositors had no proprietary remedy at common law. But it was held that in equity the money could be traced. The building society could not be a party to an *ultra vires* act. If its agents, having no power to borrow, borrowed money on its behalf, the money still belonged in equity to the lenders. Therefore they could trace and follow the money and assert their equitable ownership of it. Obviously some of the assets of the society represented money of the depositors which the society had no right in equity to retain, because, having taken it from its agents with notice of the facts, it held it in a fiduciary capacity. On the other hand, some of the property represented the property of the shareholders. The equities were equal as between these two classes of creditors, and therefore the property was divided amongst them in proportion to the amounts advanced by the shareholders and the depositors.

I think that the proprietary remedy given by the common law as thus supplemented by equity is, where this remedy is available, adequate to redress cases of unjustifiable enrichment. But there are many cases in which this remedy is not available. This happens when there is no chattel over which ownership can be asserted, and when there is no produce of the conversion of a chattel which can be traced. In such cases the remedy of a plaintiff, who asserts that the defendant has been unjustifiably enriched at his expense, is a personal remedy.

The Personal Remedy

In the eighteenth century the action of *indebitatus assumpsit* had emerged as a form of action, by means of which the law could compel a defendant, who had been unjustifiably enriched at the expense of the plaintiff, to refund his gains.[1] Lord Mansfield gave a wide extension to this action in the case of *Moses* v. *Macferlan*.[2] He said:[3]

'It lies for money paid by mistake; or upon a consideration which happens to fail; or for money got through imposition (express or implied); or extortion; or oppression; or an undue advantage taken of the plaintiff's situation, contrary to the laws made for the protection

[1] Holdsworth, *H.E.L.* viii. 92–8.
[2] (1760) 2 Burr. 1005.
[3] At p. 1012.

of persons under those circumstances. In one word the gist of this kind of action is, that the defendant, upon the circumstances of the case, is obliged by the ties of natural justice and equity to refund the money.'

As the last cited words in this judgment indicate, Lord Mansfield thought that he had found in the action of *indebitatus assumpsit* an instrument by which he could realize his wish to make some sort of a fusion between the rules of law and equity.[1] Blackstone was of the same opinion. This form of action, he said, is 'almost as universally remedial as a bill in equity'.[2] But though Mansfield did succeed in making the action a remedy for many cases of unjustifiable enrichment, he did not succeed in equating it with the remedial scope of a bill in equity. His attempts, by means of this form of action and in other ways, to give effect to equitable rights in a court of law were rejected by his successors.[3] Increased attention was paid to the basis upon which the action of *indebitatus assumpsit* rested; and this tendency to analyse the basis of the action was accentuated by the new pleading rules introduced in the Hilary Term, 1834, which drastically curtailed the liberty to plead the general issue.[4] Just as an increased attention to the logical requirements of the action of assumpsit caused the rejection of many of Lord Mansfield's ideas as to the doctrine of consideration, so an increased attention to the logical requirements of the action of *indebitatus assumpsit* caused the rejection of his ideas as to the conditions under which the law could give a remedy for unjustifiable enrichment. The judges laid it down that it lay, not to recover any unjustifiable enrichment which a defendant ought *ex aequo et bono* to refund, but only in cases where they could say that it was fair that the law should imply a promise by the defendant to repay. In other words, the remedy given by this action depended, not on the fact that it was the right and fair thing that a repayment should be made, but on a true quasi-contract, i.e. upon the question whether the circumstances of the case were such that it was right that the law

---

[1] For Lord Mansfield's attempts to effect some fusion between the rules of law and equity, see Holdsworth, *H.E.L.* xii. 584–94.

[2] *Comm.* iii. 432.

[3] Holdsworth, *H.E.L.* xii. 595–601.

[4] See *Camb. Law Journal,* i. 273–8.

should imply an obligation analogous to a contract to repay.¹ I think it is clear that, throughout the nineteenth century, the judges applied the personal remedy for unjustifiable enrichment—the action of *indebitatus assumpsit*—in this way. As Mr. Jackson says,² 'as long as the forms of action lasted, whenever the Court gave judgment for the plaintiff on an *indebitatus* count, the Court must have implied a contract, whether anything to that effect was said or not'. The House of Lords in the case of *Sinclair* v. *Brougham* laid it down that this was the basis of the action, and concluded that therefore the law 'cannot *de jure* impute promises to repay, whether for money had and received or otherwise, which, if made *de facto*, it would inexorably avoid'.³ It followed, as we have seen,⁴ that the depositors could not recover anything by means of an action for money had and received, because to allow them to recover by this action would mean that the court was implying a contract which the law pronounced to be void.

Thus, although the contract implied is a fictitious contract because there is no consent, the liability is so analogous to a contract that some of the rules relating to a true contract must be applied to determine whether in the circumstances it is possible to impose it. In other words, the question whether the enrichment is unjustifiable depends partly upon whether it is fair and right that the defendant should repay, and partly upon whether the relations of the parties are such that it is legally possible to imply a contract. The analogy to a contract, which is indicated by the word 'quasi-contract', is thus logically made part of the test which determines in what circumstances it is possible to give a remedy for unjustifiable enrichment. That this is the logical conclusion to be drawn from the decision in the case of *Sinclair* v. *Brougham* is made quite clear from Romer L.J.'s judgment in the case of *Re Simms*.⁵ After citing the opinions of Lords Haldane and Sumner in the case of *Sinclair* v. *Brougham*, and after saying that a promise cannot be implied unless it is

---

¹ See *Sinclair* v. *Brougham*, [1914] A.C. 398, 455–6, *per* Lord Sumner; cp. Holdsworth, *H.E.L.* xii. 543–4.
² *The History of Quasi-Contract*, 126.
³ [1914] A.C. 398, 452, *per* Lord Sumner.
⁴ Above, p. 140.   ⁵ [1934] Ch. 1, 31–2.

inequitable that the defendant should retain the money as against the plaintiff, he went on to show that the promise to be implied must be one which, having regard to the principles of the law of contract, is legally possible as between the plaintiff and the defendant. He said:

'Furthermore it is obvious that the promise to be implied must be a promise made to the plaintiff or his agent; he could not otherwise sue upon it. Where, therefore, A, who owes a certain sum to B, pays the sum to C under the mistaken impression that he is thereby discharging himself of his indebtedness to B, a promise by C to repay A would be readily and properly implied; as might conceivably a promise given by C to A to pay the money to B, though my attention has not been called to any case in which a promise to pay the money to a third person who was in no way a party to the transaction of payment has ever been implied; but I fail to see how the law can imply a promise given by C to B to pay him the money, for, in the first place, B has been in no way affected by A's payment to C; the debt owing by A to B still remains undischarged and B can sue for its recovery. In the second place, B was no party to the transaction of the payment, and a contract between C and B cannot be implied as arising out of the transaction between A and C. Besides, as I have already pointed out, the law would imply a contract by C to repay the money to A, and could not reasonably imply another and co-existing one to repay the same money to B. In such a transaction as I have supposed C would probably hand over the money to B and have done with it; for B could recover judgment against A, and A against C.'

It is on this principle that it has been held that if work is done by the plaintiff for the defendant under a void contract, and the defendant has accepted it, the plaintiff can sue for the value of his services, and recover on a *quantum meruit*.[1] In such a case it is clear, first, that the defendant has been enriched by the services rendered, and, secondly, that, consistently with the principles of the law of contract, the law can imply a promise to pay. The contract under which the plaintiff thought he was acting is a nullity; valuable services have been given and accepted; and so, just as acceptance of goods not ordered raises an implied promise to pay what they are worth, and just as services rendered by a plaintiff under a contract which the defendant has wrongfully determined can be sued for on a *quantum meruit*, the law can in this case consistently imply a promise to pay.

[1] *Craven-Ellis* v. *Canons, Ltd.*, [1936] 2 K.B. 403.

It would seem, therefore, that there is overwhelming authority for saying that the common law personal remedy for unjustifiable enrichment depends both on the question whether in the circumstances it is fair and right that the defendant should pay, and on the question whether the relations of the defendant and plaintiff to each other are such that the law can imply a contract to repay. It is true that in the case of *Brook's Wharf and Bull's Wharf* v. *Goodman*[1] the Court of Appeal said, after citing the cases of *Pownal* v. *Ferrand*[2] and *Dawson* v. *Linton*,[3] that the statements of principle in those cases 'do not put the obligation on any ground of implied contract or of constructive or notional contract. The obligation is imposed by the court simply under the circumstances of the case and on what the court decides is just and reasonable, having regard to the relationship of the parties.'[4] But since there was abundant authority for saying that on the facts of this case the courts would imply a contract, it cannot be supposed that the long line of cases in which liability is based on the implication of a contract is thereby overruled.[5] But of this matter, and of the new basis of the liability for unjustifiable enrichment suggested by this *dictum*, I shall have more to say in the following section of this paper.

In the meantime we should note that the personal, like the real, remedy was supplemented by the rules of equity. Thus the doctrine of equitable estoppel, which has been taken over by the common law,[6] may help to adjust the equities in a case of unjustifiable enrichment. In the case of *Holt* v. *Markham*,[7] the Court of Appeal held, and in the case of *Jones* v. *Waring and Gillow*[8] two dissenting Lords thought, that this doctrine prevented a recovery of money paid under a mistake of fact. The rule that money paid under a mistake in law is not recoverable—a rule which is, as Professor Gutteridge has said, based on a confusion of thought,[9] was mitigated by equity if there were some fiduciary relationship between the

---

[1] [1937] 1 K.B. 534. [2] (1827), 6 B. & C. 439.
[3] (1822), 5 B. & Ald. 521.
[4] [1937] 1 K.B. 534, 545, *per* Lord Wright M.R.
[5] See Mr. Landon's note in *L.Q.R.* 53. 302–4.
[6] Holdsworth, *H.E.L.* ix. 161–2. [7] [1923] 1 K.B. 504.
[8] [1926] A.C. 670. [9] *Camb. Law Journal*, v. 225–6.

parties, or some other equity which made it inequitable for a person who had received money to retain it;[1] and, as Dr. Friedmann has pointed out,[2] the liability imposed by equity in cases of resulting and constructive trusts gives a remedy for unjustifiable enrichment. The strict application of the maxim *in pari delicto potior est conditio defendentis*, which may prevent a recovery for unjustifiable enrichment, was modified by equity both in cases in which it appeared that the defendant was oppressed or in some way taken advantage of,[3] and in cases where nothing had been done in pursuance of the illegal transaction.[4] Professor Gutteridge has pointed out that in the case of *Liggett* v. *Barclays Bank*[5] 'the equitable doctrine of subrogation was applied to prevent the plaintiffs from acquiring a profit in the shape of an unjustified enrichment'. He has also pointed out that maritime law, in the shape of salvage actions and actions to recover general average contributions, has helped to mitigate the strictness of the common law by giving other remedies for unjustifiable enrichment.[6]

The Controversy as to the Principle upon which the Common Law Remedy is Based

Professor Winfield, in his *Province of the Law of Tort*,[7] opened the attack upon the principle that the personal remedy is based upon a contract implied by law. His view is that the action should be based, not upon a contract implied by law, but upon 'the idea of unjust benefit'.[8] In 1937, in a note in the *Law Quarterly Review*, he says:[9]

'Suppose that an action for money had and received comes before a judge at the present day. If it is covered by an earlier decision that there was or was not an "implied contract" in the circumstances he can take refuge in that blessed phrase, without bothering further about what is "just and reasonable"; but if the case before him is not exactly

---

[1] *Rogers* v. *Ingham* (1876), 3 Ch. D. 351, 355–6, *per* James L.J., and at p. 357, *per* Mellish L.J.
[2] 'The Principle of Unjust Enrichment', *Canadian Bar Rev.* xvi. 247, 369.
[3] Holdsworth, *H.E.L.* xii. 548, and the cases there cited.
[4] Ibid. 549, and the cases there cited.
[5] [1928] 1 K.B. 48.　　　　　　　[6] *Camb. Law Journal*, v. 224–5.
[7] At pp. 131–41.　　　　　[8] Ibid. at p. 141.　　　　[9] 53. 448.

covered by any earlier decision, he will have to consider whether it
is fair and reasonable that he should imply a contract. To put it in
another way, "implied contract" is not the foundation of liability of
this kind; it is only the façade of it.'

Mr. Jackson thinks that the technique of a fictitious contract
is objectionable. He says:[1]

'First, we can get the result we want without this fiction; the present
process is akin to using algebraic formulae to solve problems of simple
mental arithmetic. Second, the use of "fictitious contract" means that
some of the limitations of contract are applied to quasi-contract, and
there is no apparent reason for thinking that that is desirable. The
law of contract may well provide that the agreements of persons, or of
particular persons such as corporations, should take certain forms or
have certain limits if they are to be enforced, whereas such forms
or limits should not necessarily apply to obligations imposed by law.'

Dr. Friedmann is of the same opinion. He says:[2]

'The limitation of quasi-contractual remedies to cases where the
fiction of an actual contract is possible, has, it is submitted, a deplorable
effect upon the development of that branch of English law, an effect
from which English law is now trying to free itself.'

By far the weightiest of these criticisms has recently come
from Lord Wright. His eminence as a lawyer and his position as a Lord of Appeal has given a much increased importance to this controversy.[3] Lord Wright's criticisms can
be grouped under three main heads: in the first place, he
thinks that the rule that, in the case of the purchase by
infants, lunatics, or drunkards of necessaries, the law implies
a contract to pay a reasonable price, is inconsistent with the
principle stated in *Sinclair* v. *Brougham* that 'the law cannot
de jure impute promises to repay, whether for money had
and received or otherwise, which, if made *de facto*, it would
inexorably avoid'.[4] In the second place, he argues that the
notion of a contract implied in law was a fiction which under
the old pleading rules was necessary to ground an action
of *indebitatus assumpsit*, but that, since the old forms of
action are abolished, the fiction is now otiose.[5] Therefore a
plaintiff's claim should be based upon the ground that the

[1] *The History of Quasi-Contract*, 123.   [2] *L.Q.R.* 53. 451.
[3] In his article on *Sinclair* v. *Brougham*, *Camb. Law Journal*, vi. 305–26.
[4] *Camb. Law Journal*, vi. 318–19, 320.
[5] Ibid. 317, 318, 324–5.

defendant has been unjustifiably enriched at his expense, and not upon the ground that the law will imply fictitious a contract to repay, if, in the circumstances, the court thinks that a defendant has been unjustifiably enriched. 'I cannot', says Lord Wright, 'see any justification now (if ever there was) for paying regard in considering matters of substance in law to fictions or doing otherwise than applying to the actual facts the appropriate juristic rules and remedies.'[1] Though it is true that in many cases the same results are reached whether or not the concept of a fictitious contract is used, yet 'the room of the fiction is better than its company'.[2] Moreover, 'the ghost of this fiction has, I fear, actually delayed and hindered the systematic and scientific study of this important branch of the law'.[3] Only by discarding this fiction can the essential principles of the law as to unjustifiable enrichment be properly elucidated. In the third place, other systems of law give a remedy for unjustifiable enrichment as such, without using the fiction of a contract implied by law.[4] Let us now consider these criticisms.

(1) Is it true that when the law imposes a liability upon an infant, a lunatic, and a drunken person to pay for necessaries supplied to them it is acting contrary to the principle that the contract implied by the law must be legally possible, because such persons are incapable of contracting? I do not think that it is true for the two following reasons. In the first place, an infant's contract for necessaries is a valid contract;[5] there is some authority for saying that the same proposition was always true of a lunatic's contracts;[6] and there is no reason why it should not also apply to a drunkard's contracts.[7] The law, therefore, can quite consistently imply a contract to pay for necessaries. The Sale of Goods Act, 1893, simply

---

[1] *Camb. Law Journal*, vi. 325.   [2] Ibid. 326.
[3] Ibid.   [4] Ibid. 322–3.

[5] In fact there is reason to think that in medieval law and later the contract price for necessaries was recoverable; for there is reason to think that debt lay and in that action only the stipulated price could be recovered, see Holdsworth, *H.E.L.* iii. 519 n. 5; but the usual form of action came to be *assumpsit* on a *quantum meruit*, and that gave rise to the modern idea that the infant is only liable to pay a reasonable price, ibid. viii. 52.

[6] *Manby* v. *Scott* (1663), 1 Sid. 109, 112; that this is the law was laid down in *Re Rhodes* (1890), 44 Ch. D. 94.

[7] *Gore* v. *Gibson* (1845), 13 M. & W. 623, 625, *per* Pollock C.B.

restates the existing law on this matter.[1] In the second place, the question of the liability of persons under these disabilities belongs to the law of status; and as Professor Winfield has said of the obligation created by a foreign judgment, it is 'part of a substantive branch of the law which has its own principles and which had better be respected as such'.[2]

(2) I pass now to Lord Wright's second argument that, since the old pleading rule which made the fiction of a contract necessary is now abolished, the fiction has become otiose. The answer is, I think, this: those fictions which were merely pleading fictions were no doubt got rid of by the Common Law Procedure Act and the Judicature Act. It is no longer necessary to allege a loss and finding in an action for goods, a lease entry and ouster in an action to recover land, or a promise in an action for money had and received. But some of these pleading fictions have made substantive law, and the changes made in the law of pleading have not got rid of the substantive law which they have made. Take, for instance, the case of the common recovery. Because the fictitious real action was a real action, it was necessary to bring it against the tenant in possession of the freehold. Because that in practice meant that the son could not completely bar the estate tail without his father's consent, this result of the fictitious real action survived, after the abolition of common recoveries, in the rule of substantive law that an estate tail cannot be completely barred without the consent of the protector of the settlement. Similarly the exigencies of a particular form of action may leave deep marks on substantive law. The conditions in which the action of assumpsit could be brought were the parents of the doctrine of consideration; and though the doctrine of consideration may be open to criticism if it is to be the sole test of the validity of a simple contract, as *a* test of that validity it is, in the opinion of Pollock, 'plain and sensible'.[3] I maintain that the fiction that the remedy for unjustifiable enrichment was based on a contract has given rise to the rule of substantive law that in these cases of unjustifiable enrichment the court must ask 'Is it fair that the court should imply a contract between the

---

[1] 56 & 57 Vict. c. 71, s. 2.
[2] *Province of the Law of Tort*, 150.
[3] *Genius of the Common Law*, 91.

plaintiff and defendant?' and not 'Is it fair that the defendant should make a repayment?' That the fiction has given rise to a rule of substantive law is, I think, taken for granted by Lords Sumner and Haldane in *Sinclair* v. *Brougham* and by Romer L.J. in *Re Simms*.[1] If it is said that the fiction of a contract is a 'mere façade', and that it is more logical and straightforward to test liability by asking whether in the circumstances it is just that such liability should be imposed, than to ask whether in the circumstances it is just that the court should imply a contract to pay, the answer is, I think, this: The liability is a quasi-contractual liability, that is, as we have seen, a liability to a particular person. This characteristic of a quasi-contractual liability is, Dr. Friedmann tells us, recognized by German law. 'The action for unjust enrichment', he says,[2] 'is clearly an action *in personam*, and whether the defendant's enrichment is unjustified in relation to someone else, is irrelevant.' Therefore, in order to determine whether such a liability should be imposed it is logical to look to the analogy of contract; because a contractual liability is, unlike a delictual liability, a liability to a particular person. If it is said that thus to import the analogy of a contract unduly restricts the scope of the remedy for unjustifiable enrichment, the answer is that the common law is here, as in other cases, supplemented by the rules of equity and the rules of maritime law. It seems to me that the rule of the common law, though it is based upon a fictitious contract, and though it is, historically, the result of a particular form of action, has here, as in other cases, produced a doctrine which, when supplemented by the rules of equity and the rules of maritime law, is neither illogical nor, as a general rule, unjust. It seems to me that the results so produced are preferable to the results produced by systems of law which base the remedy merely upon what the court considers to be the justice of the case, because to ask whether the relations of the parties are such that a contract between them ought to be implied by law, is a more explicit and therefore a less vague inquiry than to ask is it fair that the defendant should make a payment to the plaintiff. But this brings me to the third of Lord Wright's arguments.

[1] Above, pp. 243, 244.
[2] *Canadian Bar Rev.* xvi. 260.

(3) It is said that other systems of law give a remedy for unjustifiable enrichment without using the fiction of a contract implied by law. In the first place, it must be remembered that the fiction of a contract implied by law was a necessary part of the machinery of the action of *indebitatus assumpsit*. It logically determined the conditions under which it lay; and, as we have seen, it gives effect to its quasi-contractual character. In the second place, in other legal systems which have applied to the case of unjustifiable enrichment a ·particular form of action, the conditions under which relief is given are determined by the character of that action. Scots law makes use of the *condictio*—the *condictio indebiti*, the *condictio causa data causa non secuta*,· or the *condictio ob turpem causam*.[1] Though the difference in the form of action creates some differences in the rules of substantive law,[2] the analogy between the use made of *indebitatus assumpsit* and the *condictio* is close. Both actions aim at producing just and fair results. 'As in Roman law, it is essential under the law of Scotland that a claim for repayment of money paid in error should be based on equity.'[3] Both in England and Scotland the right to recovery is based partly on the equity of the case, but immediately and directly on the exigencies of the form of action by which the relief is given; so that in both countries the method of approach is similar —is it equitable that the courts should imply a contract, is it equitable that in the circumstances a *condictio* of one sort or another should lie? In the third place, French law, which bases the right to recover directly upon the equity of the case, seems to me to have succeeded in producing a body of rules which are both complex and uncertain. M. David, in the *Cambridge Law Journal*,[4] has shown that in French law this has been the effect of adopting a remedy based upon this principle. He tells us that there are three conditions which a plaintiff must satisfy before he can recover on the ground

---

[1] *Encyclopaedia of the Laws of Scotland, sub voce* 'Repetition'.

[2] See, e.g., Lord Dunedin's remarks in *Cantiare San Rocco S-A* v. *Clyde Shipbuilding and Engineering Co.*, [1924] A.C. 226, 247–8, on the difference of Scots and English law as to the treatment of the rights of the parties when the contract has become impossible of fulfilment by no fault of either party.

[3] *Encyclopaedia of the Laws of Scotland*, loc. cit.

[4] Vol. v. 205–23.

that the defendant has been unjustifiably enriched at his expense. They are as follows:

'(1) The defendant must have been enriched, and the plaintiff must have been impoverished. (2) The enrichment of the defendant must be "*sine causa*", i.e. it must not have arisen from any circumstances which the law will recognize as giving rise to a right to retain the benefit. (3) There must be no other remedy available to the plaintiff. It must be admitted that some difficulty is created by the fact that some of the decisions of the French Courts go beyond the limits imposed by these conditions; in fact, the very existence of the third condition must be regarded as doubtful.'[1]

So many doubtful questions have arisen on the interpretation to be put on these conditions that, though M. David emphasizes the advantage of a doctrine which 'is always at hand to prevent injustice', he admits that it gives the judges 'a power to act at their discretion in each individual case'.[2] He adds that the danger that this power will be abused has 'hitherto only existed in theory'; and that 'French legal writers are unanimous in praising the caution and wisdom which has always hitherto been displayed in this instance by our judges'.[3] German law, like French law, bases the action for unjust enrichment on the lack or failure of a *causa*. Dr. Friedmann's analysis of the ways in which in German law an unjust enrichment can take place, shows that by different machinery English and German law give remedies in much the same class of cases.[4] No doubt the German remedy is more uniform than English law; and it is also much more general—so general that it is 'a kind of subsidiary claim put forward whenever the plaintiff cannot get what he wants by other actions, e.g. for damage, account, or by actions *in rem* arising out of ownership'.[5] This generality must, as in French law, make it very uncertain whether any given claim will succeed. In fact, Dr. Friedmann, like M. David, admits the danger of this vagueness, but, like M. David, he maintains that it is not serious because it has been checked by the courts and by the legal profession.[6]

Two morals can, I think, be drawn from this study of Scots and French and German law. First, whatever theory is

[1] *Camb. Law Journal*, v. 212.   [2] Ibid. 223.
[3] Ibid.   [4] *Canadian Bar Rev.* xvi. 253–60.
[5] Ibid. 261.   [6] Ibid.

adopted, the law must adopt some technical rules to determine whether or not an action for unjustifiable enrichment
will lie; and there seems to me to be no advantage in substituting the French or German technical rules for our own.
Secondly, if the result of the adoption of the French or German technical rules is to leave the matter wholly to the discretion of the judge, it means in effect that the law has thrown
up the sponge, and has abandoned the attempt to produce
any workable rules on this question. It means in effect that a
lawyer asked to advise on a doubtful case will be obliged to
study, not so much the principles of the law, as the mentality
of his judges. It is true that, whichever view is adopted,
much must be left to the discretion of the court. But I think
that the English principle based upon a contract implied by
the law makes it more possible to work out some definite
rules than the continental system and the system advocated
by Lord Wright. I cannot think that English law would be
improved if it adopted this system in place of the English
concept of a contract implied by law, which is after all
a logical concept, supplemented by the rules of equity and
the rules of maritime law. The fact that they are thus supplemented is sometimes forgotten, as is shown by the expressions
used by Dr. Friedmann in his note in the *Law Quarterly
Review* which I have cited above.[1] The saner way is that
indicated by Professor Gutteridge when he says that 'perhaps it may be possible to legislate and to extend the scope
of the old *indebitatus* counts so as to remove the hardships
which now exist if the circumstances are such as to negative
the implication of a fictitious contract'[2]—though the price
for any such reform would be an increased vagueness in a
necessarily vague body of law. It is the saner way because,
as Lord Wright himself says, 'precedent must come first,
recognized rules of law and equity must be regarded, otherwise all certainty of law would disappear'.[3] In fact, if reform
is needed, it is the only method of reform which will preserve
the continuity of the principles of English law. No doubt,
as Dr. Friedmann points out,[4] if the opposite course were

---

[1] Above, p. 247. But Dr. Friedmann in his articles in the *Canadian Bar
Rev.* xvi. 243, 365, shows that he is well aware of the fact that they are thus
supplemented.   [2] *Camb. Law Journal*, v. 229.
[3] Ibid. vi. 321.   [4] *L.Q.R.* 53. 452–3.

pursued, many reforms in the law could be effected, and the law could be made to serve any social needs which counsel could persuade the judge were ripe for satisfaction. But the common law, if subjected to this process, would soon cease to exist as a system of logical and interrelated principles and rules. It would soon be cut adrift from its historic past. No doubt those who value quick reforms to satisfy popular or semi-popular cries above logic and continuity would not grieve. But it would mean the sacrifice of all the qualities which have made English law one of the great legal systems of the world.

Maine, speaking of the way in which the progressive Greek communities got rid of old forms and rigid rules, says:[1]

'It was not for the ultimate advantage of mankind that they did so, though the immediate benefit conferred on their citizens may have been considerable. One of the rarest qualities of national character is the capacity for applying and working out the law, as such, at the cost of constant miscarriages of abstract justice, without at the same time losing the hope or the wish that the law may be conformed to a higher ideal. The Greek intellect, with all its mobility and elasticity, was quite unable to confine itself within the strait waistcoat of a legal formula; and, if we may judge by the popular Courts of Athens, of whose working we possess accurate knowledge, the Greek tribunals exhibited the strongest tendency to confound law and fact. . . . No durable system of jurisprudence could be produced in this way. A community which never hesitated to relax rules of written law whenever they stood in the way of an ideally perfect decision on the facts of particular cases, would only, if it bequeathed any body of judicial principles to posterity, bequeath one consisting of the ideas of right and wrong which happened to be prevalent at the time. Such a jurisprudence would contain no framework to which the more advanced conceptions of subsequent ages could be fitted. It would amount at best to a philosophy, marked with the imperfections of the civilization under which it grew up.'

Roman and English law became great legal systems because they resisted this temptation, and acted upon the principle stated by Hale that 'it is a reason for me to preferre a Law by which a Kingdom hath been happily governed four or five hundred yeares then to adventure the happiness and Peace of a Kingdome upon Some new Theory of my owne tho'

[1] *Ancient Law*, 75–6.

I am better acquainted with the reasonableness of my owne theory then with that Law'.[1]

I conclude that the conditions in which English law gives a remedy for unjustifiable enrichment are not unreasonable. It may be that they require amendment in some particulars. If so let them be amended. But it would be a remedy far worse than the disease if the basis of the common law rule was scrapped, and for it was substituted a rule which left the whole matter to the discretion of the judge; and if, in consequence, the equitable modifications of, and supplements to, both the proprietary and the personal remedies given by the common law were left in the air. Professor Winfield has said:[2]

'If I may venture to suggest an *eirenicon*, it is this. If some distinguished lawyers prefer to use the old, winding country road of "implied contract", by all means let them do so. But they must not frown upon others of us who would rather travel by the new and speedier by-pass of "unjust benefit". At the journey's end we can congratulate each other on our arrival at the same place, whatever we may think of the different routes that have been taken.'

But, if my argument is correct, the supposition that those who travel by the narrow way will reach the same destination as those who travel by the broad road is as unsound in law as it is in theology. Better a system which is too rigid than no system at all.

[1] Reflections by Hale on Hobbes's *Dialogue of the Law,* Holdsworth, *H.E.L.* v. 504.
[2] *L.Q.R.* 54. 530.

TERMINOLOGY AND TITLE IN EJECTMENT
—A REPLY[1]

THE student of legal history is often tempted to question the correctness of developments in the modern law which run counter to some of the rules and principles of the old law; and the temptation is the keener when, like Mr. Hargreaves, he is a master of the old learning. One example in the sphere of tort is the doubt which lawyers learned in the history of the law have cast upon the correctness of the decision in the case of *Stanley* v. *Powell*, [1891] 1 Q.B. 86. Another is to be found in Mr. Hargreaves's very learned article (*L.Q.R.* 56. 376–98) on 'Terminology and Title in Ejectment', in which Mr. Hargreaves tries to persuade us that English law still knows nothing of ownership comparable to the Roman *dominium*, but, as in the Middle Ages, knows only seisin and rights thereto—relatively good or relatively bad. His thesis is that the conception of tenure is still the basis of the land law, that without this conception the conception of an estate with land is 'meaningless', and that, since it is very difficult for a tenant of an estate in fee simple to prove a title good against the whole world, it is useless and misleading to talk of the 'ownership of land'— 'whether we like it or not, we are driven back to the medieval principles of relativity of title; we cannot base our law of land on the theory of *dominium*'. In the first place, I do not think that the conception of tenure is so intimately connected with the conception of an estate as Mr. Hargreaves imagines. Tenure indicates the quality, estate the quantity, of an interest in land. It is quite possible to envisage the existence of estates in the land in a system of law which does not recognize the conception of tenure. In the second place, I think that nobody would deny that the English theory of possession and ownership differs from the Roman theory of *possessio* and *dominium*. 'The medieval principle of the relativity of titles' still holds. The man seised or possessed is still regarded as owner as against all the world except as against the man who can prove a better right in himself or someone else; and that

[1] Reprinted from (1940) 56, *Law Quarterly Review*, 479.

is why the Real Property Limitation Act is given, as Mr. Hargreaves puts it, only a negative operation. It is sufficient to bar the right of action and the title of all who can prove a better right than that of the man seised or possessed. But the question is whether in the course of its long history, and mainly through the action of ejectment, modern, as distinct from medieval, English law has not come to recognize that a plaintiff seeking to recover land must prove not merely a better right than the defendant in possession, but a right which is better than any existing right known to and provable by the defendant. In my opinion it follows from the cases which show that a defendant can set up a *ius tertii* that the plaintiff must prove a right which is better than any existing right known to and provable by the defendant; and, if this proposition is true, it seems to me that modern, unlike medieval, English law recognizes a conception which may fairly be called ownership.

Naturally Mr. Hargreaves attempts to question both the cases in which this plea has been admitted, and the distinction drawn by them between cases where a defendant is a trespasser or otherwise a wrongdoer as against the plaintiff, and the cases where he is not—in spite of Pollock and Wright's statement (*Possession in the Common Law*, 91) that if a plaintiff's 'actual possession has not been disturbed by the act complained of, he may be defeated by showing that someone else, who need not be the defendant or anyone through whom the defendant claims, had a better right to possession'. In order to substantiate his point Mr. Hargreaves distinguishes a class of case which, he says, has sometimes been cited to establish, but in reality has no bearing upon, this plea of *ius tertii*. In this class of case the defendant proves that the plaintiff has not got an interest which would entitle him to bring an action of ejectment. Thus, Mr. Hargreaves says, 'if the defendant shows that when the plaintiff was in possession he was tenant at sufferance, holding of one A, this is not setting up the better right of A, but simply showing that the plaintiff's possession was neither seisin nor possession by virtue of such a chattel interest as entitles him to recover'. Other similar cases are those in which the plaintiff is an intruder as against the Crown, or, as in *Crisp* v. *Barber* (1788), 2 T.R. 749, is relying on a void lease. But these cases in which the plaintiff's right was negatived on this ground may be equally well regarded as cases in which his right was negatived because either the defendant or a third person had a better right. I think that because they helped to introduce the rule that, since the plaintiff must establish his right, proof that either the defendant or a third person has a better right is an answer to his claim. Similarly Mr. Hargreaves explains away cases like *Wilkins* v. *Cleveland* (1829), 9 B. & C. 864 by saying that they are only authority for the rule that a seisin for at least twenty years must be proved to justify a presumption that a livery of seisin had taken place. But here again, since a feoffment without livery of seisin gave no title, these cases may be regarded equally well as cases in which the plaintiff failed because, in the absence of livery of seisin, he could not prove his title (Cole, *Law and Practice of Ejectment* (ed. 1857), 212; cp. Lightwood, *Possession of Land*, 113).

It was inevitable that this manner of regarding these cases should gain ground as the old learning which centred round the real actions decayed, and the new learning which centred round the action of ejectment prevailed. The action of ejectment was, like the action of trover, an offshoot of the action of trespass. At all periods in the history of the law the principles and rules relating to the seisin of land and the principles and rules relating to the possession of chattels have exercised an influence upon one another. No doubt the rules as to seisin, developed in and through the real actions, came to differ both formally and substantially from the rules as to possession developed in and through the personal actions. But there was a fundamental similarity between them. It was inevitable, therefore, that the rules as to seisin and possession developed in and through the action of ejectment should be influenced by the rules as to possession developed in and through the action of trover. As I have shown, the rule that a plaintiff in trover whose possession, to use Pollock's expression, has not been disturbed by the defendant, must prove a right of property, so that his claim may be met by pleading a *ius tertii*, was recognized in trover about the same period as it was recognized in ejectment (Holdsworth, *H.E.L.* vii. 426–9). It is true that until the abolition of the real actions this rule that a plaintiff in ejectment, like a plaintiff in trover, must show a right of property better than any right known to or provable by the defendant and that if he could show such a right he established ownership of the land, was not universally true. As Lightwood (*Possession of Land*, 112) has pointed out, a disseisor could recover in ejectment against a disseisee whose right of entry was tolled. But it is true to say that, so far as a plaintiff's rights were governed by the action of ejectment, he must show a right to enter which could be defeated, not only by showing a better right in the defendant, but also a better right in some third person, so that, in effect, he must establish an absolute right of ownership (Holdsworth, *H.E.L.* vii. 63, n. 3). That is why, when the real actions were abolished, and with them the rules as to discontinuances and descents cast, the conception of ownership, as developed in and through the action of ejectment, came to be recognized. The recognition of this conception was due to this cause, and not, as Mr. Hargreaves thinks, to a 'spate of loose language which set in with the sentimental liberalism of the 'fifties'.

In my view, Mr. Hargreaves's article is a very learned and ingenious attempt to make us believe that the old learning which centred round the real actions has still sufficient vitality to modify the new learning which grew up round the action of ejectment. In my opinion, this gallant attempt to prove that these real actions still 'rule us from their graves' fails.

THE RELATION OF ENGLISH LAW TO INTERNATIONAL LAW[1]

I HAVE dealt with the early history of this topic in the tenth volume of my *History of English Law*. I need not, therefore, do more than summarize what I have there written as a preliminary to a discussion of the modern English law on this topic.

In the sixteenth and seventeenth centuries this question had not begun to be considered by the common lawyers. The rules of international law were regarded as matters which concerned the Crown, and fell within its wide prerogative in relation to foreign affairs.[2] But after the Revolution it was necessary to reconcile this wide prerogative with the principles of English constitutional law which had prevailed as the result of the Revolution. One of these principles was that the prerogative could not be used in any way which conflicted with those principles. This restriction on the prerogative of the Crown in relation to foreign affairs is recognized at the present day, and has affected the development and the content of some of its branches—notably the treaty-making power. It also affected this question of the relation of English to international law, since the judges, if asked to give effect to a rule of international law, might be obliged to consider whether it conflicted with a rule of English law by which they were bound.

The episode of the arrest of the Czar's ambassador in 1708 raised this question of the relation of the rules of international law to the common law.[3] The particular question at issue—the immunity of ambassadors—was settled by statute. But it is clear from cases arising later in the century, which turned upon the construction of this statute, that this episode had led many of the judges to consider the whole question of the relation of English law to international law; and that the trend of legal opinion was moving in the direction of asserting the broad principle that international law

[1] Reprinted from the *Minnesota Law Review*, 1941.
[2] Holdsworth, *H.E.L.* (1938), x. 369–70.
[3] Ibid. 370–3.

is part of the law of England.[1] It would, I think, have been
admitted that, if a statute or a rule of the common law conflicted with a rule of international law, an English judge must
decide in accordance with the statute or the rule of the common law.[2] But, if English law was silent, it was the opinion
of both Lord Mansfield and Blackstone that a settled rule of
international law must be considered to be part of English
law, and enforced as such.

During the late eighteenth and in the nineteenth centuries this view of the relation of English to international
law continued to be held by many distinguished lawyers. In
1792, Serjeant Hill's opinion in favour of the Crown's power
to extradite criminals, was partly grounded upon this view.[3]
He thought that there was a rule of international law that
a sovereign ought to extradite criminals, and that therefore
the Crown must possess this power. In 1805 Lord Eldon,
in the case of *Dolder* v. *Huntingfield*,[4] lays it down, in effect,
that where a question is not concluded by a rule of English
law, and is one to which international law applies, the courts
must apply the principles of international law. The question
at issue in that case was whether stock vested in trustees
for the Swiss government could be claimed by a new
Swiss government, which had, by a revolution, superseded
the old government, though the new government had not
been recognized by England. This he said was 'a question
to be discussed upon great principles of the law of nations';[5]
and he distinguished it from the questions arising in the case
of *Barclay* v. *Russell*[6] as to property belonging to the colony
of Maryland before the war of independence. The colony
was, as Lord Eldon said, 'only a corporation under the great
seal dissolved by means which a court of justice was obliged
to consider rebellious';[7] and therefore the questions in that
case fell to be decided by the rules of English law. In 1817,.

---

[1] Holdsworth, *H.E.L.* (1938), x. 371–3.
[2] Ibid. 372, n. 7. See *infra*, pp. 270-2.
[3] Ibid. 399.
[4] (1805), 11 Ves. 283.
[5] (1805), 11 Ves. 283, 294; he did not decide the point as the question at issue in the case was one of pleading only.
[6] (1797), 3 Ves. 424; for a good account of this case and the case of *Dolder* v. *Huntingfield*, see Moore, *Act of State in English Law*, 157–61.
[7] (1805), 11 Ves. 283, 294.

in the case of *Wolff* v. *Oxholm*,[1] Lord Ellenborough made an elaborate examination of the rules of international law as to the right to confiscate enemy property, in order to come to a decision as to the validity of a Danish ordinance confiscating the property and debts due to British subjects—thus in effect recognizing that the rules of international law should be given effect to by the law of England. In 1823, in the case of *Novello* v. *Toogood*,[2] which turned on the immunity of the house of an ambassador's servant, Abbott C.J. said that the Act of Anne 'must be construed according to the common.law, of which the law of nations must be deemed a part'.[3] In the same year the law officers of the Crown[4] gave it as their opinion that 'subscriptions in favour of one of two belligerent states, being inconsistent with the neutrality declared by the government of the country and with the law of nations, would be illegal, and subject the parties concerned in them to prosecution for a misdemeanor'.[5] In the following year, in the case of *De Wutz* v. *Hendricks*,[6] Best C.J. held that this was the law. He said:

'... it occurred to me at the trial that it was contrary to the law of nations (which in all cases of international law is adopted into the municipal code of every civilized country) for persons in England to enter into engagements to raise money to support the subjects of a government in amity with our own, in hostilities against their government, and that no right of action would arise out of such a transaction;'[7]

and in 1861, in the case of *The Emperor of Austria* v. *Day*,[8] that principle was recognized and restated. In 1853 Lord Lyndhurst said, 'the offense of endeavouring to excite revolt against a neighbouring state is an offense against the law of nations. No writer on the law of nations states otherwise. But the law of nations, according to the decision of our

---

[1] (1817), 6 M. & S. 92, 100–6.
[2] (1823), 1 B. & C. 554, 2 Dow & Ry. K.B. 833, 1 L.J. (O.S.) K.B. 181.
[3] (1823), 1 B. & C. 554, 562, 2 Dow & Ry. K.B. 833, 1 L.J. (O.S.) K.B. 181.
[4] R. Gifford A.G., and J. S. Copley S.G.
[5] (1823), 2 State Tr. (N.S.) 1016.
[6] (1824), 2 Bing. 314, 9 Moore, C.P. 586, 2 State Tr. (N.S.) 125.
[7] (1824), 2 Bing. 314, 315–16, 9 Moore, C.P. 586, 2 State Tr. (N.S.) 125.
[8] (1861), 3 De G.F. and J. 217, 244, 30 L.J.Ch. (N.S.) 690, 4 L.T. 494, 7 Jur. (N.S.) 639, 9 W.R. 712, *per* Lord Campbell L.C., cited below p. 269, note 1.

greatest judges, is part of the law of England'; and this statement was concurred in by Lords Brougham, Truro, and Cranworth.[1] In 1861 Stuart V.C. held that, because inter national law was part of the law of England, the Court of Chancery could, by means of an injunction, protect the public rights of foreign sovereigns.[2] In 1876 Sir R. Phillimore, Mr. Montague Bernard, and Sir Henry Maine were of opinion that English courts were justified in applying modern rules of international law; that these modern rules condemned slavery; and that therefore the captain of a British ship of war, in the port of a state which allowed slavery, was justified in refusing to give up a slave who had taken refuge on his vessel.[3]

The whole question as to the relation of English to international law was elaborately argued before all the judges in the Court of Crown Cases Reserved in the case of *Regina* v. *Keyn*[4] in 1876. The accused, a German, was the captain of the *Franconia*. He negligently ran down the *Strathclyde*,

[1] Lewis, *Foreign Jurisdiction*, 66–7.

[2] 'The regulation of the coin and currency of any State is a great prerogative right of the sovereign power. It is not a mere municipal right, or a mere question of municipal law, but a great public right recognized and protected by the law of nations. A public right recognized by the law of nations is a legal right, because the law of nations is part of the common law of England.... The friendly relations between civilized countries require for their safety the protection by municipal law of those existing sovereign rights recognized by the law of nations,' *Emperor of Austria* v. *Day* (1861) 30 L.J.Ch. (N.S.) 690, 700; we shall see (below), p. 268, that this decision, so far as it rested on those grounds, was overruled by the Court of Appeal.

[3] 'International law, it is to be observed, is not stationary; it admits of progressive improvement, though the improvement is more difficult and slower than that of municipal law, and though the agencies by which change is effected are different. It varies with the progress of opinion and the growth of usage; and there is no subject on which so great a change of opinion has taken place as slavery and the slave trade. . . . The trade in Negro slaves, which was formerly competed for as a legitimate source of profit, has in a great number of treaties been assimilated to the crime of piracy. These considerations are sufficient to justify Great Britain in instructing her officers not to enforce slave laws, or permit them to be enforced, on board her ships of war in foreign territorial waters', *Royal Commission on Fugitive Slaves*, xxv; on the whole of this subject see Stephen, *History of the Criminal Law of England* (1883), ii. 43–58; Stephen was one of the Commissioners, and reprints his memorandum, contained in the Report, in his history.

[4] (1876), 2 Ex. Div. 63, 46 L.J.M.C. 17, 41 J.P. 517, 13 Cox C.C. 403; see also Stephen, *History of the Criminal Law of England* (1883), ii 29–42.

and, as a result of the collision, a passenger on the latter vessel was killed. His act, according to English law, amounted to manslaughter. The question before the court was whether an English court had jurisdiction to try him. Since the collision occurred within the three-mile limit, that question depended upon whether the English courts would recognize the rule of international law that the sea within that limit was for all purposes part of the territory to which it was adjacent. A minority of the judges[1] held that, since international law is part of the law of England, and since international law recognized this three-mile limit, the court had jurisdiction. That the views of these judges were substantially in accordance with the views of Lord Mansfield and Blackstone, and with the later decisions and dicta which follow these views, can be seen from a comparison between the words used by Blackstone in his *Commentaries*, and by Lord Coleridge C.J. in this case. Blackstone says:[2]

'The law of nations is a system of rules, deducible by natural reason, and established by universal consent among the civilized inhabitants of the world. . . . This general law is founded on this principle, that different nations ought in time of peace to do one another all the good they can; and, in time of war, as little harm as possible, without prejudice to their own real interests. And, as none of these states will allow a superiority in the other, therefore neither can dictate or prescribe the rules of this law to the rest; but such rules must necessarily result from those principles of natural justice, in which all the learned of every nation agree; or they depend upon mutual compacts or treaties between the respective communities; in the construction of which there is also no judge to resort to, but the law of nature and reason, being the only one in which all the contracting parties are equally conversant, and to which they are equally subject. In arbitrary states this law, wherever it contradicts or is not provided for by the municipal law of the country, is enforced by the royal power; but since in England no royal power can introduce a new law, or suspend the execution of the old, therefore the law of nations (wherever any question arises which is properly the object of its jurisdiction) is here adopted in its full extent by the common law, and is held to be a part of the law of the land.'

Lord Coleridge C.J., after saying that the dominion of a state over its territorial waters was 'established as solidly as

---

[1] Lord Coleridge C.J., Brett and Amphlett J.J.A., Grove, Denman, and Lindley J.J. [2] 4 Bl. *Comm.* 66–7.

any proposition of international law can be', proceeded as follows:

'Law implies a law-giver, and a tribunal capable of enforcing it and coercing its transgressors. But there is no common law-giver to sovereign states; and no tribunal has power to bind them by decrees or coerce them if they transgress. The law of nations is that collection of usages which civilized states have agreed to observe in their dealings with one another. What these usages are, whether a particular one has or has not been agreed to, must be matter of evidence. Treaties and acts of State are but evidence of the agreement of nations, and do not in this country at least *per se* bind the tribunals. Neither, certainly, does a consensus of jurists; but it is evidence of the agreement of nations on international points; and on such points, when they arise, the English courts give effect, as part of English law, to such agreement.'[1]

But the judges who thus followed the Mansfield and Blackstone tradition on this matter were in a minority. Cockburn C.J., who delivered the leading judgment on the opposing side, and the majority of the judges,[2] held that only those parts of international law are part of English law which could be proved to have been received into English law. That reception might be effected by statute incorporating a rule of international law, or it might be proved by the assent of the nations who were bound by international law to the particular rule.

'This assent may be express as by treaty, or the acknowledged concurrence of governments, or may be implied from established usage —an instance of which is to be found in the fact that merchant vessels on the high seas are held to be subject only to the law of the nation under whose flag they sail, while in the ports of a foreign state they are subject to the local law as well as to that of their own country. In the absence of proof of assent derived from one or other of these sources, no unanimity on the part of theoretical writers would warrant the judicial application of the law on the sole authority of their views and statements.'[3]

In other words, it is not true to say that all the rules of inter-

---

[1] *Regina v. Keyn* (1876), 2 Ex. Div. 63, 153–4, 46 L.J.M.C. 17, 41 J.P. 517, 13 Cox C.C. 403.

[2] Cockburn C.J., Kelly C.B., Bramwell J.A., Lush and Field J.J., Sir R. Phillimore, and Pollock B.

[3] *Regina v. Keyn* (1876), 2 Ex. Div. 63, 202–3, 46 L.J.M.C. 17, 41 J.P. 517, 13 Cox C.C. 403.

national law, as and when they are evolved by the jurists, become part of English law; but only those parts which, by legislation, judicial decision, or established practice, have been received into English law. The mere fact that there was a unanimous consensus of jurists in favour of a particular rule did not (as the judges who took the opposite view held) make that rule a rule of international law, which must, without more, be enforced as part of the law of England. Since there was no evidence that all the states bound by international law had assented to the rule that a state has jurisdiction over its territorial waters,[1] this was not a rule which could be enforced as part of the law of England. The assent of the jurists may, indeed, make it reasonable for Parliament to legislate so as to give effect to their views. But

'it is obviously one thing to say that the legislature of a nation may, from the common assent of other nations, have acquired the full right to legislate over a part of that which was before high sea, and as such common to all the world; another and a very different thing to say that the law of the local state becomes thereby at once, without anything more, applicable to foreigners within such part, or that, independently of legislation, the courts of the local state can *proprio vigore* so apply it.'[2]

As Stephen points out, we can see the same divergence of opinion as to the relation of international law to English law in the report of the Royal Commission on Fugitive Slaves.[3] Cockburn C.J. differed from the opinion expressed by Phillimore, Bernard, Maine that the development of rules of international law *per se* modified the rules of English law,[4] and expressed the opinion that no such modification could take place without some evidence that these developed rules had been received into and become a part of English law.[5]

---

[1] *Regina* v. *Keyn* (1876), 2 Ex. Div. 63, 203–7, 46 L.J.M.C. 17, 41 J.P. 517, 13 Cox C.C. 403.
[2] *Regina* v. *Keyn* (1876), 2 Ex. Div. 63, 207, 46 L.J.M.C. 17, 41 J.P. 517, 13 Cox C.C. 403.
[3] Stephen, *History of the Criminal Law of England* (1883), ii. 44.
[4] Above, p. 263.
[5] 'The principles of international law laid down by Lord Stowell remain the same: so far as we know, no compact or understanding has been come to since between our own and other governments inconsistent with them; and with regard to exterritoriality as now contended for, I deny, in the first place, that there is any proof that it has in point of fact been generally acquiesced in;

This view in effect amounts to saying that international law is not so much a part, as a source, of English law. In each case in which the question arises the court must consider whether the particular rule of international law has been received into, and so become a source of, English law.[1]

The Territorial Waters Jurisdiction Act 1878 gave the courts the jurisdiction which the minority of judges in this case had held that they possessed;[2] and its declaratory form is some evidence that the legislature considered that their views were correct. Nevertheless, I think that the opinion of Cockburn C.J. and the majority of the judges had come to be more in accord with the principles of modern English law than the opinion of the minority which represents the older view that international law is *per se* part of the law of England. The reasons for this change are mainly three—the manner in which these questions came before the courts, a growing perception of the differences in the character and ambit of the rules of international and the rules of municipal law, and the course of legislation. Let us look briefly at the matter from these three points of view.

In the first place, though many judges and jurists had laid it down in broad terms that international law is part of the law of England,[3] these broad statements were merely prefaces to the ruling in particular cases, which turned upon the application of a particular rule of international law to cases concerning the immunities of foreign sovereigns or ambassadors, questions as to the criminal liability of subjects for breaches of truces, or for raising subscriptions or doing other acts to help revolutions against friendly powers, or questions arising in civil actions in which the existence of some rule of international law was relevant to the issues in the case. Thus the attention of the judges was concentrated upon the question whether a particular rule, alleged to be a rule of international law, and as such part of the law of England,

and I venture, with all due deference, to think that it would be no improvement on the law of nations if it had. And I must here, in passing, observe that no improvement in our own views on any principle of international law will justify us in forcing the law, as we view it, on another state, which does not take the same view that we do', *Royal Commission on Fugitive Slaves*, xxxvi.

[1] (1935), *L.Q.R.* li. 24, 31.
[2] 41–2 Vic. c. 73.
[3] Holdsworth, *H.E.L.* (1938), x. 371–3; above, pp. 261–3.

was in fact a rule of international law. They were obliged therefore to scrutinize the evidence as to whether that particular rule had been received as a rule of international law. The influence of this mental attitude is very obvious in the judgments of Cockburn C.J. and the other judges who agreed with him. In the second place, the growing perception of the differences between the character and ambit of the rules of international and the rules of municipal law, led the courts to distinguish between rights and duties enforceable in a municipal court, and rights and duties which, though not so enforceable, were yet recognized by international law. Thus in *Barclay* v. *Russell*, Lord Loughborough distinguished between political equities which might be made 'the foundation of representations to be made from state to state', and judicial equities.[1] In *The Emperor of Austria* v. *Day*[2] Lord Campbell and Turner L.J. denied the truth of the principle laid down by Stuart V.C. in the court below, that since international law was part of the law of England, and since the Emperor of Austria's prerogative rights were recognized by international law, the Court of Chancery could interfere to protect those rights by injunction.[3] Turner L.J. said:[4]

'The prerogative rights of sovereigns seem to me ... to stand very much on the same footing as acts of state and matters of that description with which the municipal courts of this country do not and cannot interfere. Such acts and matters are recognized by international law no less than the prerogative rights of sovereigns; but the municipal courts of this country have disclaimed all right to interfere with respect to them. If the subject of one state infringes the prerogative of the sovereign of another state, the remedy, as I apprehend, lies in an appeal by the offended sovereign to the sovereign of the state to which the offender belongs.'

It is true that helping to plot revolution against the sovereign of a friendly state is a misdemeanour. To that extent English law recognizes and enforces international obliga-

---

[1] (1797), 3 Ves. 424, 435.
[2] (1861), 3 De G.F. and J. 217, 30 L.J.Ch. (N.S.) 690, 4 L.J. 494, 7 Jur. (N.S.) 639, 9 W.R. 712.   [3] Above, p. 263 and note 2.
[4] *Emperor of Austria* v. *Day* (1861), 3 De G.F. and J. 217, 251–2, 30 L.J.Ch. (N.S.) 690, 4 L.J. 494, 7 Jur. (N.S.) 639, 9 W.R. 712; cf. the judgment of Lord Campbell L.C. at pp. 231–2; it appears that counsel for the plaintiff admitted in the Court of Appeal that they could not base their claim for an injunction on an invasion of the Emperor's prerogatives.

tions.[1] But English law stops short of giving a remedy in its courts to a foreign sovereign who complains of the infringement of his sovereign rights. In the third place, this attitude of mind was helped by the course of legislation in regard to topics which touch upon the rules of international law. In the Middle Ages, before international law had become a definite system, there had been legislation against breakers of truces and safe-conducts.[2] The statute of 1708,[3] which dealt with the immunities of ambassadors, though said by Lord Mansfield and others to be only declaratory of the common law,[4] really introduced this principle of international law into the common law, and for the first time provided penalties for its breach.[5] Later, the statutes dealing with such subjects as foreign enlistment and extradition made certain topics connected with international law part of English law. In these circumstances it is possible to understand Cockburn C.J.'s refusal to supply by judicial action 'the absence of actual legislation'.[6]

The view taken by Cockburn C.J. and the majority of the court in *Regina* v. *Keyn* is the view which has prevailed. This is clear from the case of *West Rand Central Gold Mining Co.* v. *Rex*.[7] Lord Alverstone C.J., delivering the judgment of the court said:[8]

'The proposition . . . that international law forms part of the law of England, requires a word of explanation and comment. It is quite

---

[1] Above, p. 262; 'fitting out a warlike expedition in England to bring about a revolution in the dominions of a sovereign in alliance with Queen Victoria would certainly amount to a misdemeanor . . . and the manufacture of twenty tons of promissory notes for the same purpose may amount to the same offence', *Emperor of Austria* v. *Day* (1861), 3 De G.F. and J. 217, 244. 30 L.J.Ch. (N.S.) 690, 4 L.J. 494, 7 Jur. (N.S.) 639, 9 W.R. 712.

[2] Holdsworth, *H.E.L.* (1938), ii. 473–4; Bl. *Comm.* iv. 68–70.

[3] 7 Anne, c. 12; Holdsworth, *H.E.L.* (1938), x. 370–1.

[4] Holdsworth, *H.E.L.* (1938), x. 372.   [5] Ibid. 369–71.

[6] 'The question is whether, acting judicially, we can treat the power of Parliament to legislate as making up for the absence of actual legislation. I am clearly of opinion that we cannot', *Regina* v. *Keyn* (1877), 2 Ex. Div. 63, 208, 46 L.J.M.C. 17, 41 J.P. 517, 13 Cox C.C. 403; with this view Stephen agrees, *History of Criminal Law of England* (1883), ii. 41–2.

[7] [1905] 2 K.B. 391, 74 L.J.K.B. 753, 93 L.T. 207, 53 W.R. 660, 21 T.L.R. 562, 49 Sol. Jo. 552.

[8] [1905] 2 K.B. 391, 406–7, 74 L.J.K.B. 753, 93 L.T. 207, 53 W.R. 660, 21 T.L.R. 562, 49 Sol. Jo. 552.

true that whatever has received the common consent of civilized nations must have received the assent of our country, and that to which we have assented along with other nations in general may properly be called international law, and as such will be acknowledged and applied by our municipal tribunals when legitimate occasion arises for those tribunals to decide questions to which doctrines of international law may be relevant. But any doctrine so invoked must be one really accepted as binding between nations, and the international law sought to be applied must, like anything else, be proved by satisfactory evidence, which must show either that the particular proposition put forward has been recognized and acted upon by our own country, or that it is of such a nature, and has been so widely and generally accepted, that it can hardly be supposed that any civilized state would repudiate it. The mere opinions of jurists, however eminent or learned, that it ought to be so recognized, are not in themselves sufficient.'

Moreover, there is another condition which must be satisfied before a rule of international law can be accepted by the courts as a part of English law—a condition which also applies to all exercises of any of the prerogatives of the Crown. That is the condition that the rule of international law must not conflict with a rule of English law. If it conflicts with a rule of English law no effect can be given to it. In *Regina* v. *Keyn*[1] Cockburn C.J. held, in effect, that, by the rules of English law, the English courts had no jurisdiction over the offences of foreigners (not being part of the crew of a British ship) committed by them on the high seas; that English law had never recognized that the English State had a general dominion over territorial waters; that, except for special purposes defined by statute, it held such territorial waters to be part of the high seas; and that therefore to assert a criminal jurisdiction over a foreigner in the case before the court would amount to changing the law of England. Even if all other nations could be proved to have assented to this jurisdiction, such assent would not

'be sufficient to authorize the tribunals of this country to apply, without an Act of Parliament, what would practically amount to a new law. . . . The assent of nations is doubtless sufficient to give the power of parliamentary legislation in a matter otherwise within the

[1] (1877), 2 Ex. Div. 63, 46 L.J.M.C. 17, 41 J.P. 517, 13 Cox C.C. 403.

sphere of international law; but it would be powerless to confer without such legislation a jurisdiction beyond and unknown to the law, such as that now insisted on, a jurisdiction over foreigners in foreign ships on a portion of the high seas.'[1]

It may perhaps be thought that the limitations and conditions placed by English law on the recognition of the rules of international law, which flow from the view that international law is not a part, but a source, of English law, are unduly restrictive. In particular cases this may be so. Thus the law, as it existed before the Foreign Enlistment Act, 1870, was inadequate to prevent breaches of neutrality; and the result was that this country was involved in heavy liabilities for the damage caused by these breaches. But generally this state of the law has not been found to be inconvenient. There are two reasons for this. In the first place, the legislature has always been willing to intervene to bring English law into harmony with the latest developments of international law. In the second place, some of the results of the meaning given to acts of state in English law enable the Crown, by virtue of its wide prerogative over foreign affairs, to give effect to the rules of international law provided that they do not conflict with the rules of English law. For instance, the Crown can recognize the status of a foreign sovereign or a foreign public ship, and thereby confer the immunity which is given by the rules of international law.

Lastly, it should be noted that these doctrines as to the relation of English law to international law are the doctrines which are applied by the ordinary courts of law and equity. The position of the Prize Court, which administers international law,[2] is different. It is bound by a statute; so that, if a statute compels a departure from the rules of international law, the court must decide in accordance with the statute.[3] But, if the decision in the case of the *Zamora*[4] is correct, it is not bound by an Order in Council which purports to alter

---

[1] (1877), 2 Ex. Div. 63, 203, 46 L.J.M.C. 17, 41 J.P. 517, 13 Cox C.C. 403.

[2] Holdsworth, *H.E.L.* (1938), i. 565, 566; xii. 653, 654, 670, 693.

[3] Ibid. i. 566.

[4] [1916] 2 A.C. 77, 85 L.J.P. 89, 114 L.T. 626, 32 T.L.R. 436, 60 Sol. Jo. 416, 13 Asp. M.L.C. 330.

a rule of international law, whether or not it is a rule of international law which has been accepted by the common law[1]—a proposition which I have given reasons for thinking is as doubtful in law as it is politically inexpedient.[2]

[1] [1916] 2 A.C. 77, 90–4, 85 L.J.P. 89, 114 L.T. 626, 32 T.L.R. 436, 60 Sol. Jo. 416, 13 Asp. M.L.C. 330.

[2] Holdsworth, *H.E.L.* (1938), i. 567.

A CHAPTER OF ACCIDENTS IN THE LAW OF LIBEL[1]

DOWN to the year 1910, when the case of *Hulton* v. *Jones*[2] was decided, it was generally thought that two of the conditions for success in an action for libel were, first, that the meaning of the statement complained of was defamatory of the plaintiff, and, secondly, that the statement must have been made of and concerning him, i.e. with the intention of defaming him. The effect of two decisions of the Court of Appeal since the case of *Hulton* v. *Jones*—*Cassidy* v. *Daily Mirror*[3] and *Newstead* v. *London Express*[4]—is to eliminate the second of these conditions. In the latter of these two cases du Parcq L.J. approved the statement of Russell L.J., in the former,[5] that 'liability for libel does not depend on the intention of the defamer; but on the fact of defamation'.[6] I propose to consider first the technical reasoning by means of which this, to my mind, unfortunate development in the law of libel has been achieved, and, secondly, its practical consequences.

The Technical Reasoning

In the case of *Hulton* v. *Jones*[7] a paragraph in a newspaper, purporting to describe happenings at Dieppe, cast imputations on the morals of a person called Artemus Jones. The writer of the paragraph proved that the person whom he was describing was, like the information in the paragraph, wholly fictitious. A real Artemus Jones sued for libel, and produced evidence to prove that persons who knew him thought that the paragraph referred to him. There was no doubt in this case that the statement was defamatory, so that the first condition for success in the action was satisfied. The sole question was whether, since it had not been published of and concerning the plaintiff, i.e. with the intention of defaming

[1] Reprinted from (1941), 57 *Law Quarterly Review*, 74.
[2] [1909] 2 K.B. 444; [1910] A.C. 20.
[3] [1929] 2 K.B. 331.
[4] [1940] 1 K.B. 377.
[5] Ibid., at p. 396.
[6] [1929] 2 K.B. 331, 354.
[7] [1909] 2 K.B. 444; [1910] A.C. 20.

him, the action lay. The Court of Appeal by a majority held that, though it was not so published, the action lay, and the House of Lords affirmed this decision. From the decision of the Court of Appeal Fletcher Moulton L.J. dissented, on the ground that an action for libel could not lie unless the libel was published of and concerning the plaintiff, i.e. with the intention of defaming him. He said:[1]

'The learned judge directs that it is immaterial whether the defendant intended the words to refer to the plaintiff or not, and that if persons who know of the existence of the plaintiff might reasonably think they referred to him, the plaintiff is entitled to succeed. He holds that you may accidentally libel a man of whose very existence you do not know. In my opinion an unintentional libel in this sense is as impossible in English law as an honest fraud, and the gist of the action is, as Lord Mansfield said, the person of and concerning whom the words are spoken or written.'

With this reasoning Sir Frederick Pollock concurred. He considered that the judgment of the Court of Appeal and the House of Lords laid down 'very new law'.[2] Farwell L.J. did not dissent from the principle laid down by Fletcher Moulton L.J.; but he dissented from his conclusion because he thought that the rule that there must be an intention to defame the plaintiff was satisfied if the defamatory statement was made recklessly, that is, without knowing or caring whether the plaintiff existed or not. He said:[3]

'Fraud is proved in an action of deceit, not only when a false representation is made knowingly, but also when it is made recklessly, careless whether it be true or false, and although there was no intention to cheat or injure the person to whom the statement was made—and yet the fraudulent intent is of the essence of the action. So the intention to libel the plaintiff may be proved not only when the defendant knows and intends to injure the individuals, but also when he has made a statement concerning a man by a description by which the plaintiff is recognized by his associates, if the description is made recklessly, careless whether it hold up the plaintiff to contempt or ridicule or not.'

Therefore, 'if the libel was true of another person and honestly aimed at and intended for him, and not for the

---

[1] [1909] 2 K.B. 444, 471.
[2] L.Q.R. xxvi. 103–4; cp. L.Q.R. xxv. 341.
[3] [1909] 2 K.B. 444, 480–1.

plaintiff, the latter has no cause of action, although all his friends and relations may fit the cap on him'.[1]

It follows that in the opinion of Farwell L.J. both the two conditions set out above must be satisfied—the statement must be defamatory, and it must be published of and concerning the plaintiff, i.e. with the intention of defaming him; but the second condition is satisfied if it is made recklessly, i.e. without caring whether it defames him or not.

It was in the judgment of Lord Alverstone C.J. that the rival theory, which has for the present prevailed, made its appearance. His view was that,

'If in the opinion of a jury a substantial number of persons who knew the plaintiff, reading the article, would believe that it refers to him, in my opinion an action, assuming the language to be defamatory, can be maintained; and it makes no difference whether the writer of the article inserted the name or description unintentionally, by accident, or believing that no person existed corresponding with the name or answering the description. If upon the evidence the jury are of opinion that ordinary sensible readers, knowing the plaintiff, would be of opinion that the article referred to him, the plaintiff's case is made out.'[2]

Lord Alverstone based his opinion upon the following grounds: first, upon the ground that, 'apart from the question of express malice' the intention or motive with which the statement is made is immaterial.[3] No one would deny this proposition. But the question is not the existence of a motive or intention with which the statement is made, but the intention of the makers of the statement to refer to the plaintiff. Lord Alverstone denied that there was any such distinction, and said the same principle must apply to both.[4] Secondly, upon the ground that the cases show that if 'the libel designates the plaintiff in such a way as to let those who knew him understand that he was the person meant',[5] he has a good cause of action. But, as both Fletcher Moulton and

---

[1] [1909] 2 K.B. at p. 481.   [2] Ibid. at p. 454.
[3] Ibid. at p. 455.
[4] 'I know of no case in which this distinction has been drawn', ibid. at p. 453—a contention sufficiently answered by the authorities cited by Fletcher Moulton L.J., ibid. at pp. 459–62.
[5] *Bourke* v. *Warren* (1826), 2 Car. & P. 307, 309–10, *per* Abbott C.J.; *Le Fanu* v. *Malcolmson* (1848), 1 H.L.C. 637.

Farwell L.JJ. point out, the reasoning in these cases is directed to prove that if, on the construction of the document, the jury find that the defendant intended to publish · the libel of and concerning the plaintiff, the plaintiff will have a good cause of action.[1] They do not mean that if it is proved that the defendant did not intend to publish the libel of and concerning the plaintiff, the plaintiff will have a good cause of action. These cases assume that the libel must be published with the intention of defaming the plaintiff, and are concerned with the question whether, on the construction of the document, it is proved that such an intention exists. Thirdly, upon the ground that the question was concluded by a passage in Lord Blackburn's judgment in the case of *Capital and Counties Bank* v. *Henty*, in which he said:[2]

'In construing words to see whether they are a libel the Court is, when nothing is alleged to give them an extended sense, to put that meaning on them which the words would be understood by ordinary persons to bear, and say whether the words so understood are calculated to convey an injurious imputation. The question is not whether the defendant intended to convey that imputation; for if he, without excuse or justification, did what he knew or ought to have known was calculated to injure the plaintiff, he ·must (at least civilly) be responsible for the consequences, though his object might have been to injure another person than the plaintiff, or though he may have written in levity only.'

But it is clear that Lord Blackburn was considering the question whether the statement was of a defamatory character, and whether, as a matter of construction, it could refer to the plaintiff. He assumed that it must be proved that it did in fact refer to the plaintiff. In fact, the fallacy of Lord Alverstone's argument consists in his refusal to distinguish between two very different questions—the question of the defamatory meaning of the statement, and the question of the intention of the defendant to publish that statement of and concerning the plaintiff. In considering the first question the intention of the defendant is, as the cases he cited show, irrelevant; in considering the second question it is all important.

The decision of the House of Lords in the case of *Hulton* v.

[1] [1909] 2 K.B. 444, 462–4, 477–8.
[2] (1882), 7 App. Cas. 741, 772.

Jones[1] is most unsatisfactory. It dismissed the appeal on two contradictory grounds. Lords Loreburn and Shaw adopted the view of Lord Alverstone. As Lord Loreburn concisely put it: 'If the intention of the writer be immaterial in considering whether the matter written is defamatory, I do not see why it need be relevant in considering whether it is defamatory of the plaintiff.'[2] In other words, the intention to refer to the plaintiff is as immaterial as the intention to defame. But Lords Atkinson and Gorrell, while concurring in the judgment of Lord Loreburn, also expressed their concurrence with the judgment of Farwell L.J. which, as we have seen, by no means gave the go-by to the need to prove an intention to refer to the plaintiff.

Thus the case of *Hulton* v. *Jones* left the question whether a plaintiff in an action for libel must prove that the statement was made of and concerning him in a very uncertain state. In the case of *Cassidy* v. *Daily Mirror*[3] the majority of the Court of Appeal adhered to the view taken by Lords Alverstone and Loreburn and for the same reasons.

The facts of that case were as follows: The defendants published a photograph of one Corrigan *alias* Cassidy and Miss X, with the caption 'Mr. M. Corrigan, the race-horse owner, and Miss X whose engagement has been announced'. Cassidy was a married man. His wife, from whom he was living apart, brought this action alleging that the picture and caption meant, and was by her friends understood to mean, that she was not Cassidy's wife. The defendant proved that he did not know of the existence of Mrs. Cassidy, so that he could not have published the statement of and concerning her; and that he was not reckless or even negligent in publishing it, since he had the information from Cassidy. Nevertheless, the majority of the Court of Appeal (Scrutton and Russell L.JJ.) held that Mrs. Cassidy had a good cause of action.

[1] [1910] A.C. 20.
[2] Ibid. at p. 24; Lord Shaw at p. 26 also cited a dictum of Lord Coleridge C.J. in *Gibson* v. *Evans* (1889), 23 Q.B.D. 384, 386 that 'it does not signify what the writer meant. The question is whether the alleged libel was so published by the defendant that the world would apply it to the plaintiff'; this was said in the course of the argument, and it clearly refers, not to the question whether the defendant intended to refer to the plaintiff, but whether on the construction of the words used it could refer to the plaintiff.
[3] [1929] 2 K.B. 331.

Scrutton L.J. based his judgment on the same cases as those cited by Lord Alverstone in *Hulton's Case*, and said:[1]

'In my view, since *E. Hulton & Co.* v. *Jones*, it is impossible for the person publishing a statement which, to those who know certain facts, is capable of a defamatory meaning in regard to A to defend himself by saying: "I never heard of A and did not mean to injure him." If he publishes words reasonably capable of being read as relating directly or indirectly to A, and, to those who know the facts about A, capable of a defamatory meaning, he must take the consequences of the defamatory inferences reasonably drawn from his words.'

Russell L.J. gave judgment to the same effect.

It is clear that their judgments, like the judgments of Lords Alverstone and Loreburn, confuse the question of the meaning of the statement, with the question whether the statement was intended to refer to the plaintiff. The two different conditions which a plaintiff must satisfy to succeed in an action for libel—the condition that the statement must be defamatory, and the condition that it must be intended to refer to the plaintiff—were held to be governed by the same rule; with the results that just as there is no need to prove an intention to defame when the statement is defamatory, so there is no need to prove that the defendant intended to refer to the plaintiff. From this decision Greer L.J. dissented.[2] He pointed out that this case differed from the case of *Hulton* v. *Jones* first in that in this case the statement was not on the face of it defamatory, and the facts which might make it defamatory were not known to the defendant, in which case, as Brett L.J. pointed out[3] in *Capital and Counties Bank* v. *Henty*, the defendant could not be made liable; and secondly, in that the defendant was not reckless or even negligent in publishing it. Therefore there was no intention actual or constructive to publish the statement of and concerning the plaintiff. It is clear therefore that, in the opinion of Greer L.J., to support an action for libel it is necessary first that the statement should be defamatory of the plaintiff, and secondly that it must be published of and concerning him, that is, with the intention of defaming him, or recklessly, i.e. without caring whether it defames him or not.

[1] [1929] 2 K.B. 331, 341.   [2] Ibid. at pp. 342–50.
[3] (1880), 5 C.P.D. 514, 539.

The result then is that Fletcher Moulton, Farwell, and Greer L.JJ. were in favour of the rule that there must be an intention to defame the plaintiff; that Lords Alverstone, Loreburn, Shaw, and Scrutton and Russell L.JJ. denied the existence of this rule; and that Lords Atkinson and Gorrell committed themselves to the impossible position of assenting to both views.

In the case of *Hulton* v. *Jones* Farwell L.J. said that the result of holding that a defendant was liable at the suit of A when he made a statement true of B and intended to refer to him, would be that 'no newspaper could ever venture to publish a true statement of A, lest some other person answering the description should suffer thereby'.[1] The truth of this dictum is illustrated by *Newstead* v. *London Express*,[2] the facts of which were as follows: the defendant published an account of a trial for bigamy, and described the man convicted as 'Harold Newstead, 30-year-old Camberwell man'. This description was true of a Camberwell barman. It was not true of another Camberwell man of the same name who was a hairdresser. The hairdresser sued the *London Express*. It was held that the evidence justified a finding by the jury that reasonable persons might think that the words referred to the plaintiff, and that the fact that the statement was true of another person, to whom the defendant intended to refer, was no defence. We shall see that the case illustrates the difficulties of applying the law as thus laid down to concrete cases. At this point we must consider its purely legal aspect. From this point of view it is interesting, first, by reason of the very lucid account given by Greene M.R. of the two opposing views which the judges have taken upon this matter, and of the state of confusion existing in the minds of some Lords who decided the case of *Hulton* v. *Jones*; and, secondly, by reason of his misunderstanding of the reasoning of those who took the view opposed to that taken by the court in this case.

Greene M.R., after pointing out that the reasoning of Lord Loreburn was incompatible with the reasoning of Farwell L.J., notwithstanding the statement of Lords Atkinson and Gorrell that they agreed with both sets of reasoning,

[1] [1909] 2 K.B. 444, 481.
[2] [1940] 1 K.B. 377.

discussed the question which of the two sets of reasoning was to be preferred. He dissented from the reasoning of Farwell L.J. cited above for the following reason:[1]

'It appears to me that the analogy of the action of deceit is not a true analogy. In that action the necessity for the presence of a fraudulent intention is satisfied if it be shown that the defendant made the statement in question recklessly, careless whether it were true or false. But this recklessness and this carelessness have nothing to do with the meaning of the statement—they are relevant only to the question of the fraudulent intent of the person making it. But in applying the analogy to the case of libel, Farwell L.J. applies the test of recklessness to the meaning of the words used, which is quite a different matter. If the words used when read in the light of the relevant circumstances are understood by reasonable persons to refer to the plaintiff, refer to him they do for all relevant purposes.'

With this reasoning the other members of the court agreed. But it is clear that it is based upon the old confusion between the meaning of the statement, and the intention of the defendant to refer to the plaintiff. It is not true to say that Farwell L.J. 'applies the test of recklessness to the meaning of the words used'. He applies it to the question whether the words were intended by the defendant to refer to the plaintiff. His view was that though 'the meaning of the words', that is, their defamatory character, must be tried by the objective test of the understanding of reasonable people, the question whether the words were published of and concerning the plaintiff must be tried by the subjective test of the intention of the defendant. So far as the Court of Appeal can decide the matter Farwell L.J.'s view is rejected. But considering the weight of opinion in favour of the opposite view, and the very confused opinions given by the House of Lords in the case of *Hulton* v. *Jones*, it is probably open to the House to reconsider its view of the matter.[2] As we shall now see, the practical consequences which have followed from the law laid down by the Court of Appeal make such a reconsideration advisable.

---

[1] [1940] 1 K.B. 377, 387.

[2] Such a reconsideration would not involve a reversal by the House of its decision in *Hulton* v. *Jones*. That decision would stand. All that the House need do would be to say that it preferred the reasoning of Farwell L.J. to that of the Court of Appeal in *Newstead* v. *London Express*.

The Practical Consequences of the Present Law

Fletcher Moulton L.J. gave some cogent reasons for his approval of the old law which required the presence of an intention on the part of the defendant to refer to the plaintiff. He said:[1]

'The limitation of the action of defamation to cases where the defendant has spoken or written the words "of and concerning the plaintiff" is not an example of the weakness of common law remedies, but of their wisdom. It constitutes the protection of the innocent individual from being guilty of defaming others of whom he has never intended to speak, and also from being himself defamed. On the one hand to hold a person responsible for every application that his words may bear in the minds of persons who either possess knowledge that he does not possess or are ignorant of that which he knows would be to put on him a burden too heavy to be borne. But on the other hand it constitutes the protection of the individual from being defamed, because it nullifies all attempts to libel by language which as a matter of construction cannot refer to the plaintiff, but which persons reading between the lines would understand to refer to him by reason of the surrounding circumstances. . . . All these devices are in vain to shelter a libeller, because the issue is not whether the language is, as a matter of construction, applicable to the plaintiff, but whether the writer intended it to refer to the plaintiff, and if he did so he is responsible if anyone can discover his intention, however much in words he may have striven to conceal it. This great and beneficial amplitude of the remedy is, however, only possible because the law makes the intention to refer to the plaintiff the critical issue.'

In fact, the law as it at present stands is unjust to the defendant, is difficult to apply, and is productive of undesirable litigation.

That the present law is unjust to the defendant some of the illustrations given by Greer L.J. in the case of *Cassidy* v. *Daily Mirror* show.

'A writer might state that A B is an ignoramus. Unknown to the writer A B may have spent five years under the tuition of X Y at Eton. Could X Y allege that this was a libel upon him, the writer having been ignorant, and having no reason to suppose that A B had been at Eton? Take another case. A, being under the mistaken impression that he saw Mr. B walking away from a theatre with Miss C, says next morning to an acquaintance: "I saw B and C leaving the

[1] [1909] 2 K.B. 444, 466–7.

theatre together last night." Unknown to A, but to the knowledge of his acquaintance, C had been murdered by the man with whom she left the theatre. Could A be successfully sued by B for saying he had murdered C ?"[1]

As he said, it followed from the decision in this case that if A were introduced to B and C as an engaged couple, and he said in a letter to a friend that they were engaged, he might be sued by a woman, unknown to him, who was in fact the wife of B.[2] Moreover, its injustice is increased by what is, in effect, its logical consequence. If there are any persons who know the special facts which would make an otherwise innocent statement defamatory, the plaintiff has a good cause of action, although it is not proved that any person in fact construed the statement in a defamatory sense.[3]

That the present law is difficult to apply is shown by the case of *Newstead* v. *London Express*.[4] Under the present law, if it is proved that the defendant had no intention of referring to the plaintiff, but the plaintiff alleges that he is defamed, the difficult question must arise, Are the words capable of defaming him? What are the tests which must be applied to answer this question? In the case of *Newstead* v. *London Express*, MacKinnon L.J. was inclined to differ from his brethren on the question whether the words were capable of defaming the plaintiff.[5] As he pointed out, the question must be, Would a reasonable man apply the words to the plaintiff? To answer this question 'not merely the actual words, but the circumstances of time and place must be taken into account, and also the constitution of the audience to whom they were addressed'.[6] It is not surprising that the jury failed to agree upon this question, seeing that it caused a difference of opinion amongst the members of the Court of Appeal. But this difficulty would not arise if the fact that the defendant had no intention of referring to the plaintiff were a defence to the action.

---

[1] [1929] 2 K.B. 331, 348.   [2] Ibid. at p. 350.
[3] *Hough* v. *London Express*, [1940] 2 K.B. 507.
[4] [1940] 1 K.B. 377.   [5] Ibid. at pp. 390, 393.
[6] Ibid. at p. 391; so, too, in *Hough* v. *London Express*, [1940] 2 K.B. 507, 516. Goddard L.J. doubted whether the statements in this case or in the case of *Cassidy* v. *Daily Mirror*, [1929] 2 K.B. 331, ought to have been held to be defamatory.

That the law as it stands is productive of undesirable litigation is shown by this same case. It encourages purely speculative actions. In this case, though the jury failed to agree upon the question whether the words referred to the plaintiff, they did agree in assessing the plaintiff's damages at one farthing. If the fact that the defendant had no intention of referring to the plaintiff were a defence, this speculative litigation would be stopped. In my opinion it is desirable that the law should be settled either by the legislature or the House of Lords in accordance with the opinion of Farwell L.J. in the case of *Hulton* v. *Jones*. Obviously, newspapers must be discouraged from making defamatory statements about fictitious persons, which may be taken to refer to real persons, by placing upon them the duty of making it clear that these statements are fiction and not news. On the other hand, the law now places upon them an impossible burden because, before publishing either an apparently innocent statement or a statement true of a particular person, they must satisfy themselves either that there is no one in the world who can put a defamatory meaning on the apparently innocent statement, or that there is no one in the world to whom it may refer and of whom it is not true. I think that the technical means by which the law should be reformed is the establishment of the rule that an intention to defame the plaintiff in the sense explained by Farwell L.J. is an essential condition for success in an action for libel.

LAW REPORTING IN THE NINETEENTH AND TWENTIETH CENTURIES[1]

AT the beginning of the nineteenth century the law reports fell into two classes—the authorized and the unauthorized reports. The authorized reports had the privilege of exclusive citation. But in 1832 Lord Denman allowed other reports to be cited in the Court of King's Bench, and the other courts gradually followed suit. In 1863 Lord Westbury laid down the rule, which now prevails, that any report signed by a barrister may be cited, and the rule, against which Bentham[2] and Watkins the conveyancer protested,[3] that an unpublished report vouched for by a barrister may also be cited. Nevertheless, the authorized reports still retained certain privileges. The judges corrected them, and if the reports differed the version in the authorized reports was preferred. But the authorized reports were expensive—a complete set cost £30, and did not include any digest. They appeared long after the case had been decided, and the times of their publication were irregular. The result was that many sets of unauthorized reports appeared—the *Law Journal* in 1822, the *Legal Observer* in 1830, the *Jurist* in 1837, the *Law Times* in 1843, the *Weekly Reporter* in 1852, the New Reports in 1862, and other sets of collateral reports in most of the courts of law and equity. This competition reduced the profits of each set of reports, and therefore the remuneration of the reporters, to a low level; the number of cases reported was excessive, and the profession was put to great expense. The result was that in the fifth decade of the nineteenth century a movement began which ended in the establishment of the Law Reports.

As early as 1843 a society called The Verulam Society ventilated a scheme for the exercise of professional control

---

[1] An address delivered to the Holdsworth Club of the Faculty of Law of the University of Birmingham at a Club Luncheon on May 23, 1941. Reprinted from *Anglo-American Legal History Series*, 1941.

[2] *Works*, vi. 389, 10 ibid. at 78.

[3] 'Principles of Conveyancing', cited by Daniel, in *The History and Origin of the Law Reports*, 10.

over the composition and publication of law reports. But the scheme came to nothing and the Society ceased to exist.[1] In 1848 the Law Amendment Society, at the instance of Serjeant Pulling, appointed a committee to consider the present system of law reporting. The committee issued its report in 1849. It pointed out that no provision was made for the official promulgation of the law made by the courts; and, alluding to the tale that in old days there were official reporters, which thus once more emerged for a purpose, lamented the discontinuance of this practice. It pointed out the bad effects of unrestricted competition in the production of reports, and it advocated the restoration of the system of official reporters.[2] This report was not productive of any results; but the Society did not let the matter drop, and in 1853 it appointed a special committee on law reporting. The committee issued an elaborate report. It discussed and rejected the idea of a voluntary association amongst the profession for the production of reports, and advocated the creation of a Board, appointed by the Crown, to superintend the production of reports. It pointed out that it was as much the duty of the State to undertake this work as it was its duty to undertake the work of publishing the statutes and Parliamentary papers.[3] As a result of this report various proposals were made for the establishment by statute of a body of officially authorized reporters.[4]

But the rival scheme—the scheme of a voluntary association amongst the members of the profession for the production of reports—was advocated by W. T. S. Daniel in a paper which he circulated to the Bar in 1863.[5] The principle upon which he based his suggestions is contained in the following passage in his paper:[6]

'I venture to suggest that without either a royal commission or a government grant [which would imply government control],[7] it is within the power of the Bar to supply an adequate remedy. I recognize and base my suggestions upon the principle that the proper preparation and publication of those judicial decisions, which are expositions of the law *ex non scripto*, is a public duty, and that the public have a right to

[1] Daniel, *The History and Origin of the Law Reports*, 3.
[2] Ibid. 3–14. [3] Ibid. 14–21.
[4] Ibid. 22.   [5] Ibid. 23–6.   [6] Ibid. 24.
[7] Inserted here from a preceding sentence.

expect that it will be discharged by a recognized body in the State qualified for the purpose. The qualifications of such a body should be—independence of the Government, co-operation with but not dependence upon the Judicature, adequate knowledge of the law and experience in the practice of the courts, combined with special skill and experience in the art of reporting. These several qualifications are possessed in the highest degree by the Bar, and by no other body of men—and the Bar form a recognized body in the State. Why should they not combine and undertake the duty? My proposal is that they should.'

It was largely owing to Daniel's exertions and to the help of Roundell Palmer, then Solicitor—and shortly afterwards Attorney-General, that this proposal eventually took shape in the constitution of the Council of Law Reporting and the Law Reports issued by it.

Many members of the Bar and many of the Vice-Chancellors expressed their approval of Daniel's paper.[1] Thus encouraged, he addressed a long letter to Roundell Palmer in which he discussed the following questions: what a proper system of law reporting ought to be, what the present system was, and what was the remedy; and to it he added as an appendix a paper on these questions written by the future Lord Lindley. He suggested that a meeting of the Bar should be called by the Attorney-General, and that a scheme should be submitted to the meeting for the establishment of a Council of Law Reporting, composed of the law officers and three representatives from each of the four Inns, to undertake and superintend the publication of law reports.[2] A sufficient number of members of the Bar having joined in the request that a meeting of the Bar be summoned, Roundell Palmer summoned it, and the meeting was held in Lincoln's Inn Hall on December 2, 1863. The meeting appointed a committee of twenty-two to prepare a scheme of reform.[3]

The committee appointed a sub-committee to consider the practice of reporting the decisions of the courts in foreign countries—India, the colonies, and Scotland—and issued a circular to the profession inviting suggestions.[4]

The committee negatived a proposal supported by Serjeant Pulling, Joshua Williams, and Westlake for a scheme

[1] Daniel, op. cit. 27.   [2] Ibid. 28–67.
[3] Ibid. 67–81.   [4] Ibid. 98–9.

by which the registrars were to prepare from notes made by official shorthand writers, records of the arguments and judgments, which were to be printed by the King's Printers and sold at a low cost. This suggestion was also made by John Pearson, afterwards Pearson J.; and we shall see that a somewhat similar scheme has recently been suggested by Professor Goodhart. Another proposal that the government should appoint and pay official reporters was not pressed. The committee recommended the scheme which, after two further meetings of the Bar, was adopted on November 28, 1864. A Council was to be set up consisting of the law officers, two representatives from Lincoln's Inn, two from the Inner, and two from the Middle Temples, one from Gray's Inn, two from the Law Society, and one from Serjeant's Inn. This Council was to be incorporated and to have the help of a paid secretary. It was to appoint the reporters and editors, but the existing authorized reporters were to have the first offer of appointment in their respective courts; and it was to make arrangements with printers and publishers for printing and publication. There were also recommendations as to the nature of the reports—there was to be a weekly series and a permanent series, and as to the amount of the subscription to the reports. The committee did not recommend that these reports should have the privilege of exclusive citation; and a proposal to that effect moved by Joshua Williams was lost.

The Law Society and three of the Inns consented to appoint representatives to the Council. Gray's Inn stood out because it was not satisfied as to the financial soundness of the scheme, and Serjeant's Inn, because the judges thought that adverse interests might be involved on which they might have to adjudicate. The Council met, issued a prospectus, made arrangements with Messrs. Clowes,[1] the printers, and induced nearly all the authorized reporters to take service under the Council.[2] The only exception to the appointment

---

[1] The law publishers were approached, but they refused to have anything to do with the scheme, Daniel, op. cit. 256–61.

[2] Ibid. 250–62, 273–81. Best and Smith, the Queen's Bench reporters, refused to accept appointment. Best objected to the supervision of an editor; Hurlstone and Coltman, the Exchequer reporters, also refused. Hurlstone was not satisfied with the financial soundness of the scheme, and when he was

of reporters by the Council is in the case of the reporters in the House of Lords. There the appointment is made in theory by the House, in practice by the Lord Chancellor.[1] The judges were asked to approve the reporters appointed, to permit the editors and reporters to have access to their written judgments, to revise their unwritten judgments before publication, and to

'. . . recognize the editors and reporters as members of the Bar exercising a professional privilege for a public object, under responsibility, through the Council, to the Judges, the Bar, and the Profession at large.'[2]

The first numbers of the Law Reports were published in January 1866; and the financial success of the scheme was so great that in the following year the Council was able to establish and supply to subscribers the *Weekly Notes*, and to supply also a King's Printer's copy of the statutes.[3] In 1870 the Council was incorporated under the Companies' Acts. Its first two objects, as set forth in its Memorandum of Association, were

'(1) the preparation and publication, in a convenient form, at a moderate price, and under gratuitous professional control, of reports of judicial decisions of the superior and appellate courts in England. (2) The issue, periodically or occasionally, of any subsidiary or other publications relating to legal subjects which it may be considered expedient to combine with the publication of such reports, including the statutes of the realm, or any part thereof, if deemed expedient.'

Lord Lindley accurately summed up the principle underlying the new system thus established, and its contrast with the system which it superseded when he said:[4]

'The leading idea of Mr. Daniel's scheme and of the present system is co-operation as distinguished from competition. The various members of the Profession were urged to combine and produce what

---

satisfied his retractation of his refusal came too late, ibid. 293–4; Lord Romilly M.R. refused to withdraw from Beavan, the authorized reporter, the exclusive right to have copies of his judgments and to have the transcripts of his oral judgments corrected, J. C. Fox, *A Handbook of English Law Reports*, 60; but Beavan was made examiner in Chancery in 1866, and Romilly consented to give these privileges to the reporters of the Council, Daniel, op. cit. 300; Beavan was thus, as he said, the last of the authorized reporters.

[1] (1903), *L.Q.R.* xix. 453, n. 1.   [2] Daniel, op. cit. 276–81.
[3] Ibid. 301.   [4] (1885), *L.Q.R.* i. 139.

they wanted for themselves, and not to rely on the efforts of individuals acting without any system and simply with a view to their own interests.'

The fact that this new system was thus started and organized and conducted by the profession had two very considerable merits. First, it was free from governmental control. This was its most important merit. From very early times the judges had been a very separate part of the machinery of government; the idea that they were guardians of a supreme law and obliged to administer justice impartially, not only between private persons, but also between the King and his people, had never been lost sight of;[1] and Blackstone had rightly regarded this independence of the judges as one of the main safeguards of constitutional liberty.[2] Similarly from very early times the legal profession had been equally self-governing and independent.[3] It followed from these facts that the publication of the law made by the judges with the assistance of the legal profession ought to be controlled by the judges and the profession. Effect was given to this consequence by the scheme adopted. And not only was this scheme consistent with the constitutional position of the judges and the legal profession, it also had the further advantage that, because it was organized and controlled by experts, it worked without friction, and was wholly free from the minute regulations and time-wasting formalities which are the inevitable accompaniments of governmental control. As Pollock, then editor of the Law Reports, said:[4]

'Disciplined co-operation is, of course, a necessity; though some learned persons, when the establishment of the Law Reports was under discussion, did not see of what use an editor would be.[5] But our bond is more like that of a college crew than that of a government office. What rules we have . . . are mostly unwritten. I admit that I set some value on two rules I have made for myself, to give my colleagues as free a hand as possible, and never to write a formal letter if I can help it. We confer freely and confidentially, as occasion requires, with the judges, with the counsel engaged in cases to be

[1] Holdsworth, *H.E.L.* ii. 196, 253–4, 435–6; v. 435–6, 493.
[2] Ibid. x. 417, 715.
[3] Holdsworth, *H.E.L.* ii. 484–512; iv. 263–7; xii. 15–46.
[4] (1903), *L.Q.R.* xix. 453; xxv. 65.
[5] See p. 287, n. 2.

reported, and with one another. .... In short, we imitate on our small scale that method of proceeding by customary and unwritten understandings, and settling the really important matters, so to speak, out of court, which is the pride of Anglo-Saxon political institutions and the despair of almost all foreign students.'

The existence of this professional Council of Law Reporting provides a body which is responsive to professional opinion, and enables improvements suggested by experience to be made easily. Thus, at the outset, the tradition of separate courts and separate reporters in those courts led to the appointment of separate editors for the different series of the reports. It was not till 1895 that Sir F. Pollock was appointed the general editor of the Law Reports.[1]

Secondly, this new departure in the history of law reporting was a development of the older system. There was no breach in historical continuity. The Law Reports took the place of the authorized reports, and most of the existing authorized reporters took service under the Council. Like the authorized reports, the Law Reports have no privilege of exclusive citation; and, as with the authorized reports, so with the Law Reports, 'it has been generally but not universally the custom in the courts to demand that, if a case is reported in the Law Reports, it should be cited from those Reports and no other'.[2] Moreover, this new departure was, like other departures in the long history of law reporting, initiated and carried out by the legal profession. In the sixteenth century the change over from the Year Books to the reports of named reporters, and the changes in the character and style of their reports; and in the eighteenth century further changes in the character and style of the reports, the beginning of the regular publication of contemporaneous reports, and the establishment of the authorized reports— had been similarly initiated and carried out. If in the future changing conditions demand a change in the organization of law reporting, it is to be hoped that this long line of historical precedents will be followed; for it is only lawyers controlled by professional opinion who can decide upon the

---

[1] (1903), *L.Q.R.* xix. 451.
[2] Report of the Law Reporting Committee March 17, 1940; the Committee said that they hoped that 'this practice may except in very special circumstances be rigidly enforced'.

best methods of publishing that judge-made law which, from the point of view of the scientific exposition of the principles of English law, is the most important of all its sources. In fact it was followed when in 1939 the Lord Chancellor appointed a committee presided over by Simonds J. to report upon the difficulties arising from the increasing number of law reports.

That committee issued a valuable report which recommended no essential changes in the existing system. But from its findings Professor Goodhart dissented, and proposed a scheme for the reorganization of law reporting which has, it seems to me, considerable merits. His arguments and suggestions can be summarized as follows:

Under the present system, except in the case of judgments reported in the Law Reports or when the judgment is written, there is no guarantee that the report represents what the judge intended to say—

'The practice adopted by certain business men of stating at the end of their letters "dictated but not read" has been held by the courts not to excuse any inaccuracies which such letters might contain. Nevertheless, under our present system of law reporting, the great majority of cases are "dictated but not read" by the judges.'

If a case is unreported in the regular reports, there is no authentic record of it, and yet such cases can be cited from an incomplete newspaper report; and this causes embarrassment to both counsel and the court. To cure these evils

'. . . official shorthand writers should be attached to all courts of record to take and transcribe all judgments and the transcripts should be sent to the judges for such revision as they might consider it desirable to make in them. After a reasonably short period, not exceeding if possible a week, these transcripts would be returned to a central office at the Law Courts, when copies could be obtained by the reporters and by any other persons on payment of a fee. All judgments would be filed in the central office, and would be indexed by an official specially appointed for this purpose.'

The cost would not be great as it would be in large part met by the fees charged for copies. The advantages of the scheme would be that inaccurate reports would be reduced to a minimum; the judges could correct anything which did not express their considered opinion; all judgments would be recorded; and editors of law reports could more easily decide what cases were reportable. Finally Professor Goodhart pointed out that—

'Although the Dominions and India have accepted many of the features of the English legal system, not one of them has adopted our haphazard method of reporting, or not reporting, judgments. As one of the witnesses said, "In Australia, New Zealand, and Canada anybody can go to an associate of the Court, pay his money and get a copy of the judgment".'

It should be observed that this scheme does not in any way weaken the control of the legal profession over law reporting. It does not subject it to the control of a government department. But it does insure that the law reporter shall have an authentic supply of raw material, and it insures it at a relatively small cost. It does insure that authentic information shall be available as to the judgment given in a case which has not found its way into the regular reports. It does recognize the obvious fact that in a system of law which depends largely upon judgments in reported cases, the State ought to do something to safeguard the accuracy of the reports of all cases and especially of those cases which, in the opinion of the judges and the profession, contain important statements of legal principles or explanations of legal rules or interpretations of the statute law. For these reasons I think that after the war Professor Goodhart's suggestions ought to be carefully considered, and that a reform on the lines which he has suggested should be undertaken. After all, if we look at the long history of law reporting, we can realize that it is perhaps a less radical reform than the change over from the Year Books to the named reporters in the sixteenth century, than the institution of the authorized reporters at the end of the eighteenth century, or the institution of the Law Reports in the nineteenth century.

TABLE OF CASES

INDEX OF NAMES

GENERAL INDEX

Ambassador's servant, question of immunity of house, 262.
Ancien régime, administrative law under, 94.
Aragon, Cortes of, 41 ff., 76, 77, 78.
Archaionomia, 74.
Articles of war, 7.
Articuli ad novas narrationes, 34.
Assets, legal and equitable, 177.
Assizes of Henry II, 81.
Assumpsit, writ of, 132 ff., 249.
  indebitatus assumpsit, 241 ff.
Athens, Courts of, 254.
Attainder, Acts of, 65.

Bailment, 189.
Benchers' table, exercise at, 27.
Bill, procedure by, in Parliament, 50, 53, 64.
Bill and answer, 195.
Building schemes, 175.

Cambridge, legal education at, 33.
Canon Law, 77, 130, 131, 189, 193, 194.
Castile, Cortes of, 41 ff., 76, 77, 78.
Causa, in contract, 130, 252.
Chambres des Enquêtes, 45.
  des Requêtes, 45.
  de la Tournelle, 45.
Commentaries on the Laws of England, 30, 31, 227, 228, 264.
Commons, rights of, 50.
Communeros, revolt of, 41.
Condictio, in Scots law, 251.
Conscience, relation to law, 167.
Consideration, doctrine of, 132 ff., 249.
Consolidation, 175.
Constable and Marshal, Court, 1 ff.
Conveyancing, lectures on, 32.
Corporate personality, theories, 209–14.
Corporation, characteristics of, 104.
Corpus Juris, 128, 192.
Council, in thirteenth century the core of Parliament, 49, 79, 208.
  predominant partner in Tudor constitution, 83.
Courts-Martial, 12.
Covenant, writ of, 131.

Culpa lata aequiparatur dolo, view adopted by equity, 169.
Curia Regis of Henry II, comprehensive and various powers of, 9.

Debt, writ of, 132.
Detinue, 239.
Diversité des Courtes, 34.
Doctor and Student, 28, 167, 190.
Dominium politicum et regale, 57, 81.

Ecclesiastical Polity, The Laws of, 86.
Education, legal, absence of continuity, 25 ff.
Ejectment, terminology and title, 256–9.
Election, equitable doctrine of, 214.
Enemy property, right to confiscate, 262.
Equitable rights, whether *jura in rem* or *jura in personam*, 215, 216, 239 ff.
Equities, kept off title by legislation of 1925, 125.
Equity:
  lectures on, 32.
  distinction from law, 138 ff.
  did not interfere when law adequate, 139.
  remedies contrasted with legal remedies, 140.
  not fused with law by Judicature Acts, 145, 168.
  analysis of progress, 1885–1935, 165 ff.
  acts *in personam*, 170, 197, 198.
  administered in separate courts from law, 171.
  text-books, 178, 179.
  should still be taught as separate whole, 185.
  how far influenced by Roman Law, 188 ff.
Estate tail, 105.
Estates General of France, 41 ff., 76, 77, 78, 82.

Featherstone Riots, Lord Bowen's report, 17.
Fideicommissum, 191, 196.
Fines, 112.

www.ingramcontent.com/pod-product-compliance
Lightning Source LLC
Chambersburg PA
CBHW031425180326
41458CB00002B/457